JANE'S MAIN BATTLE TANKS

Second edition

Christopher F. Foss

JANE'S

First published in the United Kingdom in 1983
This edition published in 1986 by
Jane's Publishing Company Limited
238 City Road, London EC1V 2PU

ISBN 0 7106 0372 X

Distributed in the Philippines and the USA and its
dependencies by Jane's Publishing Inc.,
115 5th Avenue (4th Floor), New York, NY 10003

Typesetting by D. P. Media Limited, Hitchin, Hertfordshire

Printed in the United Kingdom by
Biddles Ltd, Guildford, Surrey

Introduction

Although new types of anti-tank weapons continue to be developed and employed the Main Battle Tank is likely to retain its position as the key element on the battlefield for the foreseeable future.

There are a number of Main Battle Tanks currently at the design stage which will enter service in the 1990s and some of these will be quite different in appearance to the vehicles currently in service today.

The first of these is likely to be the French EPC which will have a very high power-to-weight ratio and have a 120 mm smooth-bore gun fed by an automatic loader. The latter will enable the crew to be reduced to three men, commander, gunner and loader. If one excludes the Swedish S-tank, the EPC will be the first operational tank in the West to have this feature. The Soviet Union however fielded its first tank with an automatic loader, the T-64, in the late 1960s and the more recent T-72 also has this feature.

The United States is also studying a number of new concepts for the future including the Tank Test Bed (TTB) which is essentially a M1 Abrams hull with a 120 mm smooth-bore gun mounted externally above the roof and all of the crew within the safety of the hull. When firing in the hull down position the vehicle would be very difficult to detect let alone hit. The weight saved by not installing a turret could be used to provide increased armour protection to the hull front and/or on the hull roof.

A number of the new anti-tank weapons now entering service attack the upper surfaces of the tank which in most cases is only thinly armoured to protect the crew from shell splinters. Future vehicles will have to be designed with much increased emphasis on protecting against top attack weapons.

For many years MBTs have been fitted with smoke dischargers but more recently new decoys have been introduced which, when fired, will confuse anti-tank guided weapons so improving the tank's survivability on the battlefield.

The development of new armours such as the British Chobham has enabled MBTs to be protected over their frontal arcs from virtually all battlefield weapons including Anti-Tank Guided Weapons (ATGW) with their High Explosive Anti-Tank warheads. As a result of the appearance of these new types of armour many ATGWs have had to be improved and fitted with larger diameter warheads.

New generation Main Battle Tanks such as the Leopard 2, M1/M1A1 Abrams and Challenger all have very significant improvements in the key areas of armour protection, mobility, firepower and night fighting capability than their predecessors.

The first part of *Jane's Main Battle Tanks* contains a detailed description of each MBT and its variants, full technical specifications, list of user countries, current status and manufacturer.

Wherever possible each vehicle is also provided with a side drawing (all of 1/76th), a selection of photographs of the basic vehicle, and where applicable, some of the specialised variants such as armoured recovery vehicles, bridgelayers, engineer vehicles and so on.

Only Main Battle Tanks that have been developed since the Second World War and are still in service or currently being offered by manufacturers for sale are included. There is however an entry of the Israeli Sherman family of tanks which have been adopted for a wide range of specialised roles.

Tanks that are still under development, or in some cases, still projects, are also included where information on this has been released.

There are a number of new MBTs included in this edition for the first time, many of which have been developed with company funding specifically for the export market, although in some cases the government has provided some financial or other support. These include the Brazilian ENGESA EE-T1 Osorio, Chinese Type 69, French EPC and AMX-40, Israeli Merkava Mark 2, South Korean XK-1 and the British Vickers Defence Systems Mark 7 which has features of the West German Leopard 2 and the earlier Vickers Valiant.

Part Two of *Jane's Main Battle Tanks* contains brief notes on the almost 100 countries that now operate MBTs or which are expected to do so in the future.

Where possible an outline on the country's battalion/ brigade/divisional/corps employment of tanks is given together with very approximate figures on how many tanks the country has, including those used for training or held in reserve. Some countries, especially Italy, Spain, United Kingdom and the United States are still in the process of reorganisation so some of the tables of organisation and equipment may well be overtaken by events.

Some of these tank holding figures are very accurate but in all cases they must be treated with caution as they are constantly changing in some countries as new vehicles come in and older vehicles are placed in reserve, exported or sold for scrap.

The author would like to take this opportunity of thanking the many armed forces, companies and private individuals who have provided material for this edition. Information, photographs and other material for revised editions should be forwarded to the author via the publisher.

Christopher F Foss
Hampshire, England
December 1985

PART 1

MAIN BATTLE TANKS

TAM Medium Tank

Development

The West German company of Thyssen Henschel has developed a medium tank called the TAM (Tanque Argentino Mediano) to meet the requirements of the Argentinian Army. The first prototype of the TAM was completed in West Germany in 1976 and the second prototype in 1977. Argentina has a requirement for at least 200 TAMs to replace old Sherman tanks currently in use. Chassis construction and final assembly are taking place in Buenos Aires with turret construction and integration of the gun and fire-control system at Rio Tercero. Some major components will continue to be supplied by Thyssen Henschel. The TAM was not deployed in the Falklands during the 1982 campaign. Full details of the TAM are given under the entry for the TAM Medium Tank in West Germany. An MICV called the VCTP has been developed to work with the TAM.

In mid-1983 Peru placed an order with Argentina for 80 TAMs and deliveries were expected to take place between 1984 and 1985. At a later date Peru may undertake licence production of the TAM or partial assembly of the vehicle. Early in 1984 it was announced that Panama had ordered 60 TAMs, including some VCTP APC variants.

Argentina has ordered 25 turrets as fitted to the Palmaria 155 mm self-propelled gun for installation on a lengthened (seven instead of six road wheels) and widened chassis. The installation of this turret is expected to increase the TAM's weight to just under 45 tonnes, so a more powerful engine may be fitted to maintain the power-to-weight ratio.

Status: In production. In service with Argentina, Panama and Peru.

Manufacturer: TAMSE, Avda, Rolon 1441/43, 2609, Boulgone Sur Mer-Provincia de Buenos Aires, Argentina.

TAM medium tank from rear showing turret detail ▶

TAM medium tank with driver's hatch open and 7.62 mm machine gun on commander's cupola

BRAZIL

ENGESA EE-T1 Osorio Main Battle Tank

Development

The EE-T1 Osorio main battle tank has been developed by ENGESA to meet the requirements of both the home and export markets. The first prototype was completed in October 1984, a second prototype followed in April 1985. Vickers Defence Systems of the UK has designed and built two turrets for the Osorio, the first of these was delivered to Brazil in spring 1985. It was fitted with a Royal Ordnance 105 mm L7A3 gun with a modified recoil system, the second turret was armed with a 120 mm GIAT smooth-bore gun. The first prototype of the MBT went to Saudi Arabia for trials in mid-1985. Production is expected to start in São José dos Campos in 1986. The Brazilian Army has a requirement for 500 MBTs of this type. To reduce development time and cost, available well-proven components have been used wherever possible in the design.

The concept of the EE-T1 is that the basic design can be adapted to individual customer requirements and it is capable of modernisation in the future as the threat changes and new systems and equipment become available.

Description

The layout of the EE-T1 is conventional with the driver's compartment at the front, turret in the centre and engine and transmission at the rear. The hull and turret are of all-welded steel construction with the front and sides well-sloped to provide the maximum possible protection within the weight limits of the vehicle.

The driver sits at the front of the hull on the left and has a single-piece hatch cover and a periscope for driving closed down; the periscope can be replaced by a passive periscope for night driving.

The commander sits on the right of the turret with the gunner forward and below his position, the loader sitting on the turret left. Both commander and loader have hatch covers in the turret roof.

The water-cooled turbo-charged V12 diesel is mounted at the rear and coupled to a fully automatic transmission. Power-to-weight ratio is an excellent 25.6 hp/tonne and acceleration from 0 to 32 km/h is 5.4 seconds. The fully automatic transmission has a torque converter (with lock up) and a hydraulic brake (retarder) with four forward and two reverse gears. The EE-T1 has a combined brake system in which only the retarder (installed in the transmission) works in the first stage with the disc brakes coming into operation in the second stage. A parking brake is also fitted.

Suspension is of the hydro-pneumatic type with each side having six dual rubber-tyred road wheels, idler at the front, drive sprocket at the rear and three track return rollers. Dampers are provided on the first, second and sixth road wheel stations. In late 1983 Dunlop Aviation Division of the UK was awarded a contract for the design and development of the hydro-pneumatic suspension system for the Osorio; this has been given the company name of Dunloride and the

Side view of prototype of ENGESA EE-T1 Osorio MBT

Rear view of prototype of ENGESA EE-T1 Osorio MBT

Prototype of ENGESA EE-T1 Osorio MBT with mock-up turret. Driver's hatch is open

Prototype of ENGESA EE-T1 Osorio MBT fitted with mock-up of turret showing 7.62 mm machine gun at loader's station

first two sets were delivered late in 1984. The centre guide, double pin tracks have replaceable rubber pads.

Main armament is a Royal Ordnance L7A3 rifled 105 mm or GIAT 120 mm smooth-bore tank gun with an elevation of +20 degrees and a depression of −10 degrees, and turret traverse is 360 degrees. Turret traverse and weapon elevation are electric with both the commander and gunner having controls, the former having overriding control. A 7.62 mm electrically-fired machine gun is mounted coaxially with the main armament and a 7.62 mm or 12.7 mm machine gun can be mounted on the roof for anti-aircraft defence. Mounted either side of the turret is a bank of four electrically-operated smoke dischargers.

Two main fire-control options are offered for the EE-T1. The first is an integrated fire-control system with a day/night gunner's periscope with laser rangefinder and a day/night commander's periscope. The advanced fire-control system, which allows the main armament to be laid and fired while the tank is moving, includes a gyro-stabilised day gunner's periscope with laser rangefinder, gyro-stabilised panoramic day commander's periscope with laser rangefinder and a gyro-stabilised panoramic thermal periscope with monitors for both gunner and commander. Optional equipment for both versions includes a loader's periscope with a night-vision option and a combat periscope.

The EE-T1 MBT has two fire-extinguishing systems. The engine bay system is operated manually or automatically, the crew bay fire-suppression system is operated automatically.

Turret options include radios, collective or individual NBC protection, azimuth indicator in mils, clinometer in mils, electronic compass and a laser detector. Chassis options include a passive periscope for the driver, crew heater and a land navigation system.

Variants

ENGESA is currently studying the possibility of installing a 155 mm gun turret on the chassis of the EE-T1 as well as twin 30 mm or twin 35 mm anti-aircraft turrets. Armoured recovery and bridgelayer versions of the EE-T1 will also probably be developed.

SPECIFICATIONS

CREW	4	MAX ROAD SPEED	70 km/h	coaxial	1 × 7.62 mm MG
COMBAT WEIGHT	39 000 kg	MAX RANGE	550 km	anti-aircraft	1 × 7.62 mm or
POWER-TO-WEIGHT		FORDING	1.2 m		1 × 12.7 mm MG
RATIO	25.6 hp/tonne	with preparation	2 m	smoke dischargers	2 × 4
GROUND PRESSURE	0.76 kg/cm²	GRADIENT	60%	AMMUNITION	
LENGTH GUN		SIDE SLOPE	40%	main	50 rounds of 105 mm or 42
forwards	9.995 m	VERTICAL OBSTACLE	1.15 m		rounds of 120 mm
rear	9.425 m	TRENCH	3 m	machine gun	5000 rounds of 7.62 mm or
LENGTH HULL	7.08 m	ENGINE	4-stroke, 12-cylinder,		600 rounds of 12.7 mm and
WIDTH	3.26 m		water-cooled turbo-charged		3000 rounds of 7.62 mm
WIDTH OVER TRACKS	3.2 m		diesel developing 1000 hp at	GUN CONTROL	
HEIGHT TO TURRET			2300 rpm	EQUIPMENT	
TOP	2.371 m	TRANSMISSION	fully-automatic with torque	Turret power control	electric/manual
GROUND CLEARANCE	0.46 m		converter, four forward and	by commander	yes
TRACK	2.63 m		two reverse gears	by gunner	yes
TRACK WIDTH	570 mm	SUSPENSION	hydro-pneumatic	Commander's override	yes
LENGTH OF TRACK ON		ARMAMENT		Gun elevation/depression	+20°/−10°
GROUND	4.49 m	main	1 × 105 mm		
			(or 120 mm)		

Status: Prototypes undergoing trials. Expected to enter production in 1986.

Manufacturer: Engesa Engenheiros Especializados SA, Avenue das Nacões Unidas, 22.833 (Santo Amaro), CEP 04795, PO Box 12.705 (CEP 01000), São Paulo, SP, Brazil.

MB-3 Tamoio Battle Tank

Development

In the late 1970s Bernardini designed the X-30 tank based on an M41 light tank chassis. It weighed 30 tonnes and would have been armed with a 90 mm or 105 mm gun but was not built; further work resulted in the Tamoio tank.

Construction of the first prototype began in 1982 and the chassis ran for the first time in November 1983. Turret/hull integration took place in mid-1984 and trials began later the same year. By early 1985 ten prototypes had been built and production was expected to start later the same year. The Tamoio was originally designated the XMB-3 but after trials with the prototype were successfully completed the X was dropped from the designation, so the vehicle became the MB-3. The Brazilian Army is understood to have a requirement for 500 tanks and both the ENGESA EE-T1 and MB-3 are competing for this order.

Description

The all-welded hull of the MB-3 Tamoio is divided into three compartments, the driver's at the front, fighting in the centre and the engine and transmission at the rear. Spaced armour is incorporated in some areas and laminate armour is said to be under consideration for production vehicles.

The driver sits at the left front of the vehicle and has periscopes for forward observation and a single-piece hatch cover opening to the right.

The all-welded turret is in the centre of the hull with the commander and gunner on the right and the loader on the left. Main armament comprises a Bernardini 90 mm gun that can fire a specially developed APFSDS-T round, although a 105 mm gun could be fitted on export vehicles. Mounted coaxially with the main armament is a 12.7 mm M2 HB machine gun, a 7.62 mm machine gun is mounted on the turret roof for anti-aircraft defence and a bank of four electrically-operated smoke dischargers is on either side of the turret. The fire-control system of the Tamoio includes a computer, day/passive night sights for commander and gunner, each sight has a laser rangefinder. The gunner has an auxiliary telescope mounted coaxially with the main armament.

Prototype of MB-3 Tamoio battle tank during cross-country trials (Ronaldo S Olive)

Prototype of MB-3 Tamoio battle tank with turret traversed to right (Ronaldo S Olive)

Prototype of Bernardini MB-3 Tamoio tank with same 90 mm gun as installed in Brazilian Army modernised M41 light tanks

SPECIFICATIONS

CREW	4
COMBAT WEIGHT	30 000 kg
UNLOADED WEIGHT	28 000 kg
POWER-TO-WEIGHT	
RATIO	16.6 hp/tonne
	(or 24.5 hp/tonne with
	8V-92TA engine)
GROUND PRESSURE	0.72 kg/cm²
LENGTH	
hull	6.5 m
gun forwards	8.77 m
gun rear	7.4 m
WIDTH	3.22 m
HEIGHT	
overall	2.5 m
to hull top	2.2 m
GROUND CLEARANCE	0.5 m
TRACK	2.6 m
TRACK WIDTH	530 mm
LENGTH OF TRACK	
ON GROUND	3.9 m
MAX ROAD SPEED	67 km/h
FUEL CAPACITY	700 litres
RANGE	550 km
GRADIENT	60%
SIDE SLOPE	30%
VERTICAL OBSTACLE	0.71 m
TRENCH	2.4 m
FORDING	1.3 m
ENGINE	Saab-Scania DSI-14 diesel
	developing 500 hp at
	2100 rpm (optional General
	Motors 8V-92TA developing
	736 hp at 2300 rpm)
TRANSMISSION	General Electric HMPT-500-3
	hydro-mechanical with 3
	forward and one reverse
	gears
SUSPENSION	torsion bar
ELECTRICAL SYSTEM	24 V
BATTERIES	4 × 12 V
ARMAMENT	
main	1 × 90 mm
	(or 105 mm as option)
coaxial	1 × 12.7 mm MG
anti-aircraft	1 × 7.62 mm MG
AMMUNITION	
90 mm	68
GUN CONTROL	
EQUIPMENT	
Turret power control	electric/manual
Gun elevation/depression	+18°/−6°
SMOKE-LAYING	
EQUIPMENT	2 × 4 smoke
	dischargers

The Brazilian-built Saab-Scania DSI-14 diesel will develop 500 hp at 2100 rpm, but it is hoped to increase this to 650/700 hp so raising the power-to-weight ratio to 22.5 hp/tonne. The engine is coupled to the same CD-500-3 transmission as in the M41 light tank. It has been reported that production vehicles will be fitted with the American HMPT-500 hydro-mechanical transmission as in the M2 Bradley Infantry Fighting Vehicle, and there will be a version with a Detroit Diesel 8V-92TA diesel developing 736 hp.

Suspension is of the torsion bar type and consists of six dual rubber-tyred road wheels with the drive sprocket at the rear, idler at the front and three track return rollers. Hydraulic shock absorbers are fitted at the first, second and sixth road wheel stations.

Standard equipment includes an NBC system, heater, fire extinguishers, bilge pump, hull escape hatch, radios and internal communications equipment.

Variants

At least two variants are under consideration, an armoured recovery vehicle and an anti-aircraft vehicle, the latter probably armed with a Bofors 40 mm L/70 anti-aircraft gun.

Status: Prototypes completed. Expected to enter production in 1986–87.

Manufacturer: Bernardini S/A Indústria e Comércio, Rua Hipólito Soares No 79, 04201 São Paulo, SP Brazil.

CHINA, PEOPLE'S REPUBLIC

Type 69 Main Battle Tank

Development

The Type 69 MBT made its first public appearance during a parade near Zhangiakou outside Beijing (Peking) in September 1982. A few sources state that production of the Type 69 commenced in 1969, but most sources state that production did not commence until the early 1980s.

Details of recent Chinese tank production is given in the following entry on the Type 59 MBT.

Iraq has placed an order for between 1000 and 2000 of the Type 69 MBTs armed with the 100 mm gun and first deliveries of these were made in 1983 via Saudi Arabia.

There are two versions of the Type 69 MBT, one armed with 100 mm gun with a fume extractor near the barrel (in 1985 Chinese sources called this model the Type 69 II) and the other armed with a 105 mm rifled tank gun of Western design (this has been called the Type Type II in the West although this cannot be the correct Chinese designation as this has now been applied to the model with 100 mm gun.)

Description

From the information supplied by Chinese sources, the Type 69 is almost identical to the Soviet T-55 series in terms of mobility and armour protection. Its main difference, apart from the 100 mm or 105 mm gun is in its fire control system.

Its layout is identical to the Type 59 and Soviet T-54/T-55 series with the driver at the front left and the other three crew members in the turret, commander and gunner on the left and loader on the right.

The Type 69 II has a 100 mm smooth bore gun with a 7.62 mm machine gun mounted coaxial with the main armament and a similar weapon mounted in the hull firing forwards and operated by the driver. The loader operates the 12.7 mm anti-aircraft machine gun.

The main armament is stabilised in both elevation and traverse and the fire control system includes a laser range finder and ballistic computer.

Observation equipment includes eight periscopes for the commander, gunner, driver and loader, gunner's night sight with magnification of ×7 and 6-degree field of view and a range of 800 metres. Tank commander has a sight with a day magnification of ×5 (12-degree field of view) and a night magnification of ×6 (8-degree field of view).

Standard equipment includes complete NBC protection system, automatic fire extinguishing system and the ability to

Type 69 MBT armed with 105 mm type Western gun fitted with a fume extractor (via G Jacobs)

lay its own smoke screen by injecting diesel fuel into the exhaust outlet on the left side of the hull.

Communications equipment installed includes a type 803 intercom and a type 889 radio. There are two commmand tank versions of the Type 69 II, the Mark B having one type 889 and one type 892 radio while the Mark C has two type 889 radios.

Variants

Apart from the different models mentioned above the only known variant is the Type 653 medium tank recovery vehicle

Type 69 MBTs on parade near Zhangjiakou, outside Beijing in September (Comlit, via Defence Magazine)

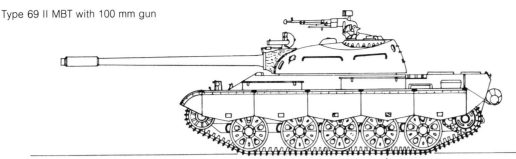

Type 69 II MBT with 100 mm gun

which uses automotive components of the Type 69. This is fitted with a hydraulically operated dozer blade at the front, hydraulically operated crane, main and auxiliary winches, radios and night vision equipment.

SPECIFICATIONS

CREW	4
COMBAT WEIGHT	36 500 to 37 000 kg
POWER-TO-WEIGHT	
RATIO	15.67 hp/tonne
GROUND PRESSURE	0.82/0.83 kg/cm²
LENGTH GUN	
FORWARDS	8.657 m
LENGTH GUN REAR	8.485 m
LENGTH HULL	6.243 m
WIDTH	3.298 m
HEIGHT TO AXIS OF	
AA MG	2.807 m
HEIGHT TO AXIS OF	
MAIN ARMAMENT	1.75 m
GROUND CLEARANCE	0.425 m
TRACK	2.64 m
TRACK WIDTH	580 mm
LENGTH OF TRACK	
ON GROUND	3.485 m
MAX ROAD SPEED	50 km/h
MAX ROAD RANGE	420 to 440 km
FORDING	1.4 m
GRADIENT	60%
VERTICAL OBSTACLE	0.8 m
TRENCH	2.7 m
ENGINE	Model 12150L-7BW V-12 diesel developing 580 hp at 2000 rpm
TRANSMISSION	manual, 5 forward, 1 reverse gears
STEERING	clutch and brake
SUSPENSION	torsion bar
ARMAMENT	
main	1 × 100 m
co-axial	1 × 7.62 mm MG
bow	1 × 7.62 mm MG
anti-aircraft	1 × 12.7 mm MG
SMOKE LAYING	
EQUIPMENT	diesel fuel injected into exhaust system

Status: In production. In service with China and Iraq.

Manufacturer: Chinese state arsenals. Enquiries to China North Industries Corporation, 7A, Yuetan Nanjie, Beijing, People's Republic of China.

Type 59 Main Battle Tank

Development/Description
In the early 1950s the Soviets supplied China with a quantity of T-54 MBTs, production of which was subsequently undertaken in China under the designation Type 59. The first production models were similar to the Soviet T-54 and not fitted with infra-red night vision equipment or a stabiliser for the main armament. Later models were fitted with a fume extractor as on the T-54A. More recent production Type 59s have been fitted with an infra-red searchlight for both the commander and gunner and a larger infra-red searchlight has been mounted above the main armament and moves in elevation with it. Some vehicles have been seen fitted with what is assumed to be a laser rangefinder to the right of the infra-red searchlight mounted over the main armament.

In 1981 it was reported that for trials purposes a Chinese Type 59 had been fitted with a Barr and Stroud IR-18 thermal imager. The British company of MEL have supplied China with 30 kits of passive night vision equipment for the Type 59 MBT. These include the commander's image intensified periscope Type DC 1026/00, gunner's image intensified periscope Type DC 1024/00 and the driver's image intensified periscope Type DC 1028/00.

In a parade held in Beijing in 1984 a number of Type 59 MBTs were observed with a Western type 105 mm rifled gun with a fume extractor.

It is believed that production of the Type 59 tank began in 1957 to 1960 at Baotou in the Beijing military region. Throughout the 1970s between 500 and 700 Type 59 tanks were produced each year. In 1979 this rose to 1000, dropping to 500 in 1980 due to budgetary restrictions, then increasing to 600 in 1981, 1200 in 1982 and 1500 to 1700 in 1983. The 1982 and 1983 figures probably incude the Type 69 series tanks as well.

Close-up of infra-red searchlight and what is assumed to be laser rangefinder on recent production Type 59 MBTs

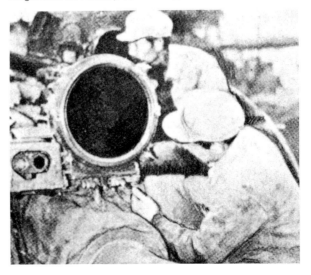

Chinese Type 59 MBT with 105 mm gun (via G Jacobs)

Outline drawing of MEL passive night vision equipment for Type 59 MBT. It is also applicable to other tanks such as the T-54/T-55

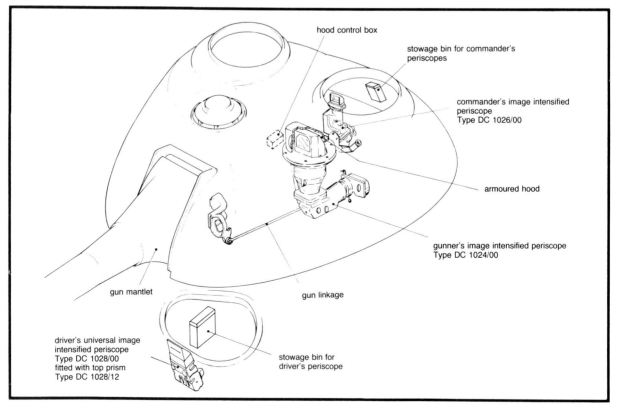

Type 59 MBT captured in South Viet-Nam and now on display in Australia (Paul Handel)

Type 59 MBT with turret removed and plated over for use in recovery role (via David Isby)

Chinese tank plant producing Type 59 MBTs with infra-red night vision equipment and what is assumed to be laser rangefinder (Tank Magazine)

Variants

Basic ARV

This may well be a local modification and is essentially a Type 59 with its turret removed, armed with a single 12.7 mm machine gun. As this vehicle is not believed to be fitted with a winch it is limited to towing operations.

AVLB

An AVLB on a Type 59 chassis is known to exist.

SPECIFICATIONS

CREW	4	FORDING		ARMOUR		
COMBAT WEIGHT	36 000 kg	without preparation	1.4 m	Hull front upper	97 mm at 58°	
POWER-TO-WEIGHT		with preparation	5.5 m	Hull front lower	99 mm at 55°	
RATIO	14.44 hp/tonne	GRADIENT	60%	Hull sides upper	79 mm at 0°	
GROUND PRESSURE	0.8 kg/cm²	VERTICAL OBSTACLE	0.79 m	Hull sides lower	20 mm at 0°	
LENGTH GUN		TRENCH	2.68 m	Hull rear upper	46 mm at 0°	
FORWARDS	9 m	ENGINE	V-12 Model 12150L	Hull rear lower	46 mm at 0°	
LENGTH HULL	6.17 m		liquid-cooled diesel	Hull top	33 mm	
WIDTH	3.27 m		developing 520 hp at	Hull floor – front	20 mm	
HEIGHT	2.59 m		2000 rpm	Hull floor – rear	20 mm	
GROUND CLEARANCE	0.425 m	TRANSMISSION	manual, 5 forward and	Turret front	203 mm at 0°	
TRACK	2.855 m		1 reverse gears	Turret sides	150 mm at 0°	
TRACK WIDTH	580 mm	SUSPENSION	torsion bar	Turret rear	64 mm at 0°	
LENGTH OF TRACK		ELECTRICAL SYSTEM	24 V	Turret roof	39 mm at 79°	
ON GROUND	4.135 m	ARMAMENT (but see text)		Mantlet	included in above	
MAX ROAD SPEED	50 km/h	main	1 × 100 m Type 59		figures	
FUEL CAPACITY		coaxial	1 × 7.62 mm Type 59T MG			
main	815 litres	bow	1 × 7.62 mm Type 59T MG			
external	400 litres	anti-aircraft	1 × 12.7 mm Type 54 MG			
RANGE		AMMUNITION				
main fuel supply	400 km	main	34			
main + external		coaxial/hull	3500			
supply	600 km	anti-aircraft	200			
		GUN ELEVATION/				
		DEPRESSION	+17°/−4°			

Status: Production probably complete. In service with Albania, China, Congo, Iran, Iraq, Kampuchea, North Korea, Pakistan, Sudan, Tanzania, Vietnam, Zaire, Zambia and Zimbabwe.

Manufacturer: Chinese state arsenals. Enquiries to China North Industries Corporation, 7A, Yuetan Nanjie, Beijing, People's Republic of China.

FRANCE

Engin Principal de Combat

Development

In December 1982, following the collapse of the French/West German MBT project, the French prime minister advised Parliament that studies would begin in 1983 for a successor to the current AMX-30 and AMX-30 B2 MBTs used by the French Army. At the same time he stated that France was ready to consider proposals by other European partners for such an MBT.

Project definition on the Engin Principal de Combat (EPC) was completed by the Atelier de Construction d'Issy-les-Moulineaux in 1985 and by that time five test rigs were already being used in component development, one for the suspension, three for automotive trials and the fifth for the weapon system.

It is expected that six EPC prototypes will be built, the first being completed in 1989. Production should start at the Atelier de Construction Roanne in 1991 and first production tanks completed in 1992. The new tank is not expected to be released for export until the mid-1990s.

Description

The EPC will have a conventional layout with the driver at the front, turret in the centre and engine and transmission at rear. The turret will have a low profile and an automatic loader in the bustle. The commander will sit on the right and the gunner on the left, both will be able to aim and fire the main armament. Turret traverse and weapon elevation will be electric with manual controls for emergency use. Gun elevation will be +18° and depression −8°.

The EPC will be powered by a Poyaud V8X-1500 Hyperbar diesel developing 1500 hp coupled to a SOMA Minerva ESM 500 transmission with four forward and two reverse gears and a hydrostatic transmission. An auxiliary power unit will be fitted to allow the main engine to be shut down if required. With a maximum combat weight of 50 tonnes the EPC would have a power-to-weight ratio of 31 hp/tonne, more than any MBT in service today, including the Leopard 2 and the M1.

The suspension will be hydro-pneumatic with six road wheels either side, the idler at the front and drive sprocket at the rear.

Main armament of the EPC will be an improved 120 mm smooth-bore gun firing both French and West German ammunition with combustible cartridge cases. The barrel will be the same length as that of the 120 mm smooth-gun fitted to the AMX-40 MBT but will have a shorter recoil and a new breech for a higher muzzle velocity. An APFSDS round with a long rod penetrator would have a muzzle velocity of between 1700 and 1750 metres a second. A HEAT round with an anti-helicopter capability has also been mentioned. The weapon will be fed by an automatic loader holding 20 rounds so enabling the tank crew to be reduced to three, commander, gunner and driver.

A 12.7 mm machine gun will be mounted coaxially with the main armament but this will not have independent elevation as on the earlier AMX-40/AMX-32 and AMX-30. A 7.62 mm anti-aircraft machine gun will be mounted on the turret roof and could be used by the commander or gunner.

The fire-control system will include a modular thermal imaging camera developed by SAT/TRT. Sights for the commander and gunner will be by SFIM and have a day/night capability.

The tank will have a basic steel armour shell to which will be added a layer of reactive armour which will react when hit by HEAT and other projectiles. This type of armour is already in service with the Israeli Army fitted on M60 and Centurion series MBTs. Increased protection will also be given to the tank against top effect weapons. With such a high power-to-weight ratio the EPC will be able to accept additional armour, if required, without decreasing the ratio to an unacceptable degree.

Like the AMX-30 series, the EPC will have an NBC system and the ability to be fitted with a snorkel for deep fording.

Status: Development.

Manufacturer: When placed in production the EPC will be manufactured by the Atelier de Construction Roanne (ARE). Enquiries to Groupement Industriel des Armements Terrestres (GIAT), 10 place G Clémenceau, 92211 Saint-Cloud, France.

AMX-40 Main Battle Tank

Development

The AMX-40 MBT has been designed by the Atelier de Construction d'Issy-les-Moulineaux specifically for the export market, with the first prototype completed in 1983 and first shown at the 1983 Satory Exhibition. By late 1984 three prototypes of the AMX-40 had been completed, the fourth prototype was completed in 1985.

Whereas the AMX-32 was essentially an upgraded AMX-30 with a lower power-to-weight ratio, the AMX-40 is a new vehicle and offers significant advantages over the

Main components of AMX-40 MBT
(1) night-vision camera **(2)** smoke dischargers **(3)** gunner's telescope M581 **(4)** gunner's panel **(6)** AA52 machine gun **(7)** tank commander's tv monitor **(8)** tank commander's panel **(9)** tank commander's telescope M496 **(10)** cupola **(11)** commander's stabilised sight M527 **(12)** radios **(13)** NBC compartment **(14)** north sensor **(15)** vehicle tool chest **(16)** air supply dust extractor **(17)** radiator (engine cooling) **(18)** hydraulic mechanism box **(19)** air filter (cyclones and paper filters) **(20)** anti-blast wall **(21)** extraction loading aid **(22)** skirts **(23)** loader's panel **(24)** loader's seat **(25)** tank commander's seat **(26)** lateral vehicle tool chests **(27)** gunner's seat **(28)** servomechanism electronics **(29)** instrument panel **(30)** driver's seat **(31)** gear shift **(32)** steering wheel **(33)** 20 mm gun with super-elevation device **(34)** hull ammunition magazine **(35)** 120 mm gun **(36)** protection bays **(37)** connector-fitted track

Front view of AMX-40 MBT with turret traversed to front and driver's hatch closed (GIAT)

earlier tank in the key areas of armour protection, mobility and firepower. As the AMX-32 is only offered now with a 105 mm gun the AMX-40 is the only French export MBT with a 120 mm gun, a further development of which will be the main armament of the EPC MBT which will enter service with the French Army in the 1990s. The AMX-40 has already been offered to Spain which has previously manufactured the AMX-30 under licence for the Spanish Army.

Description

The layout of the AMX-40 is similar to the AMX-32's with the driver's compartment at the front, turret in the centre and engine and transmission at the rear. Protection is provided against infantry anti-tank weapons and tank rounds up to 100 mm in calibre over the frontal arc by laminate type armour.

The driver sits on the left and has a single-piece hatch cover and three forward facing periscopes, one of which is integral with the hatch cover. The centre periscope can be replaced by an image intensification periscope for night driving. To the right of the driver is some 120 mm ammunition stowage.

The turret is similar to that of the AMX-32 with the commander sitting on the right side and the gunner forward and below him. The commander's cupola can be traversed through a full 360 degrees, has a single-piece hatch cover, eight periscopes for all-round observation and a gyro-stabilised SFIM M527 sight mounted on the left side of the cupola roof. This can be used for target acquisition, laying of main armament and for observation, and has a magnification of ×2 and ×8 in the day mode and ×1 in the night mode.

The AMX-40 is fitted with the integrated COTAC fire-control system also fitted in the AMX-32 and AMX-30 B2 MBTs and fully described in the latter entry. Mounted on the right side of the mantlet (on the AMX-32 on the left) is the DI VT 13A Thomson-CSF LLLTV camera which moves in elevation with the main armament. This passive system, with both the commander and gunner provided with a monitor screen, enables the AMX-40 to engage targets between 1000 and 2000 metres away, depending on the environmental conditions, with the same accuracy as in daylight. The commander also has a roof-mounted M496 sight with a magnification of ×8.

The gunner has an APX M581 sight with a magnification of ×10 and an M550/TCV 80 laser rangefinder with a maximum range of 10 000 metres. In addition the gunner has two roof-mounted periscopes for observation.

The loader sits on the left of the turret and has a single-piece hatch cover opening to the rear and three periscopes, the ones to his front and rear are turntable mounted. In the left side of the hull is an ammunition resupply hatch. Stowage baskets are provided on either side of the turret and at the rear are a stowage box and basket.

The AMX-40 is powered by a Poyaud V12X 12-cylinder diesel developing 1100 hp coupled to a West German ZF transmission; on production vehicles this would be replaced by the French ESM 500 automatic transmission which has also been selected for the EPC.

Suspension is of the torsion bar type with six dual rubber-tyred road wheels, idler at the front, drive sprocket at the rear and track return rollers. The tracks are wider than those of the AMX-32 and AMX-30 MBTs and can be fitted with grousers if required, these being carried on the top of the glacis plate to the right of the driver's position. The front two road wheel stations have improved Messier dampers. The upper parts of the tracks are covered by armoured skirts that hinge upwards to allow access to the engine for maintenance. The skirts over the front four road wheels are much thicker than the remainder as these provide lateral protection for the crew compartment.

Main armament of the AMX-40 is a 120 mm smooth-bore gun which fires fixed ammunition with a combustible cartridge case. An assisted loading device is installed which enables ammunition to be loaded into the breech while the tank is moving or stationary. The 120 mm smooth-bore gun can fire APFSDS-T, APFSDS-T (practice), or HEAT multi-purpose rounds.

A 20 mm F2 cannon is mounted coaxially to the left of the main armament and has independent elevation from −8 degrees to +40 degrees to enable it to be used against slow-flying aircraft. A 7.62 mm machine gun with a white light searchlight is mounted on the right side of the tank commander's cupola. Mounted either side of the forward part of the turret is a bank of three electrically-operated smoke dischargers firing forwards.

Of the 35 rounds of ammunition carried for the main armament, 21 are in the hull front to the right of the driver,

AMX-40 MBT from rear showing side skirts which provide additional armour protection to forward part of vehicle (GIAT)

AMX-40 MBT with turret traversed to left and showing extensive external stowage on bustle. This vehicle has the Galix protection system fitted on forward part of turret (GIAT)

Latest prototype of the AMX-40 MBT with commander's hatch open (GIAT)

two drums each with five rounds and two separate racks of two rounds each are in the turret bustle with armour protection between them and the crew.

Standard equipment for the AMX-40 includes a fire-extinguishing system for both crew and engine compartments, emergency escape hatch to rear of driver's position, NBC pack, facility to inject diesel fuel into the exhaust to lay a smoke screen and built-in test equipment (BITE).

The fourth prototype of the AMX-40 MBT made its first appearance in June 1985 and was expected to go to Egypt for trials late in 1985. The fourth prototype has been designed specifically for hot climates and can operate in temperatures of up to 50 degrees Centigrade without any degradation in performance.

The fuel tanks of the AMX-40 contain 1100 litres of fuel, sufficient for 600 km. This can be extended by two long-range fuel drums mounted at the rear which can be quickly jettisoned by the driver. The AMX-40 shown at Satory in June 1985 was fitted with one long-range fuel tank and another drum containing a further seven rounds of 120 mm ammunition. Depending on the tactical situation, the AMX-40 would carry two drums of fuel or two drums of ammunition, or one of each.

Mounted under the nose of the fourth AMX-40 prototype is a sectionalised dozer blade that is released manually by one

of the crew and when in position enables the tank to prepare its own fire position so reducing immediate requirements for engineer support.

As an alternative to the normal electrically-operated smoke dischargers either side of the turret, the AMX-40 can also be fitted with the GIAT/Lacroix Galix protection system. This can launch three types of grenade, fragmentation, smoke and decoy.

SPECIFICATIONS

CREW	4
COMBAT WEIGHT	43 000 kg
POWER-TO-WEIGHT RATIO	25 hp/tonne
GROUND PRESSURE	0.89 kg/cm²
LENGTH GUN FORWARDS	10.04 m
LENGTH HULL	6.8 m
WIDTH	
overall	3.36 m
over tracks	3.18 m
HEIGHT	
to turret roof	2.38 m
to commander's sight	3.08 m
GROUND CLEARANCE	0.45 m
TRACK WIDTH	570 mm
MAX ROAD SPEED	70 km/h
AVERAGE ROAD SPEED	55 km/h
AVERAGE CROSS-COUNTRY SPEED	50 km/h
FUEL CAPACITY	1100 litres
MAX RANGE	600 km
with long-range fuel tanks	850 km
FORDING	
without preparation	1.3 m
with preparation	2.3 m
with snorkel	4 m
GRADIENT	70%
SIDE SLOPE	30%
VERTICAL OBSTACLE	1 m
TRENCH	3.2 m
ENGINE	Poyaud V12X 12-cylinder diesel developing 1100 hp at 2500 rpm
TRANSMISSION	ZF automatic
STEERING	hydrostatic
SUSPENSION	torsion bar
ELECTRICAL SYSTEM	24 V
ARMAMENT	
main	1 × 120 mm
coaxial	1 × 20 mm cannon
anti-aircraft	1 × 7.62 mm MG
smoke dischargers	2 × 3
AMMUNITION	
main	37
coaxial	578
anti-aircraft	2250

Status: Prototypes.

Manufacturer: If and when placed in production the AMX-40 will be manufactured by the Atelier de Construction Roanne (ARE).

Enquiries to Groupement Industriel des Armements Terrestres (GIAT), 10 place G Clémenceau, 92211 Saint-Cloud, France.

AMX-32 Main Battle Tank

Development

The AMX-32 has been developed from 1975 by the ARE specifically for the export market with the first prototype, armed with the same 105 mm gun CN-105-F1 as the AMX-30 MBT completed in 1979.

Second prototype of AMX-32 MBT which was first shown in June 1981. This photograph clearly shows the new side skirt which provides increased lateral protection (GIAT)

The second prototype, shown for the first time in June 1981, has a redesigned turret and hull incorporating laminate armour, new mantlet, no searchlight, repositioned DI VT 13 (from the right to the left side of the main armament) and redesigned track; these and other improvements have increased the weight of the AMX-32 from 38 000 to 40 000 kg.

The second prototype of the AMX-32 was armed with a 120 mm gun but early in 1983 it was announced that this was no longer being offered although it is available for the AMX-40. Four prototypes of the AMX-32 have been built and one of which has been demonstrated in the Middle East.

Description
The layout of the AMX-32 is almost identical to the AMX-30 described in the following entry but with major improvements in the areas of fire-control, mobility and armour protection.

Armament/ammunition
Main armament of the AMX-32 is identical to the AMX-30 which is fully described in the next entry as is its range of GIAT produced ammunition.

Mounted to the left of the main armament is a 20 mm M693 (F2) cannon which can be elevated independently to +40 degrees or linked to the main armament. A total of 480 rounds of ammunition are carried for this weapon of which 230 are for ready use. A 7.62 mm machine gun is mounted on the right side of the commander's cupola with a total of 2150 rounds of ammunition of which 650 are for ready use.

Mounted either side of the forward part of the turret are three electrically-operated smoke dischargers firing forwards. An ammunition resupply hatch is provided in the left side of the turret. At the rear of the turret on the left is a stowage box, on the right side is a stowage basket. The AMX-32 MBT has an NBC system fitted as standard, the filters being changed from outside the vehicle.

Fire-control
The integrated COTAC fire-control system is a further development of the system installed in the AMX-10RC (6 × 6) reconnaissance vehicle which is in service with France and Morocco.

The commander's cupola, designated the TOP 7 VS, is fixed, whereas the TOP 7 cupola on the AMX-30 B2 and the basic AMX-30 can be traversed through a full 360 degrees. The 7.62 mm machine gun can be aimed and fired by the tank commander from inside his cupola as the weapon is mounted externally and rotates by itself around the cupola.

Mounted in the roof of the commander's cupola, on the left side, is a gyro stabilised SFIM M527 sight which gives the commander all-round observation and allows him to aim and fire the main armament, even when moving across country. The commander can also designate the target for the gunner and then resume his role of tank commander. The M527 has a day mode (with a magnification of ×2 or ×8) and a night mode (with a magnification of ×1), the commander's cupola also has eight periscopes for all-round observation.

Mounted on the left of the mantlet is a DI VT 13A Thomson-CSF LLLTV camera which moves in elevation with the main armament, this is the same model as installed on the AMX-30 B2 and the AMX-10RC.

This passive system enables the AMX-32 to engage targets between 1000 and 2000 metres away, depending on the environmental conditions, with the same degree of accuracy as in daylight.

The system consists of three main components, a tv camera, monitors and a control unit.

Second prototype of AMX-32 MBT with redesigned hull front (GIAT)

Front view of second prototype of AMX-32 showing redesigned hull front and turret (GIAT)

The CC8A tv camera has a Thomson-CSF 25 mm diameter supernocticon image tube and gives a 4° × 5° 30′ field of view with 625 lines and 50 images per half second. The commander and gunner each have a RR 107 C tv monitor with an 11 cm screen. On each of these screens the observed and aiming axes are displayed, the latter in the form of a single electronic graticule automatically positioned by the fire-control computer. The BC 458 B control unit is operated by the tank commander and provides boresighting and introduction of firing corrections.

The gunner has an APX M581 telescope with a magnification of ×10 and an M550/TCV 80 laser range-finder with a maximum range of 10 000 metres and an accuracy of ±5 metres. The fire-control system also takes into account the following parameters: target elevation and traverse speed, slant, outside temperature, wind speed, altitude and ammunition.

The fire-control system enables stationary or moving targets to be engaged under day and night conditions over all combat ranges with a 90 per cent hit probability.

The gunner has a roof-mounted periscope while the loader has three periscopes; the front and rear ones are turntable-mounted and the side one is fixed.

Mobility

The AMX-32 can be fitted with the same HS 110-2 700 hp engine as installed in the AMX-30 or the more recent HS 110-S2 cooled super-charged engine developing 800 hp. This is coupled to the ENC 200 gearbox with lock up torque

Second prototype of AMX-32 MBT showing main components **(1)** elevation sensor **(2)** gunner's telescope M581 **(3)** gunner's panel **(4)** gunner's tv monitor **(5)** gun gyro-accelerometer box **(6)** tank commander's tv monitor **(7)** tank commander's panel **(8)** turret gyro-accelerometer box **(9)** cupola **(10)** tank commander's telescope M527 **(11)** radio-sets **(12)** NBC compartment **(13)** flux valve **(14)** case **(15)** radiator (engine cooling) **(16)** oil cooler (gearbox cooling) **(17)** mechanism box **(18)** air supply dust remover **(19)** air filter (cyclones and paper filters) **(20)** loader's seat **(21)** tank commander's seat **(22)** gunner's seat **(23)** gyro box **(24)** system electronics box **(25)** tv camera DI VT 13 **(26)** driver's seat **(27)** reverser control **(28)** steering wheel **(29)** gear shifting station **(30)** 20 mm gun with superelevation device **(31)** main gun (105 mm) **(32)** connector-fitted track (GIAT)

converter with five forward and one reverse gears and hydrostatic steering.

Suspension is similar to the AMX-30 but the torsion bars, shock absorbers and bump stops have been strengthened to take account of the improved mobility.

Protection

The hull and turret are a combination of spaced armour, conventional armour and composite armour, with maximum possible protection being provided over the frontal arc of the tank. Side skirts protect the upper part of the suspension and these hinge upwards through 180 degrees to give access to the suspension for maintenance.

Second prototype of AMX-32 MBT showing commander's cupola with externally mounted 7.62 mm MG and SFIM M527 stabilised periscopic sight (GIAT)

Optional equipment

This includes an air-conditioning system, fire-extinguishing system, exhaust-type smoke generator and connector-type tracks (basic equipment) or metal tracks.

SPECIFICATIONS

CREW	4	GRADIENT	60%	AMMUNITION	
COMBAT WEIGHT	39 000 kg	SIDE SLOPE	30%	main	47
UNLOADED WEIGHT	37 000 kg	VERTICAL OBSTACLE	0.9 m	coaxial	480
POWER-TO-WEIGHT		TRENCH	2.9 m	anti-aircraft	2150
RATIO	17.94 hp/tonne	ENGINE		GUN CONTROL	
GROUND PRESSURE	0.9 kg/cm²	(see text)	Hispano-Suiza HS 110	EQUIPMENT	
LENGTH GUN			12-cylinder, water-cooled	Turret power control	electro-hydraulic with
FORWARDS	9.45 m		super-charged multi-fuel		manual controls
LENGTH HULL	6.59 m		developing 700 hp at	by commander	yes
WIDTH	3.24 m		2400 rpm	by gunner	yes
HEIGHT	2.96 m	TRANSMISSION	Minerva ENC 200	commander's override	yes
turret roof	2.29 m	(see text)	comprising hydraulic torque	Commander's fire-	
GROUND CLEARANCE	0.45 m		converter, 5 speed gearbox,	control override	yes
TRACK WIDTH	510 or 570 mm		forward/reverse lever and	Gun elevation/depression	
LENGTH OF TRACK ON			hydrostatic steering system	main armament	+20°/−8°
GROUND	3.84 m	STEERING TYPE	double differential	coaxial cannon	+40°/−8°
MAX ROAD SPEED		STEERING CONTROL	hydrostatic, infinitely	AA MG	+45°/−10°
1st gear	10 km/h		variable	Max rate power	
2nd gear	17 km/h	SUSPENSION	torsion bar	traverse	360° in 12–13 s
3rd gear	26 km/h	WHEEL TRAVEL		Max rate power	
4th gear	42 km/h	bump	180 mm	elevation	5.5°/1 s
5th gear	65 km/h	rebound	100 mm	Gun stabiliser	
ROAD RANGE	530 km	ARMAMENT		vertical	no
FORDING	1.3 m	main	1 × 105 mm	horizontal	no
with preparation	2.2 m	coaxial	1 × 20 mm cannon	Elevation quadrant	yes
with snorkel	4 m	anti-aircraft	1 × 7.62 mm MG	Traverse indicator	yes
		SMOKE-LAYING			
		EQUIPMENT	3 smoke dischargers either side of turret		

Status: Demonstration prototypes. Not yet in production.

Manufacturer: When placed in production the AMX-32 would be manufactured by Atelier de Construction Roanne (ARE).

Enquiries to Groupement Industriel des Armements Terrestres (GIAT), 10 place G Clémenceau, 92211 Saint-Cloud, France.

AMX-30 Main Battle Tank

Development

In 1956 a joint French, West German and Italian requirement was drawn up for a European Main Battle Tank which would be well-armed, lighter and more mobile than tanks in service at that time such as the American M47/M48 and British Centurion tanks.

In 1958 France and West Germany started design work on their respective tanks of which it was expected that one tank would be selected for production. Prototypes built by both countries were tested in 1963 at Mailly-de-Camp, Bourges and Satory in France and at the Meppen ranges in West Germany. But in the end West Germany adopted the Leopard as it was later called, France the AMX-30, while Italy chose the American M60A1 which was subsequently built under licence in Italy by OTO Melara.

Design work was carried out on the AMX-30 at the Atelier de Construction d'Issy-les-Moulineaux under the direction of the Direction des Études et Fabrications d'Armement (now Direction Technique des Armements Terrestres), with the first two prototypes being completed in 1960. A further seven prototypes built with the Hispano-Suiza HS 110 12-cylinder multi-fuel engine which was also fitted to production tanks were completed early in 1963 and in July of that year the tank was adopted by the French Army as the replacement for its American-supplied M47 tanks. Before production began two pre-production tanks were built.

Production of the AMX-30 began in 1966 at the Atelier de Construction Roanne (ARE) which had previously been building the AMX-13 light tank, production of which was transferred to Creusot-Loire to enable the factory to concentrate on the AMX-30. It was also produced under licence in Spain, additional details of Spanish AMX-30 production are given under Spain in the second part of this book. As of May 1985 a total of 1900 AMX-30 and 190 AMX-30 B2 MBTs had been built.

Description

The hull of the AMX-30 is made of rolled steel plates welded together. It is divided into three compartments: driver's at the front, fighting in the centre and the engine at the rear.

The driver is seated at the front of the vehicle on the left with a single-piece hatch cover opening to the left and three periscopes. The centre periscope, depending on the model of the tank, can be either a day periscope which can be replaced by an infra-red or image intensification night periscope (Thomson-CSF TH 9478), or a SOPELEM OB-16-A periscope. This has a binocular system for infra-red light by night and a monocular system for day driving. The infra-red system has a magnification of ×1 and a 35-degree field of view

AMX-30 MBT with coaxial 20 mm cannon elevated independently of 105 mm gun (GIAT)

and the day system has a similar magnification and a 24-degree field of view.

The other three crew members are seated in the turret with the commander and gunner on the right and the loader, who also operates the radio, on the left. The commander's cupola is a TOP 7 with ten periscopes for all-round vision and a single-piece hatch cover opening to the rear. Mounted on the forward part of the commander's cupola is a SOPELEM M 270 prism head. This comprises an armoured housing and a thick glass behind which is a prism, swivelling in elevation and reflecting the image of the terrain towards the M 267 day sight or the OB-23-A infra-red telescope (magnification ×4, 9-degree field of view), the object lenses of which fit in its lower part. On the right of the prism is a swivelling arm which supports the 7.62 mm machine gun and its PH-9-A infra-red searchlight which has a 500-metre range when being used in the infra-red mode and a 700-metre range in the white light mode. The weapon can be elevated from −10 to +45 degrees by a handwheel in the turret roof. The prism may also be used to aim the coaxial 20 mm cannon, in which case the head (of the prism) is electrically servo-controlled by the elevation swivel of the 20 mm cannon. The M 270 has a magnification of ×10 and allows the tank commander to locate and identify targets and bring the turret to bear onto the target. The tank commander also operates the SOPELEM M 208 rangefinder which can be used either as a telescope with a magnification of ×6 and a range of 600 to 3500 metres or by means of a superimposed image when it has a magnification of ×12 and a similar range.

Mounted on the left side of the turret, coaxial with the main armament, is a SOPELEM PH-8-B searchlight, which has a maximum range of 2000 metres when used in the white

AMX-30 MBT

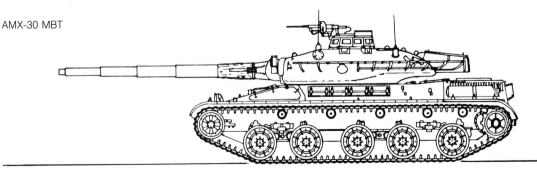

light mode and a range of 1000 metres in the infra-red mode.

The gunner, who is seated below and in front of the commander, has an M 271 day sight with a magnification of ×8 which can be changed for an OB-17-A sight. This is mounted in the roof of the turret and has a luminous graticule, magnification of ×5.4 and a 7-degree field of view. When used with the PH-8-B infra-red searchlight it has a range of 800 metres. The gunner also has two periscopes.

The loader is seated on the left of the turret and is provided with a single-piece hatch cover that opens to the rear and two periscopes. A small circular hatch in the left side of the turret is used for replenishing ammunition and ejecting spent cartridge cases manually.

The engine is to the immediate rear of the bulkhead separating the engine compartment from the fighting compartment. The Hispano-Suiza HS 110 engine is manufactured by Renault, and operates on oil, petrol or paraffin. The engine is water-cooled and air is drawn in above the chassis in the rear part of the tank and blown down through the radiator by a fan driven by the engine. The speed of the fan is governed by the water temperature.

The complete powerpack, comprising the engine, combined gearbox and steering unit, and clutch assembly can be removed in 45 minutes by a three-man team. The powerpack can also be run outside the tank before installation.

The transmission consists of an automatic clutch, combined gearbox and steering unit, brakes and two final drives. In the basic version the centrifugal type clutch is activated electrically by the gear shift lever; a non-synchronised reverser enables the same number of gears to be engaged in reverse as forwards. The combined gearbox and steering mechanism contains the mechanically-operated gearbox giving five speeds both forwards and in reverse and a triple differential steering system.

The brakes are hydraulically operated and are used as both service and parking brakes. Each final drive comprises spur-type right-angle gears and an epicyclic gear train.

The torsion bar suspension consists of five rubber-tyred twin road wheels with the idler at the front and the drive sprocket at the rear. There are five track return rollers which support the inside of the track only. The first, second, fourth and fifth road wheels are mounted on bogies and the first and fifth road wheels are provided with hydraulic shock absorbers. The centrally-guided steel track has removable rubber

AMX-30 MBT of French Army with all hatches closed. This particular vehicle is not fitted with the infra-red/white searchlight to left of 105 mm gun (GIAT)

Rear view of AMX-30 MBT showing turret bustle (GIAT)

pads and each track weighs 1580 kg. When new it has 83 links.

The AMX-30 can ford to a maximum depth of 1.3 metres without preparation and 2 metres with preparation. When deeper rivers are encountered a snorkel is erected over the loader's hatch. Two types of snorkel are available, a wide one for training and a much thinner one for operations, ie similar in concept to the Soviet snorkels fitted to the T-54/T-55 and T-62 MBTs. Before entering the water a ring is inflated around the turret, mantlet and cupola using the electrically-driven compressor, and two blanking plates are fitted over the engine compartment louvres; these are carried on the right side of the glacis plate when not in use.

Standard equipment on all AMX-30s includes a battery-operated electric pump for refuelling and a lubricating pump using the tank's compressed air circuit. The power receptacle in the driver's compartment can be used for recharging the tank's batteries from another tank, and also for supplying the electric pump used for refuelling. The tank is also equipped with an NBC system, heater, automatic fire alarm system, radios, crew intercom system and an infantry telephone at the rear.

Main armament of the AMX-30 is a 105 mm rifled gun designated the CN-105-F1 with a length of 56 calibres. The gun does not have a muzzle brake or a fume extractor but is fitted with a magnesium alloy thermal sleeve. A compressed air system removes any fumes from the barrel. The recoil system consists of two diametrically-opposed hydraulic brakes and an oleo-pneumatic recuperator for counter-recoil of the barrel.

The 105 mm gun can fire HEAT, HE, phosphorous smoke or illuminating rounds of a French design and can also fire standard 105 mm ammunition as used with the L7 series of weapons mounted in the Leopard 1 and M60 series of MBTs.

The HEAT round is known as the Obus à Charge Creuse de 105 mm Modèle F1, or OCC 105 F1 or Obus G for short. It has been demonstrated that up to a range of 3000 metres a 75 per cent hit probability can be achieved, increasing to over 90 per cent at 2500 metres. The projectile has a very small dispersion and the weapon has maximum stated rate of fire of eight rounds per minute.

The HE shell has an effective range of 3500 metres in direct fire and with the gun elevated to +20 degrees a maximum

DESIGNATION (NATO) (French)	APFSDS* OBUS FLÈCHE	HEAT† OCC(OBUS A)	HE‡ OC	Smoke OBUS Fumigène Incendiare	Illuminating OBUS Eclairant
WEIGHT OF COMPLETE ROUND	17.1 kg	22 kg	20.8 kg	21.7 kg	17.8 kg
WEIGHT OF PROJECTILE	5.8 kg	10.95 kg	12.1 kg	12.77 kg	11.7 kg
WEIGHT OF FILLING	n/app	0.78 kg	2 kg	1.77 kg	0.46 kg
TYPE OF FILLING	n/app	Hexolite	HE	WP	illuminant
LENGTH OF PROJECTILE	541.5 mm	465 mm	444 mm	444 mm	444 mm
MUZZLE VELOCITY	1525 m/s	1000 m/s	700 m/s	695 m/s	20 m/s

* Sub-projectile weighs 3.8 kg, will penetrate 150 mm of armour at an incidence of 60° at range of 5000 m
† Practice version is SCC. OCC will penetrate 400 mm of armour at 0° and 150 mm of armour at 65°
‡ Practice version is PLPN

range of 11 000 metres can be achieved. Other rounds available include a phosphorous smoke incendiary and an illuminating round which will illuminate a circle 800 metres in diameter for 35 seconds. The latest round to enter production for the French Army is the GIAT APFSDS. Basic specifications of the 105 mm rounds are listed above.

A total of 47 rounds of 105 mm ammunition is carried of which 19 are in the turret (18 in the bustle) and 28 in the hull to the right of the driver.

Mounted to the left of the main armament is a 20 mm Model F2 (Type M693) cannon, which can be elevated with the main armament but can also be elevated on its own to a maximum of +40 degrees for use against slow-flying aircraft and helicopters. The cannon has a maximum effective range of 1500 metres and can be fired by the gunner or the tank commander. The 20 mm cannon can be either dual feed (with HEI rounds with a muzzle velocity of 1050 metres per second and armour-piercing rounds with a muzzle velocity of 1250 metres per second), or single feed firing American M56 type ammunition. A total of 500 rounds of ready use ammunition is carried with a further 550 rounds held in reserve. When originally introduced into service a 12.7 mm machine gun was mounted to the left of the main armament. This was provided with 600 rounds of ammunition.

AMX-30 MBT with turret traversed to rear. Tank transporter being used is Tidelium 40 Ampliroll T 40 A (GIAT)

AMX-30 with thin snorkel entering river showing stowage space for snorkel on hull rear (ECP Armées)

CILAS/SOPELEM M409 sight as fitted to AMX-30S with optical sight on left and laser rangefinder on right

Mounted to the right of the commander's cupola is a 7.62 mm Model F1 machine gun which can be aimed and fired from within the cupola. The weapon has an elevation of +45 degrees and a depression of −10 degrees. A total of 2050 rounds of 7.62 mm ammunition is carried of which 550 are ready for immediate use. The empty cartridge cases are automatically ejected outside the tank. Maximum effective range of the 7.62 mm machine gun is quoted as 700 metres.

Two smoke dischargers mounted either side of the turret can lay a smoke screen which will cover the tank in eight seconds.

The hydraulic aiming control system is a SAMM CH 27-1S with elevation controlled through a hydraulic actuating cylinder/shock absorber and traverse controlled through a hydraulic motor. The gunner is provided with dual handle controls and the tank commander has a single handle control which can also be used to override the gunner.

A more simplified version of the AMX-30 was developed for export with no night vision or NBC system and the commander's cupola replaced by an S 470 cupola with an externally-mounted 12.7 mm machine gun rather than a 7.62 mm machine gun as installed on French Army AMX-30s, and the coaxial weapon a 7.62 mm machine gun rather than a 12.7 mm machine gun or a 20 mm cannon.

For trials an AMX-30 was fitted with the 142 mm ACRA guided missile system, but this was subsequently cancelled, not for technical reasons, but because of the high cost of the missile rounds.

It is expected that in the future the French Army's AMX-30 MBT fleet will be fitted with additional armour protection on turret front, sides and top.

AMX-30S

For desert operations the AMX-30S has been developed with the following modifications: the fitting of sand shields, reduction in the ratios of the gearbox which limits its speed to 60 km/h and an engine developing only 620 hp at 2400 rpm. At least one foreign army has adopted the AMX-30S and its tanks are fitted with a CILAS/SOPELEM M 409 sight. This has a day sight with a magnification of ×8 and an 8-degree field of view, infra-red night sight with a magnification of ×4.5 and a 10-degree field of view and a laser rangefinder with a range of between 400 and 10 000 metres. This development allows the tank commander to range onto a target without having to traverse the turret. In addition the laser rangefinder increases the first-round hit probability.

AMX-30 B2

The AMX-30 B2, announced in June 1979, is essentially an AMX-30 with an integrated fire-control system based on a laser rangefinder and an LLLTV system, new gearbox and other improvements. The French Army ordered 50 vehicles in both the 1981 and 1982 defence budgets and first deliveries were made to the 503rd Regiment at Mourmelon in January 1982. The French Army is expected to take delivery of some 271 AMX-30 B2 MBTs. In addition, 693 AMX-30s will be converted to the AMX-30 B2 configuration. Between 1984 and 1988 it is expected that 511 modernised AMX-30 B2 tanks will have been delivered to the French Army with a further 182 being delivered after 1988. Orders were for 182 conversions in 1984–85 and 273 for the period 1986–1988. GIAT is now offering the AMX-30 B2 conversion kit to existing overseas users of the AMX-30.

The COTAC FCS, officially designated the APX M581, has been designed by the AMX-APX in collaboration with the Ateliers de Construction de Tarbes. Its main components are the gunner's APX M544 telescopic sight which is combined with an APX M579 electronic control system and an APX M421 optical module containing a computer-

The complete 105 mm APFSDS round (left) with the projectile and sabot (right)

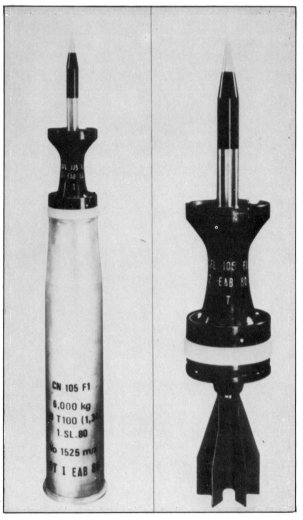

The AMX-30S has been designed specifically to meet the requirements of countries in the Middle East and is known to be used by Saudi Arabia (GIAT)

AMX-30 B2 from front showing coaxial 20 mm cannon and the amount of 105 mm, 20 mm and 7.62 mm ammunition carried (Christopher F Foss)

controlled graticule. The laser rangefinder is the APX M550 and is made by CILAS under the designation TCV 80. It has a maximum range of 10 000 metres and is accurate to ±5 metres. The SOPELEM telescopic sight has a magnification of ×10 and is directly coupled to the main armament. In

AMX-30 B2 MBT showing LLLTV camera mounted externally to the right of the mantlet (GIAT)

addition to the M581 rangefinder telescope the gunner has a rotatable M282 periscope, a fixed M223 periscope and a tv monitor associated with an LLLTV monitor.

The COTAC FCS also incorporates an accelerometer-type trunnion tilt sensor and a control panel. The tank commander manually inserts information via the control panel concerning the type of ammunition being fired, drift and jump angles, cross wind velocity, altitude and ambient temperature. Apart from the ammunition information, most of this information has to be inserted only once a day. To determine lead angles for the engagement of moving targets, a two-axis gyroscope is mounted on the sight to measure target tracking rates in both azimuth and elevation.

Other parameters are automatically acquired by the gunner's rangefinder telescope including target distance, its displacement speed in elevation and azimuth and turret slant. These parameters are processed by a lead computer built into the telescope which transmits the elevation and azimuth corrections to the gunner's day sight by means of an optical compensator and the graticule of the LLLTV camera for engaging targets at night.

In addition to the ten M268 periscopes in his cupola the commander also has an M496 telescope with a magnification of ×8 for firing the 105 mm gun, for the secondary armament (eg 20 mm cannon and 7.62 mm machine gun) and aiming assembly comprising an M591-02 prism head and an OB 49 monocular telescope.

Mounted externally on the right side of the turret is the LLLTV camera with both the tank commander and gunner being provided with a tv monitor screen. The screens display an aiming mark which enables the commander or gunner to engage targets at ranges of up to 1000 metres. Additional details of this system are given in the previous entry for the AMX-32.

The loader has a rotatable M282 periscope and two fixed M223 periscopes with the driver having a central M223 periscope (or an OB 31A image intensification periscope) and two fixed M223 periscopes.

The engine of the AMX-30 B2 has been developed from that of the AMX-30 and develops 700 hp at 2600 rpm; as an option GIAT can offer a super-charged version with an output of 800 hp.

Two different gearboxes are offered. First the ENC 200 which is a gearbox of the lock-up torque converter type with

AMX-30 ARV in travelling order with spare engine on top of hull (ECP Armées)

five forward and reverse speeds and hydrostatic steering controlled by a conventional steering wheel instead of sticks. This system allows on-the-spot turning and gear changing in bends.

The second gearbox is the 5 SD which is a further development of that installed in the AMX-30 with five speeds with interlocked pneumatic control.

The suspension uses new torsion bars which give improved cross-country mobility. As an option it is possible to fit the AMX-30 B2 with connector tracks which are quieter and offer less resistance than conventional tracks.

The AMX-30 B2 is also fitted with a new collective pressurisation system with two circuits, one with complete filtration for improved NBC protection. Supplementary armouring of the turret front and sides is under development.

Variants

AMX-30 Armoured Recovery Vehicle
This is designated the AMX-30D and is designed to carry out three major tasks: the recovery of disabled and damaged vehicles, replacement of major components such as engines, and engineer work. Equipment provided includes a hydraulically-operated dozer blade at the front of the hull which is used to stabilise the vehicle while the crane is being used or during winching or for dozing. Mounted on the right side of the vehicle is a hydraulic crane which can lift 12 000 kg through 240 degrees or 15 000 kg when being used to the front of the vehicle. The main winch has a maximum capacity of 35 000 kg and is provided with 100 metres of 34 mm diameter cable while the auxiliary winch has 3500 kg capacity and is provided with 120 metres of 11.2 mm diameter cable. There are two variants of the AMX-30D, the AMX-30DI which can lift a maximum load of 15 000 kg through a full 240 degrees rather than just to the front of the vehicle and the AMX-30D(S) which is for desert operations and has modifications similar to those fitted to the AMX-30S MBT. The AMX-30D has a loaded weight of 38 000 kg and normally carries a spare engine at the rear.

AMX-30 Bridgelayer
The AMX-30 bridgelayer is not in service with the French Army and is basically an AMX-30 MBT with its turret removed and replaced with a scissors type bridge which is launched over the rear of the hull in five minutes. The bridge is a class 50 and when opened out is 22 metres

AMX-30 bridgelayer in travelling order (ECP Armées)

AMX-30 with Pluton tactical nuclear missile system with missile elevated into ready to launch position (ECP Armées)

AMX-30 Combat Engineer Tractor (EBG) using its telescopic arm to remove a tree (GIAT)

long and will span a gap of up to 20 metres. The bridge is 3.1 metres wide or 3.92 metres when fitted with widening panels. Weight is 42 500 kg with the bridge and 34 000 kg without.

Pluton Surface-to-surface Missile System
This is the AMX-30 chassis fitted with a launcher system for the Pluton tactical nuclear missile system and is used only by the French Army. The Pluton has a maximum range of 120 km and can be fitted with a tactical nuclear warhead of either 15 or 25 kt. The French Army has five regiments of Pluton, each of three batteries with each battery having two launchers.

AMX-30 Combat Engineer Tractor
The AMX-30 Combat Engineer Tractor, or Engin Blindé de Génie, is being developed and will replace the AMX-13 VCG, at present used by the French Army engineers, in the late 1980s. By early 1985 two prototypes of the EBG had been built but production had yet to commence.

The EBG is designed for use in forward areas and is equipped with a front-mounted hydraulically operated dozer blade which is fitted with six scarifying teeth, hydraulic winch with a maximum capacity of 20 000 kg, hydraulic PTO and a working arm pivoted at the front of the hull on the right side. The arm is used to lift obstacles out of the way and can be fitted with pincers to remove tree trunks (similar to those fitted to the Soviet IMR combat engineer vehicle) or an auger which can bore 220 mm diameter holes to a depth of three metres.

Armament consists of a 7.62 mm machine gun, four smoke dischargers, launching tube for demolition charges and four mine launching tubes. The 142 mm demolition charge has four folding fins, weighs 17 kg of which 10 kg is explosive and has a maximum range of 300 metres. Each of the four mine-launching arms has a tube containing five 139 mm diameter anti-tank mines, each of which weighs 2.34 kg and contains 0.7 kg of explosive. The vehicle has a three-man crew: the commander, a sapper and a driver, maximum road speed of 65 km/h and can ford to a depth of 2.5 metres without preparation or four metres with preparation.

AMX-30 MDR Flail Tank
Development of this vehicle has now been stopped.

Roland Anti-aircraft Missile System
The Euromissile anti-aircraft missile system based on a rede-signed AMX-30 MBT chassis has two missiles in the ready to launch position with a further eight missiles being carried inside the hull ready for rapid reloading, eg four missiles for each launcher arm.

The French Army uses two versions of the system, the Roland 1 clear weather system and the Roland 2 all weather system. Roland is also used by a number of other countries including Argentina (less than 10 Shelter units), Brazil (four on Marder chassis), France (on AMX-30 chassis), Iraq (15 Roland 2 on AMX-30 chassis), West Germany (144 on Marder 2 chassis in service with Army, additional shelter mounted systems on order), US Army (on 6 × 6 truck chassis). On order for Nigeria (16 on AMX-30 chassis), Jordan (20 fire units via Iraq), Venezuela (4 to 6 on AMX-30 chassis) and Spain (18 fire units ordered on AMX-30 chassis).

Shahine Anti-aircraft Missile System
This has been developed specifically for Saudi Arabia by Thomson-CSF who developed the earlier Crotale SAM based on a 4 × 4 wheeled chassis.

A typical battery consists of an acquisition unit and four firing units. The former has a surveillance radar and an automatic information and threat evaluation system that

Roland 2 on AMX-30 chassis in travelling configuration

Thomson-CSF acquisition unit for Shahine SAM system

Thomson-CSF firing unit for Shahine SAM system with six missiles in ready to launch position

allows up to 40 targets to be registered on the computer and 18 targets to be handled simultaneously.

The firing unit has a triple-channel fire control radar and can simultaneously guide two missiles to the target. Six R460 missiles are carried in the ready to launch position. The Shahine is only in service with Saudi Arabia.

AMX-30 DCA twin 30 mm self-propelled anti-aircraft gun
This is the AMX-30 chassis fitted with a SAMM TG 230A two-man turret armed with twin 30 mm cannon and 53 were purchased by Saudi Arabia to provide close range protection for its Shahine SAM systems under the designation AMX-30 SA.

Each 30 mm cannon has 300 rounds of ready use ammunition with 600 rounds being carried in reserve in the hull. Types of ammunition that can be fired by the Hispano-Suiza HSS-831A automatic cannon include SAPHEI/T, HEI/T, HEI, TP/T and TP. For travelling the Thomson-CSF Green Eye radar can be retracted into the turret bustle.

AMX-30S Sabre twin 30 mm self-propelled anti-aircraft gun
This has been developed by Thomson-CSF and SAMM with the assistance of GIAT. It is based on the AMX-30S chassis

AMX-30S fitted with Sabre turret armed with twin 30 mm cannon

and the turret is a further development of that installed on the DCA described previously, main difference being that that Sabre has improved electronics and the turret is welded instead of cast. This system is still at the prototype stage.

155 mm GCT Self-propelled Howitzer

This is an AMX-30 chassis with its turret removed and replaced by a new fully enclosed turret fitted with a 155 mm howitzer. The latter has an elevation of +66 degrees, depression of −4 degrees and turret traverse of 360 degrees. A total of 42 projectiles and 42 cartridge cases are carried in the turret rear arranged in seven racks of six cartridge cases. Various ammunition combinations are available but a typi-

155 mm GCT self-propelled howitzer (GIAT)

cal load would consist of 36 HE plus six smoke or 30 HE, six smoke and six illuminating.

The gunner can select single shots or bursts of six rounds and firing can continue until the ammunition is exhausted. Average rate of fire is eight rounds per minute when being used in automatic mode. Range depends on the type of ammunition being used, for example 155 mm Model 56 HE has a maximum range of 21 800 metres and 155 mm Thomson Brandt RAP has a range of 30 500 metres.

A 7.62 mm or 12.7 mm anti-aircraft machine gun is mounted on the turret roof and two smoke dischargers are mounted on the forward part of the turret, below the 155 mm howitzer, firing forwards. The four man crew of the GCT consists of commander, gunner, loader and driver.

The 155 mm GCT self-propelled howitzer is in service with France, Iraq and Saudi Arabia. It is normally employed in batteries of six weapons.

SPECIFICATIONS
(specifications in square brackets relate to AMX-30 B2 where this differs from AMX-30)

CREW	4
COMBAT WEIGHT	36 000 [37 000] kg
UNLOADED WEIGHT	34 000 [35 300] kg
POWER-TO-WEIGHT RATIO	20 [18.91] hp/tonne
GROUND PRESSURE	0.77 [0.85] kg/cm²
LENGTH GUN	
forwards	9.48 m
rear	8.73 m
LENGTH HULL	6.59 m
WIDTH	3.1 m
HEIGHT	
to hull top	1.5 m
to turret top	2.29 m
overall, including searchlight	2.86 m
FIRING HEIGHT	1.81 m
GROUND CLEARANCE	0.45 [0.44] m
TRACK	2.53 m
TRACK WIDTH	570 mm
LENGTH OF TRACK ON GROUND	4.12 m
MAX SPEED	
1st gear	7 km/h
2nd gear	15 km/h
3rd gear	26 km/h
4th gear	43 km/h
5th gear	65 km/h
AVERAGE SPEED	
road	50 km/h
cross-country	35–40 km/h
FUEL CAPACITY	970 [900] litres

MAX ROAD RANGE	500–600 [400–450] km
FORDING	1.3 m
with preparation	2.2 m
with snorkel	4 m
GRADIENT	60%
SIDE SLOPE	30%
VERTICAL OBSTACLE	0.93 m
TRENCH	2.9 m
ENGINE (see text)	Hispano-Suiza HS 110 12-cylinder, water-cooled super-charged multi-fuel developing 720 hp at 2000 rpm
AUXILIARY ENGINE	none
TRANSMISSION (see text)	mechanical with 5 gears in both directions triple differential
STEERING (see text)	
CLUTCH	centrifugal
SUSPENSION	torsion bar
ELECTRICAL SYSTEM	28 V
BATTERIES	8 × 12 V, 100 Ah
ARMAMENT	
main	1 × 105 mm
coaxial	1 × 20 mm cannon (or 1 × 12.7 mm MG)
	1 × 7.62 mm MG
anti-aircraft	
SMOKE-LAYING EQUIPMENT	2 smoke dischargers either side of turret
AMMUNITION	
main	47
coaxial	1050 (480)
anti-aircraft	2050 (2070)

GUN CONTROL EQUIPMENT	
Turret power control	electro-hydraulic with manual controls
by commander	yes
by gunner	yes
commander's override	yes
Commander's fire-control override	yes
Max rate of power traverse	360° in 12–13 s
Max rate of power elevation	5.5°/1 s
Main armament elevation/depression	+20°/−8°
Secondary armament elevation/depression	+40°/−8°
7.62 mm armament elevation/depression	+45°/−10°
Gun stabiliser	
vertical	no
horizontal	no
Elevation quadrant	yes
Traverse indicator	yes
ARMOUR (estimated)	
Hull front	79 mm
Hull sides front	57 mm
Hull sides rear	30 mm
Hull top	15 mm
Hull bottom	15 mm
Hull rear	30 mm
Turret front	80.8 mm
Turret sides	41.5 mm
Turret rear	50 mm
Turret top	20 mm

AMX-30 DCA twin 30 mm SPAAG with radar erected

Driver Training Tank
This is basically the AMX-30 MBT with its turret replaced by an observation type turret and is used for driver training.

Status: In production. In service with Chile (50 ordered but in March 1982 France announced that it had suspended delivery of the final 29 vehicles), France (1173 MBTs plus 134 ARVs, GCT, Pluton and Roland variants), Greece (and ARV), Iraq (plus Roland 2 and GCT), Qatar (and ARV), Saudi Arabia (AMX-30S used plus ARV, AVLB, DCA, GCT and Shahine), Spain (299 MBTs in Army and 36 in Marines, ARV, qv Spain in Part 2), United Arab Emirates (and ARV), and Venezuela (and four ARVs).

Manufacturer: Atelier de Construction Roanne (ARE).

Enquiries to Groupement Industriel des Armements Terrestres (GIAT), 10 place G Clémenceau, 92211 Saint-Cloud, France.

GERMANY, FEDERAL REPUBLIC

New West German MBT

In 1985 it was announced that a whole new generation of armoured vehicles would be developed for the West German Army.

Prior to this announcement it was fairly certain that priority was to be given to the new MBT, usually referred to as the Leopard 3 with an in service date of 1993.

Under the new plans the first vehicle to be fielded will be an anti-tank vehicle of which 1700 are required with first deliveries due in 1994.

The second vehicle will be an anti-tank/anti-helicopter vehicle with 800 required from 1995.

The third new vehicle will be an MICV of which 2500 are required from 1996.

The last vehicle to enter service will be a new MBT, with 1300 being required with first deliveries due from 1998 at the earliest.

Leopard 2 Main Battle Tank

Development
Once production of the Leopard 1 was under way Porsche was awarded a contract to carry out further development of the tank to increase its combat effectiveness. This contract expired in 1967, at which time West Germany and the United States were already developing the MBT-70 and the agreement covering it did not allow for a national tank development programme.

West Germany did however develop new components for the Leopard 1, some of which were to provide a basis for a new tank. In 1968 Krauss-Maffei was subsequently awarded a contract worth DM25 million to build two prototypes of a new MBT. This resembled the late production Leopard 1A3/1A4 and had an improved fire-control system, different stabilisation systems, new engine and transmission and was armed with a 105 mm rifled tank gun, 7.62 mm coaxial machine gun and a remote-controlled 7.62 mm anti-aircraft machine gun.

In 1969 it became apparent that the MBT-70 would not get past the prototype stage and efforts were made to adapt

Leopard 2 MBT armed with 120 mm smooth-bore gun

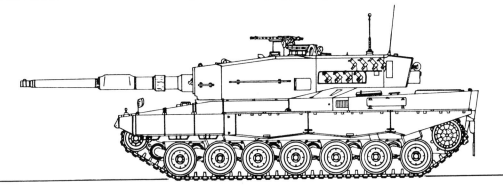

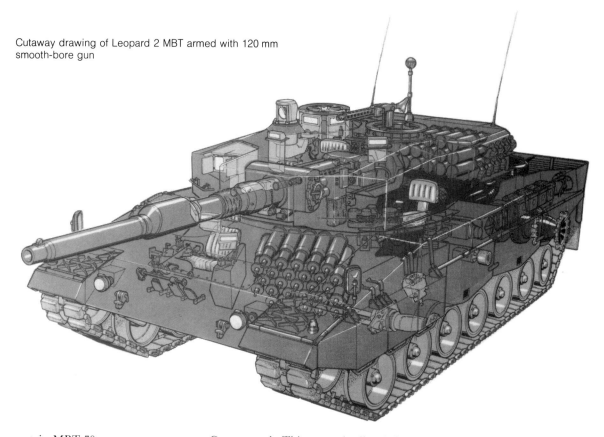

Cutaway drawing of Leopard 2 MBT armed with 120 mm smooth-bore gun

certain MBT-70 components to a new German tank. This development study was known as the Eber (or Boar). There was also a study based on the previously mentioned two prototypes, for a new tank called the Keiler (Wild Boar).

In 1970 the MBT-70 project was cancelled and the USA went on to develop a more austere version of the MBT-70 called the XM803 which was soon cancelled by Congress because of its rising costs. The USA then started on a new MBT project that culminated in the XM1 MBT, first production models of which were completed early in 1980.

In 1970 West Germany took the decision to proceed with a new tank called the Leopard 2 and a total of 16 hulls and 17 turrets were completed by Krauss-Maffei between 1972 and 1974. All of the prototypes used the Renk transmission out of the MBT-70 prototypes and 12 powerpacks used the MTU engine of the MBT-70. A study was also made of mounting the American 152 mm Shillelagh weapon system into the Leopard 2 but this idea was soon dropped.

Ten of the prototypes were equipped with a Rheinmetall 105 mm smooth-bore gun and the remainder were fitted with a Rheinmetall 120 mm smooth-bore gun. Two of the chassis were fitted with a hydro-pneumatic suspension but the advanced torsion bar suspension with integrated friction dampers was adopted.

Various types of fire-control systems were fitted in the prototype vehicles and one even had a remote-controlled 20 mm anti-aircraft cannon mounted on the turret roof.

The prototypes underwent engineer series tests between 1972 and 1974, then troop tests and in early 1975 cold weather trials in Canada, followed by desert trials in Yuma, Arizona.

In 1974 the USA and West Germany signed a Memorandum of Understanding (MoU) under which both countries affirmed their intention to make all reasonable efforts to

standardise their tank programmes. In July 1976 the MoU was amended to include efforts to standardise some tank components between the two countries. These included the engine, transmission, gunner's telescope, night vision equipment, fire-control system, tracks and main armament.

To meet the requirements of the USA, West Germany built another model called the Leopard 2 AV (Austere Version). It had a different and more simple fire-control system, a standard 105 mm rifled tank gun as fitted to the Leopard 1 and M60 series and a turret and hull which incorporated a spaced multi-layer armour, as well as many other detailed improvements influenced by the conflict in the Middle East in 1973. Two Leopard 2 AV hulls and three turrets were built. One complete Leopard 2 AV tank and one chassis

Production Leopard 2 MBT from front with driver's hatch closed and 7.62 mm MG at loader's station

Production Leopard 2 MBT from rear

Production Leopard 2 MBT

were delivered to the USA for trials in September 1976. But as expected, the USA chose one of the two competing American designs, the Chrysler XM1. The USA did however adopt the Rheinmetall 120 mm smooth-bore gun and first production M1A1s with this weapon were completed in August 1985. At present there are no plans to retrofit earlier M1s with this new gun.

In 1977 the Federal German Army selected Krauss-Maffei as prime contractor for series production for the Leopard 2 and placed an order, with options, for 1800 MBTs of which 990 will be built by Krauss-Maffei, the remaining 810 by Krupp MaK of Kiel.

The first pre-production Leopard 2 MBT was delivered to the Federal German Army late in 1978 for training. Krauss-Maffei and MaK of Kiel delivered three pre-

production Leopard 2 MBTs in 1979 and after firing trials at Rheinmetall's range at Unterlüss, it was delivered to Troop Combat School 2 at Münster. The first production Leopard 2 was handed over by Krauss-Maffei in October 1979 in Munich. Four tanks were delivered in 1979, 100 in 1980, 180 in 1981 and by 1982 production was running at 300 a year (25 a month). In 1982 it was announced that the total cost of the Leopard 2 programme for the West German Army was DM 8150 million with the first production lots being for 380, 450 and 300 tanks. The last two production lots comprise 300 and 370 tanks. Production for the Federal German Army

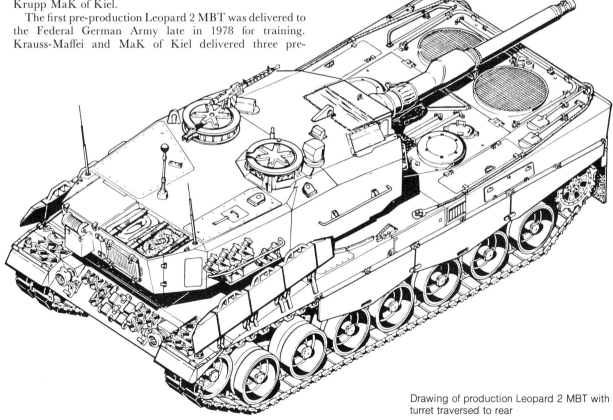

Drawing of production Leopard 2 MBT with turret traversed to rear

should be completed in 1987. Both companies installed new production and integration facilities at Munich and Kiel.

All West German tank brigades (with the exception of 4) will be issued with the Leopard 2.

Meanwhile an updating programme is underway, bringing the first production lot up to the technical standards of the current series tanks. This programme is due to be completed in 1987.

Dutch Leopard 2 Programme
In March 1979 the Dutch placed an order for 445 Leopard 2s for delivery from 1982 to 1986 to replace 369 Centurion MBTs and 130 AMX-13 light tanks; of these MaK will build 167 and Krauss-Maffei the remainder. The order is worth Fl 2400 million. Dutch industry will participate in the production of parts and components at approximately 60 per cent of the value of the order. In addition Dutch industry will be provided with new export possibilities for products not directly concerned with the Leopard 2 contract. The price is based on the price of the West German vehicles, including the additional costs of moving production to the Netherlands and amounts to about DM 3.2 million (basis 1980) per vehicle, not including the cost of peripheral equipment for the vehicle's weapon. The first four Leopard 2 MBTs for the Dutch Army were completed in mid-1981. Main contract deliveries began in July 1982 and by November that year ten vehicles were being delivered a month with final deliveries expected to take place in May 1986. They have different 7.62 mm machine guns (FN in place of Rheinmetall MG3s), smoke dischargers, passive night periscope for the driver, radios and intercom equipment from the West German version.

In 1983 the Royal Netherlands Army's 41st Armoured Brigade stationed in West Germany became the first Dutch Army unit to be equipped with the Leopard 2.

Swiss Leopard 2 Programme
In August 1983, the Swiss Army announced that after evaluating the Leopard 2 and M1 MBTs the former had been selected. A total of 380 will be ordered in one lot, the first 35 coming direct from Krauss-Maffei in West Germany and the remainder made under licence in Switzerland. The first 35 tanks, called the Pz 87, will be delivered in 1987 and used for training. The first Swiss tank battalion is expected to become operational in 1988.

Production Leopard 2 MBT showing armoured skirts towards front of vehicle and latest camouflage paint scheme of West German Army

Leopard 2 MBT climbing a slope clearly showing suspension detail and armour protection above first and second road wheel stations

Prime contractor for the licence production in Switzerland will be Contraves with final assembly taking place at the Federal Construction Works at Thun, where the Pz 61 and Pz 68 MBTs were built and where these and Centurion MBTs are overhauled today.

Production of the Leopard 2 in Switzerland will be at the rate of six tanks a month with final deliveries taking place in 1993.

It is expected that between 60 and 70 per cent of the Leopard 2 will be built in Switzerland with Saurer (NAW) building the engine and SLM the transmission.

Swiss Leopard 2s will be similar to the West German Leopard 2s but have Swiss radios and intercoms, Swiss coaxial and anti-aircraft machine guns. Switzerland has also decided to install the British Graviner Crew Bay fire and explosion suppression system.

Description
The hull of the Leopard 2 has a spaced multi-layer armour and is divided into three compartments: driver's at the front, fighting in the centre and engine at the rear.

The driver is seated at the front of the hull on the right side and is provided with a single-piece hatch cover that opens to the left and three observation periscopes. The centre periscope can be replaced by a passive night periscope. Some of the ammunition supply is stowed to the left of the driver.

The turret is in the centre of the vehicle with the commander and gunner on the right and the loader on the left. The commander is provided with a circular hatch cover that opens to the rear and periscopes for all-round observation. A PERI-R 17 primary stabilised panoramic periscope mounted in front of the commander's hatch can be traversed through 360 degrees enabling the commander to observe the terrain and lay the main armament, with magnification of ×2 and ×8.

The gunner has a dual-magnification stabilised EMES 15 sight with integrated laser rangefinder, and thermal image unit (WBG) which are linked to the fire-control computer. He also has an auxiliary sighting telescope FERO-Z 18 with a magnification of ×8 and the RPP 1-8 computer-controlled board testing system.

The EMES 15 is a primary stabilised binocular sighting

instrument for the gunner. The mirror head of the periscope is stabilised around two axes, the day path has a magnification of ×12 and a 5-degree field of view.

The laser rangefinder has a range of 9990 metres and is accurate to ±10 metres with measuring distances shown to three digits together with the fire preparation and selected type of ammunition in the lower part of the gunner's sight.

The fire-control computer calculates successively the angle of sight and lateral angular lead for the main armament. The following parameters are taken into account, target distance (from laser rangefinder), angle of tilt of the vehicle, direction of motion in regard to the target, lateral wind and ballistic data of ammunition. The data calculated by the fire-control computer is fed into the weapon slave system which guides the weapon to the line of sight of the EMES 15 or PERI-R 17. The thermal image unit integrated in the EMES 15 enables the armament to be aimed and fired at night or in bad weather or at camouflaged targets.

The gunner also has a roof-mounted observation periscope. The loader is seated on the left side of the turret and has a single-piece hatch cover that opens to the rear and a single observation periscope. An ammunition resupply hatch is provided in the left side of the turret and there is a stowage basket at the turret rear.

The engine compartment at the rear of the hull is separated from the fighting compartment by a fireproof bulkhead. The MTU MB 873 engine is coupled to a Renk HSWL 354 hydro-kinetic planetary gear shift with an integral service brake.

Rheinmetall-developed 120 mm ammunition for the Leopard 2, APFSDS-T on left and HEAT-MP-T on right. Both have a combustible cartridge case

The suspension with torsion bars consists each side of seven dual rubber-tyred road wheels with the idler at the front and the drive sprocket at the rear, and four track return rollers. Advanced friction dampers are provided at the first, second, third, sixth and seventh road wheel stations. The Diehl tracks have rubber-bushed pins with removable rubber pads, which can be replaced by snow grousers. The rear two-thirds of the top of the tracks are covered by steel-reinforced rubber skirts which can be folded up to allow access to the suspension for maintenance. The front third of the top of the track is covered by special armoured boxes which can be rotated upwards both for maintenance and to reduce the overall width of the vehicle for rail travel.

Standard equipment on the Leopard 2 includes an NBC system, powerpack preheating, crew compartment heater, fire-extinguishing system, electric bilge pumps and a hull escape hatch behind the driver.

The 120 mm smooth-bore gun has been developed by Rheinmetall and weighs 1905 kg (barrel, thermal shroud, bore evacuator and breech) with a barrel length of 5.3 metres and has a dropblock breech mechanism. Firing is electric with emergency firing induced by means of an impulse generator. When fired, the weapon recoils and is brought back into position by a recuperator. At the same time the breech block opens automatically. The 120 mm smooth-bore gun fires two types of ammunition, APFSDS-T and HEAT-MP-T, each of which has a practice version. The APFSDS-T has an effective range of well over 2000 metres and the HEAT-MP-T has a high degree of effectiveness against both soft and hard targets. Both fin-stabilised rounds have a semi-combustible cartridge case with a metal base stub which is ejected into a bag under the gun. Brief details of the ammunition are as follows:

Type of projectile	APFSDS-T	APFSDS-T(P)	HEAT-MP-T	HEAT-MP-T(P)
DESIGNATION	DM-13	DM-28	DM-12	DM-13
CARTRIDGE WEIGHT (incl. propellant)	19 kg	17 kg	23 kg	23 kg
CARTRIDGE LENGTH	884 mm	884 mm	981 mm	981 mm
PROJECTILE WEIGHT	7.3 kg	5.6 kg	13.5 kg	13.5 kg
PROPELLANT WEIGHT	7.1 kg	7.1 kg	5.4 kg	5.4 kg

Of 42 rounds of ammunition carried some are stored to the left of the driver and some in the left side of the turret bustle. If the latter is hit it will explode outwards due to blow-out panels.

A 7.62 mm Rheinmetall MG3 machine gun is mounted coaxially to the left of the main armament and a similar weapon can be mounted on the loader's hatch. Mounted on either side of the turret are eight smoke dischargers.

Variants

Krupp MaK is developing a new armoured engineer tank (Engineer Tank 2), although no production contract has been awarded so far.

Porsche and Krupp MaK are developing a new armoured recovery vehicle based on the chassis of the Leopard 2 under the designation Bergepanzer 3.

The chassis of the Leopard 2 could also be used to mount

the turret of the Gepard anti-aircraft tank now in service with Belgium, West Germany and the Netherlands (with Dutch rather than West German radars).

A Leopard 2 prototype was fitted with the American Avco-Lycoming AGT-1500 gas turbine in 1978 for trials purposes by Krupp MaK at Kiel.

Details of the Vickers Mk 7 MBT which uses the chassis of the Leopard 2 MBT are given under the United Kingdom.

SPECIFICATIONS

CREW	4	FUEL CAPACITY	1200 litres	AMMUNITION	
COMBAT WEIGHT	55 150 kg	MAX RANGE		main	42
POWER-TO-WEIGHT		road	550 km	MG	4750
RATIO	27.27 hp/tonne	FORDING	1 m	GUN CONTROL	
GROUND PRESSURE	0.81 kg/cm²	with preparation	2.35 m	EQUIPMENT	
LENGTH GUN		with snorkel	4 m	Turret power control	electro-hydraulic/manual
FORWARDS	9.668 m	GRADIENT	60%	by commander	yes
LENGTH GUN REAR	8.51 m	SIDE SLOPE	30%	by gunner	yes
LENGTH HULL	7.722 m	VERTICAL OBSTACLE	1.1 m	commander's override	yes
WIDTH SKIRTS		TRENCH	3 m	Commander's fire-	
UNFOLDED	3.54 m	ENGINE	MTU MB 873 Ka 501 4-stroke,	control override	yes
WIDTH INCLUDING			12-cylinder multi-fuel,	Gun elevation/	
SKIRTS	3.7 m		exhaust turbo-charged,	depression	+20°/−9°
HEIGHT			liquid-cooled developing	Gun stabiliser	
to turret top	2.46 m		1500 hp at 2600 rpm	vertical	yes
to commander's		TRANSMISSION	Renk HSWL 354 hydro-	horizontal	yes
periscope	2.79 m		kinetic planetary gear shift, 4	Range setting device	yes (laser)
hull top	1.769 m		forward and 2 reverse gears	Elevation quadrant	yes
firing height	1.99 m	CLUTCH	torque converter	Traverse indicator	yes
GROUND CLEARANCE		SUSPENSION	torsion bar		
front	0.53 m	ELECTRICAL SYSTEM	24 V		
rear	0.48 m	BATTERIES	8 × 12 V, 125 Ah		
TRACK	2.785 m	ARMAMENT			
TRACK WIDTH	635 mm	main	1 × 120 mm		
LENGTH OF TRACK		coaxial	1 × 7.62 mm MG		
ON GROUND	5.245 m	anti-aircraft	1 × 7.62 mm MG		
MAX ROAD SPEED		SMOKE-LAYING			
forwards	72 km/h	EQUIPMENT	8 smoke dischargers		
reverse	31 km/h		either side of turret		

Status: In production. In service with Dutch and West German Armies. Ordered by the Swiss Army and will be manufactured under licence in Switzerland. Krauss-Maffei have proposed a new MBT called Lince to Spain, details of this are given in Part 2.

Manufacturers: Krauss-Maffei AG, Ordnance Division, Krauss-Maffei Strasse 2,8000 Munich 50, Federal Republic of Germany. Krupp MaK Maschinenbau GmbH, PO Box 9009, 2300 Kiel 17, Federal Republic of Germany.

Leopard 1 Main Battle Tank

Development

In November 1956 a Military Requirement was issued for a new MBT with the following specifications: combat weight of 30 tonnes, power-to-weight ratio of 30 hp/tonne, width of 3.15 metres, height of 2.2 metres, maximum road speed of 65 km/h, air-cooled multi-fuel engine, 105 mm gun and two machine guns. In June 1957 the Federal Republic of Germany and France agreed to develop a tank to meet these specifications and in July 1957 the Joint Technical Characteristics were issued, the only difference between the two countries being in the overall width of the tank. In September 1958 Italy joined the project which resulted in supplements to the Technical Characteristics being issued in October 1961.

West Germany formed two design teams, Team A and Team B. In France the Direction des Etudes et Fabrication d'Armement (now the Direction Technique des Armements Terrestres) was the overall contractor with the design work being carried out at the Atelier de Construction d'Issy-les-Moulineaux at Satory.

The West German Team A comprised Porsche, Jung, Luther and Jordan and MaK and Team B comprised Ingenieurbüro Warneke, Rheinstahl Hanomag and Henschel. Turrets and armament were designed by Rheinmetall and Wegmann.

Team A's first prototype was completed in June 1960 and the second in August the same year. Team B completed its first prototype in May the same year.

The four prototypes were delivered for trials early in 1961. The trials, which were carried out at Trier and later at Meppen, were completed in April 1962. It was then decided to concentrate on the Team A design, even though it was found to have a number of deficiencies during trials; this was hardly surprising considering the very short development period and the fact that tank development in Germany had been stopped since 1945. Before the trials were completed in April 1962 a further order was placed with Team A for 26 tanks with turrets designed by Wegmann, and Team B was awarded a contract for a further six tanks with turrets designed by Rheinmetall. Following the decision to concentrate on the Team A design only two of the second series from Team B were completed. The 26 tanks were known as the second series and had numerous improvements including increased armour protection, improved suspension, ten-cylinder diesel engine coupled to a new transmission, modified fire-control equipment and the British 105 mm L7 series gun. Trials with the second series were completed early in 1963.

Before the second series had even completed their trials a pre-production batch of 50 tanks was ordered, which incorporated many improvements as a result of the earlier trials including the replacement of the 12.7 mm ranging machine

Leopard 1A1A1 of West German Army fitted with appliqué armour to turret sides and mantlet. 105 mm gun does not have thermal sleeve

Leopard 1A1A1 MBT climbing vertical obstacle. Note additional turret and mantlet armour

gun with an optical rangefinder. During trials with the ranging machine gun (which was fitted on late Centurion tanks with the 105 mm gun, and later fitted to the Chieftain), it was found that it limited the range of the 105 mm gun to between 1500 and 1800 metres.

Comparative trials between the West German design and the French AMX-30 were carried out from 1962, but in July 1963 the Defence Committee of the Federal German Parliament decided to go ahead with the production of the West German design, which later became known as the Leopard, even though the main comparative trials had yet to take place.

In July 1963 Krauss-Maffei of Munich was nominated prime contractor for the Leopard 1 MBT and Krupp MaK of Kiel was selected as general contractor for production of the armoured recovery vehicle, armoured engineer vehicle and the armoured bridgelayer. Krupp MaK also built a small number of Leopard 1 MBTs.

The first production Leopard was handed over to the Federal German Army in September 1965, and since then the tank has been adopted by nine other countries including Italy, where it has been manufactured under licence by OTO Melara (qv). Production of the Leopard 1 was completed by Krauss-Maffei in 1979 but resumed again by both manufacturers early in 1981 to meet the requirements of Greece and Turkey.

Description (Leopard 1A1)

The all-welded hull is divided into two compartments, the crew compartment at the front and engine compartment at the rear.

The driver is seated at the front of the hull on the right and is provided with a single-piece hatch cover that opens to the left. In front of the hatch are three periscopes, the centre one of which can be replaced by an infra-red or image-intensification periscope for night driving.

The all-cast turret is mounted in the centre of the hull with the commander and gunner seated on the right and the loader on the left. Both the commander and the loader have a single-piece hatch cover that opens to the rear. The commander is provided with eight periscopes for all-round observation, one of which can be replaced by an image intensification periscope for night observation. The gunner

has one observation periscope while the loader has two. Mounted in the turret roof in front of the commander's hatch is a TRP 2A zoom periscope with a magnification of ×6 up to ×20. This is swivel-mounted and can also be moved vertically by hand within the gun elevation range. When the commander actuates a switch the periscope is automatically slaved to the gun. For night observation the commander can replace the zoom periscope with an infra-red sight.

The gunner is seated in front of and below the commander and is provided with a TEM 2A rangefinder which can be used in either the coincidence or stereoscopic modes. It has magnifications of ×8 and ×16 and is mechanically linked to the gun and provided with super-elevation cams to compute the super-elevation angle for two types of ammunition. The gunner also has a TZF 1A telescope mounted coaxially with the main armament which has a magnification of ×8 and is provided with a movable scaled graticule to set the super-elevation for the different types of ammunition. There is an ammunition resupply hatch in the left side of the turret and a stowage basket at the turret rear. Mounted over the main armament is an XSW-30-U infra-red/white searchlight, which can be removed and stowed at the rear of the turret when not required. In the infra-red mode in conjunction with an infra-red sight which can be mounted in place of the commander's TRP 2A periscope it has a range of 1200 metres and in the white light mode a range of 1500 metres.

The engine compartment at the rear is separated from the fighting compartment by a fireproof bulkhead. The complete powerpack, consisting of the engine, transmission and cooling system, is provided with quick-disconnect couplings which allow the entire powerpack to be replaced in the field within 20 minutes.

The steer/shift transmission is coupled directly to the engine and has four forward and two reverse gears as well as a pivot turn capability, and a torque converter and lock-up clutch. The gears can be shifted electro-hydraulically without interruption of tractive forces and the speed range can be pre-selected manually, gear changing being automatic.

The running gear consists each side of seven dual light metal rubber-tyred road wheels with the drive sprocket at the rear, idler at the front and four track return rollers. The first, second, third, sixth and seventh road wheel stations are provided with hydraulic shock absorbers. The Diehl tracks are provided with rubber-bushed connectors and the

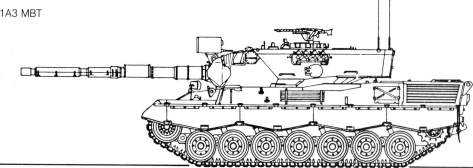

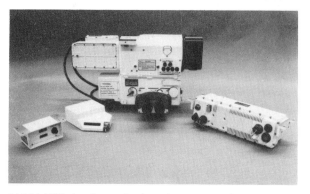

SABCA FCS showing system's major components

rubberised track pads can be replaced by snow grousers. Steel-reinforced rubber skirts for the top of the tracks can be folded vertically for maintenance. The track skirts perform two functions: they increase the ballistic protection and also reduce the whirl-up of dust.

The NBC system is installed at the front of the hull and produces an over-pressure in the crew compartment. In normal use the system provides the crew with clean dust-free air, and in the NBC mode removes contaminated particles by an additional purification process.

Standard equipment includes an automatic fire-extinguishing system, heater, hull escape hatch and infra-red reflecting paint.

For underwater operations there are two fording shafts available, one for fording to a depth of 2.25 metres and an extra shaft for fording to a depth of 4 metres. Either shaft is fitted over the commander's hatch, down which air for the engine is drawn and the exhaust leaves via the exhaust pipes in the normal manner. Before entering the water all openings are sealed; the turret ring by an inflatable rubber ring. A hydraulic system controls the engine combustion air intake, dust ejection blower valves of the combustion air cleaners, exhaust flaps of the engine and heater, pressure ventilation in the engine compartment as well as the dust ejection valves and air intake of the NBC system. Two bilge pumps remove any water that enters the vehicle.

Main armament of the Leopard 1 is a British-supplied 105 mm L7A3 rifled tank gun which consists of a single-piece barrel with a screwed-on breech-block and a bore evacuator. The barrel can be changed in the field in about 20 minutes. The semi-automatic breech mechanism automatically opens after each round is fired, ejecting the empty cartridge case into the bag under the breech.

The Leopard 1 can fire all the standard 105 mm rounds manufactured by West Germany, the United Kingdom and the USA. Some countries use West German ammunition and others British.

Of 55 rounds of ammunition carried, 42 are in the hull and 13 in the turret. Details of the ammunition are given in this section under M60 series (USA) and Centurion (UK).

Krauss-Maffei states that the first round hit probability of the Leopard 1, even when on the move and firing at moving targets, was significantly increased by the incorporation of the gun stabilisation system and of modern fire-control systems, the latest of which has a primary stabilised line of sight, laser rangefinder and an integral thermal imaging system.

Mounted coaxially with the main armament is a 7.62 mm Rheinmetall MG 3 machine gun which is provided with 1250 rounds of ready-use ammunition. The coaxial machine gun is operated by the gunner but can also be operated by the tank commander in the override mode. A second MG 3 machine gun is mounted at the commander's or loader's station for anti-aircraft defence. Four electrically-operated smoke dischargers are mounted on either side of the turret.

Variants

Leopard 1A1A1

The first model of the Leopard to enter service with the Federal German Army was called the Leopard 1 of which 1845 were built in the first, second, third and fourth batches. From 1971 they were fitted with a thermal sleeve for the main armament, gun stabilisation system, new tracks, lateral skirt,

Leopard 1A1A1 of Federal German Army fitted with Hoffmann-Werke AFV gunfire simulator over 105 mm gun

Leopard 1A2 fitted with thermal sleeve for 105 mm gun, and infra-red/white light searchlight over main armament

Leopard 1A3 which was the first production model Leopard 1 to have a turret of all welded construction incorporating spaced armour

modified turret hatches and modified wading equipment. The stabilisation system controls the gun in elevation and traverse so that the gunner is able to observe the terrain, acquire and then engage the target while moving across country with a high degree of first-round hit probability. With these modifications the Leopard 1 became the Leopard 1A1. These tanks have since been fitted with add-on armour to the turret and gun shield and are now known as the Leopard 1A1A1. The additional add-on armour consists of flexibly-mounted, screwed-on armour steel plates with two-faced rubber lining. The armour also covers the turret bustle back and the gun shield is also reinforced with armour steel plates. In addition, armour steel plates are welded onto the sloped front roof section. The extra weight caused by the fitting of this additional armour is about 760 kg, which makes the vehicle approximately the same weight as the Leopard 1A4.

Leopard 1A2

The fifth production batch of Leopards for the Federal German Army consisted of 343 tanks of which 232 were built with the modifications of the Leopard 1A1 (but without the spaced armour on turret and mantlet) but in addition have a turret of stronger cast steel, improved NBC system and passive image-intensification night vision equipment for both the commander and driver.

Leopard 1A3

A total of 110 Leopard 1A3 tanks out of the fifth production batch were delivered to the Federal German Army, incorporating all the improvements of the Leopard 1A1 and 1A2 but with a new welded turret of spaced armour with a wedge-shaped mantlet. The turret rear stowage bin has been incorporated into the contour of the turret which accommodates the searchlight when it is not mounted over the main armament. In addition, the loader's periscope is adjustable in both elevation and azimuth. In 1981 the Greek Government ordered 106 Leopard 1A3 MBTs plus an option for an additional 110 vehicles for delivery from February 1983 through to April 1984. Krauss-Maffei of Munich built 73 MBTs and Krupp MaK of Kiel 33 MBTs and four ARVs. The Turkish order for 81 Leopard 1s comprised four ARVs to be built by Krupp-MaK and 77 Leopard 1A3 MBTs (54 built by Krauss-Maffei and 23 by Krupp MaK).

Leopard 1A4

This was the final production model of the Leopard 1 for the Federal German Army of which 250 were built, 215 by Krauss-Maffei and 35 by Krupp MaK. It is similar to the Leopard 1A3 but has an integrated fire-control system consisting of a stabilised panoramic telescope for the tank commander, gunner's primary sight with integral stereoscopic rangefinder coupled to the fully-stabilised main armament and controlled by a ballistic computer.

West German Army Modification Programme

In 1982–83 six West German Army Leopard 1 MBTs were fitted with different fire-control systems for comparative trials. These were the AEG-Telefunken Lemstar M/EMES 17, Krupp-Atlas Elektronik FLP-10/EMES 18 and the Zeiss AFLS-L/EMES 12A4. All of these had a thermal imaging system for use under poor sighting and night combat conditions.

The West German Army finally accepted the Krupp-Atlas EMES 18 combined with the thermal imaging system in 1984.

It is expected that a certain quantity, probably about 1300, of the West German Army Leopard 1 MBT fleet will be retrofitted from 1986 through to the early 1990s.

Leopard 1A4 MBT with spaced armour turret

In order to overcome future battlefield threats, measures are also to be undertaken to enhance the protection of the Leopard 1 by add-on armour and of secondary protective devices such as an explosion suppression system for the crew compartment.

Optional equipment for Leopard 1 MBT

Krauss-Maffei offers a large number of modification kits for the Leopard 1 MBT: such as all ammunition stowed below the turret ring, additional armour for the turret and mantlet, armoured skirts, automatic transmission and gear shift, Belgian SABCA FCS (already adopted by Australia, Belgium and Canada), brackets on glacis plate for snow grousers, dozer blade (already adopted by Australia), driver's periscopes fitted with washers and a wiper blade (already adopted by Denmark), improved turret and trunnion bearings, modifications to FCS to allow a 105 mm gun to fire APFSDS rounds, improved combustion cleaners, external stowage boxes on hull sides (already adopted by Australia and the Netherlands), snorkel, passive periscope for commander and driver, replaceable track pads, new West German fire control system EMES 18 that can have an integral thermal imaging system based on US common modules, passive LLLTV sighting system PZB 200, stabilisation system for the main armament, and a tropical kit.

The PZB 200 system consists of a combined low-light-level tv camera for terrain surveillance and sighting of targets, which is mounted on the gun mantlet and so moves in elevation with the main armament, monitor that can be seen both by the commander and gunner, control panel with on/off switch, dimmer control for graticule illumination, focusing switch and selector switch for extreme illumination levels and simple built-in test equipment.

The complete dozer blade unit consists of the dozer blade, two pivot-mounted push arms and a hydraulic unit for lifting and lowering the blade. The complete dozer blade can be attached or removed in approximately ten minutes without the need of a crane or an ARV and can be locked mechanically for travelling. All control elements are packaged into a watertight unit so that earth moving is possible during fording operations. A utility outlet for power supply is standard equipment on the vehicle. A simple control panel is attached to the driver's station and the power supply and control cable passes through the open driver's hatch or alternatively, one of the slots normally occupied by the vision block.

Leopard 1A1A1 MBT armed with 120 mm Rheinmetall smooth-bore gun as installed in Leopard 2 MBT

Product improved Leopard ARV lifting a complete turret off a Leopard 1 MBT. Note stabiliser in lowered position at hull rear of ARV

Leopard AEV using dozer blade

Export Leopard 1 MBTs

Almost every country that has ordered the Leopard 1 MBT and its many variants have specified modifications to suit their own specific needs. Details of these, where applicable, are given in the individual country entries, eg Australia, Belgium, Canada, Denmark, Greece, Italy, Netherlands, Norway and Turkey.

Leopard 1 with 120 mm Gun

For trials purposes, Rheinmetall have fitted three Leopard 1 series MBTs of the West German Army with the same 120 mm smooth-bore gun as installed in the Leopard 2 MBT.

Leopard Armoured Recovery Vehicle

The Leopard ARV was designed by Porsche and the first production vehicle was completed in September 1966 by Krupp MaK of Kiel. The ARV is based on the chassis of the MBT but has a new hull. Standard equipment includes a dozer blade at the front of the hull, hydraulically-operated crane on the right side of the hull which is pivoted at the front, main winch with a capacity of 35 tonnes (which can be increased to 70 tonnes with a guide pulley), electric wrench and a welding system. The vehicle, which weighs 39 800 kg and has a four-man crew, has been designed for recovery of damaged vehicles, towing disabled vehicles, changing vehicle components and lifting complete vehicles weighing up to 20 tonnes, carrying a spare Leopard MBT powerpack, dozing, and refuelling and defuelling other vehicles. Armament consists of a bow-mounted 7.62 mm MG 3 machine gun, 7.62 mm MG 3 anti-aircraft machine gun and smoke dischargers. In 1978 the Federal German Army took delivery from Krupp MaK of 100 product-improved Leopard ARVs which have a hydraulic jack mounted at the rear of the hull on the right side and a more powerful crane.

Leopard Armoured Engineer Vehicle
This is based on the Leopard ARV and entered production in 1968. The only differences between the ARV and the AEV are that a heat exchanger has been installed, explosives are carried for demolition work, an auger is carried in place of the spare powerpack on the rear of the hull and the dozer blade can be fitted with scarifiers to rip up the surface of roads.

Leopard Bridgelayer
After trials with two competing designs, model B was selected for production and the first production vehicles were completed by MaK in 1975. The aluminium bridge is launched over the front of the vehicle as follows: on arrival at the obstacle the vehicle lowers the support blade at the front of the hull, the lower half of the bridge slides forwards until its end is lined up with the end of the upper half, the two sections are locked together, extended over the gap and lowered into position, the cantilever arm is withdrawn, the support blade raised and the vehicle can then be driven away. The bridge is 22 metres long when opened out and can span a gap of up to 20 metres. Weight of the bridge and vehicle is 45 300 kg.

Leopard Driver Training Tank
This is essentially an MBT with its turret removed and replaced by an observation cabin with seats for the instructor and two trainee drivers with the third trainee driver seated in the normal position at the front of the hull. If required the instructor can take over control of the vehicle at any time. The driver training tanks used by Belgium and the Netherlands do not have the dummy gun barrel as fitted to the West German Leopard driver training tanks.

Leopard driver training tank of Federal German Army

Gepard twin 35 mm self-propelled anti-aircraft gun showing amount of on-board ammunition carried

Leopard GPM Engineer Vehicle
After evaluating prototypes submitted by Krupp MaK and EWK, EWK's has been selected for service with the Federal German Army. So far no production order has been placed for this vehicle.

Gepard Anti-aircraft Vehicle
To replace the twin 40 mm SPAAGs used by the West German Army prototypes of both twin 30 mm and twin 35 mm systems were built based on a Leopard 1 chassis. After trials the latter was selected for production and 420 were built by Krauss-Maffei for West Germany (delivered between 1976 and 1980), Belgium (55 delivered from 1977 to 1980) and the Netherlands (95 delivered from 1977 to 1979 and called the CA 1). Of the 420 West German vehicles the first 195 are called the B2 and the remaining 225, which have a Siemens laser rangefinder, are designated the B2L.

The Belgian and West German vehicles have AEG-Telefunken (target tracking) and Siemens (search) while the Dutch vehicles have the Hollandse Signaalapparaten surveillance and tracking radars.

The Gepard is armed with twin 35 mm Oerlikon KDA cannon each of which have a cyclic rate of fire of 550 rpm.

Biber armoured bridgelayer of West German Army laying its bridge in position

Each cannon is provided with 310 rounds of anti-aircraft and 20 rounds of APDS ammunition, the latter for engaging ground targets. The guns have powered elevation from −10 degrees to +85 degrees and the turret can be traversed through a full 360 degrees. The West German and Belgian versions have four smoke dischargers either side of the turret while the Dutch vehicles have six.

ATAK 35

As a private venture, the Swiss company of Contraves has upgraded a Dutch CA 1 to ATAK 35 configuration, although this turret can be installed on other chassis. This version has much improved electronics and has been demonstrated in West Germany and Austria.

Roland 2 SAM on Leopard 1 Chassis

In 1982 Krupp MaK, Blohm and Voss and Euromissile proposed that the chassis of the Leopard ARV could be modified to accept the Roland 2 SAM system. The latter is at present produced mounted on the AMX-30 MBT chassis, Marder MICV chassis and in a mobile shelter.

Leopard 155 mm Self-propelled Gun

This was developed as a private venture by Krauss-Maffei and GIAT of France and basically consists of a Leopard chassis with the turret of the French 155 mm GCT self-propelled gun which is normally mounted on the AMX-30 chassis. This has not so far been adopted by any country.

76 mm Anti-aircraft Tank

Krupp MaK and OTO-Melara of Italy have suggested that the Leopard chassis be fitted with the same turret armed with the 76 mm gun as fitted to the OTO 76/62 76 mm self-propelled anti-aircraft gun. Details of the latter are given in the entry for the OF-40 MBT under Italy.

SPECIFICATIONS

Model	Leopard 1	Leopard 1A4
CREW	4	4
COMBAT WEIGHT	40 000 kg	42 400 kg
UNLOADED WEIGHT	38 700 kg	40 400 kg
POWER-TO-WEIGHT RATIO	20.75 hp/tonne	19.57 hp/tonne
GROUND PRESSURE	0.86 kg/cm²	0.88 kg/cm²
LENGTH GUN FORWARDS	9.543 m	9.543 m
LENGTH HULL	7.09 m	7.09 m
WIDTH OVERALL	3.25 m (without skirts)	3.37 m (with skirts)
HEIGHT to top of commander's periscope	2.613 m	2.764 m
FIRING HEIGHT	1.88 m	1.88 m
GROUND CLEARANCE	0.44 m	0.44 m
TRACK	2.7 m	2.7 m
TRACK WIDTH	550 mm	550 mm
LENGTH OF TRACK ON GROUND	4.236 m	4.236 m
MAX ROAD SPEED	65 km/h	65 km/h
FUEL CAPACITY	955 litres	955 litres
MAX RANGE road	600 km	600 km
cross-country	450 km	450 km
FORDING	2.25 m	2.25 m
with preparation	4 m	4 m
GRADIENT	60%	60%
SIDE SLOPE	30%	30%
VERTICAL OBSTACLE	1.15 m	1.15 m
TRENCH	3 m	3 m
ENGINE	MTU MB 838 Ca M500, 10-cylinder multi-fuel developing 830 hp at 2200 rpm	
TRANSMISSION	ZF 4 HP 250 planetary-gear shift with hydraulic torque converter, 4 forward and 2 reverse gears	
STEERING	regenerative double differential	
CLUTCH	torque converter with mechanical interlock	
SUSPENSION	torsion bar	torsion bar
ELECTRICAL SYSTEM	24 V	24 V
BATTERIES	8 × 12 V, 100 Ah	8 × 12 V, 100 Ah
ARMAMENT main	1 × 105 mm	1 × 105 mm
coaxial	1 × 7.62 mm MG	1 × 7.62 mm MG
anti-aircraft	1 × 7.62 mm MG	1 × 7.62 mm MG
SMOKE-LAYING EQUIPMENT	4 smoke dischargers either side of turret	

Model	Leopard 1	Leopard 1A4
AMMUNITION main	55	60
7.62 mm	5500	5500
GUN CONTROL EQUIPMENT		
Turret power control by commander	electro-hydraulic/manual	electro-hydraulic/manual
by gunner	yes	yes
commander's override	yes	yes
Commander's fire-control override	yes	yes
Max rate of power traverse	360° in 15 s	360° in 15 s
Max rate of power elevation	4.1°/s	4.1°/s
Gun elevation/depression	+20°/−9°	+20°/−9°
Gun stabiliser vertical	yes (refitted)	yes
horizontal	yes (refitted)	yes
Range setting device	yes	yes
Elevation quadrant	yes	yes
Traverse indicator	yes	yes
ARMOUR		
Hull nose	70 mm at 55°	70 mm at 55°
Hull glacis	70 mm at 60°	70 mm at 60°
Hull glacis top	25 mm at 83°	25 mm at 83°
Hull sides upper	35 mm at 50°	35 mm at 50°
Hull sides lower	25 mm at 90°	25 mm at 90°
Hull top	10 mm	10 mm
Hull floor	15 mm	15 mm
Hull rear	25 mm at 88°	25 mm at 88°
Turret mantlet	60 mm	n/av
Turret front	52 mm	n/av
Turret sides	60 mm	n/av
Turret rear	60 mm	n/av

Status: Production as required. In service with Australia, Belgium, Canada, Denmark, West Germany, Greece, Italy, Netherlands, Norway and Turkey.

Manufacturers: Krauss-Maffei AG, Ordnance Division, Krauss-Maffei Strasse 2, 8000 Munich 50, Federal Republic of Germany. Krupp MaK Maschinenbau GmbH, PO Box 9009, 2300 Kiel, Federal Republic of Germany.

ATAK 35 twin 35 mm system based on Leopard I chassis

CA 1 twin 35 mm self-propelled anti-aircraft gun as used by Dutch Army which has different radars to those fitted to the model used on West German and Belgian Gepards

Leopard 1 production							
	MBT	ARV	AEV	Bridgelayer	Gepard	Training	Total
Australia	90	6	nil	5	nil	nil	101
Belgium	334	36	6	nil	55	12	443
Canada	114	8	nil	6	nil	nil	128
Denmark	120	nil	nil	nil	nil	nil	120
West Ger.	2437	544*	36	105	420	60	3602
Greece	106	4	nil	nil	nil	nil	110
Italy	920†	69	12	nil	nil	nil	1001
Netherl'd	468	52	14	14	95	12	655
Norway	78	6	nil	nil	nil	nil	84
Turkey	77	4	nil	nil	nil	nil	81

* 444 standard plus 100 product improved
† 200 from West Germany, remainder built under licence in Italy + 160 specialised versions subsequently ordered (64 bridgelayers, 68 ARVs and 28 AEVs)

TAM Tank

Development

In mid-1974 the West German company of Thyssen Henschel was awarded a contract for the design and development of a new medium tank for the Argentinian Army under the designation of the TAM (Tanque Argentino Mediano), as well as an infantry combat vehicle under the designation of the VCI (Véhiculo Combate Infanteria), subsequently renamed VCTP. The contract covered the design, development and construction of three prototypes of both the TAM and the VCI.

The main reason for the decision to develop a tank in the 30-tonne class rather than the normal 40- to 50-tonne class was that many bridges and roads in South America could not stand up to the heavier tanks. An added advantage was that it enabled Argentina to have a tank and an infantry combat vehicle that were both based on the same chassis with resulting logistical, training and economic advantages. In terms of firepower the TAM is at least as good as the Leopard 1 MBT.

The first prototype of the TAM was completed in September 1976 with the second and third prototypes being finished the following year. On completion of company trials in West Germany the TAMs were shipped to Argentina for both operational and firing trials. The TAM will replace the Sherman tanks currently used by Argentina and it is expected that about 200 TAMs and 300 VCIs will be built in Argentina. Chassis construction and final assembly are carried out in Buenos Aires while construction of the turret and the integration of the gun and fire-control system take place at Rio Tercero. Thyssen Henschel continues to supply major components to Argentina for both the TAM and VCI. Additional information on the TAM programme is given in this section under Argentina.

Description

The chassis of the vehicle is based on the one used for the Marder MICV used in large numbers by the West German Army, but strengthened to take account of the increased weight of the vehicle and the stresses caused by firing the main armament.

The hull of the TAM is all welded with the well-sloped glacis plate providing protection against small arms fire, shell splinters and armour-piercing rounds up to 20 mm in calibre.

The driver is seated at the front of the hull on the left side and steers the vehicle with a conventional steering wheel. He is provided with a single-piece hatch cover that opens to the right and three periscopes. Two escape hatches are provided, one in the floor of the vehicle and one at the rear.

The engine is mounted to the right of the driver with the glacis plate hinged on the right to allow access to the engine for maintenance. On the prototype the engine was identical to the one installed in the Marder MICV and developed 600 hp at 2200 rpm but production vehicles have a super-

TH 301 with 105 mm gun in travelling lock (Christopher F Foss)

charged engine that develops 720 hp at 2400 rpm. The engine is coupled to a Renk HSWL-194 planetary gearbox which gives four gears in both directions. The steering system is of the stepless hydrostatic type.

The all-welded turret is mounted to the rear of the vehicle with the commander and gunner on the right and the loader on the left. The commander is provided with a single-piece hatch cover and eight periscopes. Mounted in front of his hatch is a non-stabilised Steinheil Lear Siegler TRP-2A panoramic sight with a magnification of between ×6 and ×20, identical to that fitted to the Leopard 1 MBT which can be replaced by an infra-red sight. The commander also operates the coincidence rangefinder. The gunner is seated forward and below the commander and is provided with a Zeiss TZF sight with a magnification of ×8, combined with a swivelling and tilting periscope. The loader is provided with a single-piece hatch cover that opens to the rear with a tilting periscope mounted in front of him. An ammunition-loading port is provided in the left side of the turret. Mounted in the hull rear is a hatch that can be used either as an emergency exit or to reload the vehicle rapidly with ammunition.

The torsion bar suspension system consists of six rubber-tyred road wheels with the drive sprocket at the front, idler at the rear and three track return rollers. The first, second, fifth and sixth road wheel stations have hydraulic shock absorbers. The tracks are Diehl with removable rubber pads. The tops of the tracks are covered by detachable rubber skirts.

To extend the TAM's range two 200-litre long range fuel tanks can be fitted at the rear. The basic vehicle can ford to a depth of 1.4 metres but with preparation it can ford to 2.25 metres, or 4 metres with a snorkel. Standard equipment includes an NBC system, combustion heater for both cold engine starts and the crew compartment, electric bilge pumps, and a fire-extinguishing system that can be operated manually or automatically.

The main armament comprises a 105 mm gun that fires a wide range of fixed ammunition including APDS, APFSDS, HEAT, HE-T, HESH and WP-T. It is provided with a fume extractor and is fully stabilised in both planes. Fifty rounds of 105 mm ammunition are carried of which 20 are in the turret. Mounted coaxially with the main armament is a 7.62 mm machine gun manufactured under licence in Argentina from FN of Belgium. A similar weapon is mounted on the roof of the tank for anti-aircraft defence. Four Wegmann smoke dischargers are mounted on either side of the hull.

Optional equipment includes additional armour protection, radios and an intercom system.

Variants

TH 301

Using company funds, Thyssen Henschel has built a fourth prototype of the TAM called the TH 301 (this was originally called the TAM-4), which was completed late in 1978.

Externally it is very similar to the model designed for Argentina but internally has significant differences in its powerpack and fire-control system.

In addition to eight periscopes for all-round observation, the commander has a PERI R12 sight as fitted to the final production model of the Leopard 1, the Leopard 1A4. This stabilised sight has an elevation of +60 degrees, a depression of −10 degrees and can be traversed through a full 360 degrees. It has a magnification of ×2 or ×8 and is fitted with an external wiper.

TH 301 with main armament in travelling lock and long-range fuel tanks at rear undergoing trials

Prototype of 57 mm support tank showing Hughes TOW launcher to right of main armament

The gunner has a fully stabilised telescope with a magnification of ×8 and an integral laser rangefinder.

Its main armament is a Rheinmetall-developed 105 mm gun designated the Rh 105-30 firing APFSDS, APDS, HEAT and HEP projectiles and with an elevation of +18 degrees and depression of −7 degrees. The turret can be traversed through a full 360 degrees in 15 seconds and the main armament is fully stabilised.

Information on target range is fed to the computer manually by the tank commander or automatically by the laser rangefinder, which has a range of from 400 to 5000 metres. Angle of cant and lead angle is also fed automatically and the type of ammunition to be fired is fed in manually.

For engaging targets at night there is an LLLTV camera mounted on the mantlet which moves in elevation with the main armament. Both commander and gunner have a tv monitor screen and in addition to the optical cross-hairs being displayed a second set of electronically generated cross-hairs is superimposed onto the tv picture. The latter changes in accordance with the variable angle of aim (independent of ammunition type and target range), and is also corrected for vehicle cant. The two sets of cross-hairs are then brought together and the main armament fired.

The TH 301 is powered by an MB 833 Ka 500 diesel developing 720 hp coupled to a Renk transmission which is

TAM tank

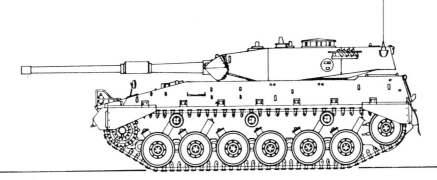

fitted with a hydro-dynamic retarder which is used to augment the steering effort in addition to being used for braking the vehicle.

Under development is another version of the TAM which has the same fire-control system as the TH 301 but with a 120 mm gun and powered by a 600 hp diesel.

VCTP MICV
Similar to West German Marder MICV but developed to meet requirements of Argentina.

Dragon 30 mm SPAAG
This system, fitted with two man turret armed with twin 30 mm cannon was developed to the prototype stage but is no longer offered.

155 mm SPG
Proposal only. Basic chassis fitted with same turret as installed on the French 155 mm GCT self-propelled gun on AMX-30 MBT chassis.

57 mm SPAAG
This is a proposal by Thyssen Henschel and Bofors and would be armed with a 57 mm gun, developed from a naval weapon of the same calibre, which would fire AP and APFSDS (pre-fragmented) ammunition and be fitted with an optronic fire-control system.

57 mm support tank
This vehicle can be based on the Marder or TAM chassis and the first prototype was shown in November 1977. It is a joint development between Bofors who are responsible for the 57 mm gun and its associated ammunition and Thyssen Henschel.

It has been designed to undertake a variety of roles on the battlefield including anti-tank, anti-helicopter, anti-APC and the destruction of soft skinned vehicles.

Armament consists of a Bofors 57 mm gun with an elevation of +45 degrees, depression of −8 degrees and turret traverse a full 360 degrees. A 7.62 mm machine gun is fitted coaxial with the main armament and mounted on the right side of the turret is a launcher for a Hughes TOW ATGW. A total of 148 rounds of 57 mm (AP, HE and proximity fuzed) ammunition are carried plus six Hughes TOW ATGW.

The three man crew consists of the commander, gunner and driver, and three infantrymen can be carried in the hull at the rear.

Marder with FL-20 turret
In 1985 a Marder chassis was fitted with the new French Fives-Cail Babcock FL-20 turret armed with a 105 mm gun and a 20 mm coaxial cannon.

SPECIFICATIONS (TAM)

CREW	4	with auxiliary tanks	900 km	ARMAMENT	
COMBAT WEIGHT	30 500 kg	FORDING	1.4 m	main	1 × 105 mm
UNLOADED WEIGHT	28 000 kg	with preparation	2.25 m	coaxial	1 × 7.62 mm MG
POWER-TO-WEIGHT		with snorkel	4 m	anti-aircraft	1 × 7.62 mm MG
RATIO	23.27 bhp/tonne	GRADIENT	65%	SMOKE-LAYING	
GROUND PRESSURE	0.77 kg/cm²	SIDE SLOPE	30%	EQUIPMENT	4 smoke dischargers
LENGTH GUN		VERTICAL OBSTACLE	0.9 m		either side of turret
FORWARDS	8.23 m	TRENCH	2.5 m		
LENGTH HULL	6.775 m	TURNING RADIUS		AMMUNITION	
WIDTH	3.12 m	1st gear	6.5 m	main	50
HEIGHT TO TURRET TOP	2.42 m	2nd gear	13.5 m	machine gun	6000
GROUND CLEARANCE	0.44 m	3rd gear	20 m	GUN CONTROL	
TRACK	2.62 m	4th gear	30 m	EQUIPMENT	
TRACK WIDTH	450 mm	ENGINE	super-charged MTU MB 833	Turret power control	electro-hydraulic/
LENGTH OF TRACK			Ka 500 6-cylinder diesel		manual
ON GROUND	3.9 m		developing 720 hp at 2200	by commander	yes
MAX ROAD SPEED			rpm	by gunner	yes
1st gear	16 km/h	TRANSMISSION	Renk HSWL-194 planetary	commander's override	yes
2nd gear	31 km/h		with 4 speeds both forward	Commander's fire-	
3rd gear	47 km/h		and reverse	control override	yes
4th gear	75 km/h	STEERING	stepless hydrostatic	Gun elevation/depression	+18°/−7°
FUEL CAPACITY	650 litres	SUSPENSION	torsion bar	Gun stabiliser	
MAX ROAD RANGE	550 km	ELECTRICAL SYSTEM	24 V	vertical	yes
		BATTERIES	6 × 12 V, 100 Ah	horizontal	yes

Status: Production in Argentina. In service with Argentina, Panama and Peru.

Manufacturer: Thyssen Henschel, Postfach 102969, D-3500 Kassel, Federal Republic of Germany.

Marder MICV chassis fitted with FL-20 turret armed with 105 mm gun and 20 mm coaxial cannon

INDIA

Vijayanta Tank Production

In August 1961 following the evaluation of competing British and West German MBT designs to meet an Indian requirement for a new MBT to be manufactured in India, an agreement was signed between Vickers Limited of the United Kingdom and the Indian Government. This agreement covered building prototypes in the United Kingdom, supplying a small quantity of production tanks and building a new facility at Avadi, near Madras, to undertake production of the Vickers MBT. The Indians call the tank the Vijayanta, or Victorious.

The first two prototypes were completed in 1963 and one was sent to India and the other retained in the United Kingdom for development work. The first production tanks were delivered from Vickers Elswick works in 1965. The first Indian Vijayanta, which was mainly built from components supplied by the United Kingdom, rolled off the production line at Avadi in January 1965. Since then India has progressively undertaken the production of more and more of the tank. As originally built the Vickers Mk 1 MBT weighed just under 39 tonnes but it is believed that Indian manufacturing methods increased the weight of Indian models to between 41 and 42 tonnes. Full details of the Vijayanta tank are given in the United Kingdom section under the Vickers MBT. Early in 1981 Marconi Radar Systems was awarded a £6 million contract for its SFCS 600 tank fire-control system for the Vijayanta MBT with a £6 million option for additional systems. Each contract is for 70 systems making a total of 140, but this option has not been exercised. In 1981 Barr and Stroud supplied a Tank Laser Sight (as installed in the Chieftain and other AFVs) for trials in the Vijayanta MBT.

In 1983 Vijayantas fitted with Vickers Defence Systems powerpack (using a Rolls-Royce Condor diesel) and a Cummins powerpack (using a Cummins KTA 111 diesel) were tested in India. In mid-1983 it was announced that India was

Indian Army Vijayanta MBT (Indian Ministry of Defence)

to order 250 Leyland L60 engines for its Vijayantas in two batches, the first consisting of 150 engines. The L60 is produced in India but local production cannot meet the demand for both new and rebuilt engines for the Vijayanta fleet.

Early in 1985 Indian sources stated that MTU of West Germany was to supply 12 diesel engines to India, six for the Vijayanta and six for new Arjun MBT.

Variants
Entering service with the Indian Army is a Vijayanta chassis with an additional road wheel either side. Its turret has been replaced by a Soviet 130 mm M-46 field gun firing over the rear. The 130 mm gun has limited traverse with over 30 projectiles and charges being carried.

In 1983 it was reported that India was to ship a Vijayanta chassis to France to have the turret of the French 155 mm GCT self-propelled gun fitted for trials purposes.

Arjun MBT

In the early 1970s the Combat Vehicle Research and Development Establishment at Avadi started design work on a new MBT which finally made its first appearance in early 1985. This is called the Arjun and weighs about 50 tonnes, its external appearance is similar in some respects to the West German Leopard 2 MBT, especially in turret design. In

April 1985 it was stated that by 1988 20 prototypes of the Arjun MBT would be completed to enable extensive trials of key subsystems such as armament, fire-control, powerpack and suspension prior to the start of full-scale production. By the time the first prototype of the Arjun was unveiled in April 1984 Rs 300 millions had already been spent on the project.

The Explosives Research and Development Laboratory at Pune in Maharashtra has developed a new high-energy propellant which will be used in the 120 mm smooth-bore gun to give a higher muzzle velocity and therefore greater penetration characteristics.

Indian T-72 production

It was originally intended to order only a small number of T-72s pending the production of the new Indian MBT but as this has fallen behind schedule additional T-72s have been ordered. It is also reported that India is currently testing a number of T-72s with new powerpacks supplied by General Motors, Detroit Diesel and Cummins. The remaining 97 Centurion tanks (some of the earlier ones have found their way to South Africa) have been withdrawn from service and are awaiting disposal.

Manufacturer: Avadi Company, 29 Mount Road, Madras, India.

ISRAEL

Merkava Main Battle Tank

Development
In the 1950s Israel obtained most of its armoured fighting vehicles from France (modified Sherman tanks and AMX-13 light tanks) and the United Kingdom (Centurion MBTs). The United Kingdom provided Israel with two Chieftain tanks for trials before the 1967 Middle East war but after the war declined to provide them in quantity, but further supplies of the Centurion tank were made available. M48 tanks were supplied by West Germany until Arab pressure stopped this source of tanks as well. Israel's only source of tanks then became the USA which supplied M48s, M60s and M60A1s. If the Arabs put pressure on the USA to stop further supplies of tanks to Israel the country would be left with no source for MBTs and so it was decided to proceed with the development of an Israeli tank that would, where possible, use components from the existing M48/M60/Centurion tanks.

Merkava Mark 1 MBT clearly showing turret profile and turret basket at rear (Israeli Ministry of Defence)

Israeli experience in the 1967 campaign proved that mobility was no substitute for armour protection and they therefore decided at an early stage that the main emphasis would be placed on armour with firepower and mobility second and third priorities. Design work on the tank started as early as 1967 but detailed design work, under the direction of General Israel Tal, did not begin until August 1970. Prior to the construction of the first prototypes of the Merkava, a number of test rigs based on M48 and Centurion tank chassis were completed to prove the basic concept. The first prototype of the Merkava was completed in 1974.

In May 1977 Israel finally announced that it had developed a new MBT called the Merkava (or Chariot) to the prototype stage and that a series production run of 40 tanks was being built. First production tanks were delivered to the Israeli Army in 1979.

The Merkava Mk 1 was first used in action during the fighting in the Lebanon in 1982. First production Merkava Mk 2s were delivered to the Israeli Army in December 1983 and by early 1985 total production is believed to have amounted to over 400 vehicles.

Description

The hull of the Merkava is made of cast and welded armour with a well-shaped glacis plate with the right side higher than the left. Behind the first layer of cast armour is a space filled with diesel fuel and then another layer of armour. This spaced armour gives the tank protection from HEAT projectiles and ATGWs.

The layout of the Merkava is unconventional with the turret and fighting compartment at the rear of the vehicle. The driver is seated on the left side of the hull, forward of the turret, with the engine compartment to his right. The driver is provided with a one-piece hatch cover that opens to the left and three observation periscopes for driving with the hatch closed; the centre one can be replaced by a passive one for night driving. The driver can reach his compartment through the main crew compartment as the backrest of the driver's seat folds forwards.

The Teledyne Continental AVDS-1790-6A V-12 diesel develops 900 hp and is coupled to an Allison CD-850-6BX transmission. The engine is in fact a more powerful version of the engine fitted to the M60 and M60A1 MBTs and the transmission is also similar to that installed in these tanks. Access to the engine compartment is via two flaps which are opened by springs after the locks are released. The engine can be replaced in the field in about 60 minutes. The air cooling filter vent is positioned in the upper part of the hull, forward of the driver's seat, with the outlet being located on the opposite side. The exhaust outlet is on the right side of the hull, above the skirting plates over the second road wheel.

The wedge-shaped turret, which has been designed to accept either a 105 mm (M68) or 120 mm gun, is cast with a welded front. It has a small cross-section and a large overhang at the rear. The radios and hydraulics are mounted in the turret bustle. The commander is seated on the right side of the turret with the gunner seated forward and below the commander. The commander has no cupola but is provided with a hatch cover that opens to the rear and five periscopes for all-round observation. The commander's hatch can be raised manually to give direct all-round observation while retaining full overhead protection. Mounted forward of his hatch cover in the roof of the tank is a sight that can be traversed through 360 degrees, with a magnification of from

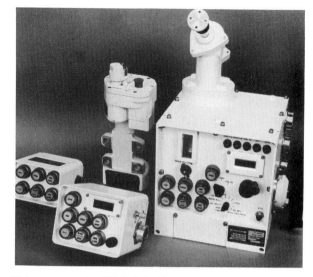

Main components of Elbit digital fire-control system for Merkava Mark 1 MBT (left to right) loader's, commander's and gunner's unit

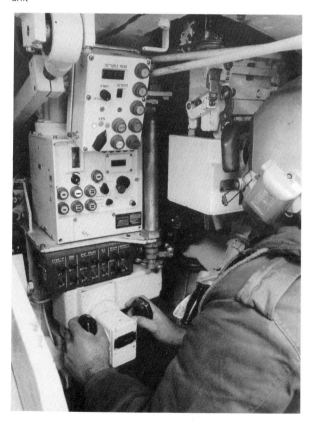

Gunner's station on Merkava Mark 1 MBT

×4 to ×20. The rotating head of the commander's periscope is linked to the turret traverse system by a counter-rotating device. The gunner's optics are in the forward part of the turret roof and right-angled ribs in front of the optics stop shell-splinters and small arms fire from damaging them. The gunner's periscope has magnifications of ×1 and ×8 and incorporates a laser rangefinder. The loader is seated on the left rear side of the turret and is provided with a single-piece hatch cover opening to the rear.

There are three hatch covers in the rear of the hull: the left one gives access to the batteries and the right one gives access to the NBC pack. The centre one is a two-part door, the upper part opening upwards and the lower part downwards, through which ammunition or wounded can be loaded. This hatch can be opened from the outside but locked from the inside. A 60-litre water tank is provided above the rear hatch. The infantry telephone is mounted at the rear of the hull on the left side. More recently some Merkava MBTs have been observed fitted with closely-spaced chains with ball ends. These detonate HEAT projectiles before they can hit the turret ring.

The Mark 1 Merkava has six Centurion-type rubber-tyred road wheels either side with the drive sprocket at the front, idler at the rear and four track return rollers. Each road wheel is suspended by a separate helical spring with suspension arms for two road wheels each caged in a housing.

A white light and an infra-red driving light mounted on either side of the glacis plate can be folded down in action to avoid damage from shell splinters and small arms fire. The 1 kW searchlight is mounted vertically in the bustle under armour protection to the rear of the loader's position and is controlled by the tank commander. The Merkava is equipped with an NBC system and a Spectronix explosion suppression system.

Main armament is a standard 105 mm M68 rifled tank gun fitted with a thermal sleeve, manufactured in Israel by Israel Military Industries and also fitted to most other Israeli tanks. It has an elevation of +20 degrees and a depression of −8.5 degrees. A travelling lock is provided for the 105 mm gun on the right side of the glacis plate. The Merkava carries a total of 92 rounds of 105 mm ammunition of which eight are stowed below the turret ring for ready use and the remainder in the hull rear, 12 in two-round containers and 72 in four-round containers. No ammunition is stowed above the turret ring, and all ammunition is in special containers. In addition to the standard 105 mm HEAT and HESH rounds the gun will fire a new APFSDS-T round developed by Israel Military Industries.

The Israel Military Industries APFSDS-T round is of the hyper-velocity kinetic energy type with a swaged tungsten alloy core. It is fin-stabilised with a slipping obturator band.

Merkava Mk 1 MBT from the rear showing external stowage basket on turret rear and entry hatches in hull rear (Israeli Ministry of Defence)

Merkava Mk 2 MBT showing additional armour protection on side of turret (Israeli Army)

A conventional three segment type sabot is used and its triple base modified M30 propellant contains an efficient titanium-dioxide reducing liner.

The manufacturer states that the APFSDS-T projectile is effective against both stationary and moving targets at ranges of up to 4500 metres at an angle of attack of 60 degrees. The projectile will penetrate 150 mm Heavy NATO Single (HNS) target of homogeneous rolled steel armour plate at an obliquity of 60 degrees at a striking velocity equivalent to 2000 metres in range.

Basic specifications of the APFSDS-T round are:

WEIGHT OF CARTRIDGE	18.7 kg
LENGTH OF CARTRIDGE	885 mm
WEIGHT OF PROJECTILE	6.3 kg
LENGTH OF PROJECTILE	417 mm
PROPELLANT TYPE	Triple base, MP, M30M
PROPELLANT WEIGHT	5.8 kg
MUZZLE VELOCITY	1455 m/second
TRACER BURNING TIME	3.5 seconds

A 7.62 mm machine gun is mounted coaxially to the left of the main armament and a similar weapon is mounted at the commander's and loader's station. The coaxial machine gun is fed from a 2000-round continuous belt which is between the plates of the spaced armour. The MGs are MAGs, manufactured under licence from FN of Belgium. A 60 mm Soltam mortar is carried by the Merkava for which 30 mortar bombs are stored in a compartment in the turret rear. This mortar fires high explosive, smoke and illuminating bombs and helps to conserve 105 mm ammunition.

During the 1973 Middle East war many Israeli tanks ran out of ammunition and so the Merkava has been designed to carry a large supply in the rear of the hull. The Merkava can also be used as a command post with the ammunition supply containers removed. By reducing the ammunition load the Merkava can also carry troops, for example ten infantry can be carried by reducing the ammunition load by 45 rounds or a three-man commando squad together with their radios if the ammunition load is reduced by 25 rounds. It must be emphasised that the ability to carry infantry is only an option for use in special circumstances as the infantry have no vision devices at all.

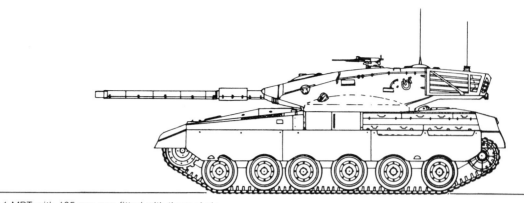

Merkava Mk 1 MBT with 105 mm gun fitted with thermal sleeve

Merkava has a digital fire-control system designed by Elbit Computers Limited of Haifa and a laser rangefinder which can be used by the commander or gunner. The laser rangefinder is manufactured by Elop-Electrical and feeds information into the computer. The system is built around a Central Processing Unit and consists of operation units, control and feedback servo loops and sensors. The system includes three operation units, gunner's, commander's and loader's. The gunner's is the main unit and provides all manual inputs necessary for ballistic computation. It also includes a logistic panel which enables system bore sighting and system BITE, as well as the display of pre-select inputs. The unit also includes the following manual inputs: type of ammunition (six types) and recoil compensation insertion for each type of ammunition, in elevation and deflection. The commander's unit provides a readout of the system's display, range and ammunition inputs. The loader's unit provides ammunition inputs.

The control loop transfers the computer super-elevation information to the hydraulic gun elevation drive and the ballistic move drive. In addition deflection data is transferred to the moving graticule. The feedback loop ensures that the actual super-elevation and graticule deflection data are identical to the computed data and will correct the error accordingly.

The system includes automatic sensors, laser rangefinder, turret cant angle indicator and target angular velocity sensor. Optional sensors include cross wind velocity, charge temperature, barrel bend and ambient air density.

Manual operation of the electrical system if the computer fails is made possible with a handwheel drum and mounted scales, connected to the mechanical gearbox, to give elevation angle compensation and range to target for all types of projectiles. The commander can, if required, take over control of the main armament and fire the gun. The main armament is stabilised in both planes as an American Cadillac Gage stabilisation system is fitted as standard. This is manufactured under licence in Israel by PML Precision Mechanism Ltd. It is probable that a thermal imaging system will be fitted in the future.

It has been confirmed that Elop-Electronic Industries Limited supplies the commander's night vision goggles, night driver's periscope, part of the fire-control system and laser rangefinder and the tank commander's turret control handle. Tadiran supplies communications equipment, Ashot Ashkelon the tank tracks, Shahal the shock absorbers, and Urdan Industries supplies hull and turret armour as well as driving sprockets, road wheels, suspension arms and tracks.

Variants

Merkava Mark 2

In 1983 the Merkava Mark 2 replaced the earlier Mk 1 in production. Main improvements over the original production model include a layer of special armour on the front and sides of the turret, 60 mm mortar is mounted on the left side of the turret and can be now loaded and fired from within the turret, steel skirts that protect the suspension are backed by special armour, fire-control system has a number of improvements including a Neodymium-YaG laser rangefinder in place of the original Neodymium-glass laser rangefinder and a more advanced computer.

The original 900 hp diesel engine has been retained but the new Israeli-designed and built transmission is much more efficient and has enabled range of the Merkava to be increased by 25 per cent to 500 km with only a slight increase in fuel capacity.

Merkava Mark 3

This is now under development and expected to enter production between 1985 and 1990. Armour will be a 100 per cent improvement over the Mark 1; Mk 3 will also incorporate improved suspension (hydro-pneumatic), new armour probably integrated with a vehicle protection system, new powerpack with engine developing 1400/1500 hp giving a power-to-weight ratio of 23 to 25 hp/tonne, acceleration of 0 to 32 km/h in eight seconds plus all of the improvements including probably a 120 mm gun. The latter may be the

Merkava Mark 1 MBT with 105 mm gun fitted with thermal sleeve

American model of the Rheinmetall 120 mm smooth-bore gun produced in the US for the M1A1.

155 mm Self-propelled gun

Early in 1984 it was reported that Soltam was developing a 155 mm self-propelled gun on the Merkava chassis.

Dozer mine-clearing equipment

Some Merkava MBTs have attachment plates under the hull front to enable them to be fitted with Israeli designed and produced mineclearing equipment and dozer blades.

SPECIFICATIONS (Mk 1)

CREW	4
COMBAT WEIGHT	60 000 kg
UNLOADED WEIGHT	58 000 kg
POWER-TO-WEIGHT RATIO	15 hp/tonne
GROUND PRESSURE	0.9 kg/cm²
LENGTH GUN FORWARDS	8.63 m
LENGTH HULL	7.45 m
WIDTH	3.7 m
HEIGHT	
to commander's cupola	2.75 m
to turret roof	2.64 m
FIRING HEIGHT	2.15 m
GROUND CLEARANCE	0.47 m
TRACK WIDTH	640 mm
LENGTH OF TRACK ON GROUND	4.78 m
MAX ROAD SPEED	46 km/h
ACCELERATION	
0 to 32 km/h	13 s
RANGE	400 km
FUEL CAPACITY	900 litres
FORDING	1.38 m
FORDING WITH PREPARATION	2 m
GRADIENT	60%
SIDE SLOPE	38%
VERTICAL OBSTACLE	0.95 m
TRENCH	3 m
ENGINE	Teledyne Continental AVDS-1790-6A V-12 diesel developing 900 hp
TRANSMISSION	Allison CD-850-6BX
SUSPENSION	Independent, helical spring and volute bumper spring
ROAD WHEEL ARM TRAVEL	+210 mm −85 mm
ELECTRICAL SYSTEM	24 V
BATTERIES	8 × 12 V (500 Ah)
ARMAMENT	
main	1 × 105 mm
coaxial	1 × 7.62 mm MG
anti-aircraft	2 × 7.62 mm MG
AMMUNITION	
main	62 (nominal, can be as high as 85)
coaxial/anti-aircraft	10 000
GUN CONTROL EQUIPMENT	
Turret power control	electro-hydraulic/manual
by commander	yes
by gunner	yes
Gun elevation/depression	+20°/−8.5°
Gun stabiliser	
vertical	yes
horizontal	yes

Status: In production. In service with the Israeli Army.

Manufacturer: Israeli Ordnance Corps facility at Tel a Shumer, near Tel Aviv, Israel.

Israeli Upgraded Centurion Main Battle Tank

Development/Description

The Centurion MBT entered service with the Israeli Armour Corps in 1959 but was not initially liked by its crews as it was more complex than the Sherman tanks used at the time.

One of the main drawbacks of the Centurion was its Meteor petrol engine which gave the tank a relatively low power-to-weight ratio and a very high fuel consumption which limited its operational range. The cooling system also gave a lot of trouble as did the air-cleaners.

In the late 1960s a decision was taken to replace the Meteor petrol engine with a diesel and after trials with three different engines, the Teledyne Continental AVDS-1790-2A diesel was selected, as it was also being installed in the Israeli Armoured Corps' M48A2 tanks which were being modernised then. The original Merritt-Brown Z51R manual gearbox was replaced by the Allison CD-850-6 automatic which greatly reduced driver fatigue as well as simplifying training.

To accommodate the new powerpack the rear of the hull had to be enlarged, but even so the engine had to be installed at an inclination of 3.5 degrees front side up. This meant that elevated top decks had to be fitted to accommodate the cooling air outlets that vented upwards through louvres above the transmission compartment. Externally the modified Israeli Centurions, officially designated the Upgraded Centurion (not the Ben-Gurion), is recognisable by its raised engine decks and air filter boxes on the trackguards.

The Upgraded Centurion, which entered service with the Israeli Armoured Corps in 1970, also has increased fuel capacity, more efficient air-cooled braking system, new fire-extinguishing system, improved ammunition layout with 72 rounds of 105 mm ammunition carried, and a new electrical system.

Some Centurions have been observed with a 12.7 mm M2 HB machine gun over the gun barrel. This was originally fitted for training but was used in urban fighting in the Lebanon in lieu of the 105 mm M68 gun. The 12.7 mm machine gun is fitted with one box of ready use ammunition and fired by an electrically-operated solenoid from within the turret.

The Upgraded Centurion has a maximum road speed of 43 km/h and twice the cruising range of the Centurion Mk 5 on which it is based.

Variants

The Upgraded Centurion can also be fitted with appliqué reactive armour and various types of mine roller (similar to the Soviet PT-55's) and a mine plough (similar to the Soviet KMT-4's) can be fitted at the front of the tank.

The RKM bulldozer attachment is produced by Urdan Industries Limited and is intended for use on the M48, M60 and Centurion tanks of the Israeli Army although it is also suitable for installation on foreign vehicles.

It consists of three major components: the bulldozer blade, which is a standard blade with some modifications to improve its performance in sandy soils as found in the Middle East; the electro-hydraulic unit, which is connected to the tank's 24 V electrical system to supply hydraulic pressure to the main cylinder. The electro-hydraulic system and all the movements of the bulldozer blade are controlled by a control unit in the driver's compartment and the main structure which houses the electro-hydraulic unit and is attached to the user tank. It carries the

Upgraded Centurion MBT of Israeli Army showing modified rear engine deck to accommodate Continental AVDS-1790-2A diesel engine with Allison CD-850-6 transmission

Israeli Army Upgraded Centurion MBT with turret traversed to left. Note turret basket, new commander's cupola, infra-red driving lights and mounting points for appliqué reactive armour on the glacis (Kensuke Ebata)

bulldozer blade and the main actuating cylinder.

The driver operates the attachment from a detachable control unit inside the driving compartment, the system has four basic modes of operation:

Blade up. In this mode the bulldozer blade is lifted to its maximum height for travel.

Blade floating. In this mode the bulldozer blade is released and lowered until it rests on the soil surface for earthmoving parallel to the soil contour.

Blade down. In this mode the blade is used for heavy duty earthmoving.

Blade down and routers extended. Used for routing surfaces when the tank is being driven in reverse.

The RKM bulldozer attachment can be installed by the tank crew in about 30 minutes and the system is fitted with standard NATO inter-tank connectors for attaching to the users' tanks' 24-volt power supplies. The system can be

Centurion MBT fitted with dozer blade. Turret is traversed to rear

Israeli Army Centurion chassis modified to carry and launch 290 mm rockets

removed in about 15 minutes. In the Israeli Army it is issued on the scale of one or two per tank company.

The Israeli Army also uses the Centurion ARV Mk 2 and some tanks have had their turrets removed for use as tugs. As a private venture Soltam has fitted a Centurion chassis with a turret-mounted 155 mm gun/howitzer, but this has yet to be placed in production.

Centurion APC
Some Israeli Centurions have had their turrets removed for use as armoured personnel carriers in Southern Lebanon. The hull armour around the turret ring has been built up to the front, sides and rear and 7.62 mm/12.7 mm machine guns have been mounted around the top to provide suppressive fire.

290 mm multiple rocket system
The Israeli Army uses a number of Centurion chassis with their turrets removed and fitted with a three-round launcher for a 290 mm rocket designed by Israel Military Industries.

Note on Israeli MBTs
During the fighting in the Lebanon in the summer of 1982 many Israeli M48, M60 and Centurion series MBTs were observed to be fitted with appliqué armour.

Late in 1983 it was confirmed that this was reactive armour developed by Rafael Armament Development Authority with production and marketing being undertaken by Israel Military Industries. This armour, called Blazer, is suitable for installation on all types of MBT and adds less than 1 tonne to the vehicle weight. It consists of small panels of armour bolted onto the hull and turret reacting to HEAT attack but not activated by small arms ammunition, artillery fire or artillery fragments. Once a panel has been hit it no longer provides protection but the manufacturer believes that the possibility of a panel being hit twice is remote.

On an M60A1 type MBT about 10 square metres are protected including the turret roof. Blazer provides a high degree of protection against attack from HEAT projectiles such as those fitted to Soviet RPG-7 and Sagger type weapons.

Israeli Centurion and M60 series tanks have also been observed fitted with smoke grenade launchers on either side of the 105 mm gun.

In early 1984 it was announced that the Israeli Ordnance Corps had developed a low cost fire-control system which would be fitted initially to Israeli M48 and Centurion tanks and at a later date to the T-55 tanks used by some reserve units. The fire-control system can be installed in under a day and includes a computer developed by Elbit Computers and optics by El-Op.

It is also reported that some Israeli M48 and Centurion tanks are to be fitted with an Astronautics fire-control system, the FCS-10 for the M48 and FCS-20 for the Centurion.

Manufacturer: The Upgraded Centurion programme was carried out at Israeli Ordnance Corps Workshops at Tel a Shumer, near Tel Aviv, Israel.

Israeli Sherman Tanks

When the state of Israel was founded in 1948 its armoured forces consisted of 12 French Hotchkiss H-35/39 tanks, two British Cromwell tanks, two American Sherman tanks plus an assortment of light armoured vehicles, many of which were made locally and suitable only for internal security operations. Between 1949 and 1954 additional Shermans were obtained from a variety of sources. These models included the M4A1 (75 mm gun), M4A1 (105 mm howitzer), M4A1 (locally fitted with ex-Swiss Krupp M1911 field gun in place of 105 mm howitzer), M4A2 (75 mm gun) and a single Sherman 17-pounder. In 1954 a single M10 tank destroyer was obtained. Israel then embarked on its own Sherman retrofit programme.

M1 Super Sherman
In 1956 France delivered a batch of 100 M4A1E3 and M4A1E8 Sherman tanks fitted with 76.2 mm guns. These tanks were renamed M1 Super Sherman by Israel and were used during the 1956 and 1967 Arab/Israeli wars, after which they were transferred to border security units or rebuilt for other roles.

M50 Mark 1 and M50 Mark 2 Shermans
During 1954 Israeli technical experts went to Bourges Arsenal in France to design a turret mounting for the Sherman using the French 75 mm CN-75-50 tank gun. Two

M50 Sherman tank of Israeli Army with turret traversed to rear (Israeli Army)

prototypes were built, one on an M4A2 hull and the other on the single M10 hull. Modifications undertaken included several to the ammunition ejection system, replacement of the welded-on steel box on the turret rear by a cast counterweight filled with lead, a specially adapted telescopic sight and a new ammunition feed system.

A pre-production model was completed in 1955 and by 1956 the first M50 Mark 1 Shermans had been rebuilt from M4A4 hulls and French-supplied turret castings in Israeli workshops. One company of M50 Mark 1s was subsequently used in the 1956 war.

As a result of combat experience several modifications were carried out on the production line. Because of the modifications the last of the initial batch of 50 Sherman M50 Mark 1 conversions was not delivered until April 1959. By this time the original Continental petrol engines, narrow tracks and VVS suspensions were beginning to present considerable maintenance problems due to the increased weight of the turret and armament. Their replacement with a 460 hp diesel and HVSS suspension was started. The M4A3 hull was considered ideal for this as it was already fitted with a radiator. Several hundred M4A3 hulls were bought from a variety of sources. The first batch of Cummins diesel engines arrived in 1960 to be fitted into the M50 Mark 2 as this version was designated. The prototypes had been tested late in 1959. Later two smoke dischargers were fitted to either side of the turret.

The 75 mm CN-75-50 gun fired the following types of ammunition:

Type	AP	AP	HE
DESIGNATION	POT-51A	PCOT-51P	n/a
WEIGHT OF COMPLETE ROUND	21 kg	21 kg	20.6 kg
WEIGHT OF PROJECTILE	6.4 kg	6.4 kg	6.2 kg
MUZZLE VELOCITY	1000 m/s	1000 m/s	1000 m/s
PENETRATION	110 mm/0°	170 mm/0°	n/app
	60 mm/60°	40 mm/60°	

M51 Sherman

Although the M50 Sherman was capable of successfully engaging Soviet T-34/85 and T-54/T-55 series tanks the Egyptians began receiving increased quantities of Soviet IS-3 heavy tanks in the early 1960s and a newer and more capable gun was needed to meet the threat.

The Israelis initially looked at the French 105 mm CN-105-F1 56-calibre tank gun with a maximum muzzle velocity of 1000 metres a second firing a HEAT projectile. However it was found that the gun was too long and the muzzle velocity too high to operate efficiently from a modified Sherman turret, primarily because of the lack of space during recoil.

The Israelis then returned to Bourges Arsenal to modify a CN-105-F1 to meet their requirements. This resulted in the barrel length being reduced by 1.5 metres to obtain an acceptable muzzle velocity of 800 metres a second. The new gun was designated the 105 mm D1504 tank gun, 44 calibre with ammunition made in Israel.

The Sherman model chosen for this conversion was the M4A1. The tanks were stripped back to their hulls, fitted with a Cummins 460 hp diesel engine, E8 HVSS suspension modified steering, transmission and exhaust, wider tracks and a new turret mantlet, turret bustle and ammunition stowage to house the new 105 mm gun and its ammunition.

M51 Sherman, armed with 105 mm gun (Israeli Army)

Other improvements included replacing the original bulky battery charger with a small and compact dynamo, fitting a white light/infra-red searchlight over the main armament, fitting two smoke dischargers either side of the turret and replacement of the locking assembly and hydraulic controls by a new SAMM CH 23-1 system based on that fitted to the AMX-13 light tank then in service with the Israeli Army. After trials with the prototypes it was found necessary to fit the gun with a muzzle brake.

The modifications took about 25 000 man hours per tank and resulted in the combat weight being increased to 39 tonnes. The maximum road speed is 45 km/h and the operational range is 270 km.

The M51 was first used operationally in the pre-1967 war border conflict with Syria. It was subsequently used in the 1967 war, 1968–70 war of attrition and the 1973 war. In 1973 it successfully engaged Soviet T-62 MBTs used by Egypt and Syria.

The 105 mm gun fires a non-rotating hollow charge anti-tank round (the OCC 105 F1), HE model 60, smoke and practice rounds. The first is similar to that fired by the French AMX-30 MBT and has a muzzle velocity of 905 metres a second and will penetrate 360 mm of armour at an incidence of 0 degrees or 150 mm at 60 degrees.

Following the 1967 war the regular armoured units were re-equipped with more modern MBTs, allowing some of the M1/M50/M51 series to be transferred to the reserve mechanised brigades and border defence units. Chile has taken delivery of about 100 M51 Sherman tanks from Israel. The remainder of the older Shermans were then reworked into a variety of specialised versions; descriptions follow.

Armoured Ambulance

This is a rebuilt Sherman M50 with the turret removed and engine repositioned in the front. It is similar in overall shape to the armoured command post vehicle and M50 self-propelled howitzer and first entered service in 1969 for use in front-line areas during the war of attrition. The patients were carried on stretchers in the rear of the vehicle which was provided with extensive medical equipment. To facilitate rapid removal of wounded men from the battlefield a trap-door was provided in the floor of the vehicle.

Artillery Observation Post Vehicle

This is a Sherman M1 with its turret removed and replaced by a scissors type hydraulically-operated arm, on top of which is mounted a platform for artillery observation personnel. It is known as the cherrypicker and was used for the first time during the war of attrition.

Armoured Command Vehicle

This is a rebuilt Sherman M50 with turret removed, engine repositioned to the front and superstructure added to the rear, on top of which is mounted the commander's cupola with a pintle-mounted 7.62 mm machine gun. Its overall shape is similar to the armoured ambulance and it entered service in 1967.

Engineer and Mine-clearing Versions

The Israeli Army is known to have used M4 flail type mine-clearing tanks and a small quantity of Sherman bridgelayers but it is not known if any of them are still in use.

The Israeli Army uses two modified Sherman tank chassis in the armoured engineer role. The first of these is a Sherman with a cast hull and horizontal volute suspension system, turret traversed to rear and armament removed, searchlights fitted, and a hydraulically-operated dozer blade fitted at the front of the hull. The bow machine gun has also been removed on this model.

The second vehicle is called the Trail Blazer by the Israeli Army and uses a modified Sherman chassis with a welded

Medical evacuation tank based on rebuilt Sherman chassis (Israeli Army)

Trail Blazer tank based on Sherman chassis with dozer blade raised, rear spades raised and hydraulic crane in travelling position on right side of hull (Israeli Army)

Sherman with hydraulically-operated dozer blade for clearing obstacles in forward areas (Israeli Army)

M51 Sherman with turret traversed to rear

hull and horizontal volute suspension system and the turret removed. Mounted at the front of the hull on the right side is a large hydraulically-operated crane, similar to that installed on the Leopard 1 and AMX-30 ARVs, which is used for removing obstacles and changing powerpacks in the field. When not required this lies along the right side of the hull. Mounted at the front and rear of the Trail Blazer are hydraulically-operated blades; the rear one is normally used when the Trail Blazer is in the recovery mode, while the front one can be used to clear obstacles as well. The winch compartment is in the centre of the hull where the turret was previously situated and stowage boxes are mounted along each side of the hull.

Sherman with AMX-13 Turret

In the 1967 campaign Israel captured a quantity of Sherman tanks from the Egyptians fitted with a French AMX-13 turret armed with a 75 mm gun. These had been supplied by the French in the early 1950s. As far as it is known these tanks were not taken into service with the Israeli Army although their chassis were probably converted to other roles.

155 mm Self-propelled Howitzer M50

This was developed in the late 1950s by France to meet the requirements of Israel and consists of a much modified Sherman tank chassis fitted with a French 155 mm Model 50 howitzer at the rear of the hull. This weapon has a maximum elevation of +69 degrees and fires a 43 kg HE projectile to a maximum range of 18 000 metres. The modifications to the hull have been extensive and include moving the engine to the front of the hull alongside the driver. The main drawback

155 mm self-propelled howitzer M50 in travelling configuration (Israeli Army)

160 mm self-propelled mortar with mortar at low elevation and full front lowered to horizontal (Israeli Army)

of this weapon is that there is no overhead protection for the gun crew and limited traverse of the armament.

155 mm L-33 Self-Propelled Gun/Howitzer

This has been designed to meet the requirement of the Israeli Army by Soltam and consists of a rebuilt Sherman M4A3E8 chassis fitted with a Cummins diesel engine, all welded fully enclosed armoured superstructure and a Soltam 155 mm M-68 gun/howitzer. The latter has an elevation of +52 degrees, depression of −3 degrees and a total traverse of 60 degrees. A total of 60 rounds of 155 mm separate loading ammunition are carried of which 16 are for ready use. Maximum range is 21 000 metres. The L-33 has a crew of eight men and a loaded weight of 41 500 kg. It entered service in 1973 and first saw action in the same year during the Yom Kippur war.

160 mm Self-propelled Mortar

This conversion was undertaken by the Soltam company of Haifa from 1969 and consists of a Sherman (or M7 Priest) chassis with the turret and superstructure removed and replaced by vertical sides, front and rear, with the front being capable of being lowered to the horizontal. The 160 mm breech-loaded mortar mounted in the centre of the vehicle fires forwards, has a limited traverse and can be elevated from +43° to +70°. The mortar fires an HE bomb weighing 40 kg to a maximum range of 9600 metres, HE content being 5 kg, or two types of smoke bomb. Average rate of fire is five to eight bombs a minute. A total of 56 mortar bombs are stowed along the sides of the vehicle and below the floor on which the mortar is mounted. Access to the latter bombs is by a hatch to the right of the driver. A 7.62 mm or a 12.7 mm machine gun is mounted on each side of the vehicle for anti-aircraft use. The vehicle has a crew of eight, loaded

155 mm L-33 self-propelled gun/howitzer showing roof-mounted 7.62 mm anti-aircraft machine gun (Israeli Army)

weight of 36 654 kg, and is powered by a 430 hp Cummins diesel, which gives the vehicle a maximum road speed of 43 km/h and a range of 300 km.

Multiple Rocket Launcher

The Sherman chassis has also been used as the launcher for trials with the Israel Military Industries 290 mm multiple rocket system. Details of this, not based on Centurion chassis, were given for the entry on the Centurion MBT under Israel on page 53.

Status: In service with the Israeli Army and Lebanese Christian Militia (M50). Some Israeli M51 Sherman tanks are known to have been supplied to Chile in recent years.

ITALY

New Italian MBT

In 1984 OTO-Melara and FIAT formed a consortium to design a new MBT and an 8 × 8 tank destroyer to meet the requirements of the Italian Army.

FIAT, or INVECO as it is now known, will be responsible for the automotive components while OTO-Melara will be responsible for the weapons.

Because of their respective experience in tracked and wheeled armoured vehicles, OTO-Melara will concentrate

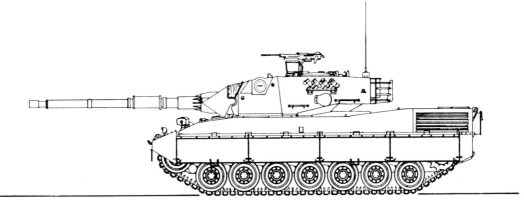

on the MBT while INVECO handles the 8 × 8 tank destroyer.

The new MBT will be a further development of the OF-40 Mk 2 produced by OTO-Melara for the United Arab Emirates and will have improved armour protection, a new 1200 hp FIAT engine coupled to a ZF transmission, new suspension, possibly hydro-pneumatic, and a 120 mm smooth-bore gun.

The 120 mm smooth-bore gun will be the West German Rheinmetall weapon as installed in the Leopard 2 and American M1A1 or the GIAT 120 mm weapon as installed in the AMX-40.

The Italian Army requires an early operational capability for its new MBT so there will be no prototypes as such. Production is expected to begin in 1987 with first deliveries in 1988. It is expected that the first production batch will be for 200 to 250 vehicles to replace part of the remaining M47 fleet.

The Italian Army Leopard 1s will need replacing in the 1990s but it is not clear whether Italy will develop a new MBT or join with France (in EPC project) or West Germany (in the new Combat MBT).

A major stumbling block in either project could be the export market as Italy would want to produce a MBT for both home and export markets to ensure a longer production run.

Status: Development.

Manufacturer: OTO-Melara, via Valdilocchi 15, 19100 La Spezia, Italy.

OF-40 Main Battle Tank

Development
The OF-40 MBT has been designed from 1977 by OTO-Melara and FIAT specifically for the export market, with the former responsible for overall design and production and the latter for the powerpack. The first prototype of the OF-40 (O for OTO-Melara, F for FIAT and 40 for the approximate weight) was completed in 1980. The United Arab Emirates placed an order for 18 OF-40 Mk 1s with the first of these being delivered in 1981. Further development resulted in the OF-40 Mk 2 of which 18 have been ordered and delivered to the United Arab Emirates together with three ARVs based on the same chassis.

The original 18 OF-40 Mk 1s are now being brought up to Mk 2 standard in the United Arab Emirates.

Description (Mk 1)
The all-welded hull is divided into three compartments: driver's at the front, fighting in the centre and engine and transmission at the rear. The driver is seated at the front on the right side and has a single-piece hatch cover that lifts and swings to the left. There are three unity periscopes in front of him, the centre one of which can be replaced by an Aeritalia image intensification periscope for night driving.

To the left of the driver is the NBC pack and 42 rounds of 105 mm ammunition and behind him there is an oval emergency hull escape hatch.

The all-welded turret is in the centre of the hull with the commander and gunner on the right and the loader on the left. The commander has a circular hatch cover that opens to the rear and eight unity periscopes for all-round observation, one of which can be replaced by an Aeritalia image intensification periscope. The commander's seat can be elevated by a manually-operated hydraulic system and a foot-operated valve enables him to lower the seat quickly in an emergency.

The commander does not have a cupola but mounted in the roof forward of his hatch is a French SFIM VS 580-B panoramic sight which can be stabilised and fitted with image intensification night vision equipment. This enables the tank commander to detect and identify the target and he can then either hand over to the gunner or engage the target himself.

The gunner is seated in front of and below the commander and has one forward facing roof-mounted periscope and an

OF-40 Mk 1 MBT from front showing wedge-shaped mantlet and thermal sleeve for 105 mm gun

OF-40 Mk 2 MBT firing OTO-Melara 105 mm rifled gun during trials in Italy

optical sight with a magnification of ×8. It is mounted coaxially with the 105 mm gun in a M114 telescopic mount.

The loader sits on the left of the turret and has a circular hatch cover that opens to the rear, in front of which are two roof-mounted periscopes that give observation to the front and left side.

The main armament of the OF-40 is an OTO-Melara designed and manufactured 105 mm 52-calibre rifled tank gun with falling wedge breech-block, concentric buffer and spring recuperator. The gun is fired electrically but can also be fired by a manually-actuated impulse generator. During counter-recoil the automatic breech-block opens and ejects the spent cartridge case into a bag under the breech.

The barrel is provided with a thermal sleeve and a bore evacuator. The gun fires all standard NATO 105 mm ammunition and a well-trained crew can achieve a rate of fire of nine rounds a minute. As an option the main armament can be stabilised in both elevation and traverse.

Fifty-seven rounds of 105 mm ammunition are carried, 42 to the left of the driver and 15 in the turret for ready use.

A 7.62 mm machine gun is mounted coaxially to the left of the main armament and a similar weapon is mounted on the turret roof for anti-aircraft use.

Mounted externally on either side of the turret are four electrically operated smoke dischargers.

The fire-control system has been designed by Officine Galileo and consists of the gunner's fire-control system, gunner's telescope which moves in elevation with the main armament, commander's stabilised day/night roof-mounted sight and the turret/gun electro-hydraulic drive system.

The gunner's fire-control system consists of an Aeritalia C125 optical sight with a magnification of ×8 and range scale for APDS, HEAT and HESH 105 mm projectiles and 7.62 mm machine gun ammunition; Selenia VAQ-33 laser rangefinder with a range of between 400 and 9995 metres; laser feeding and control equipment; fire-control computer; control device and read-out for the tank commander, gunner's controls and elevation sensor.

The commander's roof-mounted SFIM VS 580-B sight can be traversed through a full 360 degrees, has a magnification of ×8, stadiametric rangefinding capability and range scales for APDS, HEAT and HESH ammunition.

Turret traverse and gun elevation are electro-hydraulic; with turret traverse at a rate of 360 degrees in 17 seconds and gun elevation from −9 degrees to +20 degrees at 7 degrees a second. The turret/gun drive system is controlled from the gunner's handle but an override system allows the commander to take over the laying and firing of the main armament if required and manual controls are provided for emergency use.

The engine, transmission and cooling system are assembled to form the powerpack which is supplied by FIAT ready for installation in the tank and can be removed by four men with a crane in under 45 minutes. The cables and wires are provided with quick disconnect couplings and if required the powerpack can be run outside the vehicle for testing.

The engine is a MTU ten-cylinder, four-stroke, pre-combustion chamber, super-charged multi-fuel developing 830 hp at 2200 rpm and is fitted with a tropicalisation kit to control the fuel supply and prevent the engine from overheating.

Combustion air is taken in by two super-charged blowers through the two air cleaners. The two dry air cleaners are fitted in the side recess in front of the engine compartment and air enters through the intake scoops on the hull deck. Screens mounted in front of the scoops prevent large particles such as leaves entering the vehicle.

A cyclone filter battery purifies the air from coarse dust and large surfaced micro-top filters retain the fine dust. The coarse dust ejected by the cyclone filters is continuously blown outside by a dust blower installed in each air cleaner. The exhaust gases are taken from each cylinder liner by flexible corrugated tube compensators through an exhaust manifold into the exhaust mufflers in the side recesses of the engine compartment.

The engine of the OF-40 is liquid cooled through a self-contained cooling system with internal pressure controlled by a pressure relief and under pressure valve. On either side of the transmission is a cooler with a control fan on the vertical axis between the two coolers to suck the necessary cooling air from the top through the cooling air intake grille and force it through the two coolers. When deep fording, this duct is filled with water and the fan, coolers and mixing chamber are therefore completely flooded.

OTO Melara OF-40 Mk 2 MBT showing thermal sleeve for 105 mm gun and LLLTV camera on gun mantlet

Model of Otomatic 76/62 76 mm self-propelled anti-aircraft gun system with turret traversed to rear and radars in operating position

Engine torque is transmitted to a torque converter which is followed by a four-speed planetary gearbox with two reverse speeds. The individual speeds are shifted electro-hydraulically by a shift lever alongside the driver.

There is a separate clutch between the engine and ZF transmission which can be operated manually from the crew compartment. Thus provides easy starting at low temperatures as the starter has to crank the engine only and not the transmission.

The steering works through a longitudinally super-imposed gearbox so steering movements do not cause essential power losses in the gearbox. Steering movements are mechanically transmitted from the control handle at the driver's station to the control valve.

The final drives are on either side at the rear of the vehicle and are of the planetary type. The transmission is connected to the final drives by an internally toothed sleeve which can be loosened from the outside when the powerpack has to be removed.

The suspension is of the torsion bar type with seven dual rubber-tyred road wheels on each side. The first three and last two road wheels have hydraulic shock absorbers and bump stops to prevent excessive wheel travel. The adjustable idler is at the front, drive sprocket at the rear and there are five track support return rollers on each side.

The track is the rubber-bushed connector type with the individual track shoes joined by end connectors and centre guiding teeth. The upper part of the track and suspension is covered by a steel-reinforced rubber skirt which keeps dust down and provides a degree of protection against attack by HEAT projectiles.

The OF-40 has three independent braking systems; service, parking and emergency systems.

The tank can ford to a depth of 1.2 metres without preparation and an optional semi-deep fording hydraulic system enables it to cross streams to a maximum depth of 2.5 metres. A snorkel can be fitted which enables the OF-40 to ford to a depth of 4 metres. An electrically-operated bilge pump is fitted in both the engine and crew compartment, each with the capacity of 120 litres a minute.

The overpressure NBC system is mounted at the front of the hull to the left of the driver. Fresh air is drawn into the vehicle by a blower and is then separated from the coarse dust in a cyclone filter. The NBC protection filter is down-stream of the course dust filter and retains all NBC agents. The dust collection compartment of the cyclone filter is continuously kept free of dust by a dust ejector blower. Pressure in the tank is monitored by a pressure gauge in the crew compartment.

An automatic fire-extinguishing system in the engine compartment has spray tubes and nozzles connected to a battery of bottles in the crew compartment containing the fire extinguishing agent. This system is activated at 180°C through a fire wire in the engine compartment.

Variants

OF-40 Mk 2 MBT
The OF-40 Mk 2 is essentially the Mark 1 fitted with the Galileo OG14L2A fire-control system which includes a stabilisation system for the 105 mm gun and sensors for wind velocity, powder temperature, ambient temperature and type of ammunition. The OG12L2B fire control system is similar but has a stabilised line of sight.

In the OF-40 Mk 2 the tank commander has a day/night periscope that is self-stabilised during panoramic search and is slaved to the gun stabilisation when used for firing.

The gunner has a sight with a magnification of ×7 and ×14 that incorporates a laser rangefinder as well as a telescopic sight with a magnification of ×8 that is coaxial with the 105 mm gun.

Mounted coaxially on the right side of the turret is a LLLTV camera with the monitor in turret.

Deliveries of the second batch of 18 OF-40 Mk 2 tanks to the United Arab Emirates began in 1984 and were completed in 1985. The Mk 1s are now being brought up to Mk 2 standard.

OF-40 ARV
Three of these have been built for the United Arab Emirates and is essentially OF-40 chassis with a spade, hydraulic crane with a lifting capacity of 20 tonnes and a main winch with a capacity of 30 tonnes which can be increased to 60 tonnes if required.

New engine
Currently undergoing trials is the FIAT V-12 MTCA diesel which develops 1000 hp with a possible increase to 1200 hp. This may be installed in the OF-40 so increasing its power-to-weight ratio to 25 hp/tonne.

Palmaria 155 mm Self-propelled Howitzer
This has been developed from 1977 by OTO-Melara specifically for the export market with the first prototype being completed in 1981. So far orders have been placed by Libya (210) and Nigeria (25) with Argentina ordering 25 turrets for modified TAM chassis.

The chassis is similar to the OF-40 MBT, the major difference being that the Palmaria is powered by a V-8 diesel developing 750 hp instead of a V-10 developing 830 hp.

The 155 mm howitzer has an elevation of +70 degrees, depression of −5 and turret traverse of 360 degrees. The howitzer can fire HE, illuminating or smoke projectiles to a maximum range of 24 000 metres or a HE rocket assisted projectile to a range of 30 000 metres. 30 rounds of separate loading ammunition are carried; if required the system can

35 mm Self-propelled Anti-aircraft Gun

For trials purposes a Palmaria chassis has been fitted with the ATAK twin 35 mm anti-aircraft turret designed as a private venture by Contraves.

76/62 76 mm Self-propelled Anti-aircraft Gun

This is being developed as a private venture by OTO-Melara and is essentially an OF-40 MBT with a new fully enclosed turret armed with a 76 mm gun developed from a naval weapon of the same calibre for use in the anti-aircraft/anti-helicopter role firing proximity-fuzed fixed ammunition.

The 76 mm gun has a maximum range of 6000 metres and cyclic rate of fire of 120 rounds a minute, although bursts of five to six rounds would normally be fired. A total of 100 rounds of ammunition are carried, 70 in the turret (of which 28 anti-aircraft and three anti-tank are in the feeding and loading system) and 30 in the hull. Turret traverse and weapon elevation is powered and the gun has a maximum elevation of +60 degrees and a depression of −5 degrees.

Various types of fire control system can be fitted. A 7.62 mm machine gun is mounted on the turret roof for local defence and four smoke dischargers are fitted either side of the turret.

Two prototypes of the OTO-Melara 76/62 76 mm self-propelled anti-aircraft gun system are being built.

OTO Melara Palmaria 155 mm self-propelled howitzer with turret traversed to front

be fitted with an automatic loader to increase its rate of fire.

Palmaria has a five man crew consisting of the driver who is seated in the hull at the front of the vehicle and the commander, gunner, charge handler and magazine operator seated in the fully enclosed turret. Combat weight of the system is 46 000 kg and unloaded weight is 43 000 kg.

SPECIFICATIONS

CREW	4	TRANSMISSION	ZF power shifting 4-speed (4 forward and 2 reverse) planetary type with hydraulic torque converter
COMBAT WEIGHT	45 500 kg		
UNLOADED WEIGHT	43 100 kg		
POWER-TO-WEIGHT RATIO	18.24 hp/tonne	SUSPENSION	torsion bar
GROUND PRESSURE	0.92 kg/cm²	ELECTRICAL SYSTEM	24 V
LENGTH		BATTERIES	8 × 12 V
gun forward	9.22 m	ARMAMENT	
gun rear	8.114 m	main	1 × 105 mm gun
hull	6.893 m	coaxial	1 × 7.62 mm MG
WIDTH		AA	1 × 7.62 mm MG (or optional 12.7 mm MG)
without skirts	3.35 m		
with skirts	3.51 m	SMOKE DISCHARGERS	4 either side of turret
HEIGHT		AMMUNITION	
turret roof	2.42 m	main	57
commander's sight	2.68 m	MG	5000
FIRING HEIGHT	1.89 m	GUN CONTROL EQUIPMENT	
GROUND CLEARANCE	0.44 m	Turret power control	electro-hydraulic/ manual
TRACK WIDTH	584 mm		
LENGTH OF TRACK ON GROUND	4.25 m	by commander	yes
MAX ROAD SPEED		by gunner	yes
forwards	65 km/h	commander's override	yes
reverse	25 km/h	Commander's fire-control override	yes
FUEL CAPACITY	1000 litres		
MAX RANGE		Max rate power traverse	360°/17 s
road	600 km	Max rate power elevation	7° s
FORDING			
without preparation	1.2 m	Gun elevation/ depression	+20°/−9°
with preparation	2.25 m		
with snorkel	4 m	Gun stabiliser	
GRADIENT	60%	vertical	no (optional)
SIDE SLOPE	30%	horizontal	no (optional)
VERTICAL OBSTACLE	1.15 m	Range setting device	yes
TRENCH	3 m	Elevation quadrant	yes
TURNING RADIUS	pivot turns	Traverse indicator	yes
ENGINE	MTU 90° 10-cylinder, 4-stroke, pre-combustion chamber, super-charged multi-fuel developing 830 hp at 2200 rpm		

Status: In production. In service with United Arab Emirates.

Manufacturer: OTO-Melara, via Valdilocchi 15, 19100 La Spezia, Italy.

JAPAN

Future Japanese MBT

In fiscal year 1984 the Technical Research and Development Institute of the Japanese Self-Defence Agency started studies of key components for a future MBT, even though the TK-X (under the designation Type 88) is not expected to enter production and service until 1988.

Initial component development will cost 200 million yen. It is expected that the new MBT, which could enter service in the early part of the next century, will have a gas turbine or a diesel engine and have semi-active suspension.

STC (or TK-X) Main Battle Tank

Development
Research and development of a new MBT, designated the STC, began in 1976 by the Technical Research Headquarters of the Japanese Self-Defence Agency. Funding for the engine, gun, ammunition and fire-control system was started in fiscal year 1977 and funding for the suspension and new armour in fiscal year 1978. The 1979 budget provided additional funds for the gun and ammunition as well as the hull and turret.

Prime contractor for the STC is Mitsubishi Heavy Industries, with the Japan Iron Works responsible for the armament and Mitsubishi Electric for the fire-control system. Suspension of the TK-X will be a hybrid hydro-pneumatic/torsion bar type and will enable the tank to change attitude in longitudinal direction only, for example on reverse slopes. Unlike the current Type 74, it will not be able to compensate for transverse changes.

The TK-X is powered by a Mitsubishi 10ZG ten-cylinder air-cooled diesel developing 1500 hp, but the cooling system is believed to consume 300 hp so with a combat weight of 50 tonnes, power-to-weight ratio of TK-X would be about 24 hp/tonne. It was originally intended that the combat weight of the new MBT would be about 43 tonnes, but recent information has indicated that it will be between 48 and 50 tonnes.

The 120 mm smooth-bore tank gun will fire APFSDS and HEAT-FS projectiles, the former developed by Daikin Industry Co and the latter by Komatsu Machinery Co. For trials a 105 mm rifled tank gun was bored out to 120 mm smooth-bore, and for comparison a 120 mm rifled gun was also built. Comparative trials with the 120 mm guns have been completed and the first actual 120 mm smooth-bore gun was completed late in 1979. Production tanks will have a 120 mm Rheinmetall gun made under licence.

Japanese sources say that the tank will have an automatic loader. As it has a four-man crew this could mean that the magazine only holds a small number of ready use ammunition, or a load-assist device only is provided.

The armour will be of the multiple-layer type with ceramic cells, developed by a team of Japanese manufacturers including the Kyoto Ceramic Co Limited. The fire-control system will be an advanced type with a mini- or micro-computer and a tv function and it is possible that an anti-aircraft and an ECCM capability will be provided. The first two prototypes of the STC MBT were to be completed by fiscal year 1982,

with standardisation taking place in 1988. There is a possibility that standardisation of the TK-X could be delayed by one or two years, in which case it would become the Type 89 (Hachi-kyu Shiki Senshya) or the Type 90 (Kyu-Maru Shiki Senshya). The Japanese Ground Self-Defence Force has a requirement for between 600 and 800 STCs to replace its Type 61 MBTs.

SPECIFICATIONS OF TYPE 88 (provisional)

CREW	4
WEIGHT	48 000 to 50 000 kg
LENGTH HULL	7.5 m
WIDTH	3.5 m
HEIGHT	2.4 m
MAX ROAD SPEED	70 km/h
RANGE	500 km
ENGINE	Mitsubishi 1ZG turbo-charged water-cooled 10-cylinder diesel developing 1500 hp
ARMAMENT	
main	1 × 120 mm gun
coaxial	1 × 7.62 mm MG
anti-aircraft	1 × 12.7 mm MG

Status: Development. Not yet in production or service.

Type 74 Main Battle Tank

Development
Mitsubishi Heavy Industries and the Japanese Ground Self-Defence Force began project definition studies for a new MBT to succeed the Type 61 in 1962. To prove the basic concept, a number of test rigs was built and tested between 1964 and 1967. Construction of the first two prototypes began at the Maruko works of Mitsubishi Heavy Industries late in 1968 and was completed in September 1969. They were called the STB-1, and contained many features of other tanks under development at that time, for example the hydro-pneumatic suspension system of the MBT-70, hull of the

Type 74 MBT with 12.7 mm AA MG (Keiichi Nogi)

Type 74 MBT from rear showing turret bustle (Ryuta Wantanabe)

Type 74 MBT with suspension raised giving 0.2 m ground clearance (Keiichi Nogi)

Leopard 1, 105 mm gun as used by the Leopard 1, M60, Centurion and other MBTs and a turret similar to that of the AMX-30. The STB-1 had an automatic loader for the British L7A1 gun which was subsequently manufactured in Japan by the Japan Steel Works Limited with a 12.7 mm (0.50) Browning M2 HB machine gun mounted towards the rear of the turret which could be aimed and fired from within the tank.

The STB-1 was followed in 1971 by the STB-3, which had the automatic loader removed as it proved both too complex and too expensive, the remote-controlled 12.7 mm (0.50) machine gun replaced by a more simple mount and the turret slightly different in shape with a much longer bustle.

The first production contract was placed before the final model, the STB-6, appeared in 1973. The first Type 74 MBT was completed in September 1975 and by January 1980 some 225 had been built.

Under the Fourth Defence Plan, which ran from fiscal year 1972 to 1976, 160 tanks were ordered, the fiscal year 1980 order was for 100 units, fiscal year 1981 order was for 72, and the fiscal year 1982 budget was for 80 Type 74 MBTs. For fiscal year 1983 a total of 75 Type 74s were requested but only 60 were approved. For fiscal year 1984 75 Type 74s were requested but only 60 were approved. The fiscal year 1985 request was for 68 Type 74s but again only 60 were authorised.

Under the fiscal year 1981 Mid-term Defence Programme

Estimate (FY 81 MDPE) which commenced in FY 1983, 373 Type 74 MBTs will be ordered giving a total of 850 Type 74 MBTs in service by the end of 1988.

Description

The hull of the Type 74 MBT is all-welded steel and is divided into three compartments: driver's at the front, fighting in the centre and engine at the rear.

The driver is seated at the front of the vehicle on the left side and is provided with a single-piece hatch cover that opens to the left. Three JM 17 Mod 2 periscopes are mounted forward of this hatch cover and an infra-red periscope can be mounted in the centre of the hatch cover and used in conjunction with the infra-red driving lights.

The turret is all cast with the commander and gunner seated on the right and the loader on the left. The commander's cupola can be traversed through 360 degrees and has a single-piece hatch cover that opens to the rear. There is a J3 infra-red periscope sight with an integral laser rangefinder and a magnification of ×1 and ×8 in the forward part of the commander's cupola and he also has five periscopes, two on either side and one to the rear. The gunner is seated forward of the commander and is provided with a J2 IR periscopic sight with a magnification of ×1 and ×8 in the turret roof and a telescope linked to the main armament. The loader has a single-piece hatch cover that opens to the rear and a periscope mounted forward of his hatch. There is an external stowage basket at the rear of the turret.

The engine and transmission are mounted at the rear of the tank with the exhaust pipes and silencers mounted on the running boards to the rear of the turret. The maximum quoted road speed of the Type 74 is 53 km/h but reliable sources have indicated that its top speed is at least 60 km/h.

The suspension is hydro-pneumatic and can be adjusted to suit the type of terrain being crossed. There are five dual rubber-tyred road wheels with the drive sprocket at the rear and the idler at the front. There are no track return rollers. The hydro-pneumatic suspension can be operated either by the commander or the driver and enables the tank to be inclined six degrees forwards or backwards, nine degrees left or right and raised or lowered giving a minimum ground clearance of 200 mm and a maximum ground clearance of 650 mm.

Standard equipment includes infra-red driving lights, infra-red searchlight to the left of the main armament and an

Type 74 MBT with suspension lowered (Keiichi Nogi)

Type 74 MBT

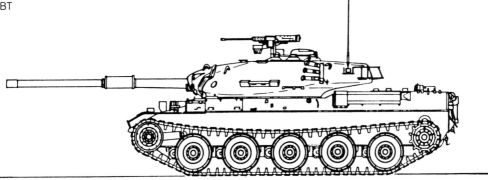

NBC system. In the white light mode the searchlight has a maximum range of 3000 metres and in the infra-red mode a range of 1000 metres. One Type 74 MBT in each company is fitted with a dozer blade.

Main armament consists of a 105 mm rifled tank gun (the British Royal Ordnance L7 series made under licence in Japan) which fires the standard range of ammunition including APDS-T and HESH-T. Unlike other tanks fitted with the gun the Type 74 is not fitted with a thermal sleeve for the main armament. The gun has a drop block-breech mechanism and a new concentric recoil mechanism to reduce the volume of the upper part of the gun as well as reducing the frontal area of the turret. The gun control equipment includes a Nippon Electric laser rangefinder mounted in the commander's sight, which also provides inputs to the Mitsubishi Electric ballistic computer connected to the gunner's sight. Target range is fed to the computer automatically but trunnion tilt, barrel wear, ammunition type and temperature are fed in manually. The main armament is stabilised in both the vertical and horizontal planes.

A 7.62 mm Type 74 machine gun is mounted coaxially with the main armament and a 12.7 mm (0.50) Browning M2 HB machine gun is pintle-mounted in the centre of the turret forward of the commander's and loader's positions. This has an elevation of +60 degrees and a depression of −10 degrees. Three smoke dischargers are mounted either side of the turret.

Variants

Type 78 Armoured Recovery Vehicle
The prototype of an ARV based on the chassis of the Type 74 MBT was completed in 1974 and standardised as the Type 78 ARV in 1978. In appearance it is very similar to the

Type 74 MBT with infra-red/white searchlight mounted to left of main armament (Keiichi Nogi)

Type 78 ARV in travelling order
(Kensuke Ebata)

Provisional drawing of the AW-X twin 35 mm self-propelled anti-aircraft gun system on Type 74 MBT chassis

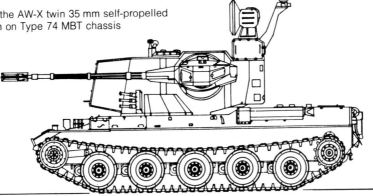

French AMX-30D and West German Leopard 1 ARVs with the crew compartment at the front, hydraulically-operated dozer blade at the front of the hull and an hydraulic crane on the right side of the hull.

AW-X SPAAG

The prototype of the twin 35 mm self-propelled anti-aircraft gun system, called the AW-X, is mounted on a modified Type 74 MBT chassis for trials.

Status: In production. In service with the Japanese Self-Defence Force.

Manufacturer: Mitsubishi Heavy Industries, Sagamihara. Mitsubishi Heavy Industries, 5-1, Marunouchi 2-chome, Chiyoda-ku, Tokyo, Japan.

Type 61 Main Battle Tank

Development

When the Japanese Ground Self-Defence Force was formed in 1950 one of its first requirements was for tanks. To meet its immediate needs the USA supplied Japan with numbers of Sherman and M24 Chaffee tanks. A few American M47 tanks supplied for trials had the drawback of not being designed for the small stature of the Japanese and their bulk and weight made them unsuitable for transportation in many parts of Japan.

Design work on the first Japanese post-war tank began under the direction of the Ground Armaments Directorate at the Technical Research and Development Headquarters of the Japanese Self-Defence Force in 1954. The first four prototypes were completed in 1957 and comprised two model ST-A1s and two model ST-A2s.

The four prototypes were followed by two ST-A3 and ten ST-A4 tanks which were almost identical to production tanks. In April 1961 the tank was standardised as the Type 61 MBT and first production tanks were completed in 1962. Production was very slow initially: ten tanks were produced in 1962 with a similar number the following year, 20 in 1964, 30 in 1965 and 30 in 1966. The 100th Type 61 was completed in November 1966. By late 1970 250 tanks had been completed and it is believed that total production amounted to about 560 units. The Type 61 is still used by the Japanese Ground Self-Defence Force but has been supplemented by the Type 74 MBT, also manufactured by Mitsubishi.

As of 1983 the Japanese Ground Self-Defence Force had 559 Type 61s on strength. The first two Type 61s were retired in December 1984. A total of 36 Type 61s were retired in 1985 with a further 25 in 1986.

Description

The all-welded hull of the Type 61 is divided into three compartments: driver's at the front, fighting in the centre and the engine at the rear.

Type 61 MBTs with nearest tank fitted with infra-red searchlight to left of main armament (Kensuke Ebata)

SPECIFICATIONS

CREW	4
COMBAT WEIGHT	38 000 kg
UNLOADED WEIGHT	36 000 kg
POWER-TO-WEIGHT RATIO	19.7 hp/tonne
GROUND PRESSURE	0.85 kg/cm²
LENGTH GUN FORWARDS	9.41 m
LENGTH GUN REAR	7.84 m
LENGTH HULL	6.7 m
WIDTH	3.18 m
HEIGHT	
including A/A MG	2.67 m (with 0.65 m ground clearance)
to turret top	2.48 m (with 0.65 m ground clearance)
to turret top	2.03 m (with 0.2 m ground clearance)
GROUND CLEARANCE	adjustable from 0.2–0.65 m
TRACK	2.7 m
TRACK WIDTH	550 mm
LENGTH OF TRACK ON GROUND	4 m
MAX ROAD SPEED	53 km/h
FUEL CAPACITY	950 litres
MAX RANGE	300 km
FORDING	1 m
with preparation	2 m
GRADIENT	60%
SIDE SLOPE	40%
VERTICAL OBSTACLE	1 m
TRENCH	2.7 m
ENGINE	Mitsubishi 10ZF Type 22 WT 10-cylinder air-cooled diesel developing 750 hp at 2200 rpm
TRANSMISSION	Mitsubishi MT75A manual with 6 forward and 1 reverse gears
STEERING	double differential
SUSPENSION	hydro-pneumatic, variable
ELECTRICAL SYSTEM	24 V
ARMAMENT	
main	1 × 105 mm
coaxial	1 × 7.62 mm MG
anti-aircraft	1 × 12.7 mm MG
SMOKE-LAYING EQUIPMENT	3 smoke dischargers either side of turret
AMMUNITION	
main	55
coaxial	4500
anti-aircraft	660
GUN CONTROL EQUIPMENT	
Turret power control	electric/manual
by commander	yes
by gunner	yes
Gun elevation	+9.5° (+15° using suspension)
Gun depression	−6.5° (−12.5° using suspension)
Gun stabiliser	
vertical	yes
horizontal	yes
Elevation quadrant	yes
Traverse indicator	yes

Type 61 MBT with commander's hatch open

Type 61 MBT modified to resemble Soviet T-54/T-55 mine-clearing tank (Tank Magazine)

The driver is seated at the front of the hull on the right side and is provided with a single-piece hatch cover that opens to the right. Three periscopes are mounted forward of his hatch.

The turret is cast with an overhanging bustle similar to that of the M47 tank and a light sheet steel stowage box at the very rear.

The commander and gunner are seated on the right of the turret with the loader seated on the left. The commander's domed-shaped cupola, which can be traversed through 360 degrees, has a single-piece hatch cover in its rear, which opens backwards. The cupola has four vision blocks and mounted in the lower part of the cupola is a coincidence rangefinder with a magnification of ×12. The commander is also provided with a periscopic sight with a magnification of ×7 mounted in the forward part of the cupola roof. The gunner is seated forward of the commander and is provided with a telescopic sight with a magnification of ×6 and a periscope with a magnification of ×4. The loader is seated on the left side of the turret and has a single-piece hatch cover opening to the rear. A single periscope is mounted in the turret roof in front of the hatch cover.

The engine is mounted at the rear of the hull and is cooled by two axial-flow cooling fans mounted over the top of the engine.

The torsion bar suspension consists of six dual rubber-tyred road wheels with the drive sprockets at the front and the idler at the rear. There are three track return rollers and the

first, second, fifth and sixth road wheel stations are equipped with hydraulic shock absorbers.

Main armament is a Type 61 90 mm rifled tank gun which is manufactured by the Japan Steel Works. This is fitted with a fume extractor and a T type muzzle brake. Types of ammunition fired include APC with the projectile weighing 10.95 kg and HE with the projectile weighing 10.62 kg. Mounted coaxially with the main armament is a 7.62 mm (0.30) Browning M1919A4 machine gun while a 12.7 mm (0.50) Browning M2 HB machine gun is mounted on the commander's cupola for anti-aircraft use. This can be aimed and fired from within the tank and some vehicles have had a shield provided for this weapon.

The Type 61 has no NBC system or deep wading equipment. Some models have been fitted with an infra-red searchlight to the left of the main armament and infra-red driving lights.

Variants

Armoured Vehicle-launched Bridge Type 67

This is the basic MBT with its turret removed and replaced by a scissors bridge laid to the front of the vehicle. When opened out the bridge is 12 metres long and will span a gap of up to 10 metres. It has a maximum capacity of 40 000 kg.

Type 61 MBT

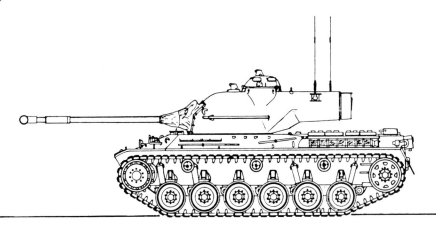

Type 70 armoured recovery vehicle with A-frame to rear and dozer blade raised

Type 61 MBT with turret traversed to rear and commander's machine gun cupola hatch open (Keiichi Nogi)

Type 67 armoured bridgelayer laying its scissors bridge in position (Kensuke Ebata)

Launching time is between three and five minutes and the bridge can be picked up from either end. The Type 67 weighs 36 700 kg with the bridge and has a crew of three men.

Armoured Engineer Vehicle Type 67
This vehicle has been designed for engineer roles on the battlefield and is equipped with a dozer blade at the front and a light crane. The Type 67 weighs 35 000 kg and has a crew of four.

Armoured Recovery Vehicle Type 70
The Type 70 ARV is the basic MBT with its turret removed and replaced by a new superstructure with a winch mounted in the bustle at the rear. An A-frame is pivoted towards the front of the hull; when not in use it lies back over the rear of the hull. A hydraulically-operated dozer blade mounted at the front of the hull is used to stabilise the vehicle during recovery operations, or when the A-frame is in use. The Type 70 weighs 35 000 kg and has a crew of four. Armament consists of an 81 mm mortar which can be mounted on the glacis plate and a 12.7 mm and a 7.62 mm machine gun.

Type 61 Training Tank
For training purposes some Type 61 MBTs have been fitted with wooden mine-sweeping equipment at the front of the hull to resemble Soviet T-54/T-55 mine-clearing tanks. Some have also been fitted with the British Weston Simfire tank gunnery and tactical training system.

SPECIFICATIONS

CREW	4	FORDING	0.99 m	ARMAMENT	
COMBAT WEIGHT	35 000 kg	GRADIENT	60%	main	1 × 90 mm
UNLOADED WEIGHT	33 500 kg	VERTICAL OBSTACLE	0.685 m	coaxial	1 × 7.62 mm MG
POWER-TO-WEIGHT		TRENCH	2.489 m	anti-aircraft	1 × 12.7 mm MG
RATIO	17.4 hp/tonne	TURNING RADIUS	10 m	SMOKE-LAYING	
GROUND PRESSURE	0.95 kg/cm²	ENGINE	Mitsubishi Type 12	EQUIPMENT	2 × 3 smoke
LENGTH GUN			HM 21 WT,		dischargers (optional)
FORWARDS	8.19 m		V-12, 4-cycle	GUN CONTROL	
LENGTH HULL	6.3 m		direct-injection,	EQUIPMENT	
WIDTH	2.95 m		turbo-charged diesel	Turret power control	hydraulic/manual
HEIGHT			developing 600 hp	by commander	yes
including A/A MG	3.16 m		at 2100 rpm	by gunner	yes
turret roof	2.49 m	AUXILIARY ENGINE	none	Gun stabilisation	
GROUND CLEARANCE	0.4 m	TRANSMISSION	mechanical, 5 forward	vertical	no
TRACK WIDTH	500 mm		1 reverse speeds with a	horizontal	no
LENGTH OF TRACK			2-speed auxiliary	ARMOUR	
ON GROUND	3.7 m		reduction unit	Hull glacis	46 mm
MAX ROAD SPEED	45 km/h	STEERING	controlled differential	Hull sides	25 mm
MAX RANGE	200 km	SUSPENSION	torsion bar	Hull rear	15 mm
		ELECTRICAL SYSTEM	24 V	Turret front	64 mm
		BATTERIES	4 × 12 V, 200 Ah		

Status: Production complete. In service only with the Japanese Ground Self-Defence Force.

Manufacturer: Mitsubishi Heavy Industries, Maruko, Tokyo. Mitsubishi Heavy Industries, 5-1, Marunouchi 2-chome, Chiyoda-ku, Tokyo, Japan.

KOREA, REPUBLIC (SOUTH)

XK-1 Main Battle Tank

Development

Following proposals from a number of armoured fighting vehicle manufacturers, in 1980 the South Korean Government selected the Land Systems Division of General Dynamics (then Chrysler Defense) to design and build two prototypes of a new MBT to meet its own specific requirements. The first of two prototypes of the XK-1 MBT was completed in 1983, this was the Automotive Test Rig (ATR). It was shipped to Aberdeen Proving Grounds in November 1983 for automotive performance, endurance and reliability testing. The ATR is a fully payloaded tank and is fitted with a non-operational turret.

The second prototype, called the Fire Control Test Rig (FCTR) was rolled out at a ceremony at Selfridge Air National Guard base in December 1983 and shipped to Aberdeen Proving Grounds in February 1984 to begin fire-control tests. Production of XK-1 is now underway in South Korea.

Description

The layout of the XK-1 is conventional with the driver at the front, turret in the centre and engine and transmission at the rear. It is similar in appearance to the American M1 MBT, also produced by General Dynamics, but is somewhat smaller as South Korea wanted a lighter tank more suitable for use in hilly terrain. Prototypes are powered by a Teledyne Continental AVCR-1790 series diesel engine developing 1200 hp that was originally designed and built to meet the requirements of the United States Army and already installed in the private venture Teledyne Continental Motors, General Products Division, Super M60 MBT. In that application it was coupled to a West German Renk RK-304 hydro-kinetic transmission but for the XK-1 it is coupled to a West German ZF transmission.

Main armament is confirmed as the 105 mm M68E1 with a 7.62 mm M60 coaxial machine gun. A 7.62 mm M60 and a 12.7 mm M2 HB machine gun are mounted on the turret roof for anti-aircraft and close defence, the commander would normally operate the 12.7 mm weapon and the loader the 7.62 mm weapon.

Suspension is of the hybrid type using both torsion bar and hydro-pneumatic units. The central road wheels have the torsion bars and the front and rear stations have the hydro-pneumatic units. When the front hydro-pneumatic units are lowered and the rear units raised the 105 mm gun can be depressed to about −10 degrees; without using the hydro-pneumatic suspension depression of the main armament is believed to be limited to −7 degrees.

The gun control equipment of the XK-1 was designed by Hughes Aircraft Company under contract to Hyundai Rolling Stock Limited of South Korea. It is similar to that

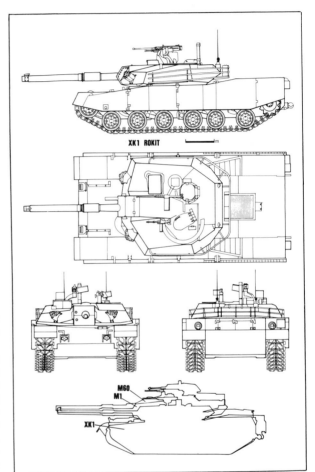

Provisional drawing of XK-1 MBT (not to 1/76th scale) (Steven Zaloga)

XK-1 Automotive Test Rig (ATR)

installed in the US Army M1 MBT with the gunner's primary sight subsystem incorporating the same laser rangefinder and thermal imaging system as the M1, but with a binocular eyepiece for the gunner instead of a monocular one. It will also have stabilised optics and a vertical sensor.

Production versions of the XK-1 will be powered by a West German MTU MB 871 Ka V-8 diesel which develops 1184 hp at 2600 rpm which is already installed in the European 155 mm SP-70 self-propelled howitzer which has yet to enter production.

Status: Prototypes built and tested in USA. in production in South Korea.

SPECIFICATIONS (provisional)

CREW	4	LENGTH HULL	7.39 m
COMBAT WEIGHT	52 000 kg	WIDTH	3.62 m
POWER-TO-WEIGHT		HEIGHT	2.25 m
RATIO	22.76 hp/tonne	ARMAMENT	
LENGTH GUN		main	1 × 105 mm
FORWARDS	9.58 m	coaxial	1 × 7.62 mm MG
		anti-aircraft	1 × 12.7 mm MG

Manufacturer: Prototypes of the XK-1 have been built in USA by General Dynamics, Land Systems Division, but production is undertaken in South Korea by Hyundai Rolling Stock Limited.

SPAIN

New Spanish MBT Lince

Now that Santa Barbara has completed production of the licence built AMX-30 for the Spanish Army, a number of proposals are being considered for the future. It is understood that the Spanish Army has a requirement for 400 to 800 new MBTs and that key requirements include a 120 mm smooth-bore gun, MLC 50, minimum power-to-weight ratio of 25 hp/tonne, transmission with torque converter, suspension with high vertical travel, tracks with replaceable pads, stabilised main armament, ability for commander or gunner to aim and fire main armament, digital fire-control computer, stabilised sights for commander and gunner, night vision equipment and good armour protection.

In summer 1984 it was confirmed that five companies had submitted proposals for the new Spanish MBT. GIAT of France is offering a selection which includes participation in the EPC MBT, licenced production of the AMX-40 or upgrading the existing fleet of AMX-30s to AMX-30 B2 standard. General Dynamics Land Systems Division is offering both the M1(105 mm) and M1E1(120 mm). Krauss-Maffei of West Germany is offering a new design called the Lince which is virtually a scaled-down Leopard 2. Thyssen

SPECIFICATIONS (Krauss-Maffei Lince)

CREW	4
WEIGHT	49 000 kg
POWER-TO-WEIGHT	
RATIO	24.48 hp/tonne
LENGTH	
gun forward	9.088 m
hull	7.1 m
WIDTH	
overall	3.74 m
over tracks	3.48 m
HEIGHT	
to hull top	1.64 m
to turret top	2.5 m
GROUND CLEARANCE	0.5 m
TRACK	2.845 m
TRACK WIDTH	635 mm
LENGTH OF TRACK	
ON GROUND	4.492 m
MAX ROAD SPEED	70 km/h
MAX RANGE	550 km
FORDING	
without preparation	0.8 m
with preparation	2.25 m
with snorkel	4 m
VERTICAL OBSTACLE	1.1 m
TRENCH	3 m
ENGINE	MTU MB 871 Ka 502 diesel developing 1200 hp
TRANSMISSION	hydro-mechanical
ARMAMENT	
main	1 × 120 mm
coaxial	1 × 7.62 mm MG
anti-aircraft	1 × 12.7 mm MG
AMMUNITION	
main	40
coaxial	2500
anti-aircraft	500
GUN CONTROL	
EQUIPMENT	
Turret power control	electric/manual
by commander	yes
by gunner	yes
Gun elevation/depression	+20°/−9°
Gun stabiliser	
vertical	yes
horizontal	yes

Artist's impression of Krauss-Maffei Lince MBT designed for Spanish Army

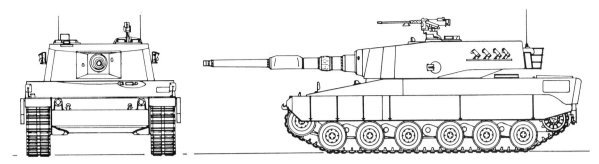

Provisional drawing of Krauss-Maffei Lince MBT for Spanish Army

Henschel of West Germany and OTO-Melara of Italy also proposed vehicles to meet this requirement. In 1985 Vickers Defence Systems entered the competition with the Valiant MBT.

Whichever tank is selected, prime contractor will be the Sevilla Artillery Factory where the AMX-30 MBTs were built for the Spanish Army.

Spanish AMX-30 Tank Production

Following delivery of the first 19 vehicles from France, Spain was building the AMX-30 MBT under licence from France from 1974, initially from components supplied by France but gradually the Spanish content increased until about 85 per cent of the tank was built in Spain. A total of 19 tanks was supplied direct from France plus 10 AMX-30D ARVs. It is estimated that five were completed in 1974, 21 in 1975, 52 in 1976, 66 in 1977 and at least 80 in 1978. No funds were allocated for AMX-30 production in 1981 and final deliveries to the Spanish Army took place in 1983–84 after 280 tanks had been completed. The Spanish tanks are almost identical to the French models but have an MG3S 7.62 mm machine gun for the commander and other minor differences. Production of the AMX-30 was undertaken by the Sevilla Artillery Factory of Empresa Nacional Santa Barbara SA (ENSB), Empresa Nacional de Optica (ENOSA) providing the optical equipment, and Experiencias Industriales SA (EISA) the electrical and hydraulic equipment.

Rear view of AMX-30 MBT built at Sevilla Artillery Factory for Spanish Army

In 1980 Spain purchased the entire licence from GIAT in order to continue development itself.

Modernised AMX-30

In 1984 Santa Barbara announced that it had successfully built and tested a modernised AMX-30 and that this had already been approved by the Spanish Army. Main improvements can be summarised as the installation of a new powerpack comprising a General Motors Detroit Diesel engine developing 920 hp, Allison CD-850-6A automatic transmission and an FAS cooling system; new suspension and tracks; new fire-control system; air-conditioning system; explosion suppression system; protective side skirts and a driving tachograph. In 1984 Spain signed a contract with Euromissile for the supply of 18 Roland 2 SAM systems and 414 missiles. Much of this work will be carried out in Spain including manufacture of the AMX-30R launcher vehicle.

Spanish AMX-30 fitted with British Weston Simfire tank gunnery and tactical training system

Talbot Main Battle Tank Conversions

In 1951 Barreiros Diesel SA was formed for the conversion of petrol engines to diesel operation. It later moved into manufacture of its own diesel engines followed by trucks and

M47E1 MBT with standard 90 mm gun and turret traversed to rear

M48A5E1 from rear showing external stowage

exhaust smoke laying system installed and four Wegmann type smoke dischargers mounted either side of turret. Retains 90 mm gun.

M47E2

Fitted with AVDS-1790-2D engine, CD-850-6A transmission, 105 mm Rh-105 30 gun, TEESS engine exhaust smoke generating system and Wegmann type smoke dischargers.

M48A3E

M48A3 with Continental AVDS-1790-2A diesel engine coupled to CD-850-6A transmission, Cadillac Gage turret and weapon control system installed, TEESS engine exhaust smoke laying system installed and four Wegmann type smoke dischargers mounted either side of turret. Retains 90 mm gun.

M48A5E

Almost same as American M48A5, has Continental AVDS-1790-2A 12-cylinder diesel engine coupled to CD-850 series transmission, main armament can be 105 mm M68 or Rh-105 30, standard fire-control system.

M48A5E1 with 105 mm M68 gun and bank of four Wegmann type smoke dischargers either side of turret. 12.7 mm anti-aircraft machine gun not fitted

M47E2 with new engine, 105 mm Rheinmetall Rh-105 30 gun and bank of four Wegmann type smoke dischargers on turret side

other vehicles. In 1965 it formed a partnership with Chrysler Corporation of the United States whose defence division was manufacturing M60 MBTs as well as supplying spare parts for the M48 MBT. In the 1960s the company built trucks for the Spanish Army and in the 1970s started to overhaul and modernise M47 and M48 tanks and M113 series armoured personnel carriers for the Spanish Army. Talbot also manufactures engines and transmissions for AFVs as well as road wheels and other suspension items. In 1978 the company went into partnership with PSA and its name was changed to Talbot SA. The main plant in Spain is at Villaverde near Madrid employing around 14 000 people. The plant has a special military division which employs over 400 people and can overhaul 12 to 15 MBTs a month on a single shift basis, though this figure could easily be doubled. It has a separate line for the complete overhaul of the M113 APC and its many variants, including the mortar carrier. MBT conversions currently offered by Talbot are listed below with a résumé of army/marine conversions.

M47E1

Basic M47 tank fitted with AVDS-1790-2A 12-cylinder diesel engine coupled to CD-850-6A transmission, bow machine gun removed, Cadillac Gage turret and weapon control system installed, coaxial machine gun is now an MG42, engine

M47E2R recovery tank in travelling configuration carrying spare engine

M47E2I engineer tank with stabilising blade lowered at front of hull, lifting M113 armoured personnel carrier

M48A5E1

As M48A5E but has AVDS-1790-2D 12-cylinder diesel and a new fire-control system. Gunner has M35 periscope, laser rangefinder, passive night vision viewer, control panel, output unit, ammunition selection unit, graticule projection unit, handgrips with switches for laser/lead/battle range, cant sensor and analogue electronic computer. Commander has M17 stereoscopic rangefinder and ammunition selection unit, loader has ammunition selection display unit and driver has three M27 periscopes the centre one of which can be replaced by an AN/VVS-2 passive night driving periscope. It has a TEESS engine exhaust smoke generating system and Wegmann type smoke dischargers installed.

M47E2I Engineer Tank

This has a new powerpack consisting of a Continental AVDS-1790-2D 12-cylinder diesel coupled to an Allison CD-850-6A transmission and a new front superstructure. Mounted at the front of the hull is a hydraulically-operated blade which can be used for clearing obstacles, preparing fire positions or to stabilise the vehicle when the winch is in use.

Main winch is provided with 100 metres of cable and has a maximum capacity of 70 tonnes. Mounted on the right side of the hull at the front is a hydraulically-operated crane which is traversed to the rear and lowered to the horizontal for travelling. The crane can be fitted with an auger for boring operations. The M47E2I has a crew of four and is armed with one 7.62 mm bow-mounted machine gun and one roof-mounted 12.7 mm machine gun. Mounted on the left side of the superstructure are six smoke dischargers firing forwards.

M47E2R Recovery Tank

This is almost identical to the M47E2I engineer tank but does not have the auger and is used to recover damaged and disabled vehicles.

M47E2VLP Bridgelayer

This is an M47 (or M48) chassis fitted with a new powerpack and can lay a scissors type bridge over the front of the vehicle in a similar manner to the M48/M60 AVLBs used by the US Army.

SPECIFICATIONS

Model	M47E1	M47E2	M48A3E	M48A5E
CREW	4	4	4	4
COMBAT WEIGHT	47 000 kg	46 700 kg	47 100 kg	49 000 kg
UNLOADED WEIGHT	41 000 kg	41 200 kg	44 400 kg	44 000 kg
POWER-TO-WEIGHT RATIO (hp/tonne)	16.17	16.27	16.13	15.51
GROUND PRESSURE	0.93 kg/cm²	0.93 kg/cm²	0.83 kg/cm²	0.86 kg/cm²
LENGTH GUN				
forwards	8.51 m	9.16 m	8.69 m	9.3 m
rear	7.09 m	7.74 m	7.42 m	8.04 m
LENGTH HULL	6.36 m	6.36 m	6.88 m	6.88 m
WIDTH	3.39 m	3.39 m	3.63 m	3.63 m
HEIGHT				
without AA MG	3.02 m	2.96 m	2.87 m	2.87 m
with AA MG	3.35 m	3.35 m	3.28 m	3.28 m
GROUND CLEARANCE	0.47 m	0.47 m	0.42 m	0.42 m
TRACK	2.79 m	2.79 m	2.92 m	2.92 m
TRACK WIDTH	580 mm	580 mm	710 mm	710 mm
LENGTH OF TRACK ON GROUND	3.91 m	3.91 m	4 m	4 m
MAX ROAD SPEED FORWARDS	56 km/h	56 km/h	50 km/h	50 km/h

Model	M47E1	M47E2	M48A3E	M48A5E
FUEL CAPACITY	1500 litres	1500 litres	1500 litres	1500 litres
MAX ROAD RANGE	600 km	600 km	550 km	550 km
FORDING	1.2 m	1.2 m	1.2 m	1.2 m
GRADIENT	60%	60%	60%	60%
VERTICAL OBSTACLE	0.91 m	0.91 m	0.91 m	0.91 m
TRENCH	2.59 m	2.59 m	2.59 m	2.59 m
ENGINE				
Continental V-12, AVDS	1790-2A	1790-2D	1790-2A	1790-2D
output (hp/rpm)	760/2400	760/2400	760/2400	760/2400
TRANSMISSION	Allison Division, GMC, model CD series 850-6A			
SUSPENSION	torsion bar	torsion bar	torsion bar	torsion bar
ELECTRICAL SYSTEM	24 V	24 V	24 V	24 V
BATTERIES	6 × 12 V	6 × 12 V	6 × 12 V	6 × 12 V
ARMAMENT				
main MG	1 × 90 mm	1 × 105 mm	1 × 90 mm	1 × 105 mm
coaxial MG	1 × 7.62 mm	1 × 7.62 mm	1 × 7.62 mm	1 × 7.62 mm
anti-aircraft	1 × 12.7 mm	1 × 12.7 mm	1 × 12.7 mm	1 × 12.7 mm
AMMUNITION				
main	77	42	62	54
coaxial	2750	2500	5900	8000
anti-aircraft	1250	2175	600	600

Status: Production. In service with the Spanish Army.

Manufacturer: Automoviles Talbot SA, Special Products Division, Apartado No 40, Madrid, Spain.

Spanish M48s

Eighteen M48s of the Spanish Marines have been fitted with the new AVDS-1790-2A series diesel engine but retain the 90 mm gun, these are the M48Es. Spain purchased 54 M48A2 tanks from West Germany and these were all upgraded to M48A5 standard (Spanish designation M48A5E). A total of 108 American supplied M48 tanks have also been brought up to M48A5E standard (54 M48s and 54 M48A1s). In 1983 the Spanish Army selected a Hughes gun control equipment for installation in the M48. Hughes Electro-Optical and Data Systems Group, Tactical Programmes Division, delivered the first of 54 systems in summer 1983. Under the second phase of the contract a further 110 systems were to be delivered from summer 1984. Many of the components of this gun control equipment will be pro-duced under licence from Hughes by EISA/ENOSA in Spain. About 70 per cent of the components of the M48's fire-control system will be the same at that of the M60A3's fire-control system currently in production in the United States for the US Army, as well as key modules for the laser rangefinder for the M1 Abrams MBT.

Spanish M47s

As of 1983 at least 330 M47s had been rebuilt for the Spanish Army, 46 to M47E1 and M47E2 standard. In 1981 an additional 100 M47s were purchased from Italy and West Germany and it is reported that 50 of these will be rebuilt to recovery versions, 25 to engineer tank and the remaining 25 to bridgelayers, in addition to the prototypes of these vehicles already built.

SWEDEN

New Swedish Main Battle Tank

Development

At present the Swedish Army has 650 MBTs in service, 350 Centurions (all of which have been fitted with the 105 mm gun) and 300 Bofors Strv 103Bs (or S-tank).

Under the direction of the Defense Materiel Administration (FMV) concept definition studies have already begun on a successor to the S-tank to enter service in the 1990s. A joint development company has been established by Bofors and Hägglund and Söner, called HB Utveckling (Hägglund-Bofors Development), with Hägglund responsible for the chassis and mobility aspects and Bofors for the armament, fire-control and other combat areas.

As of early 1985 no prototypes of the MBT had been completed and there is speculation as to whether the future Swedish defence budget would be able to fund the design, development and production of a new MBT as well as all the other equipment needed by the Swedish Army, Navy and Air Force.

The project to field a new articulated tank destroyer armed with a 120 mm Rheinmetall smooth-bore gun was cancelled after the prototype was completed. Sweden is now placing main emphasis on a new family of 20 tonne vehicles which will include a mechanised infantry combat vehicle, recovery vehicle, mortar carrier and anti-aircraft vehicle.

Developing companies: Bofors AB, Ordnance Division, Box 500, S-690 20, Bofors, Sweden. AB Hägglund and Söner, AFV Division, S-891 01, Örnsköldsvik, Sweden.

Stridsvagn 103 Main Battle Tank

Development

In the early 1950s the head of the tank design section of the Vehicle Division of the Swedish Army Ordnance, Sven Berge, studied a number of tank designs including the French AMX-13 light tank which features an oscillating turret with an automatic loader for its main armament. This tank suffers a number of disadvantages and Sven Berge then proposed a turretless tank with a fixed gun, the gun being elevated and traversed by altering the pitch of the hull and aimed in traverse by turning the whole vehicle.

One of the first problems to be overcome was that of laying the gun accurately in azimuth by relying only on its tracks. In the winter of 1957/58 an Ikv 103 assault gun was fitted with an external crowbar steering system which proved the basic concept. In 1959 a similar system was fitted to the heavier M4 Sherman tank, but this time between the tracks and the hull. The Sherman installation also proved that the system would work on a heavy vehicle rather than on a light vehicle such as the Ikv 103.

In mid-1958 Bofors was awarded a contract to design the turretless tank with its fixed gun mounting, automatic loading system, adjustable hydro-pneumatic suspension system and the new steering system. The following year Bofors was awarded a contract to build two prototype tanks and the company selected two major sub-contractors, Landsverk for the suspension and Volvo for the powerpack. Until then most tank development in Sweden had been carried out by Landsverk as Bofors was known primarily for artillery and naval ordnance. Bofors had built two armoured vehicles before the

Rear view of Strv 103B MBT showing external stowage boxes and empty cartridge case ejection port in hull rear

Strv 103B MBT with flotation screen erected before amphibious operation

turretless tank contract, a 40 mm self-propelled anti-aircraft gun called the Lvkv 42 with adjustable suspension and a 120 mm assault gun that featured an automatic loader, neither of which vehicles was placed in production.

The Swedish Army also cancelled development of the Landsverk Strv KRV tank which was to have been armed with a 150 mm smooth-bore gun with an automatic loader. The two chassis already built were subsequently used in the development of the suspension system of the turretless tank. The suspension was hydro-pneumatic and consisted of four road wheels with the idler at the front and the drive sprocket at the rear, with three return rollers, as well as the new steering system and a hydrostatic steering drive. Later, one of the chassis was fitted with a British 20-pounder (83.4 mm) gun as by that time the British Centurion tank was already in service with the Swedish Army.

In mid-1960 the Swedish Army placed a pre-production order for ten vehicles. The first two prototypes completed in mid-1961 differed in some detail from later vehicles as the suspension had no return rollers, no front support was provided for the 105 mm gun and five machine guns were fitted, one on the commander's cupola and two in boxes on each side of the hull firing forwards. They were powered by a Boeing 502/10MA gas turbine and a Rolls-Royce B81 eight-cylinder petrol engine.

The pre-production vehicles had the right pair of machine guns replaced by a 12.7 mm (0.50) ranging machine gun, and the suspension incorporated two track return rollers. Development costs of the tank, which was subsequently named the Stridsvagn 103, or ·Strv 103, amounted to £8.4 million, including the two prototype vehicles and the ten pre-production vehicles.

The first production Strv 103s were completed in 1966 and production continued until June 1971 by which time 300 had been built. The first production vehicles, known as the Strv 103A, were not fitted with a flotation screen or the dozer blade. Later production vehicles, known as the Strv 103B, had both the flotation screen and the dozer blade and earlier production tanks were subsequently brought up to Strv 103B standard. The Strv 103 is in service with three of Sweden's six armoured brigades, the other three having British-supplied Centurion MBTs.

The S-tank has also been tested by a number of other countries including the Federal Republic of Germany, United Kingdom and the USA. Components of the vehicle are used in the 155 mm Bandkanon 1A self-propelled gun

which is used only by the Swedish Army and the twin 40 mm VEAK anti-aircraft gun system which was not placed in production.

Description

The all-welded hull of the S-tank has the engine and transmission at the front, fighting compartment in the centre and the magazines at the rear. There is a series of horizontal ribs on the glacis plate to deflect armour-piercing rounds. The two engines are geared together to a common output and the diesel (which is the same as that used in the British FV432 APC and the FV433 Abbot 105 mm self-propelled gun) is normally used all the time with the gas turbine being used only when the tank is in action. The gas turbine can also be used to assist in cold weather starting and also acts as a power source when the diesel engine is not operating. Two fire extinguishers in the engine compartment can be operated from inside or outside the vehicle. The glacis plate and the main armament have to be removed before the engine can be changed, which takes about four hours.

The transmission consists of a Volvo torque converter coupled to a gearbox with two forward and two reverse gears, one gear for road driving and the other for cross-country. Steering is a regenerative double-differential system with a hydrostatic steering device, steering being accomplished by handle bars on the tiller columns.

The driver, who also lays and fires the main armament, is seated on the left side of the hull and is provided with a single-piece hatch cover, a Jungner OPS-1 combined periscope and binocular sight to his front and a single periscope to the left. The OPS-1 has a field of view of 100 degrees and a magnification of ×1, ×6, ×10 or ×18 with the sight graticule being in the right eyepiece. The radio operator seated to the rear of the driver is provided with a single-piece hatch cover and two periscopes, and is also provided with controls to drive backwards if required. The commander is seated on the right side of the tank, slightly to the rear of the radio-operator and is provided with four periscopes and a Jungner OPS-1 combined periscope and binocular sight which is identical to that of the driver's except that line-up needles are provided in the left eye-piece. The commander's OPS-1 unit is fully stabilised in elevation from −11 to +16 degrees, and his cupola can be traversed through 208 degrees. The cupola is stabilised in azimuth and enables the commander to locate the target. He then uses the handle bars on the tiller columns

Bofors Strv 103B MBT with dozer blade showing maximum hull elevation

Bofors Strv 103B MBT showing flotation screen collapsed around top of hull

automatic loader enables a high rate of up to 15 rounds per minute to be achieved. When all the ammunition has been expended the magazines are reloaded through two hatches at the rear by the crew in about ten minutes. Types of ammunition fired include APDS (with a muzzle velocity of over 1500 metres per second and an effective range of at least 2000 metres), HE (effective range 5000 metres) and smoke. The empty cartridge cases are automatically ejected outside the hull and if the automatic loading system fails the radio-operator can hand crank ammunition to the breech of the gun. Buttons on the main tiller box are used to select the type of ammunition to be fired.

Two fixed 7.62 mm Ksp 58 machine guns mounted on the left side of the hull are laid in a similar manner to the main armament and fired alternately. Once ammunition has been expended, they have to be reloaded by one of the crew leaving the vehicle. A 7.62 mm Ksp 58 machine gun mounted on the left of the commander's cupola can be aimed and fired from within the vehicle and can also be used for anti-aircraft defence. For target illumination at night some S-tanks have been fitted with two Bofors Lyran launchers on the roof.

A dozer blade is carried folded under the nose of the tank and when required is swung forward and secured by two rods. It is operated by adjusting the hydro-pneumatic suspension. The S-tank has no NBC system.

A flotation screen carried around the top of the hull takes between 15 and 20 minutes to erect and the tank is then propelled in the water by its tracks at a speed of 6 km/h. When afloat, the driver stands on top at the rear with a remote throttle control and steers by reins attached to the main tiller.

to lay the tank onto the target, selects the type of ammunition and then fires the main armament. All the periscopes and sights on the S-tank have armoured shutters, which have two functions: they provide a measure of protection against shell splinters and also prevent the tank's position being given away by the sun glinting on its periscopes. There is a hull escape hatch in the fighting compartment.

The hydro-pneumatic suspension system consists of four dual rubber-tyred road wheels identical to those used on the Centurion MBT, with the idler at the rear, drive sprocket at the front and two track return rollers. To provide a more stable firing platform the suspension is locked when the main armament is fired. The first and third road wheels are mounted on leading arms with the second and fourth on trailing arms. A positive displacement pump transfers fluid between the front and rear units while a servo system compensates for the alteration in the length of track in contact with the ground, and the height of the hull above the ground. The track is of the single dry-pin type with integral rubber pads.

Main armament of the S-tank is a 105 mm rifled tank gun 62 calibres long designated the L74. The gun, which has a bore evacuator but no muzzle brake, is basically a longer version of the British L7 series gun as installed in many other tanks, but has twin vertical sliding breech-blocks with centre cranks. The gun is fed from a magazine at the rear of the hull that holds 50 rounds of ammunition in ten racks each holding five rounds. A typical load would comprise 25 APDS, 20 HE and 5 smoke rounds, but any combination is possible. The

S-tank Modernisation Programme

Following successful trials of an S-tank with its Rolls-Royce K60 engine replaced by a Detroit Diesel 6V-53T developing 300 hp, all vehicles are to be retrofitted with this engine together with its gearing and auxiliaries.

In addition the modernised S-tank has a modified transmission consisting of a three-step automatic gearbox, bevel gearing with forward reverse function and an electronics unit, new radiators, generator, silencer and controls.

The graticule in the existing sight is to be replaced and a Simrad laser rangefinder and will be incorporated into the gunner's sight by Bofors Aerotronics. In 1983 the latter company delivered the prototype of a fire-control computer for the S-tank using the same software as in the Improved Centurion (qv Sweden in part 2) but with modified hardware.

Bofors is studying ways of compensating for barrel droop such as a muzzle reference system and add-on armour for

Bofors Strv 103B MBT

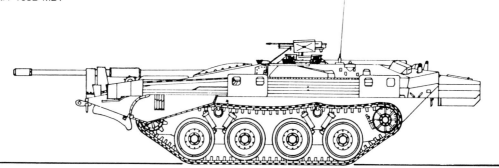

Modernised S-tank with additional fuel cans alongside of hull

improved protection against attack from HEAT projectiles.

By late 1984 ten prototypes of the modernised S-tank had been completed. The tanks are being modernised under a Kr400 million contract awarded to Bofors in late 1983 and when completed the modernised tanks will be known as Strv 103C. Deliveries will run from 1986 to 1989.

To increase range and protection, additional diesel fuel cans will be arranged alongside of the tank.

SPECIFICATIONS

CREW	3	MAX SPEED		ARMAMENT	
COMBAT WEIGHT	39 700 kg	road	50 km/h	main	1 × 105 mm
UNLOADED WEIGHT	37 000 kg	water	6 km/h	coaxial	2 × 7.62 mm MG
POWER-TO-WEIGHT		FUEL CAPACITY	960 litres	anti-aircraft	1 × 7.62 mm MG
RATIO	18.4 hp/tonne	MAX ROAD RANGE	390 km	SMOKE-LAYING	
GROUND PRESSURE	1.04 kg/cm²	FORDING	1.5 m	EQUIPMENT	8 smoke dischargers
LENGTH GUN		with preparation	amphibious	AMMUNITION	
FORWARDS	8.99 m	GRADIENT	60%	main	50
LENGTH OF HULL		VERTICAL OBSTACLE	0.9 m	MG	2750
excluding stowage		TRENCH	2.3 m	GUN CONTROL	
boxes at hull rear	7.04 m	TURNING RADIUS	pivot in neutral	EQUIPMENT	
WIDTH	3.63 m	ENGINES	Rolls-Royce K60 multi-	Turret power control	n/app
WIDTH OVER TRACKS	3.26 m		fuel developing 240 bhp	by commander	yes
HEIGHT			at 3750 rpm and Boeing	by driver/gunner	yes
to top of commander's			553 gas turbine	commander's override	yes
cupola	2.14 m		developing 490 shp at	Commander's fire-	
including machine gun	2.73 m	AUXILIARY ENGINE	38 000 rpm	control override	yes
FIRING HEIGHT	1.7 m	TRANSMISSION	none	Gun elevation/depression	+12°/−10°
GROUND CLEARANCE			Volvo with 2 forward	Gun stabiliser	
hull centre	0.5 m	STEERING	and 2 reverse gears	vertical	no
hull sides	0.4 m		regenerative double-	horizontal	no
TRACK	2.6 m		differential with hydro-		
TRACK WIDTH	670 mm	SUSPENSION	static steering drive		
LENGTH OF TRACK		ELECTRICAL SYSTEM	hydro-pneumatic		
ON GROUND	2.85 m	BATTERIES	24 V		
			2 × 12 V, 114 Ah		

Status: Production complete. In service with the Swedish Army.

Manufacturer: Bofors AB, Ordnance Division, Box 500, S-691 80 Bofors, Sweden.

SWITZERLAND

Pz 61 and Pz 68 Main Battle Tanks

Development

In 1951 the Technical Section of the Swiss General Staff carried out a study to see if an MBT could be designed in Switzerland. This study concluded that it was possible and two years later design work on the first Swiss MBT began at the Federal Construction Works in Thun. Before this deci-sion the Federal Construction Works had designed two vehicles for the Swiss Army, the NK I 75 mm self-propelled anti-tank gun and the NK II 75 mm assault gun, neither of which entered production; Switzerland then procured 152 Jagdpanzer 38(t) tank destroyers from Czechoslovakia which were delivered between 1947 and 1952, and have now been retired from service.

It was apparent that any Swiss-designed MBT would not

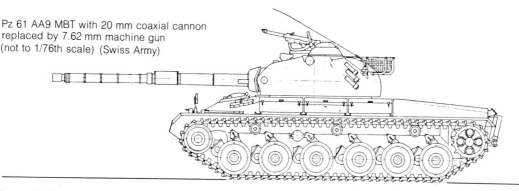

Pz 61 AA9 MBT with 20 mm coaxial cannon replaced by 7.62 mm machine gun (not to 1/76th scale) (Swiss Army)

be available until the late 1950s at the earliest so Switzerland turned to France and the United Kingdom to meet its immediate requirements for tanks. In 1951 an order was placed for 200 French AMX-13 light tanks, which are known as the L Pz 51 and were phased out of service in 1980/81, followed in 1955 by an order for 100 British Centurion Mk 5 tanks which were known as the Pz 55. A further order was placed in 1957 for 100 Centurion Mk 7s which were called the Pz 57, and in 1960 Switzerland bought 100 Centurions from South Africa which were called Pz 55.

The first prototype of the Swiss MBT, designated the KW 30 was completed in 1958 and was armed with a Swiss-designed 90 mm gun. The second prototype was completed the following year. These two prototypes were followed by ten pre-production tanks, Pz 58 (Panzer 58), which were built between 1960 and 1961 and armed with a British 20-pounder (83.4 mm) gun as installed in the Pz 55. In March 1961 a production order for 150 Pz 61s (armed with British 105 mm gun) was placed with deliveries to the Swiss Army taking place between January 1965 and December 1966. The Pz 61s are operated by the tank battalions of the Swiss 4th Mechanised Division.

Description

The hull of the Pz 61, like its turret, is a one-piece casting supplied to Thun by Georg Fischer of Schaffhausen, and is divided into three compartments: driver's at the front, fighting in the centre and the engine at the rear.

The driver is seated at the front of the hull in the centre and is provided with a one-piece hatch cover hinged at the rear. Three periscopes are mounted forward of the hatch.

The turret, which unlike most other contemporary tanks has no bustle, is in the centre of the hull with the commander and gunner seated on the right and the loader on the left. The commander's cupola has a single-piece hatch cover that opens to the rear and eight periscopes. The commander also operates the split-image coincidence rangefinder which has a magnification of ×8. The gunner is seated forward and below the commander and has a periscope with a magnification of ×8 and ×2.7. The loader's cupola is provided with six vision blocks and split hatch covers that open left and right. The loader's cupola is a little higher than the commander's whose area of observation is therefore restricted.

The engine compartment is at the rear, separated from the fighting compartment by a fireproof bulkhead. The complete powerpack, consisting of the engine, auxiliary engine, transmission, cooling and exhaust system, can be removed from the vehicle in about one hour. The engine is supplied from West Germany and is coupled to a Swiss SLM transmission consisting of a semi-automatic gearbox with six forward and two reverse gears and a double differential steering system

with a hydrostatic steering drive which provides progressive and continuous steering control.

The suspension of the Pz 61 consists of six dual rubber-tyred road wheels, each independently located and sprung by Belleville washers. The idler is at the front and the drive sprocket at the rear. There are three track return rollers. The tracks of the Pz 61 are of cast manganese and have no rubber pads.

Main armament of the Pz 61 is a British-designed 105 mm L7 series gun manufactured in Switzerland with a number of modifications, known as the Pz Kan 61 and firing a Swiss-designed HE (muzzle velocity 600 m/s) round in addition to the normal APDS (muzzle velocity 1470 m/s), HESH (muz-

Pz 61 AA9 MBT with 7.5 mm MG replacing 20 mm coaxial cannon (Swiss Army)

Pz 68 Mk 3 MBT (Swiss Army)

Pz 68 Mk 3 MBT with commander's, loader's and driver's hatches open (Swiss Army)

zle velocity 730 m/s) and smoke rounds. Of the 56 rounds of 105 mm ammunition carried, 12 are in the turret for ready use and 22 each side of the driver at the front of the hull, Switzerland has adopted the Israeli APFSDS projectile and 12 rounds of this type are carried. The gun control system for the Pz 61 is a French SAMM type CH 25 electro-hydraulic system similar to that developed for the French AMX-30 MBT except that the gun of the Pz 61 is elevated by a motor rather than a jack as in the case of the AMX-30.

Mounted on the forward part of the loader's hatch is a 7.5 mm MG 51 machine gun for anti-aircraft defence which can be elevated from −4 to +77 degrees, and mounted on either side of the turret are three L Pz 51 (80.5 mm) smoke dischargers.

Standard equipment on the Pz 61 includes NBC system, hull escape hatch and a drinking water tank. There is no provision for deep fording. The Pz 61 AA9 is the earlier Pz 61 with an SE-412 radio and dry air filter installed, the 20 mm cannon replaced by a standard 7.5 mm machine gun and improved maintenance facilities. It is probable that the Pz 61 will be modernised to enable it to remain effective into the 1990s.

Pz 68 MBT (later called the Pz 68 Mark 1)

Further development of the Pz 61 resulted in the Pz 68. The first prototype was completed in 1968 with production being authorised in 1968 at a cost of 460 million francs. Between January 1971 and July 1974 170 Pz 68s were delivered to the Swiss Army. Major differences between the Pz 61 and the Pz 68 can be summarised as the replacement of the 20 mm coaxial cannon by a standard 7.5 mm machine gun, stabilisation system for the main armament allowing the tank to engage targets accurately while moving across country, ammunition resupply hatch in the left side of the turret, more powerful engine and modified transmission, wider tracks with replaceable rubber pads and a greater length of track in contact with the ground. Mounted at the rear of the turret is a large stowage basket and deep fording equipment can be installed. The main armament is equipped with a fume extractor but no muzzle brake. Pz 68 and the Pz 61 tanks have

been fitted with a Bofors Lyran system (Swiss Army designation is the 7.1 cm Le GW 74 for which 12 projectiles are carried) on the turret roof between the commander's and loader's cupolas. This system can launch an illuminating rocket to a maximum range of 500 metres and a maximum altitude of 1300 metres. The Pz 68s are used by the 4th and 11th Mechanised Divisions. All but 13 per cent of the Pz 68 was manufactured in Switzerland, the engine, auxiliary engine and turret controls coming from abroad.

Pz 68 Mark 2

This was approved for production in 1974 at a cost of 146.3 million Swiss Francs, and is basically the Pz 68 Mark 1 with an alternator, thermal sleeve for main armament, and a system for extracting carbon monoxide. Between March and December 1977 50 Pz 68 Mk 2 tanks were delivered to the Swiss Army.

Pz 68 Mark 3

This has all the improvements of the Mks 1 and 2 but also has a larger turret. Production was authorised in 1975 at a cost of 447 million Swiss francs and 110 tanks were delivered between 1978 and September 1979.

Pz 68 Mark 4

This is similar to the Mk 3 and 60 were ordered in 1978 for delivery between October 1981 and December 1982. At present various modernisation schemes are being studied to enable the Pz 68 to remain effective through the 1990s.

Variants

Anti-aircraft Tank

In August 1978 a contract for the development of an anti-aircraft tank based on the chassis of the Pz 68 MBT was awarded to Contraves AG of Zürich by the Swiss Government Agency for Armament. The prototype of this system, which had the same twin 35 mm turret as fitted to the West German Gepard SPAAG, was handed over to the Swiss Ordnance Procurement Agency in April 1979. It has been decided that the system will not be procured at present.

Armoured Recovery Vehicle

Development of an ARV based on the chassis of the Pz 61

Entp Pz 65 armoured recovery vehicle in travelling order (Swiss Army)

Target version of Pz 68 MBT (Swiss Army)

Brü Pz 68 armoured bridgelayer in travelling configuration
(Swiss Army)

SPECIFICATIONS

Model	Pz 61	Pz 68
CREW	4	4
COMBAT WEIGHT	38 000 kg	39 700 kg
UNLOADED WEIGHT	37 000 kg	38 700 kg
POWER-TO-WEIGHT RATIO	17 hp/tonne	16.62 hp/tonne
GROUND PRESSURE	0.85 kg/cm²	0.86 kg/cm²
LENGTH GUN FORWARDS	9.43 m	9.49 m
LENGTH GUN REAR	8.28 m	8.6 m
LENGTH HULL	6.78 m	6.98 m
WIDTH	3.06 m	3.14 m
HEIGHT		
including AA MG	2.85 m	2.88 m
commander's cupola	2.72 m	2.75 m
FIRING HEIGHT	1.93 m	1.96 m
GROUND CLEARANCE	0.42 m	0.41 m
TRACK	2.59 m	2.59 m
TRACK WIDTH	500 mm	520 mm
LENGTH OF TRACK ON GROUND	4.13 m	4.43 m
MAX ROAD SPEED	50 km/h	55 km/h
FUEL CAPACITY	760 litres	710 litres
MAX RANGE		
road	300 km	350 km
cross-country	160 km	160 km
FORDING	1.1 m	1.1 m
with preparation	n/app	2.3 m
GRADIENT	60%	60%
VERTICAL OBSTACLE	0.75 m	1 m
TRENCH	2.6 m	2.6 m
ENGINE	MTU MB 837 8-cylinder diesel developing 630 hp at 2200 rpm	MTU MB 837 8-cylinder diesel developing 660 hp at 2200 rpm
AUXILIARY ENGINE	diesel developing 31 hp at 3100 rpm	diesel developing 35 hp at 2800 rpm
TRANSMISSION	SLM semi-automatic 6 forward and 2 reverse gears	SLM semi-automatic 6 forward and 6 reverse gears
STEERING	infinitely variable hydrostatic cross-drive	
SUSPENSION	Belleville washers	Belleville washers
ELECTRICAL SYSTEM	24 V	24 V
BATTERIES	4 × 6 V, 300 Ah	4 × 6 V, 300 Ah
ARMAMENT		
main	1 × 105 mm	1 × 105 mm
coaxial	1 × 7.5 mm MG	1 × 7.5 mm MG
anti-aircraft	1 × 7.5 mm MG	1 × 7.5 mm MG
SMOKE-LAYING EQUIPMENT	3 smoke dischargers either side of turret	
AMMUNITION		
main	56	56
7.5 mm	5400	5400
GUN CONTROL EQUIPMENT		
Turret power control	electro-hydraulic/ manual	electro-hydraulic/ manual
by commander	yes	yes
by gunner	yes	yes
commander's override	yes	yes
Commander's fire-control override	yes	yes
Max rate power traverse	360° in 9.5 s	360° in 9.5 s
Max rate power elevation	20.8°/s	20.8°/s
Gun elevation/depression	+21°/−10°	+21°/−10°
Gun stabiliser		
vertical	no	yes
horizontal	no	yes
Range setting device	yes	yes
Elevation quadrant	yes	yes
Traverse indicator	yes	yes
ARMOUR	20–60 mm	20–60 mm

MBT began at Thun in 1961 with the first prototype being completed in 1967/68. After trials with this prototype a modified version based on the chassis of the Pz 68 was placed in production. First production vehicles, known as the Entpannungspanzer 65 (or Entp Pz 65) were completed in 1970. The vehicle is fitted with a main winch with 120 metres of cable and a maximum capacity of 25 000 kg, which can be increased to 75 000 kg with the use of snatch blocks. The auxiliary winch used to pull out the main cable has 240 metres of cable. Mounted at the front of the vehicle is a hydraulically-operated dozer blade which is used to stabilise the vehicle or for dozing. Pivoted at the front of the hull is an A-frame with a maximum lifting capacity of 15 000 kg. A full range of tools and cutting equipment is carried. The Entp Pz 65 has a crew of five and a loaded weight of 38 000 kg. Armament consists of a single 7.5 mm machine gun and eight smoke dischargers.

Armoured Bridgelayer

The prototype of the bridgelayer was based on the chassis of a Pz 61 tank but production vehicles, designated the Brückenlegepanzer 68, were based on the Pz 68 tank chassis. The bridge is launched as follows: the vehicle stops short of the obstacle and the bridge is tilted forwards, a beam is slid over to the far bank and the bridge is then advanced along the beam. Once the bridge has reached the far bank, the beam is retracted. The bridge has an overall length of 18.23 metres and a maximum capacity of 60 000 kg, its normal capacity being 50 000 kg. The bridgelayer has a crew of three and weighs 44 600 kg complete with the bridge.

155 mm Self-propelled Gun

The prototype of a 155 mm self-propelled gun called the Panzer-Kanone 68, based on the chassis of a Pz 68 MBT, was built some time ago. It was not placed in production as the Swiss Army procured additional American 155 mm M109 SPGs.

Target Tank

A special version of the Pz 68 has been developed for training anti-tank crews, called the Schweres Panzerzielfahrzeug, or Pz Zielfz 68. It has a heavily-armoured turret with a dummy gun and additional armour is provided for the hull. The tops of the tracks are covered by armoured skirting. The Pz Zielfz 68 weighs 38 000 kg and has a two-man crew.

Status: Production complete. In service only with the Swiss Army.

Manufacturer: Federal Construction Works, Thun, Switzerland.

TAIWAN

ROC MBT Development Programme

The Republic of China Fighting Vehicles Development Centre is currently designing a medium battle tank. Very little information has become available although press releases have provided the following information:
1) The ROC MBT will be based on extracts from foreign designs;
2) The design will specifically aim at meeting the requirement of the geographical, bridge and climatic characteristics of the Taiwan area;
3) The ROC MBT will have infra-red night vision equipment, laser rangefinder, ballistic computer, modern electronic communications equipment, improved armour protection against armour-piercing and HEAT projectiles, have an all-weather combat capability and feature a powerpack made in Taiwan.

In mid-1984 Taiwan started to order M60A3 hulls from the US; details are given in Part 2.

Status: Probably early project development stage.

Developing agency: Fighting Vehicles Development Centre, ROC Army, Taichung, Taiwan 400, Republic of China.

UNION OF SOVIET SOCIALIST REPUBLICS

T-80 Main Battle Tank

It is believed that the T-80 has a chassis similar to that of the T-72/T-74 but is powered by a gas turbine engine in place of the V-12 diesel installed in the T-72/T-74.

Main armament consists of a turret-mounted gun that can fire a conventional round or an anti-tank guided missile; the latter may be laser guided. The missile may be a development of the Kobra which is also fired by the T-64B variant of the T-64 MBT which has been in service with the Soviet Army for some years.

In 1981 the US Department of Defense released an artist's impression of a new tank called the T-80. When the 1983 edition of *Soviet Military Power* was published the T-80 was shown to be nothing more than the late production T-72 which has the Soviet designation of T-74.

T-64 and T-72 Main Battle Tanks

Development

Following the commencement of full-scale production of the T-62 MBT in 1961 the Soviets produced a number of prototype tanks, of which one was placed in production in a Soviet tank plant as the T-64 and is now in service with the Group of Soviet Forces in Germany and units within the Soviet Union itself. The T-64 was first seen in 1970 and in 1980 was also deployed with the Southern Group of Soviet Forces in Hungary. As far as it is known the T-64 has not been issued to any other member of the Warsaw Pact, nor has it been exported. From all accounts the T-64 was not considered to be a satisfactory design and serious problems were encountered with its engine, suspension, fire-control system and the automatic loader for the 125 mm gun.

Production of the T-64 was finally completed in 1981 when 200 were built compared to 500 in 1980, and 1000 in 1978 and 1979, according to the US Department of Defense. Other sources indicate that production of the T-64 was completed as early as 1971–72.

The T-64 was followed by the T-72 which entered production in 1972 and was first seen in October 1977 when the French Minister of Defence, Yvon Bourges, paid an official visit to the Taman Guards Division. The tank was seen in public for the first time during the November 1977 military parade in Moscow.

During fighting in Lebanon in 1982 the Israeli Army destroyed a number of T-72 MBTs with standard 105 mm guns firing APDS ammunition, TOW ATGWs (helicopter

T-64s of the Soviet Army showing external ammunition boxes for 12.7 mm machine gun ammunition and mounting points under hull front for mine clearing attachment

T-64 showing external stowage

launched), 155 mm, 203 mm improved conventional munitions and US Rockeye cluster bombs with anti-tank sub-munitions.

In 1983 the US Department of Defense stated that production of the T-72 in the USSR in recent years had amounted to 1500 in 1978, 2000 in 1979, 2300 in 1980, 1400 in 1981 and 1300 in 1982. Production commenced in Poland and Czechoslovakia in 1981 when 20 vehicles were built, rising to 100 the following year.

Late production models of the T-72 are called the T-80 by the US although the correct Soviet designation is in fact the T-74 with 300 produced in 1980, 400 in 1981 and 1200 in 1982.

In early 1985 the US Department of Defense issued revised production figures for Soviet tank production, these were 3100 in 1980, 2000 in 1981, 2500 in 1982, 2700 in 1983 and 3200 in 1984.

There are now five plants making the T-72 MBT, Plzen in Czechoslovakia, Katowice in Poland and Kharkov, Omsk and Nizhni-Tagil in the Soviet Union. It is believed that Chelyabinsk came back on line in 1984 to build the T-74 or T-80 MBT. More recently Yugoslavia and India have started to manufacture the T-72/T-74 under licence.

The United States Army considers the M60A1 inferior to the T-72, the more recent M60A3 on a par with it and the new M1 superior to it. Initially it was thought that the armour on the T-64 and T-72 was of the normal rolled and cast type but in 1978 a United States Army report stated that the armour was of an advanced type.

Description of T-64 (Provisional)

This has a similar layout to the T-72 and the same armament and NBC system, but hydro-mechanical suspension, five-cylinder opposed diesel engine and a slightly different turret. The suspension consists of six small dual road wheels with the drive sprocket at the rear, idler at the front and four track return rollers which support the inside of the double pin track only. The first, second, fifth and sixth road wheel stations are provided with a hydraulic shock absorber. Over the top of the suspension, which slopes downward towards the rear, is a rail on which panels of additional armour can be attached.

The infra-red searchlight is mounted on the left rather than the right of the main armament as in the case of the T-72M. Three boxes of 12.7 mm ammunition are mounted on the left side of the turret, the snorkel is carried on the top of the turret at the rear and at the very rear of the turret is a detachable stowage box. The T-64 has two snorkels for deep fording, one fitted to the turret and the other over the engine compartment.

There is also a command version of the T-64 called the T-64K. When stationary a 10-metre telescopic mast is erected over the turret and held in position by stays which are pegged to the ground. The command version does not normally have the 12.7 mm anti-aircraft gun fitted. Unlike the T-72, the 12.7 mm anti-aircraft machine gun of the T-64 can be aimed and fired from within the tank.

T-64 showing external stowage on turret

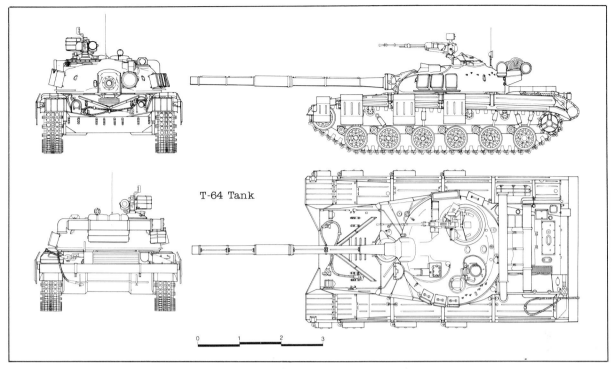

T-64 Tank

Four-view drawing of T-64 MBT showing external details (Steven Zaloga)

Variants of T-64 MBT

T-64 M1981/1, also called T-64A by the US Army, has a modified sight for the gunner with an enlarged opening, smoke mortars on the turret front, bump stop for the fourth road wheel and hinges for the attachment of side skirts;
T-64 M1980/2 is the same as the M1981/1 but with skirts;
T-64B (US designation) has the Kobra guided missile system also fitted to the T-80 MBT;
T-64B M1981/1 does not have the Kobra guided missile system but the standard 125 mm gun.

Description of T-72

The hull of the T-72 is divided into three compartments: driver's at the front, fighting in the centre and the engine compartment at the rear. It is believed that the turret has conventional cast armour with a maximum thickness of 280 mm, the nose is about 80 mm thick and the glacis is of a new laminate armour 200 mm thick, which when inclined gives between 500/600 mm of protection.

The glacis is well sloped, transversely ribbed and has a deep V splash-board. The driver is seated at the front of the hull and is provided with a single-piece hatch cover that opens to the right, in front of which is a single wide-angle observation periscope. The driver's headlamps are designated FG 125.

The other two crew members are seated in the turret with the gunner on the left and the commander on the right. The commander's contra-rotating cupola has a single-piece hatch cover that opens forward with two rear-facing vision blocks. In the forward part of the cupola is a combined day/night sight with an infra-red searchlight mounted over the top, and to either side of the combined day/night sight is another periscope. Forward and slightly below the commander's cupola is an optical stadiametric rangefinder.

The gunner's hatch opens forward and has a circular opening for mounting the snorkel for deep fording operations and two observation periscopes. In front and to the left of the gunner's hatch is a panoramic day/night sight which is used in conjunction with the infra-red searchlight mounted to the left and in front of the sight. The gunner's sight is the TPD-2 while his night sight is the TPN 1-49-23. Forward and below the gunner's hatch is a laser rangefinder which may be connected to the left side of the optical rangefinder on the commander's side.

The infra-red searchlight is mounted on the right side of the main armament rather than the left as in the case of the earlier T-64 (initial production vehicles).

Two light steel stowage boxes are mounted on the turret, one at the rear and the other on the right slightly behind the commander's position. The snorkel is carried on the left side of the turret to the rear. Whereas the turret on the T-64 is roughly circular, that of the T-72 has a distinct bulge and external stowage on the two tanks is also different. There are also significant differences in the engine deckings which indicate that they are powered by different engines.

Fuel cells extend along the right side of the hull top; while on the left hull top are stowage boxes and a single oil cell. There are four internal oil tanks in the T-72, one to the left of the driver and two to his right and one on the floor in the space between the rear of the ammunition carousel and the fire wall/engine bulkhead. An unditching beam is normally carried at the rear and there is also provision for carrying two 200-litre fuel drums at the rear to increase operational range.

The suspension each side consists of six road wheels with the idler at the front, drive sprocket at the rear and three return rollers which support the inside of the track only. Track is of the single-pin type with rubber bushed pins.

Four removable spring-loaded skirt plates fitted over the

T-72 MBT

◀ T-72 MBT from rear showing unditching beam

forward part of the track are unclipped in action and spring forward at an angle of 60 degrees from the side of the vehicle to give a measure of protection against HEAT projectiles.

A dozer blade mounted under the nose of the tank is used for clearing obstacles and preparing fire positions and, like most other Soviet tanks, the T-72 can be fitted with KMT-5 mine-clearing equipment. The dozer blade can be brought into the operating position in one or two minutes and enables the tank to prepare its own defilade position without calling on engineer support. A typical position for a T-72 MBT would be 10 metres long, 4.5 metres wide and 1.2 metres deep with a total volume of 54 cubic metres. The T-72 is provided with an NBC system and can be fitted with a snorkel for deep fording.

Main armament is a 125 mm smooth-bore gun fitted with a light alloy thermal sleeve and a bore evacuator. The gun, designated the 2A46, fires three main types of separate loading ammunition, APFSDS (possibly designated the BR-11) with a maximum range of 2100 metres, HEAT-FS with a maximum direct fire range of 4000 metres and HE-FRAG(FS) with a maximum indirect fire range of 9400 metres.

Type	APFSDS	HEAT-FS	HE-FRAG(FS)
MUZZLE VELOCITY	1615 m/s	900 m/s	850 m/s
ARMOUR PENETRATION	300 mm/1000 m	475 mm/1000 m	n/app

Of 39 rounds of ammunition carried 12 are APFSDS, 21 HE and the remaining six HEAT. The ammunition is of the separate loading type with a combustable cartridge case, all that remains of the latter after firing is a stub. The additional rounds of ammunition are stowed in racks behind the turret

T-72 MBTs parade through Red Square, Moscow, on 7 November 1980. Note attachment points under nose for mine clearing equipment (TASS)

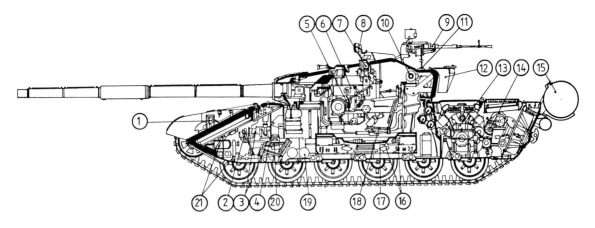

Cutaway drawing of T-72 MBT showing main components

(1) driver's FG 125 headlamp **(2)** steering tillers **(3)** NBC system **(4)** gear lever **(5)** gun elevation mechanism **(6)** TPD-2 gunner's sight **(7)** TPN 1-49-23 gunner's night sight **(8)** searchlight for use with TKN 3 observation device **(9)** 12.7 mm anti-aircraft machine gun to rear **(10)** hoist for ammunition containers **(11)** antenna base **(12)** turret bin for deep fording equipment and cold rations **(13)** 780 bhp diesel engine **(14)** gearbox **(15)** long-range fuel tanks which can be jettisoned **(16)** charges and projectiles in containers on ammunition hoist platform **(17)** ammunition hoist platform **(18)** gunner's seat **(19)** NBC decontamination equipment **(20)** driver's adjustable seat **(21)** parking brake **(22)** external stowage for spares, tools and accessories **(23)** manual drive for turret traverse gear **(24)** turret traverse indicator **(25)** 125 mm gun sliding wedge breech-block **(26)** 7.62 mm PKT coaxial machine gun **(27)** tank commander's periscopes **(28)** skirting plates **(29)** 7.62 mm PKT machine gun ammunition boxes **(30)** radio set **(31)** hydraulic turret traverse gear

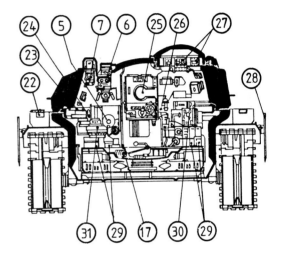

basket and in indentations in the rear floor fuel cell and second forward right fuel cell near the driver. The carousel automatic loader is mounted on the turret floor and also on the rear wall of the turret. The projectile is loaded in the lower half of a carrier while the cartridge and propellant is loaded in the upper half. When the 125 mm gun loads it must pick up the carrier and ram both the projectile and powder charge. This enables a rate of fire of eight rounds a minute to be achieved but there are some doubts about the reliability of the automatic loader. The main armament is stabilised and enables the T-72 to shoot on the move with a high probability of a first-round hit.

A 7.62 mm PKT machine gun is mounted coaxially to the right of the main armament and a new design 12.7 mm machine gun is mounted on the commander's cupola. The 12.7 mm machine gun can however only be used with the commander exposing the upper part of his body. Maximum sight range in the ground-to-ground role is 2000 metres, maximum sight range in the anti-aircraft role is 1500 metres.

T-72s built for export outside the Warsaw Pact have a slightly different fire-control system and automatic loader and do not have the internal lining that is standard on Warsaw Pact T-72s consisting of a layer of synthetic material that contains lead and provides some degree of protection against the effects of neutron radiation and electro-magnetic pulses.

Variants of T-72

T-72   Initial production model, has infra-red searchlight to left of 125 mm gun as on T-64

T-72M   Confirmed Soviet designation, standard production model with infra-red searchlight to right of main armament

Close-up of T-72 turret with commander's cupola traversed to rear (US Army)

BREM armoured recovery vehicles based on much modified T-72 MBT chassis

T-72MK Command version of T-72M, also T-72K on original T-72 tank

T-74(?) Initial version of T-74. Has no right side optics port which possibly indicated installation of a laser rangefinder. Fitted with older gill armour fold-out side plates

T-74(?) Also known as T-72 M1980/1, same as above but with new fabric armour over side containers and suspension

T-72 Also known as T-72 M1981/2, T-72 retrofitted with side armour over rear deck to discourage top attack

T-74 Also known as the T-72 M1981/3, or T-80 (in US only). Variant of previous model with at least two versions. Initial version looks almost identical to T-72 M1980/1 but has thicker frontal armour. T-72 M1981/3 is follow on fitted with smoke mortars which have also been retrofitted to older models and some T-64s

T-74 Also known as T-72 M1984, as above but with appliqué armour on turret roof

All of the above versions retain the attachment points for mine clearing equipment under the nose of the vehicle, and have cylindrical containers above the ammunition containers for the anti-aircraft machine gun on the right side of the turret, modified mount for the AA machine gun ammunition containers, which are now attached with their narrower sides downwards, and no longer have horizontal holding hoops along the lower rim of the turret.

All current production versions of the T-64/T-72 are now fitted with a quickly erectable cover to protect the driver when he is driving in the head out position.

BREM Armoured Recovery and Repair Vehicle

This is based on the chassis of T-72 and mounted at the front of the hull on the left side is a hydraulic crane which can lift 12 tonnes, a main winch with a capacity of 25 tonnes which can be increased to 100 tonnes, auxiliary winch, hydraulically-operated dozer/stabilising blade at the front of the hull, towing equipment and a complete range of tools and recovery equipment.

Model	T-64	T-72
SPECIFICATIONS (Provisional)		
Model	T-64	T-72
CREW	3	3
COMBAT WEIGHT	38 000 kg	41 000 kg
POWER-TO-WEIGHT		
RATIO	18.42 hp/tonne	19 hp/tonne
GROUND PRESSURE	1.09 kg/cm²	0.83 kg/cm²
LENGTH		
gun forwards	9.1 m	9.24 m
hull	6.4 m	6.95 m
WIDTH		
without skirts	3.38 m	3.6 m
with skirts	4.64 m	4.75 m
HEIGHT	2.3 m	2.37 m

T-72M MBT (Courtesy of Steven Zaloga)

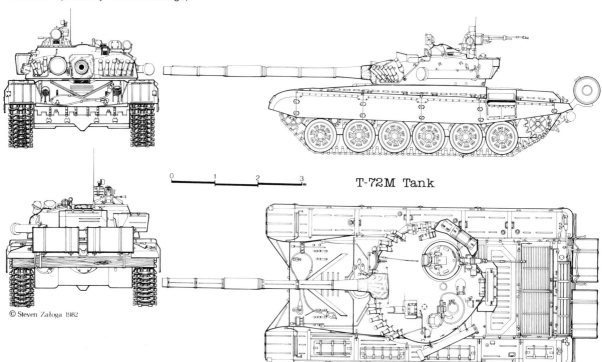

© Steven Załoga 1982

T-72M Tank

Model	T-64	T-72
GROUND CLEARANCE	0.377 m	0.47 m
TRACK WIDTH	580 mm	580 mm
LENGTH OF TRACK		
ON GROUND	4.1 m	4.25 m
MAX ROAD SPEED	70 km/h	60 km/h
RANGE		
road, without long-range fuel		
tanks	450 km	480 km
road, with long-range fuel		
tanks	700 km	700 km
FUEL CAPACITY	1000 litres	1000 litres
FORDING		
without preparation	1.4 m	1.4 m
with preparation	5.5 m	5.5 m
GRADIENT	60%	60%
VERTICAL OBSTACLE	0.915 m	0.85 m
TRENCH	2.72 m	2.8 m
ENGINE	5-cylinder opposed	V-12 multifuel
	piston, diesel,	(W-46)
	liquid-cooled,	780 hp
	700/750 hp	at 2000 rpm
TRANSMISSION	synchromesh, hydraulically assisted with 7 forward and	
	1 reverse gears	
STEERING	clutch and brake	clutch and brake
SUSPENSION	hydro-mechanical	torsion bar
ELECTRICAL SYSTEM	24 V	24 V
ARMAMENT		
main	1 × 125 mm	1 × 125 mm
coaxial	1 × 7.62 mm MG	1 × 7.62 mm MG
anti-aircraft	1 × 12.7 mm MG	1 × 12.7 mm MG
AMMUNITION		
main	40	39
coaxial	3000	3000
anti-aircraft	500	500
GUN CONTROL		
EQUIPMENT		
Turret power control	electric/manual	electric/manual
Gun elevation/depression	+18°/−5°	+18°/−5°
Gun stabiliser		
vertical	yes	yes
horizontal	yes	yes

Status: The T-72 MBT is in production. Within the USSR production is undertaken at defence plants, which have a zavod number, attached to civilian facilities managed by the Heavy and Transport Machine Building Industry.

These are Nizhni-Tagil Railroad Enterprise (Zavod No 183), Kharkhov (Malyshev) Locomotive Enterprise (Zavod No 75), Omsk Railroad Enterprise (Zavod No 13) and Chelyabinsk Heavy Machinery Enterprise (Zavod No 178).

In Czechoslovakia production is said to be undertaken at the CKD-Praga facility in Plzen, although other sources indicate that the T-72 is assembled in Martin at the Machine Enterprise with CKD carrying out transmission work.

In Poland the T-72 is made at Katowice. The T-72 is also being built in India (qv) and Yugoslavia (qv), in both cases the late production model T-74 is built.

In service in Algeria, Angola (unconfirmed), Bulgaria, Cuba, Czechoslovakia (local manufacture under licence), East Germany, Finland, Hungary, India (local manufacture under licence), Iraq, Libya, Poland (local manufacture under licence), Romania, Syria, USSR and Yugoslavia (local manufacture under licence).

Manufacturer: Soviet state arsenals.

T-62 Main Battle Tank

Development
The T-62 MBT was developed from the earlier T-54/T-55 series in the late 1950s and entered production in 1961. It was first seen in public during a parade held in Moscow in May 1965. Although no figures have been released, it is believed that production of the T-62 amounted to 20 000 units. Production of the T-62 continued in the Soviet Union until 1970 and it has been confirmed that a quantity of T-62s for the home and export markets was produced by Czechoslovakia.

Main recognition features of the T-62 compared with the earlier T-54/T-55 are a longer and wider hull, different spacing on the road wheels as the T-62 has a distinct gap between the third and fourth and fourth and fifth road wheels, shape of the turret, and the longer and fatter gun barrel with a fume extractor towards its muzzle.

The T-62 was widely used by both Syria and Egypt during the 1973 Middle East campaign and its main drawbacks were shown to be slow rate of fire and limited depression of the main armament, and its 115 mm gun and its associated fire-control system were no match for the Israeli tanks with their 105 mm rifled guns.

Description
The hull of the T-62 is divided into three compartments, driver's at the front, fighting in the centre with the engine and transmission compartment at the rear. The driver is seated at the front of the vehicle on the left side and is provided with a single-piece hatch cover that opens to the left. Two vision blocks are mounted forward of his hatch cover, each with an integral defrosting element. The left vision block can be replaced by a TVN-2 infra-red periscope which has a 30-degree field of view and a maximum range of 60 metres. A hull escape hatch behind the driver's seat opens to the inside of the vehicle. Mounted on the glacis plate is a wave deflector, and mounted to the rear of this on the right side are a white light and an infra-red headlamp.

The cast turret is in the centre of the tank with the commander and gunner seated on the left and the loader on the right. Both are provided with a single-piece hatch cover that opens to the rear and can be locked vertical. Rails outside the turret can be used by infantry or for stowing personal equipment.

The commander's cupola has four periscopes, two mounted in the hatch cover and two in the forward part of his cupola. The commander's sight, designated the TKN-3, is a day/night binocular periscope with an integral infra-red capability mounted in the forward part of his cupola. For day use it has a magnification of ×5 and a 10-degree field of view and for night it has a magnification of ×4.2 and an 8-degree

T-62 MBT

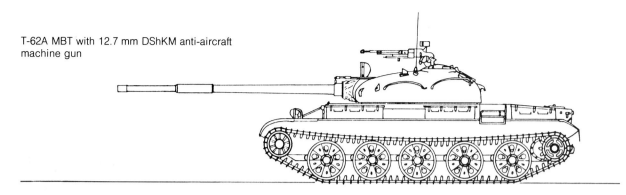

T-62A MBT with 12.7 mm DShKM anti-aircraft machine gun

Soviet T-62 tanks fitted with snorkel for deep fording

field of view. Effective range when used in conjunction with the OU-3GK searchlight is 400 metres. The handles of the sight are used to rotate the commander's cupola and operate the searchlight, target designation equipment and other systems.

The gunner has a TSh2B-41u telescope with a rotating graticule for super-elevation required for the different types of ammunition and dual magnification, ×3.5 with an 18-degree field of view and ×7 with a 9-degree field of view, filter capabilities, stadiametric rangefinder (at the bottom of the graticule) and an integral wiper. The maximum sighting ranges are 4000 metres for APFSDS, 3700 metres for HEAT, 4800 metres for HE 18 and 3600 metres for HE 11. The gunner's infra-red sight is the TPN1-41-11 periscope which is used in conjunction with the main L-2G searchlight mounted coaxially to the right of the main armament and has an effective range of 800 metres. The TPN1-41-11 has a magnification of ×5.5 and a 6-degree field of view.

The gunner is also provided with a Type TNP-165 periscope with a magnification of ×1. The loader on the right side of the turret is provided with a single TNP-165 periscope which can be used to the front or rear of the vehicle.

Mounted at the rear of the turret, to the left of the spent cartridge ejection door, is an electrically-operated blower operated by the driver using the KUV-3 ventilator control box.

To the rear of the turret, over the engine compartment, is a large rectangular sheet steel plate that covers the engine louvres when the tank is snorkelling. The engine is equipped with a pre-heater and is normally started by compressed air although an electrical auxiliary system is also provided. The engine is coupled to the manual transmission and changing up or down is accomplished by double-declutching. The

two-stage planetary steering system, which also serves as brakes, transmits torque to the final drives, each of which is a two-step, step-down reduction gear.

The torsion bar suspension consists of five dual rubber-tyred road wheels with the drive sprocket at the rear and the idler at the front. A hydraulic shock absorber is provided at the first and last road wheel stations. The all-steel track has steel pins that are not secured at the outer end and are free to travel towards the hull. A raised piece of metal welded to the hull just forward of the sprocket drives the track pins back into position each time they pass. Each track has 96 links and weighs 1386 kg when new. Like the T-54/T-55, the T-62 is now being fitted with an improved live track.

A centralised ethylene-bromide fire-extinguishing system is activated automatically by heat sensors of which there are eight in the engine, transmission and fighting compartments, or manually by the tank commander or driver.

The T-62 MBT has a PAZ nuclear collective protection system which consists of a radiation detector/actuator (RBZ-1m), five separate explosive squib mechanisms and a blower/dust separator. The box-like radiation detector/

T-62A MBT from front but without 12.7 mm anti-aircraft machine gun installed (US Army/Michael Green)

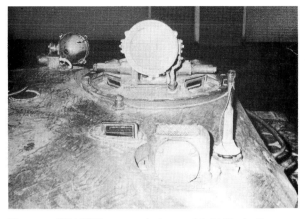

Close-up of OU-3GK commander's searchlight fitted with cover. In foreground is gunner's sight

T-62A MBT without anti-aircraft machine gun installed on display in the US (Donald Spaulding)

operational range. All vehicles have three external fuel cells on the right side of the vehicle for diesel fuel while the single tank on the left side is for auxiliary oil. The driver can select which fuel to use first, normally using the two rear drums, then the three external cells and finally the main fuel tank.

The T-62 can, like other Soviet tanks, lay its own smoke-screen by spraying diesel oil into the exhaust manifold when it is sufficiently hot, creating thick white smoke that exits from the exhaust ports on the left side of the tank. When laying the smoke-screen the tank is always in second or third gear. This consumes about ten litres of fuel per minute and produces a smoke-screen 250 to 400 metres long which lasts for some four minutes, but this does depend on the wind strength.

The tank can ford to a maximum depth of 1.4 metres without preparation. It can also ford deep water when fitted with a snorkel. It takes up to eight hours to prepare the tank for deep fording and two types of snorkel are available, a large diameter one for training and a thinner one for operational use which is normally carried in sections on the rear of the turret. The tank is usually driven across the river bed in first gear and navigated by its GPK-59 gyro-compass and a radio link to the far bank. Once ashore, it takes only one or two minutes to prepare the tank for action again.

Main armament of the T-62 MBT is a U-5TS (2A20) 115 mm smooth-bore gun fitted with a bore evacuator, with a maximum rate of fire of four rounds per minute when at a standstill. After firing the main armament of the T-62 automatically elevates to an angle of +3 degrees 30 minutes for loading. The turret cannot be traversed while the weapon is being loaded. The following rounds of fixed ammunition can be fired:

AMMUNITION TYPE	HE-FRAG (FS)	HEAT-FS	HEAT-FS	APFSDS
DESIGNATION	OF-18	BK-4	BK-4M	BM-6
FUZE MODEL	V-429E	GPV-2	GPV-2	n/app
WEIGHT OF COMPLETE ROUND	28.1 kg	26.2 kg	26.2 kg	22.5 kg
WEIGHT OF PROJECTILE	17.72 kg	11.79 kg	13.13 kg	5.39 kg
WEIGHT OF BURSTING CHARGE	2.72 kg	1.55 kg	1.45 kg	n/app
TYPE OF BURSTING CHARGE	TNT	RDX/aluminium	RDX/wax	n/app
MUZZLE VELOCITY	750 m/s	900 m/s	900 m/s	1680 m/s
ARMOUR PENETRATION AT 0°	n/app	432 mm/ at any range	440 mm/ at any range	330 mm/ 1000 m

Note: OF-18 is known as the extended range version and replaces the earlier OF-11 which has a muzzle velocity of about 915 m/s

actuator (a radiation threshold detector) is mounted on the right side of the turret compartment behind the compressed air tanks.

The detector/actuator senses the initial pulse of radiation (gamma or neutron pulse) which precedes the blast wave and then activates the explosive squib mechanism. The latter is a system of spring-loaded shutters, dampers, or louvres that are held open by a detent pin. When the squib mechanism is activated, an explosive charge detonates and forces the detent pin out of place, thus allowing the shutter, damper or louvre to close. The explosive squib mechanism's function is to close the engine louvres, sight aperture, bulkhead ventilation fan, air baffles to the transfer case and the air intake to the blower/dust separator. The latter is in the turret below the shell ejection port and is an electric motor mounted with a set of fan blades which draws air into the vehicle and spins it at approximately 7000 rpm.

It should be noted that the blower/dust separator removes nuclear fallout only: it does not protect crew from chemical or biological contaminates as the air is not passed through a chemical filter. The tank must pass through the contaminated area as quickly as possible and must then be decontaminated before becoming fully operational again.

Mounted at the rear of the hull is an unditching beam and two drum fuel tanks can be installed at the rear to increase

An integral spent shell ejection system, activated by the recoil of the gun, ejects the empty cartridge case out of the turret through a trapdoor in the turret rear. Of the 40 rounds (37 in command tanks) of 115 mm ammunition carried, two ready rounds are kept in the turret, one round by the gunner's feet, one by the loader's feet, 16 in the forward part of the tank to the right of the driver and 20 in the rear of the fighting compartment.

A 7.62 mm PKT machine gun mounted coaxially to the right of the main armament has a practical rate of fire of 200 to 250 rounds per minute and is fed by a belt containing 250 rounds.

The gun elevating and traversing mechanism consists of electric, hydraulic and manual controls. The gunner can elevate or depress the gun (electric/hydraulic) and both the

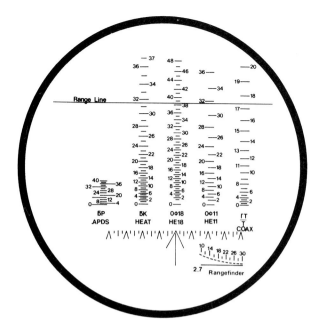

Graticule of TSh2B-41u telescope (US Army)

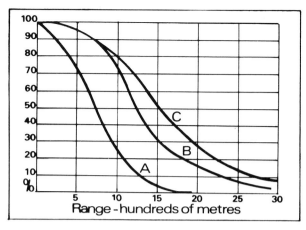

First-round hit probability of T-62 MBT with 115 mm gun showing **(A)** firing HEAT projectile from stationary T-62 at target moving at 19 km/h **(B)** firing APFSDS projectile from stationary T-62 at target moving at 19 km/h **(C)** firing APFSDS projectile from stationary T-62 at stationary target

commander and gunner can traverse the turret by electric controls through a full 360 degrees. Only the gunner can traverse the turret and elevate the gun manually. The gun is fully stabilised in both horizontal and vertical planes.

Variants

T-62A

The main differences between the T-62 and the T-62A are the contour and the size of the turret and the removal of the fixed loader's hatch on the T-62 and its replacement by a rotating cupola mounting a 12.7 mm DShKM anti-aircraft machine gun, which can be used only from outside the tank. Some machine gun ammunition boxes are stored externally on the right of the turret. There are also differences in the design of the engine covers on the T-62A. The T-62 can also be fitted with mine-clearing equipment similar to that fitted to the T-54/T-55, details of which are given in the entry for the T-54. According to American reports the T-62 tank is being updated in a similar fashion to the American M60 series improvement programme with laser rangefinder, ballistic computer, replacement of L-2G infra-red searchlight with new model and image intensification sights for both commander and gunner. The laser rangefinder is of the box type similar to that fitted on the T-54/T-55 and illustrated in the following entry.

T-62K Command Tank

In addition to having additional communications equipment, the T-62K command tank has the TNA-3 land navigation system. This appeared in 1973 and consists of six components, gyroscopic compass, one or two compass indicators, latitude correction device, an odometer, power converter and a calculator.

T-62 laying a smoke screen from the exhaust outlet in left side of tank (US Army)

The gyroscopic compass indicates on what azimuth the vehicle is travelling and is mounted in the left rear of the turret compartment and can determine direction regardless of its position within its mounting. The compass indicator is mounted in the driver's compartment or in the tank commander's cupola; some T-62Ks have two compass indicators, one at each position.

The latitude correction device, odometer, and power converter are on the left side of the tank hull in the area of the turret. This adjusts the gyroscopic compass to conform to changes in latitude. The odometer converts the rotation of the driveshaft into distance travelled in metres. The power converter supplies the electricity for the TNA-3 land navigation system.

The calculator is in the turret to the right of the gunner and takes the signal from the other components and produces a readout which is used to navigate the vehicle.

While the system is warming up, which takes about 15 minutes, the T-62K cannot be moved without damaging the gyroscopic compass. Due to drifting of the gyroscopic compass, and other mechanical factors, the system accumulates error over a period of time and after several hours needs to be reset. The system does not automatically convert slope distance travelled into correct horizontal map distances, but the operator can manually adjust for this error by moving a correction setting. In addition this correction allows for the adjustment of varying road conditions such as dry pavement, mud or snow.

Once the crew member provides the system with his initial location and the pre-determined objective's location, the calculator gives a continuous en route numerical readout of the position of the tank, and its distance and azimuth to the objective. The readout from the calculator gives the distance in metres to the right and up, from the original location. From this readout the operator can compute his grid co-ordinates.

T-62M
This is T-62A fitted with a new live track, similar in appearance to that installed on the T-72 MBT.

T-62 Flamethrower
A flamethrower version of the T-62 is in service. This has a flame gun mounted coaxially with the 115 mm gun with an effective range of 100 metres.

Modified T-62 MBT
In 1984 T-62s began appearing in the Group of Soviet Forces Germany with side skirts and smoke mortars on the turret sides. In Afghanistan similar vehicles have been seen with a thick appliqué armour panel on the hull front and a box-like appliqué armour panel on the turret front in addition to the fabric armour skirts on the sides over the suspension and side containers.

Egyptian T-62s
Some Egyptian T-62s have been observed fitted with twin launchers on either side of the turret rear for indigenously developed Sakr ground-to-ground smoke rockets.

Royal Ordnance 115 mm tank barrel
Royal Ordnance Nottingham is now manufacturing exact copies of the 115 mm tank barrel installed in the T-62 MBT for the Egyptian Army.

SPECIFICATIONS

CREW	4	FUEL CONSUMPTION		GUN CONTROL EQUIPMENT		
COMBAT WEIGHT	40 000 kg	paved road	3 – 3.3 litres/km	Turret power control	electric-hydraulic/ manual	
UNLOADED WEIGHT	38 000 kg	dirt road	1.9 – 2.1 litres/km	by commander	yes (powered only)	
POWER-TO-WEIGHT RATIO	14.5 hp/tonne	FORDING	1.4 m	by gunner	yes (electric-hydraulic/ manual)	
GROUND PRESSURE	0.83 kg/cm²	with preparation	5.5 m	Gun elevation/depression	+17°/–4°	
LENGTH GUN		GRADIENT	60%	commander's override	yes	
forward	9.335 m	VERTICAL OBSTACLE	0.8 m	Gun stabiliser		
rear	9.068 m	TRENCH	2.85 m	vertical	yes	
LENGTH HULL	6.63 m	TURNING RADIUS	skid turns	horizontal	yes	
WIDTH	3.3 m	ENGINE	Model V-55 V-12	Elevation quadrant	yes	
HEIGHT	2.395 m		water-cooled diesel with	Traverse indicator	yes	
GROUND CLEARANCE	0.43 m		injection pump fuel system,	ARMOUR		
TRACK	2.64 m		pressure lubricated,	Hull front upper	102 mm at 60°	
TRACK WIDTH	580 mm		developing 580 hp at	Hull front lower	102 mm at 54°	
LENGTH OF TRACK ON GROUND	4.15 m		2000 rpm	Hull sides upper	79 mm at 0°	
MAX SPEED		AUXILIARY ENGINE	none	Hull sides lower	15 mm at 0°	
1st gear	14.5 km/h	TRANSMISSION	manual with 5 forward and 1	Hull rear upper	46 mm at 0°	
2nd gear	20 km/h		reverse gears	Hull rear lower	46 mm at 0°	
3rd gear	29 km/h	STEERING	2-stage planetary	Hull top	31 mm	
4th gear	45.5 km/h	CLUTCH	10 driving, 9 driven steel	Hull floor front	20 mm	
5th gear	50 km/h		discs and a release	Hull floor rear	20 mm	
reverse	7 km/h		mechanism	Turret front	242 mm	
FUEL CAPACITY		SUSPENSION	torsion bar	Turret sides	153 mm	
internal	675 litres	ELECTRICAL SYSTEM	24 V	Turret rear	97 mm	
external	285 litres	BATTERIES	4 × 12 V, 150 Ah	Turret top	40 mm	
supplementary external	400 litres	ARMAMENT		Turret mantlet	included in above figures	
MAX RANGE		main	1 × 115 mm	Turret hatches	30 mm/31 mm	
paved road	450 km	coaxial	1 × 7.62 mm MG			
dirt road	320 km	anti-aircraft	1 × 12.7 mm MG (on T-62A only)			
paved road with additional fuel tanks	650 km	SMOKE-LAYING EQUIPMENT	diesel fuel injected into exhaust system			
dirt road with additional fuel tanks	450 km	AMMUNITION				
		main	40			
		coaxial	2500			
		anti-aircraft	500			

M1977 Armoured Recovery Vehicle

In the 1950s the Soviet Union developed a tank destroyer based on the chassis of the T-55 MBT. It is believed to have been called the SV-130 and was probably armed with a modified version of the 130 mm M-46 field gun. In concept and appearance it was similar to the earlier SU-100 but was produced only in small numbers as was a similar vehicle based on the chassis of the T-62 MBT. As far as it is known none of these remain in service in their original roles although some have been converted into ARVs which are very similar in appearance to the earlier SU-85-T and SU-100-T ARVs. They are limited to towing operations and as far as it is known they are not fitted with winches or other specialised recovery equipment. The Soviet designation for the ARVs based on the T-55 and T-62 assault gun chassis is not known, although the United States calls the T-62 model the M1977 ARV, or the T-62-T ARV.

Status: Production complete. In service with Afghanistan, Angola, Algeria, Bulgaria, Cuba, Czechoslovakia (limited numbers), Egypt, East Germany (limited numbers), Iran, Iraq, Israel, North Korea, Libya, Mongolia, Romania (limited numbers), Syria, USA (training), USSR, Viet-Nam, Yemen, People's Democratic Republic (South), Yugoslavia.

Manufacturer: Soviet state arsenals. The T-62 was also produced in Czechoslovakia for home and export markets. Production of the T-62 is currently being undertaken in North Korea.

T-54 and T-55 Main Battle Tanks

Development

During 1944 the Soviets designed a new medium tank called the T-44. This was produced in small numbers between 1945 and 1949, but proved unreliable in service. Main improvements over the earlier T-34/85 were its torsion bar suspension, transversely-mounted engine and transmission, well-shaped hull and a turret with a similar shape to the T-34/85 except that it did not have the thick turret neck. The T-44 was used in combat towards the end of the Second World War and again during the Hungarian uprising of 1956. Rebuilt T-44s, known as T-44Ms were still in service in the 1970s. They have also been used for training, and are still held in reserve.

The T-44 was followed by the T-54, the first prototype of which was completed in 1946 with production following in

1949. No production figures for the T-54 and T-55 have been released but it is estimated that over 50 000 were built in the Soviet Union with production also being undertaken in China (as the Type 59), Czechoslovakia and Poland. The chassis of the T-54, in a much modified form, was also used as the basis for the ZSU-57-2 self-propelled anti-aircraft gun system. The chassis of the T-54/T-55 has also been used as the basis for a 122 mm assault gun called the IT-122 which is no longer in service.

The T-54/T-55 has been used in combat in the Middle East wars of 1967 and 1973, in Angola, Viet-Nam and during the Indo-Pakistan conflicts. From all accounts it has proved to be a well-armed and armoured tank, simple to maintain and operate, has a very low silhouette, can be quickly fitted with a snorkel to allow it to ford deep rivers (a feature subsequently adopted by many Western countries), has a full range of night vision equipment and can operate in an NBC environment. Its main drawbacks are the lack of depression of its main armament, simple fire-control system which limits the range of its gun and its external fuel tanks which present a fire risk.

Description

The all-welded hull of the T-54 is divided into three main compartments: driver's at the front, fighting in the centre and the engine and transmission at the rear.

The driver is seated at the front of the tank on the left and is provided with a single-piece hatch cover that swings to the left. Two periscopes are provided forward of this hatch, one of which can be replaced by an infra-red periscope which is used

T-55 MBT used by US Army in West Germany for Opposition Forces training (US Army/Michael Green)

Soviet T-54B MBT

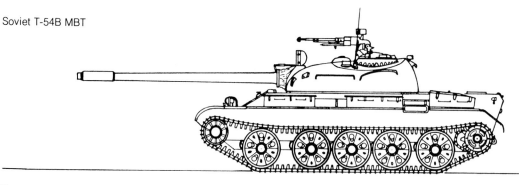

T-55 tanks on the move, with second tank (No 465) laying smoke screen

in conjunction with the infra-red light mounted on the right side of the glacis plate. The driver's infra-red system is known as the TVN-2. A narrow board mounted at right angles to the glacis plate stops water rushing up the glacis plate when the tank is fording shallow rivers. To the right of the driver are ammunition stowage, batteries and a small fuel tank. A hull escape hatch is provided behind the driver.

The turret is a one-piece casting with the top welded into position. The top consists of two D-shaped pieces of armour welded together down the centre. The commander is seated on the left of the turret, with the gunner on the same side but in front of the commander. The commander has a cupola which can be traversed through 360 degrees, with a single-piece hatch cover that opens forwards with a single periscope each side. A TPK-1 sight with a single periscope either side is mounted in the forward part of the cupola top. When in action the commander is constantly rotating his cupola for possible targets. On sighting a target he lines it up with his TPK-1 sight and then slews the turret onto the target. The gunner then lays the gun accurately onto the target and fires the main armament. The gunner has a TSh 2-22 sight with a magnification of ×3.5 or ×7. The loader is seated on the right of the turret and is provided with a single-piece hatch cover that opens to the rear and a single periscope. The T-54 does not have a rotating turret floor, but the later T-55 has, as does the T-62 MBT.

The engine is mounted transversely at the rear of the hull. The T-55 uses an electrical start-up system for the engine as its primary means, with a compressed air system for back-up in cold weather. The T-55 uses a compressed air engine start-up system primarily, with an electrical back-up. This is due to the fact that the T-55 has an AK-150 air compressor to refill the air pressure cylinders. The T-54 has no such air compressor.

The torsion bar suspension consists of five single rubber-

tyred road wheels with a distinct gap between the first and second road wheels. The drive sprocket is at the rear and the idler at the front. There are no track return rollers. The first and fifth road wheel stations are provided with a hydraulic shock absorber. The all-steel track has steel pins that are not secured at the outer end and are free to travel towards the hull. A raised piece of metal welded to the hull just forward of the sprocket drives the track pins back into position each time they pass. Like the T-62, the T-54 and T-55 are now being fitted with a new track.

The T-54 and T-55 can be fitted with a snorkel for deep fording. Two types of snorkel are available, a thin one for operational use and a thick one for training. These snorkels take between 15 and 30 minutes to fit and on reaching the far bank are blown off. The operational snorkel is mounted over the loader's periscope and when not fitted is carried disassembled at the rear of the turret, or at the rear of the hull. The

T-54 having its turret removed. Note turret has no basket (TASS)

T-54A fitted with dozer blade

T-55 MBT showing night vision equipment for commander, gunner and driver

To extend the tank's operational range two drum type fuel tanks can be fitted at the rear. On the right running board are four flat light steel tanks. The first, second and fourth tanks each contain 93 litres of fuel while the third contains lubricating oil. The driver can select which fuel tanks to use first, for example the drums at the rear, followed by the three external tanks and finally the main fuel tanks. There are three stowage boxes on the left running board, the first one for tools and other maintenance equipment, the second for gun-cleaning equipment and the third for infra-red equipment. Mounted at the very rear of the hull is an unditching beam.

When the T-54 entered service it was not fitted with night vision equipment. The first production tank to have this fitted was the T-54B and early tanks were then refitted with it. The tank is normally fitted with the following equipment: infra-red driving light which is used in conjunction with the driver's infra-red periscope and has a range of 40 to 60 metres. Mounted on the forward part of the commander's cupola is an infra-red searchlight with a range of 400 metres, while mounted to the right of the main armament is another infra-red searchlight with a range of 800 to 1000 metres.

Main armament of the T-54 is a 100 mm D-10T (originally called the M1944) rifled tank gun which was originally developed around naval gun ammunition and also used in a modified form in the SU-100 assault gun. The D-10T has a horizontal sliding wedge breech-block with the recoil system consisting of a hydraulic buffer and a hydro-pneumatic recuperator, an overall length of 5.608 metres and weight of 1948 kg. The weapon has a maximum range in the indirect fire role of 14 600 metres and can fire the following types of ammunition:

An average rate of fire for a T-54 is four rounds per minute. The D-10T gun is not stabilised but the D-10TG, first fitted to the T-54A, is stabilised in the vertical plane only while the D-10T2S, which is stabilised in both planes, is fitted in the T-54B, T-54C, T-55, T-55A and has been refitted in earlier tanks.

The turret traversing and gun elevating system was manual on early tanks but later models have full power traverse and elevation with manual controls for use in an emergency.

Mounted to the right of the main armament is a 7.62 mm SGMT machine gun and a similar weapon fixed in the centre of the glacis plate fires forward and is operated by the driver by pressing a button on the right steering lever. Mounted at the loader's position is a 12.7 mm DShKM anti-aircraft machine gun.

Variants

T-54 (Early Model)

The first model of the T-54 to enter service could not be fitted with a snorkel, had two cupolas, wide mantlet, and its turret rear had a distinctive bulbous shape.

thicker snorkel is mounted over the loader's hatch cover. The tank normally crosses the river in first gear and navigates with the aid of an onboard gyrocompass.

As originally built the T-54 was not fitted with an NBC system, which was installed on later production tanks and subsequently refitted to earlier production models. The tank can lay its own smoke-screen by injecting diesel fuel into the exhaust on the left side, producing a cloud of smoke some 300 metres long which lasts about two minutes.

AMMUNITION TYPE	AP-T	APC-T	HE	HE-FRAG	HEAT-FS	HVAPDS-T
DESIGNATION	BR-412*	BR-412D	F-412	OF-412	ZBK-5M	BM-8
FUZE MODEL	MD-8	DBR-2	RGM	V-429	VP-9	n/app
WEIGHT OF PROJECTILE	15.69 kg	16 kg	15.89 kg	15.59 kg	12.36 kg	5.69 kg
WEIGHT OF BURSTING CHARGE	0.05 kg	0.064 kg	2.159 kg	1.46 kg	1.038 kg	n/app
TYPE OF BURSTING CHARGE	RDX/aluminium	RDX/aluminium	TNT	TNT	RDX/wax	n/app
MUZZLE VELOCITY	1000 m/s	1000 m/s	900 m/s	900 m/s	900 m/s	1415 m/s
ARMOUR PENETRATION AT 0°	150 mm/1000 m	185 mm/1000 m	n/app	n/app	380 mm/at any range	200+ mm/1000 m
*Also type BR-412B which will penetrate 135 mm/1000 m						

GSP heavy amphibious ferry carrying a T-54 MBT that is fitted with long range fuel tanks and unditching beam at hull rear

T-55A(M) (foreground) clearly showing radiation covers fitted over commander's and loader's hatches with BTR-60PBs, T-54 (No 622) and T-55A(M) (No 614) tanks in background

T-54

The second production model, although the latter could have been the pre-production tank, has the normal type turret with two cupolas. On the right cupola is a 12.7 mm DShKM machine gun. When fitted with infra-red night vision equipment it is known as the T-54 (M) and is also built in China under the designation Type 59. There is a separate entry for the Type 59 MBT under China.

T-54A

This model was first seen in the mid-1950s and its main armament has a bore evacuator which was subsequently fitted to all further T-54/T-55 tanks. Its D-10TG gun is stabilised in the vertical plane only and other improvements include power elevation for the main armament, electric oil pump, bilge pump, modified air filter and an automatic fire-extinguishing system. When originally built the tanks were not fitted with infra-red night vision equipment, but most have now been fitted, and designated T-54A(M). The gunner's sight is a model TSh 2A-22.

T-54B

This model entered service in 1957/58 and was the first model to be built with infra-red night vision equipment fitted as standard. Main armament is a 100 mm D-10T2S which is stabilised in both the horizontal and vertical planes. The gunner's sight is a model TSh 2-32.

T-54C (or T-54X)

The T-54C is similar to the T-54B but the gunner's cupola has been replaced by a simple hatch that opens forwards and is not fitted with an anti-aircraft machine gun. All T-54s up to and including this model have a turret dome ventilator forward of the loader's hatch. The T-54(X) was produced during transition of production between T-54 and T-55.

T-55

The T-55 was introduced in the late 1950s and was first seen during the 1961 November parade held in Moscow. Major differences between this and the T-54 can be summarised as no loader's cupola or 12.7 mm DShKM anti-aircraft machine gun (this has since been fitted to some models), no turret dome ventilator forward of the loader's hatch, 580 hp engine, modified transmission, rotating turret floor, armament stabilised in both planes and increased ammunition

Long-range fuel drums being loaded on rear of T-54 with aid of crane

T-55A tanks fitted with laser rangefinder over main armament and two infra-red driving lights on glacis plate

stowage. When fitted with a 12.7 mm anti-aircraft machine gun the T-55 is known as the T-55(M).

T-55A

This model was seen for the first time in May 1963. Major differences from earlier members of this family are the replacement of the 7.62 mm SGMT by the more recent 7.62 mm PKT weapon, the elimination of the 7.62 mm bow machine gun (which allowed 6 more rounds of 100 mm ammunition to be carried), the base of the commander's cupola being smooth rather than bolted and both the loader's and driver's hatch covers being raised. The T-55A has an anti-radiation lining, which accounts for the thickened hatches, in the inside of the hatches as well as the turret and fighting compartment. When fitted with a 12.7 mm anti-aircraft machine gun the T-55A is known as the T-55A(M).

Differences between production tanks

Polish-produced tanks often have different stowage arrangements which include the mounting of a rectangular box on the left side of the turret, a smaller square stowage box on the left side of the turret rear and a slightly different rear decking. In 1978 a number of T-54s and T-55s were observed with a box type laser rangefinder mounted over the main armament. In 1979/80 it was reported that T-54/T-55 chassis were being converted to specialised weapons platforms of an undisclosed type.

British T-54 Retrofit Package

Late in 1984 the British company of Oceonics Vehicle Technology (OVT) announced that it had formed a consortium of companies to offer a complete retrofit pack for the T-54/T-55 tank. The two other members of the consortium were Ferranti Computer Systems who would provide the Falcon fire-control system and Rolls-Royce Motors, Military Engine Division (now part of Perkins) who would supply the CV-8 Condor diesel engine which powers the MCV-80. The CV-8 engine will be coupled to a Self-Changing Gears TN12 cross-drive transmission with six forward and one reverse gears. The original gunner's sight will be replaced by a Vickers Instruments sight. Oceonics Vehicle Technology will replace the original torsion bar suspension by a new hydro-pneumatic system based on the hydrostrut system which has already been evaluated by the British Army on a Chieftain MBT. Existing road wheels, drive sprocket and tracks will be retained.

105 mm L7 Gun Conversion

Royal Ordnance Nottingham has developed a 105 mm regunning package for the Soviet T-54/T-55 MBT.

The new weapon, the proven L7, enables a rate of fire of up to ten rounds a minute to be achieved and the elevation of +17°/−4° to be retained. The gun fires all of the standard 105 mm rounds including the L64 APFSDS-T, L52 and L28 APDS-T, L37 HESH and L38 smoke.

The crew positions in the T-55 require the gun to be loaded from the right side and controlled from the left, but the breech of the L7 normally opens in the opposite direction. The gun was therefore turned through 180 degrees.

The recoil system for the T-55s 100 mm gun included only one buffer cylinder and its operating length was greater than the requirement for the 105 mm gun. This meant the design and development of a revised recoil system, including new

Polish Army T-55 fitted with KMT-4 plough type mine clearing equipment, provision for mounting roller type mine clearing equipment on nose and launcher bins for rocket-propelled explosive hose for mine clearing at hull rear

buffer components and modified recuperator, maintaining trunnion pulls consistent with the original system and re-balanced elevating mass.

Ammunition stowage in the T-55 included 18 rounds of 100 mm within two internal fuel tanks. The larger calibre 105 mm meant redesign and manufacture of new ammunition racks and fuel tanks, together with modified clamps, and modified main and emergency firing circuits. A new telescopic graticule was required to suit the British ammunition and the coaxial machine gun. First customer for this regunning kit is Egypt. A photograph of a modified T-55 with 105 mm gun appears in Part 2 under Egypt.

T-54-T Armoured Recovery Vehicle

This ARV is equipped with a loading platform on which a spare engine can be carried, spade at the rear and jib crane which can lift a maximum weight of 1000 kg. No winch is fitted so this model has limited capabilities. A snorkel can be fitted for deep fording operations. Empty weight is 32 000 kg and crew is between three and five. The Soviet designation for this vehicle is BTS-2 (Medium Tank Towing Vehicle–2.)

T-54 (A) Armoured Recovery Vehicle

This has been developed by East Germany and standard equipment includes a push/pull bar, full range of tools, dismountable crane with a lifting capacity of 1000 kg, radiation warning equipment and a chemical warfare agent detector. The T-54 (A) ARV does not have a winch or a spade but can be fitted with a snorkel for deep fording. PT-54 or PT-55 roller mine-clearing equipment can be fitted at the front if required.

T-54 (B) Armoured Recovery Vehicle

This is also an East German development and is similar to the above but with brackets for securing tow ropes at the rear of the hull and a protective plate on the front of the hull. Like the model T-54 (A) it has no winch or spade. Weight is 32 000 kg and crew is between three and five.

T-54 (C) Armoured Recovery Vehicle

This is also an East German development and has a stowage platform, snorkel, rear-mounted spade, front-mounted dozer blade, and a heavy duty crane with a telescopic jib which can lift a maximum weight of 20 000 kg. Weight is 34 000 kg and crew is between three and five.

Czechoslovak T-55 ARV

This is similar to the T-55-T ARV but the commander is provided with a cupola on the right side of the hull. It is believed that this cupola is similar to that fitted on the T-54/T-55 MBTs and is equipped with an infra-red search-light. Armament consists of a 7.62 mm machine gun. A jib crane is provided for unloading components from the loading platform and mine-clearing rollers can be mounted at the front. This is designated MT-55, the same designation being given to the Czechoslovak designed AVLB on the T-55 chassis.

Polish T-54/T-55 ARVs

Poland has developed at least two ARVs based on T-54 or T-55 MBT chassis, designated WZT-1 and WZT-2. The WZT-1 is Polish equivalent of the BTS-2 with some differences while the WZT-2 is new design and equivalent to the T-55-K or Soviet BREM-1 on T-72 chassis.

Czechoslovak MT-55 Bridgelayer

This has been developed by Czechoslovakia as the replacement for the earlier MT-34 which was based on the T-34 tank chassis. The MT-55 is fitted with a scissors bridge which is launched hydraulically over the front of the vehicle. When opened out it is 18 metres long and will span a gap of 16 metres, and will take a maximum load of 50 000 kg. Weight is 37 000 kg and crew is two men.

East German BLG-60 Bridgelayer

This is a joint development by East Germany and Poland and is used by them in place of the Czechoslovak MT-55 bridgelayer. The scissors bridge is launched over the front of the vehicle; it is 21.6 metres long and will span a gap of 20 metres. Maximum capacity is 50 000 kg. The BLG-60 weighs 37 000 kg and has a crew of two or three men.

T-54(A) ARV with snorkel mounted for deep fording operations

T-55 MTU bridgelayer in travelling configuration

IMR combat engineer vehicle using pincer type crab to hull rear

Israeli T-54/T-55 tanks

Details of these versions are given in Part 2 under Israel.

Soviet MTU-20 Bridgelayer

The MTU-20 was developed in the late 1960s as the replacement for the older MTU and is launched in a similar manner except that when travelling the ends of the bridge are folded on top to reduce the overall length of the equipment. When opened out the bridge is 20 metres long and will span a gap of up to 18 metres; maximum capacity is 60 000 kg. The MTU-20 weighs 37 000 kg and has a crew of two.

Soviet MTU Bridgelayer

The MTU bridgelayer entered service with the Soviet Army in the late 1950s and is basically a T-54 with its turret removed and replaced by a launching system for a bridge 12.3 metres long. The bridge will span a gap of up to 11 metres and has a maximum capacity of 50 000 kg. The MTU weighs 34 000 kg and has a crew of two men.

Combat Engineer Vehicle (IMR)

This is essentially a T-55 MBT with its turret removed and replaced by a hydraulically-operated crane that can be traversed through a full 360 degrees. This is fitted with a pair of pincer type grabs which are used to remove trees and other obstacles, the grabs can be replaced by a small bucket. Mounted at the front of the hull is a hydraulically operated dozer blade which can be used in a straight or V-configuration, but cannot angle doze.

Dozer T-54

The T-54 and T-55 can be fitted with either the BTU bull-dozer blade for clearing soil and obstacles or the STU blade for clearing snow.

T-55 flamethrower tank showing flame gun mounted coaxial with 100 mm gun

flamethrower for which 460 litres of liquid are carried. Maximum range of the flame gun is 200 metres. The 100 mm main armament of the T-55 is retained.

Mine-clearing T-54 and T-55 tanks

These tanks can be fitted with a wide range of mine-clearing equipment including Czechoslovak roller and plough type systems, Soviet roller system models PT-54, PT-54M and PT-55, Soviet plough system type KMT-4, and the Soviet plough and roller type system called the KMT-5. A more recent development is the mounting on the rear of the tank of rocket-propelled charges which are launched across the minefield and once on the ground are detonated.

Local modifications

Many countries have modified the T-54/T-55 to meet their own requirements and details of such conversion work undertaken by Egypt, India, Israel, Romania and Viet-Nam will be found under their respective countries in the second part of this book.

Flamethrower TO-55

A flamethrower version of the T-55 is known to be in service with the Soviet Army and Marines under designation TO-55. This has its 7.62 mm coaxial machine gun replaced by a

SPECIFICATIONS

Model	T-54	T-55
CREW	4	4
COMBAT WEIGHT	36 000 kg	36 000 kg
UNLOADED WEIGHT	34 000 kg	33 700 kg
POWER-TO-WEIGHT RATIO	14.44 hp/tonne	16.11 hp/tonne
GROUND PRESSURE	0.81 kg/cm²	0.81 kg/cm²
LENGTH GUN		
forwards	9 m	9 m
rear	8.485 m	8.485 m
LENGTH HULL	6.45 m	6.45 m
WIDTH	3.27 m	3.27 m
HEIGHT TO TURRET ROOF	2.4 m	2.4 m
FIRING HEIGHT	1.75 m	1.75 m
GROUND CLEARANCE	0.425 m	0.425 m
TRACK	2.64 m	2.64 m
TRACK WIDTH	580 mm	580 mm
LENGTH OF TRACK ON GROUND	3.84 m	3.84 m
MAX ROAD SPEED	48 km/h	50 km/h
TOTAL FUEL CAPACITY	812 litres	960 litres
MAX ROAD RANGE	400 km	500 km
MAX RANGE		
with long range fuel tanks	600 km	600 km
FUEL CONSUMPTION	1.9 litres/km	1.9 litres/km
FORDING	1.4 m	1.4 m
with preparation	4.546 m	4.546 m
GRADIENT	60%	60%
VERTICAL OBSTACLE	0.8 m	0.8 m
TRENCH	2.7 m	2.7 m
ENGINE MODEL	V-54	V-55
ENGINE TYPE	V-12 water-cooled diesel	
ENGINE hp/rpm	520/2000	580/2000
AUXILIARY ENGINE	none	none
TRANSMISSION	manual with 5 forward and 1 reverse gears	
STEERING	clutch and brake	clutch and brake
CLUTCH	multi-plate	multi-plate
SUSPENSION	torsion bar	torsion bar
ELECTRICAL SYSTEM	28 V	28 V
BATTERIES	4 × 12 V, 280 Ah	4 × 12 V, 280 Ah

Model	T-54	T-55
ARMAMENT		
main	1 × 100 mm	1 × 100 mm
coaxial	1 × 7.62 mm MG	1 × 7.62 mm MG
bow	1 × 7.62 mm MG	none
anti-aircraft	1 × 12.7 mm MG	none
SMOKE-LAYING EQUIPMENT	diesel fuel injected into exhaust system	
AMMUNITION		
main	34	43
7.62 mm	3000	3500
12.7 mm	500	none
GUN CONTROL EQUIPMENT		
Turret power control	electro/hydraulic with manual controls for emergency use	
by commander	yes	yes
by gunner	yes	yes
Max power traverse rate	360° in 21 sec	360° in 21 sec
Gun elevation/depression	+17°/−4°	+17°/−4°
Gun stabiliser		
vertical	no	yes
horizontal	no	yes
Rangefinder type	stadiametric	stadiametric
Elevation quadrant	yes	yes
Traverse indicator	yes	yes
ARMOUR		
Hull front upper	97 mm at 58°	97 mm at 58°
Hull front lower	99 mm at 55°	99 mm at 55°
Hull sides upper	79 mm at 0°	79 mm at 0°
Hull sides lower	20 mm at 0°	20 mm at 0°
Hull rear upper	46 mm at 0°	46 mm at 0°
Hull rear lower	46 mm at 0°	46 mm at 0°
Hull top	33 mm	33 mm
Hull floor front	20 mm	20 mm
Hull floor rear	20 mm	20 mm
Turret front	203 mm at 0°	203 mm at 0°
Turret sides	150 mm at 0°	150 mm at 0°
Turret rear	64 mm at 0°	64 mm at 0°
Turret roof	39 mm at 79°	39 mm at 79°
Mantlet	included in above figures	

Status: Production complete. In service with Afghanistan, Albania, Algeria, Angola, Bangladesh, Bulgaria, Central African Republic, China, Congo (and Type 59), Cuba, Czechoslovakia, Egypt, Equatorial Guinea, Ethiopia, Finland, East Germany, Guinea, Guinea-Bissau, Hungary, India, Iraq (and Romanian M77), Israel, North Korea (and Type 59), Kampuchea, Laos, Libya, Mali, Mongolia, Morocco, Mozambique, Nicaragua, Nigeria, Pakistan (and Type 59), Peru, Poland, Romania, Somalia, Sudan, Syria, North and South Yemen, USSR, Yugoslavia, Viet-Nam, Zambia and Zimbabwe (including some from North Korea).

Manufacturers: Three Soviet tank plants plus Labedy in Poland and Martin in Czechoslovakia. Poland produced the T-54A and T-54A(M) from 1956 to 1964 and the T-55 from 1964 onward. Also manufactured in China as the Type 59.

UNITED KINGDOM

Future Tank Project

In 1983 Alvis, Royal Ordnance Leeds and Vickers Defence Systems were each awarded £100 000 contracts by the British Ministry of Defence to carry out studies for a new MBT to replace Chieftain and then Challenger in the British Army.

This project is called the Future Tank Project by the Royal Armament Research and Development Establishment (Chertsey), previously the Military Vehicles and Engineering Establishment.

It is speculated that the tank could weigh between 40 and 45 tonnes rather than the 62 tonnes of the Challenger. All possible configurations were studied including crews of two, three and four, turret-mounted gun, externally mounted gun and fixed main armament.

It is understood that all three companies proposed a tank with three crew in the hull and an overhead gun with an automatic loader.

It is believed that a concept demonstrator programme is now underway to enable the user, the Royal Armoured Corps, to decide the future crewing and configuration of the tank before a prototype is built.

Talks are also underway with other NATO countries about possible future tank collaboration for the 1990s as part of the Independent European Programme Group (IEPG).

At present, Royal Ordnance is the sole producer of Challenger MBTs for the British Army and there will be a long gap between the end of Challenger production and start of production of the new MBT, assuming that Royal Ordnance Leeds is prime contractor.

Challenger Main Battle Tank

Development

The United Kingdom began design work on a successor to the Chieftain in the late 1960s, but this was superseded in 1970 by the Anglo-German MBT which was cancelled in March 1977, as the two national replacement timetables

'have gradually diverged to such a degree that in the view of both governments collaboration on a project is no longer practicable'.

However, well before this date, in 1968, the Military Vehicles and Engineering Establishment built the prototype of a tank with an externally-mounted main gun which was followed in 1971 by another tank which incorporated Chobham armour. The latter was based on the Chieftain MBT and designated the FV4211.

In September 1978 the British Ministry of Defence issued the following statement regarding the successor to the Chieftain MBT:

'The studies of the Chieftain tank replacement have now reached the stage where it is necessary to enter into more intensive component development. Work on the first stage of the project, known as Project Definition, has therefore been started.

'The new tank must be in service by the late 1980s, when the Chieftain, despite improvements, will be coming to the end of its useful life. The successor to Chieftain will be required to match anticipated Warsaw Pact armoured and anti-armour capabilities well beyond the turn of the century and will be designed to the highest practicable standards of firepower, protection and mobility.

'Project Definition will be based on a tank of conventional turreted design carrying a four-man crew, protected by Chobham armour, and mounting a British rifled bore 120 mm gun. In the interest of standardisation and interoperability with our NATO Allies, the possibility of a closer association between our project and their own tank replacement programmes will continue to be given particularly careful consideration. We shall keep them fully informed of the progress of Project Definition.'

It was announced in Parliament in July 1979 that the Rolls-Royce Motors CV12 diesel engine had been selected for the MBT-80 in preference to the American AVCO-Lycoming AGT-1500 gas turbine engine.

In July 1980 the following Parliamentary Statement was made of future British tank policy:

Turret being lowered onto Challenger MBT chassis at Royal Ordnance Leeds (Royal Ordnance Leeds)

Challenger MBT (Royal Ordnance Leeds)

Challenger MBT hulls on the production line at RO Leeds (Royal Ordnance Leeds)

Challenger (left) and Khalid (right) turrets on the production line at RO Leeds (Royal Ordnance Leeds)

'The Army's future main battle tank requirements have been reviewed against the latest assessment of the Warsaw Pact threat and the progress of Project Definition of MBT-80. The Warsaw Pact have for many years been able to deploy more tanks in war than NATO; this advantage now stands at some 3 to 1. In addition the Soviet tanks that have entered service in recent years are technically advanced and highly effective. There is every indication that new tanks, incorporating further improvements, will come into service in the 1980s.

'BAOR's present main battle tank, Chieftain, has been in service since the 1960s. Although it is the most effective NATO tank of its generation and continues to be improved, its performance will not be fully adequate against the increasing threat. Under existing plans it would be replaced by MBT-80. But it is now clear the MBT-80 cannot be available until the early 1990s and in order to meet the threat a much earlier enhancement of BAOR's armoured capability is required.

'I have therefore decided to bring into service by the mid-1980s a new tank known as Challenger. Challenger incorporates a number of technological advances including Chobham armour and a 1200 horsepower diesel engine. Its firepower will be similar to the improved Chieftain's but its level of protection and mobility will be markedly better. An immediate order is to be placed with ROF Leeds for enough Challengers to equip one of BAOR's four armoured divisions. The estimated cost is some £300 million. The final number of Challengers to be bought will be the subject of a further study but the present assumption is that they will replace up to half the existing Chieftains in BAOR.

'The MBT-80 programme will be discontinued but a programme of tank development, building on work already done for MBT-80, will continue. The longer term requirement including the replacement of the remaining Chieftains will be the subject of further study, which will encompass the possibility of some form of collaborative project within NATO as well as the option of an improved Challenger.

'The purchase of Challenger will lead to a significant qualitative improvement in BAOR's armoured capability from the mid-1980s and by the retention in service of replaced Chieftains, will make it possible to deploy more tanks in war. In order to effect an immediate enhancement of our armoured capability I have also decided that a ninth armoured regiment should be formed in BAOR this November by reroling an armoured reconnaissance regiment. It will be equipped with Chieftains currently held in reserve for war. These measures are consistent with the objectives of the NATO Long Term Defence Programme and will, I am sure, be warmly welcomed within the Alliance.'

The first British Army order for Challenger MBTs was for 243 tanks, sufficient to equip four regiments and the first of these was handed over to the British Army by Royal Ordnance Leeds in March 1983.

In June 1984 the British Ministry of Defence placed an additional order for 64 Challenger tanks, sufficient to equip a fifth regiment in BAOR. Since then a further order for 18 Challenger MBTs has been placed and the actual size of the regiments reduced.

Challenger has already been tested in Abu Dhabi and in mid-1985 two vehicles were tested in Saudi Arabia, these had a number of modifications including the replacement of IFCS by the Marconi Command and Control Systems SFCS 600 system.

Description

Challenger is essentially the FV4030/3 (Shir 2) modified to suit the requirements of the British Army. The layout of Challenger is similar to that of Chieftain with the driver's compartment at the front, turret and fighting compartment in the centre, and engine and transmission at the rear. The turret and hull incorporate Chobham armour for increased battlefield survivability.

The driver has a single-piece hatch cover that lifts and swings forward horizontally to allow him to drive in the head out position. To the rear of this is a single wide-angle periscope which can be replaced by a Pilkington PE Badger passive periscope for driving at night. The driver can also leave the vehicle via the fighting compartment.

The commander is seated on the right of the turret with the gunner forward and below the commander and the loader on the left side of the turret.

The commander has a modified No 15 cupola which has been designated the No 32 cupola. This has a No 37 day sight which is capable of being quickly replaced by a Rank Pullen image intensification swap sight. The Rank Pullen No 37 night sight (SS 120) provides the tank commander with night surveillance, target acquisition and, if used with the PRI AV No 22 or No 24, the ability to lay the main armament. In the day mode it has a magnification of ×1 and ×5 while in the night mode when filters allow it to be used as a standby sight in full light. The cupola also has nine periscopes for all-round observation.

The No 37/swap sight is an interim solution as in July 1981 the Ministry of Defence awarded a development contract to Barr and Stroud for the Thermal Imaging Surveillance and Gun Sighting System (also known as TOGS – Thermal Observation and Gunnery System). A major sub-contractor to Barr and Stroud will be Pilkington PE. The turret has been designed to accept this system when it is available. A single thermal imager in an armoured box on the right of the turret will provide separate outputs for both commander and gunner in the relaxed mode or as a gun sight.

Delivery of Class II Thermal Imaging Common Modules for TOGS commenced late in 1983 for both Challenger and Chieftain MBTs. Rank Taylor Hobson provides the infra-red scanning modules while Marconi Avionics provides the processing electronics.

The loader has a roof-mounted ×1 periscope swivel mounted forward of the two-piece hatch cover that opens front and rear.

Main armament of the Challenger consists of a 120 mm L11A5 rifled tank gun for which between 48 and 52 rounds of ammunition are carried, this depends on the mix according to the tactical situation. This gun and its ammunition is described in the entry for the Chieftain MBT later in this section.

There are up to 42 charge stowage and 64 projectile stowage positions. Each charge location takes either one DS or two HESH/smoke charges and a typical mix would be 20 DS

Production Challenger MBT fitted with Simfire S Series weapon simulator

Production Challenger MBT from above with all hatches closed (Royal Ordnance Leeds)

and 44 HESH/smoke with all charges stowed in special containers below the turret ring. A fire suppressant fluid in these containers reduces the risk of fire.

In the future the 120 mm L11A5 gun will be replaced by a 120 mm rifled high technology gun.

A 7.62 mm L8A2 machine gun is mounted coaxially with the main armament and a 7.62 mm L37A2 machine gun is mounted at the commander's cupola. Mounted either side at the front of the turret is a cluster of five electrically-operated smoke dischargers, each with a coverage of 100 degrees. The smoke dischargers will be replaced in the future by the Royal Ordnance Visual and Infra-Red Smoke Screening System (VIRSS).

The Challenger has the Marconi Command and Control Systems Improved Fire-Control System (IFCS), this is fully described in the entry for the Chieftain MBT and has a target tracking rate of 30 mils/s in traverse and 10 mils/s in elevation. Slewing rate in traverse is 0.2 to 4000 mils/s and 0.2 to 1000 mils/s in elevation. The computer used in IFCS is a more modern design giving greater stretch potential for the future. The gun control system is similar to that installed in Chieftain but a number of units have been designed to replace the thermioc valve equipment with solid-state equivalents.

The gunner has a periscope Tank Laser Sight No 9 Mark 1 with a magnification of ×1 and ×10 with an 8.5 degree field of view. The laser rangefinder is an Nd-YAG with an operating range of 300 to 10 000 metres and an accuracy of ±10 metres for 90 per cent of shots. The gunner will also have an emergency No 87 periscopic sight.

Mounted at the rear of the turret is an NBC No 6 Mk 2 environmental control system.

Challenger is powered by a Rolls-Royce Motors, Military Engine Division, Condor 12V 1200 diesel developing 1200 bhp at 2300 rpm, this is fitted with two Garret-AiResearch turbochargers. The transmission is a David Brown Gear Industries TN37. Torque converter is a Borg Warner with lock-up clutch giving four forward and three reverse gears. Steering is a Commercial Hydraulics STN37 double differential with hydrostatic, infinitely variable control. Additional details of the engine are given in the entry for the Khalid MBT.

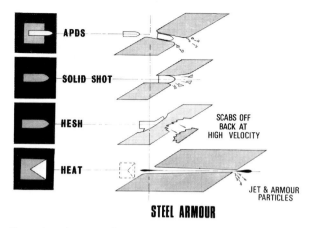

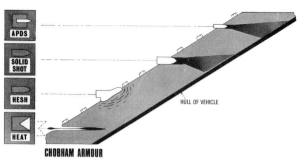

STEEL ARMOUR

Examples of present day weapons against conventional steel armour (Ministry of Defence)

Examples of present day weapons against Chobham armour (Ministry of Defence)

In July 1981 Rolls-Royce Motors was awarded a £20 million contract for Challenger powerpacks. David Brown sends the transmission and Airscrew Howden the cooling group direct to Rolls-Royce which assembles and tests the complete powerpack before it is sent to Royal Ordnance Leeds for installation in the Challenger.

The Challenger powerpack weighs 5.49 tonnes and has been designed for quick replacement in the field and can be removed by a REME LAD in under 45 minutes.

The hydrogas suspension of Challenger has been designed and developed by MVEE in conjunction with Oceonics Vehicle Technology (previously Laser Engineering Development), with production being undertaken by Royal Ordnance. Challenger has six aluminium road wheels with the drive sprocket at the rear, idler at the front and four track return rollers. The upper part of the track is covered by conventional steel skirts similar to those fitted to Chieftain.

Challenger improvements

A number of automotive improvements have been under development and most of them have now reached the stage where they have been tested on Challenger. Some of these may be retrofitted to Challengers in the future provided that sufficient funding is available.

Current production Challengers are fitted with the David Brown Gear Industries TN37 transmission with four forward and three reverse gears, using a torque converter and epicyclic gear trains controlled by multi-plate clutches. Undergoing trials is the David Brown Gear Industries TN54 transmission which would be a direct replacement for the TN37. It uses the same epicyclics but has a different clutch layout and six forward and two reverse gears. The TN54 transmission would give improved handling when manoeuvring in confined space.

Dowty Controls has developed the Digital Automotive System Control Unit (DASCU) which replaces and carries out all the functions of the present Main Engine Control Unit (MECU) mounted on the rear bulkhead and the Gearbox Controller Automatic (GCA) mounted in the driver's compartment. Existing fittings and harness are retained with the DASCU which contains built-in test equipment to monitor all systems. A key feature is the reversionary mode which allows the vehicle to keep moving with reduced performance if an essential input fails. The DASCU can be interrogated from outside the Challenger using a Husky M-208 hand-held computer.

Oil-cooled generators may be installed in Challenger; these have a generator regulator panel that is not interchangeable with the standard now fitted.

Production Challengers have a single dry pin track with removable rubber pads. Trials have already been carried out with a new double-pin track, made by Blair, to a RARDE(C) design. This is a rubber-bushed live track joined by two end connectors and a centre connector, with replaceable rubber track pads held in place by pad retainers. The new track is reversible and has a longer life and reduced rolling resistance.

When fitted with the new track, a new drive sprocket is required and a modified final drive incorporating a dipstick and filler plug on the backplate. Road wheels of a new pattern would also be installed.

Already undergoing trials on a Challenger is a hydraulic track tensioner which uses a grease-filled hydraulic ram to position the front idler.

Challenger MBT chassis being fitted with Marconi Command and Control System Marksman twin 35 mm anti-aircraft turret

Challenger with Marksman Anti-aircraft Turret

In June 1985 the Marconi Command and Control Systems Marksman twin 35 mm anti-aircraft gun turret was taken to Royal Ordnance Leeds mounted on the Centurion tank chassis which had been used for firing trials. The complete turret was then transferred to a Challenger hull which had been fitted with a suitable adaptor ring. This took 1 hour 29 minutes after which Challenger Marksman was taken out and driven at speed on the Royal Ordnance Leeds test track facility. While on the test track the radar was operating and the gun stabilisation system successfully tested.

Challenger Armoured Repair and Recovery Vehicle (CHARRV)

In June 1985 it was announced that Vickers Defence Systems of Newcastle-upon-Tyne had been awarded a contract for the development and initial production of 30 Challenger Armoured Repair and Recovery Vehicles for the British Army. Royal Ordnance Leeds was also competing for this contract and future contracts for the CHARRV will again be open to competitive tendering.

It is estimated that total value of this contract is £60 million. The first six CHARRVs will be completed from early 1987 and be used for extensive troop trials, the remaining 24 will be delivered from late 1988.

The CHARRV will be fitted with a front-mounted blade used to stabilise the vehicle when the main winch is in use or as a dozer blade, an Atlas hydraulic crane for changing complete Challenger powerpacks in the field and a winch. The vehicle will have a crew of three and four additional seats for the crew of the tank being towed.

The commander's cupola will have an externally-mounted 7.62 mm machine gun and Royal Ordnance Visual and Infra-red Smoke Screening System will be fitted as standard.

Status: In production. In service with the British Army.

Manufacturer: Royal Ordnance Leeds.

Enquiries to Sales and Marketing Director, Royal Ordnance, Griffin House, The Strand, London WC2N 5BB, England.

Model of Challenger armoured repair and recovery vehicle in travelling configuration with dozer blade raised and crane traversed to rear

SPECIFICATIONS

CREW	4
COMBAT WEIGHT	62 000 kg
UNLOADED WEIGHT	60 000 kg
POWER-TO-WEIGHT RATIO	19.35 bhp/tonne
GROUND PRESSURE	0.97 kg/cm²
LENGTH	
gun forward	11.56 m
gun rear	9.86 m
hull	8.39 m
WIDTH	
overall	3.518 m
over tracks	3.42 m
HEIGHT	
top of commander's sight	2.95 m
turret roof	2.5 m
GROUND CLEARANCE	0.5 m
Track	2.12
Track width	650 mm
Length of track on ground	4.79 m
MAX ROAD SPEED	60 km/h
FORDING	1.07 m
GRADIENT	58%
VERTICAL OBSTACLE	0.9 m
TRENCH	2.34 m
FUEL CAPACITY	1797 litres
ENGINE	Rolls-Royce Motors Condor 12V 1200 12-cylinder diesel, water-based cooled, developing 1200 bhp at 2300 rpm
AUXILIARY ENGINE	Coventry Climax H30 diesel, 3-cylinder, developing 37 bhp at 3000 rpm
TRANSMISSION	David Brown Gear Industries TN37. Borg-Warner torque converter with lock-up clutch giving 4 forward and 3 reverse gears
STEERING	Commercial Hydraulics STN 37 double differential, hydrostatic, infinitely variable
SUSPENSION	hydrogas
ELECTRICAL SYSTEM	24 V
BATTERIES	6 × 6TN (4 in hull, 2 in turret)
ARMAMENT	
main	1 × 120 mm L11A5
coaxial	1 × 7·62 mm L8A2 MG
anti-aircraft	1 × 7·62 mm L37A2 MG
SMOKE-LAYING EQUIPMENT	2 × 5 smoke dischargers
AMMUNITION	
main	44 to 52 rounds
7.62 mm	4000
GUN CONTROL EQUIPMENT	
Turret power control	electric/manual
Gun elevation/ depression	+20°/−10°
by commander	yes
by gunner	yes
Max rate power traverse	400 mils/s
Max rate power elevation	100 mils/s
commander's override	yes
Commander's fire-control override	yes
Gun stabiliser	
vertical	yes
horizontal	yes
Range setting device	yes
Elevation quadrant	yes
Traverse indicator	yes

Khalid Main Battle Tank

Development

In December 1974 Iran ordered 125 Shir 1 (FV4030/2) or FV4032, and 1225 Shir 2 (FV4030/3) or FV4033 MBTs but

Main external differences between Chieftain and Khalid are larger engine compartment of latter and different cupola

the order was cancelled by the new Iranian Government in February 1979. The first three FV4030/2 prototypes were completed by January 1977. By this time production of the FV4030/2 was well under way at the Royal Ordnance Leeds with first production tanks scheduled for delivery in 1980.

In November 1978 Jordan placed an order with the United Kingdom for 278 Khalid MBTs worth £275 million for delivery from 1981.

Further development of the Shir 2 (FV4030/3) resulted in the Challenger MBT which entered service with the British Army in 1983 and for which there is a separate entry.

Description

The Khalid is essentially the FV4030/2 with minor modifications to suit Jordanian requirements and is based on a late production Chieftain with major changes in the fire-control system and the powerpack.

The powerpack consists of the Rolls-Royce Motors Military Engine Division Condor 12V 1200 (previously designated the CV12 TCA) diesel, the David-Brown Gear Industries TN37 transmission and a cooling system by Airscrew Howden. Rolls-Royce receives the transmission and cooling system at the Shrewsbury factory, integrates them with the engine, tests the complete powerpack and sends it to Royal Ordnance Leeds for installation in the tank.

The Rolls-Royce Condor 12V 1200 is a 60-degree Vee form 12-cylinder direct injection four-cycle compression ignition engine which develops 1200 hp at 2300 rpm. The powerpacks for the Khalid (FV4030/2) and Challenger are almost identical, the only difference being that the Khalid (FV4030/2) has one hydraulic and one electric starter whereas the FV4030/3 has two electric starters.

The TN37 fully automatic transmission has been designed to provide four speeds forwards and three in reverse, using a three-element single-stage torque converter in conjunction with epicyclic gear trains. These are operated by multi-plate clutches, activated by an automatic electronic controller. Steering is by regenerative double differential type hydrostatic systems. The main vehicle service and parking brakes are incorporated within the transmission. The TN37 is arranged with a single input and two in-line outputs at right angles to

Airscrew Howden cooling group developed for FV4030/2 and FV4030/3

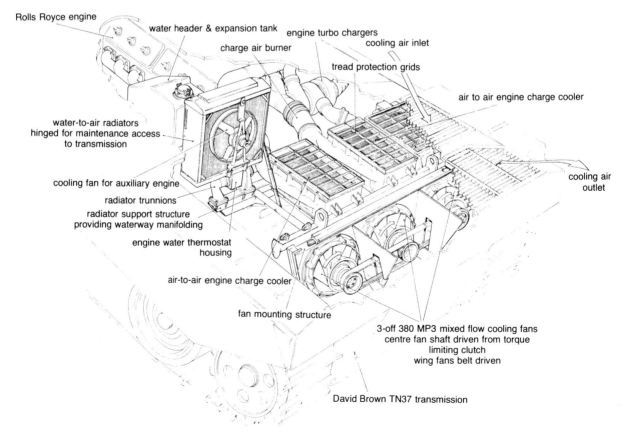

Rolls Royce engine
water header & expansion tank
charge air burner
engine turbo chargers
cooling air inlet
tread protection grids
air to air engine charge cooler
water-to-air radiators hinged for maintenance access to transmission
cooling air outlet
cooling fan for auxiliary engine
radiator trunnions
radiator support structure providing waterway manifolding
engine water thermostat housing
air-to-air engine charge cooler
fan mounting structure
3-off 380 MP3 mixed flow cooling fans centre fan shaft driven from torque limiting clutch wing fans belt driven
David Brown TN37 transmission

Khalid MBT showing commander's cupola with Pilkington PE Condor day/night sight and 120 mm L11A5 rifled tank gun fitted with thermal sleeve and muzzle reference system

the input. Flexible gear couplings are fitted to the outputs for connection to the final drives.

The requirement of the cooling group was to remove at an ambient temperature of 52°C the heat dissipated from the Condor 12V 1200 engine and the TN37 transmission, provide cooling air for the charge air, provide an additional 10 per cent of the air volume for cooling ancillaries and to provide an auxiliary power unit.

This requirement was achieved by designing a system consisting essentially of two air-to-water radiators, two air-cooled charge air-coolers and three 380 mm mixed flow fans, mounted on top of the vehicle drive transmission. Cooling air enters through armoured louvres, passes through the heat exchangers to the fans and discharges through armoured louvres. A separate fan was required for cooling the auxiliary power unit when used during the vehicle 'silent watch' situation.

The Khalid has a bogie type suspension which is a further development of that fitted to Chieftain but with nearly twice the suspension travel.

The fire-control system of the Khalid is the Marconi Command and Control Systems Improved Fire-control System which is described in the entry for the Chieftain. The Barr and Stroud Tank Laser Sight is also fitted to the Khalid.

The commander's cupola is a No 15 which has been modified to accept the Condor sight. The Condor has been developed by Pilkington PE Limited and is a combined day/passive night sight plus projector recticle image unit, and provides the commander with a 24-hour day/night vision and firing capability. Condor incorporates two independent channels for day and night use and interfaces with the main armament via the projector reticle image unit which injects optical graticule information into the sight and also enables

spot injection for the IFCS. It has a fully armoured hood, can be elevated from −10 to +35 degrees and is also provided with a wiper blade.

In December 1980 Pilkington PE Limited announced that it had been awarded a contract worth more than £6 million to supply the commander's day/night sight and driver's night driving periscope for the Khalid MBT. The contract includes the supply of the No 84 sight, reticle image projector, armoured hood and night driving periscope.

The main armament consists of a standard 120 mm L11A5 rifled tank gun, 7.62 mm L8A2 machine gun mounted

David Brown TN37 transmission

coaxially with the main armament, 7.62 mm L37A2 machine gun which can be aimed and fired from inside the commander's cupola and six electrically operated smoke dischargers either side of the turret.

The driver can exchange his day driving periscope for a Pilkington PE image intensification night periscope.

SPECIFICATIONS (as for Chieftain Mark 5 except)

WEIGHT	58 000 kg
POWER-TO-WEIGHT RATIO	20.68 hp/tonne
LENGTH (hull)	8.39 m
WIDTH	3.518 m
HEIGHT	3.012 m

Status: Production complete. In service with the Jordanian Army.

Manufacturer: Royal Ordnance Leeds.

Enquiries to Sales and Marketing Director, Royal Ordnance, Griffin House, The Strand, London WC2N 5BB, England.

Chieftain 900 Main Battle Tank

Development

Late in 1981, following the results of a market survey carried out by its own headquarters' marketing division, a decision was taken by the Royal Ordnance to go ahead as a private venture with another main battle tank subsequently named Chieftain 900. The first of two prototypes of Chieftain 900 were completed at the Royal Ordnance Leeds in April 1982 and after carrying out automotive trials, were shown for the first time at the 1982 British Army Equipment Exhibition.

Description

Chieftain 900 is based on late production Chieftain chassis with significant improvements to the three key areas of tank technology: armour protection, firepower and mobility. All this has been achieved within a weight limit of approximately 56 tonnes.

The layout of Chieftain 900 is similar to the basic Chieftain with driver at the front, commander, gunner and loader in the turret and the engine and transmission at the rear.

Chieftain 900 is fitted with the British-developed Chobham armour which provides the best known protection against all battlefield weapons including ATGW and tank guns. The glacis and hull sides are well sloped and the turret is a considerable improvement on Challenger's and other second generation main battle tanks' such as Leopard 2 and M1.

A major effort has also been made on Chieftain 900 to improve hull protection against damage from anti-tank mines.

If required, an NBC filtration system providing clean, pressurised air to the crew compartment can be fitted in the turret bustle. Another option is a roof-mounted infra-red detector, the turret-mounted control box giving audible and visual warning of a threat.

The tank can also be fitted with a standard Graviner fire warning and extinguishing system.

Chieftain 900 is armed with the semi-automatic Royal Ordnance Nottingham 120 mm L11A5 rifled tank gun which is fitted with a fume extractor, thermal sleeve and muzzle reference system for easier sighting and gun alignment. The gun fires the standard L15A4 APDS-T projectile which is effective out to 3000 metres, and the L31 HESH can be used against a variety of battlefield targets out to 8000 metres.

Chieftain 900 MBT fitted with MRS and thermal sleeve for 120 mm L11A5 rifled tank gun (Royal Ordnance Leeds)

Chieftain 900 MBT fitted with Number 15 cupola and Pikington PE Condor commander's day/night sight. Driver is in head out position (Royal Ordnance Leeds)

Training versions of both projectiles are available, as is a smoke projectile.

Inside the turret and hull are 42 charge containers which can each take one APDS or two HESH charges. Stowage for 64 projectiles is provided, the mix depending on the tactical environment, but a typical ammunition load would consist of 20 APDS and 44 HESH projectiles. The following types of ammunition can be fired:

Type	APDS-T	DS-T	HESH*	Smoke-WP
DESIGNATION	L15A4	L20A1	L31	L34
WEIGHT OF PROJECTILE	10.35 kg	5.81 kg	17.08 kg	17.35 kg
WEIGHT OF PROPELLANT, BAGGED	9.04 kg	5.77 kg	3.03 kg	3.03 kg
PROPELLANT TYPE	NQ/S53-12	NQ/S27-09	NQ/S27-09	NQ/S27-09
MUZZLE VELOCITY	1370 m/s	1370 m/s	670 m/s	670 m/s

*SH/Practice is L32A5

The 120 L11A5 gun can also fire the new APFSDS round designated the L23.

The main armament is stabilised in both azimuth and elevation and the tank commander can override the gunner and lay and fire the main armament.

A 7.62 mm L8A2 machine gun is mounted coaxially with the main armament and the tank commander has a 7.62 mm L37A2 machine gun on his cupola which can be cocked, elevated and fired from above and below the cupola. The cupola-mounted machine gun can also be dismounted for use in the ground role.

Mounted either side of the turret front is a batch of five Peak Engineering smoke dischargers, each of which provides 1800 mils coverage.

Chieftain 900 is fitted with the Barr and Stroud Tank Laser Sight (TLS) No 9 Mk 1 with a magnification of ×1 and ×10 and a NdYag laser rangefinder with an operating range of 300 to 10 000 metres. The gunner also has an emergency telescopic sight.

To give the user the widest possible selection, the prototype has not been fitted with a fire-control system. Types that could be fitted include the Marconi Command and Control Systems Improved Fire-control System (as fitted to Chieftain, Khalid and Challenger), Marconi Command and Control SFCS 600 (ordered for Indian Vickers Mk 1 and Nigerian Mk 3 MBTs), the Marconi Command and Control Systems Centaur, Ferranti Falcon and a number of systems from Barr and Stroud. All these systems are in volume production or have been widely tested in a variety of AFVs in many parts of the world and require only integration with Chieftain 900.

The tank commander has a modified Number 15 cupola with full manual contra-rotation which is provided with a day sight with a magnification of ×15 and nine periscopes for all-round observation. As in Chieftain, the tank commander can lay and fire the main armament and override the gun-laying system when it is being operated by the gunner. Alignment of the cupola with the main armament allows injection of ballistic graticule into the commander's main sight.

The loader has a single day periscope and the driver has a single wide angle day periscope that can quickly be replaced with a passive night periscope such as the Pilkington PE Badger.

Chieftain is powered by the proven Rolls-Royce Condor 900E engine which develops 900 bhp at 2300 rpm, and is turbo-charged with air-to-water charge cooling and uses a conventional mechanical governor.

The engine is coupled to the well-tried Self-Changing Gears TN12/1000 transmission with six forward and two reverse gears, engaged through a centrifugal clutch and fully automatic gear controller. As an option a semi-automatic controller is available. The regenerative drive steering brakes incorporated into the TN12/1000 gearbox are hydraulically controlled from the driving compartment.

The engine compartment is cooled by hydraulic fans designed by Airscrew Howden, which allow efficient continuous main engine operation in ambient temperatures of up to 52°C. In some tank designs a considerable amount of engine power is taken up by the cooling system, so there is less bhp at the sprocket. The cooling group for Chieftain 900 uses only about 125 bhp.

Steering is the standard hydraulic-operated regenerative disc type with the steering brakes incorporated in the gearbox.

For improved acceleration and higher top speed a spur gear final drive unit with a modified ratio of 4.14 is fitted, compared with 5.1 for Chieftain.

For silent watch a standard Coventry Climax H30 two-stroke diesel engine with a rating of 37 bhp at 3000 rpm is installed in the engine compartment.

Chieftain 900 with turret traversed right and driver's, commander's and loader's hatches closed (T J Gander)

SPECIFICATIONS

CREW	4
COMBAT WEIGHT	56 000 kg
POWER-TO-WEIGHT	
RATIO	16 bhp/tonne
GROUND PRESSURE	0.95 kg/cm²
GUN LENGTH	
forwards	10.8 m
rear	9.75 m
HULL LENGTH	7.52 m
WIDTH	
skirts	3.51 m
over tracks	3.33 m
HEIGHT	
turret top	2.44 m
TRACK	2.72 m
MAX ROAD SPEED	52 km/h
FORDING	1.07 m
GRADIENT	60%
SIDE SLOPE	30%
VERTICAL OBSTACLE	0.9 m
TRENCH	3.15 m
ENGINE	Rolls-Royce 900E 12-cylinder Condor, 60° direct injection turbo-charged 4-stroke diesel developing 900 bhp at 2300 rpm
AUXILIARY ENGINE	Coventry Climax H30 No 4, 3 vertical cylinders, 6 opposed pistons, 2-stroke compression ignition, developing 23 bhp at 2000 rpm or 37 bhp at 3000 rpm
TRANSMISSION	TN12/1000 epicyclic, 6 forward and 2 reverse gears
STEERING	hydraulically-operated regenerative disc steering brakes incorporated into gearbox
MAIN BRAKES	hydraulic-powered disc
FINAL DRIVE	spur with ratio of 4.14:1
SUSPENSION	improved bogie
ELECTRICAL SYSTEM	24 V
BATTERIES	
hull	4 × 200 Ah
turret	2 × 100 Ah
ARMAMENT	
main	1 × 120 mm L11A5
coaxial	1 × 7.62 mm L8A2 MG
anti-aircraft	1 × 7.62 mm L37A2 MG
SMOKE-LAYING	
EQUIPMENT	2 × 5 smoke dischargers
AMMUNITION	
main	64 projectiles
machine gun	4000
GUN CONTROL	
EQUIPMENT	
Turret power control	electric/manual
by commander	yes
by gunner	yes
commander's override	yes
Commander's fire-	
control override	yes
Max rate of power	
traverse	18 s per complete revolution
Max rate of power	
elevation	6 s through 30° of travel
Gun depression	−10° (180 mils)
Gun elevation	+20° (355 mils)
Gun stabiliser	
vertical	yes
horizontal	yes
Range setting device	yes
Elevation quadrant	yes
Traverse indicator	yes

Status: Two prototypes completed. Ready for production.

Manufacturer: Royal Ordnance Leeds.

Enquiries to Sales and Marketing Director, Royal Ordnance, Griffin House, The Strand, London WC2N 5BB, England.

The suspension on either side consists of three equalised bogie type units with four rubber bonded steel wheels. The front and rear stations are provided with telescopic dampers and the suspension has twice the travel of that fitted to Chieftains currently in service.

The dry pin, steel wheelpath tracks each have 98 links per side when new and for road use rubber pads can be fitted as an option.

In designing Chieftain 900, Royal Ordnance Leeds has tried to keep the initial cost as low as possible. This has been achieved by allowing the user to select from a wide range of optional equipments those which meet his own specific requirements.

In 1984 Royal Ordnance Leeds announced that a number of new options were being offered for Chieftain 900. These include the Visual and Infra-Red Smoke Screening System (VIRSS) already adopted by the British Army for its Chieftain and Challenger MBTs, new advanced auxiliary generating unit incorporating a 300 to 500-amp, air-cooled, brushless generator, air conditioning system, laser detection device, Archer advanced radio harness, solid-state gun control equipment, sighting options now include both panoramic and thermal imaging systems, Pilkington commander's day/night sight, Vickers Instruments L23 sight with laser rangefinder and the Hydrostrut suspension system which has been designed by Royal Ordnance Leeds and Oceonics Vehicle Technology.

Hydrostrut has been successfully tested on Chieftain 900 and basic Chieftain and additional details are given in the entry for the Chieftain MBT.

Chieftain Main Battle Tank

Development

In the early 1950s there were a number of proposals for a new MBT to replace both the Centurion and Conqueror tanks, but none progressed beyond the drawing board. In 1956 Leyland Motors, which was the design parent for the Centurion Mk 7, built three prototypes of a vehicle called the FV4202. This was similar in some respects to the earlier Centurion but had only five road wheels and a new turret without a mantlet, and the driver was seated reclining at the front of the hull allowing the hull's height to be reduced. Both the latter characteristics were subsequently adopted for the Chieftain MBT(FV4201), the characteristics of which were issued in 1958. The first mockup was completed in early 1959 and the first prototype late in the same year. The Chieftain was first shown to the public in 1961 when it was fitted with a false covering over the front of its hull to conceal the well-shaped glacis plate.

A further six prototypes were built between July 1961 and April 1962 and in May the following year the Chieftain was accepted for service with the British Army. Two production lines for the Chieftain were established, one at Royal Ordnance Leeds and the other at Vickers' plant at Elswick.

About 900 Chieftain MBTs were built for the British Army, with production completed early in the 1970s. In 1971 Iran placed an order for about 707 Chieftain MBTs: the Mk 3/3P and Mk 5/5P plus a quantity of ARVs and bridgelayers, all of which were delivered by 1978. Iran was considering the possibility of retrofitting its complete Chieftain fleet with the new Rolls-Royce CV-12 diesel, developing 800 hp (as against the 1200 hp for the Shir 1 and Shir 2).

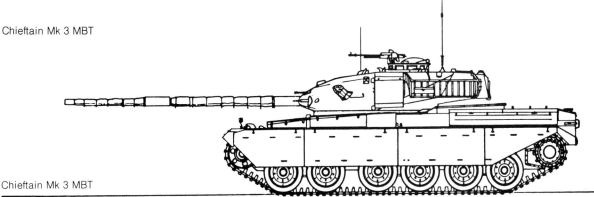

Chieftain Mk 3 MBT

Iran also took delivery of 187 improved Chieftains called the FV4030/1. These carried more fuel than the Mark 5/5P, had improved mine protection and additional shock absorbers on the rear station. They also incorporated electronic control of the Self-Changing Gears TN12 transmission to permit automatic operation and easier driver training.

In 1974 Iran ordered 125 Shir 1 and 1225 Shir 2 MBTs for delivery from 1980 but the order was cancelled in 1979 before deliveries could begin from the Royal Ordnance Leeds.

The Shir 1 (FV4030/2) was subsequently ordered by Jordan under the name Khalid and the Shir 2 (FV4030/3) is the basis for the Challenger MBT for the British Army. There are separate entries for both vehicles earlier in this section.

During fighting in the Middle East Iraq captured between 200 and 300 Chieftain MBTs from Iran, many of which were undamaged. It is reported that some of these are now being overhauled prior to delivery to Jordan.

In August 1981 Oman took delivery of 12 British Army Chieftain Mk 7/2C MBTs, which were on loan until 15 new Chieftains, called the Qayis Al Ardh by Oman, were delivered between 1984 and 1985. These Chieftains, as well as the Scorpions used by Oman, are fitted with the Vickers Instruments L20 sight which incorporates the Ferranti Type 520 laser rangefinder. It is understood that Oman has more recently increased its order to between 40 and 50 Chieftains.

Description (Mk 5)

The hull of the Chieftain is of cast sections welded together and is divided into three compartments: driver's at the front, fighting in the centre and engine at the rear. Of all tanks

Chieftain MBT with turret traversed to rear and using its front mounted dozer blade

developed in the 1950s and produced in the 1960s the Chieftain has the most powerful armament and the best armour protection. Whereas most other tanks (eg Leopard 1 and AMX-30) were developed with priority given to mobility, followed by firepower and protection last, Chieftain was designed to have firepower first, protection second and mobility last.

The driver is seated at the front of the hull and is provided with a single-piece hatch cover that lifts and opens to the right. To the rear of the hatch cover is a single wide-angle AFV No 36 Mk 1 periscope which can be replaced by an infra-red periscope for night driving, which is being superseded by a Badger passive night driving periscope developed by Pilkington PE Limited.

The turret is a two-piece casting with the loader seated on the left and the commander and gunner on the right. The commander's cupola can be traversed through 360 degrees by hand and has a single-piece hatch cover that opens to the rear, nine AFV No 40 Mk 2 observation periscopes and a single AFV No 37 Mk 4 sighting periscope. Mounted on the right side of the commander's cupola is an infra-red searchlight which is mounted coaxially with the cupola-mounted machine gun.

The gunner is seated in front of and below the commander and has a sight periscope No 59 with a magnification of ×1

Chieftain MBTs with turrets traversed to rear being driven onto an LST at Marchwood, England, for shipment to West Germany (Ministry of Defence)

Chieftain hulls on the assembly line at Royal Ordnance Leeds in 1976 (Ministry of Defence)

internal flashing indicators and creates an audible signal in the crew's headphones.

The Horstmann suspension consists of three bogies each side each with two dual road wheels and a set of three horizontal springs. The drive spocket is at the rear, idler at the front and there are three track return rollers. The first and last road wheel stations are provided with a hydraulic shock absorber. The tracks are of cast steel with dry pins and replaceable rubber pads. Each track has 96 links when new and the total weight of the pair of tracks on the Chieftain is 4719 kg. The top half of the track is covered by an armoured skirt which can be removed for maintenance.

An air ventilation and filtration system is mounted in the rear of the turret which provides the crew with clean air for normal ventilation and works in conjunction with an NBC filter pack (No 6 Mark 2) which does not require the crew to wear respirators inside the tank.

Mounted on the turret roof is an infra-red detector which has three silicon photo-voltaic cells covering 360 degrees. Any infra-red light source detected can be localised to within an arc of about 62 degrees. A snorkel kit developed for the Chieftain was not issued for service use. The Chieftain can be fitted with a navigational aid.

Block diagram of Marconi Command and Control Systems Improved Fire-control System

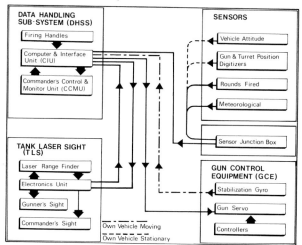

Barr and Stroud TLS No 1 Mk 2 System

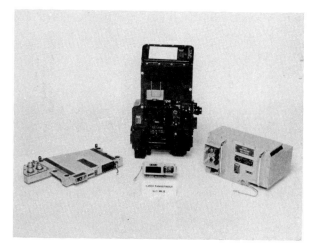

and ×8 or a Barr and Stroud Tank Laser Sight Unit. The gunner also has a No 7 telescopic sight. Both the commander and gunner can replace their day sights with an infra-red sight with a magnification of ×3: the commander's night sight is the L1A1 and the gunner's an L3A1.

The loader has a two-piece hatch cover that opens to the front and rear of his position and a folding rotatable periscope AFV No 30 Mk 1.

Mounted on the left side of the turret is a Marconi Command and Control Systems infra-red/white light searchlight. The very high intensity light operates as a target illuminator and is mounted directly onto the gun turret so that it remains in line with the gun during traverse. In elevation a servo-control system on the mirror assembly ensures that the light beam remains aligned automatically onto the target. The searchlight has a range in the infra-red mode of at least 1000 metres and a range in the white-light mode of at least 1500 metres. The searchlight overhangs the side of the turret and has an armoured cover.

The NBC system is mounted in the rear of the turret and at the very rear of the turret is a stowage basket.

The engine is at the rear of the tank and is coupled to a TN12 gearbox.

The TN12 epicyclic gearbox incorporates a Merritt-Wilson differential steering system and electro-hydraulic gear selector. It has six forward and two reverse gears plus an emergency mechanical selector of second gear forward and low reverse.

Of five portable fire extinguishers provided two large ones are mounted in the engine compartment. A Firewire automatic fire-detection system actuates a warning horn and

Chieftain Mk 6 MBT (Simon Dunstan)

Some Chieftains have a dozer blade mounted on the front of the hull consisting of an electro-hydraulic power pack which is fitted in place of the right hand front stowage bins. The blade itself is aluminium and is operated by the driver who is provided with a joystick control unit. A plough type mine clearing unit has been developed for the Chieftain.

Main armament is a 120 mm L11A5 rifled tank gun which is provided with a fume extractor and a thermal sleeve. It has a vertical sliding breech-block and a maximum rate of fire of eight to ten rounds for the first minute and six rounds a minute thereafter.

The ammunition is of the separate loading type, ie projectile and charge. The projectiles are stowed alongside the driver, under the gun and in the turret and the charges are stored in pressurised water bins below the turret bin. The gun can fire the following types of Royal Ordnance ammunition:

Type	APDS-T	DS-T	HESH*	Smoke-WP
DESIGNATION	L15A4	L20A1	L31	L34
WEIGHT OF PROJECTILE	10.35 kg	5.81 kg	17.08 kg	17.35 kg
WEIGHT OF PROPELLANT,				
BAGGED	9.04 kg	5.77 kg	3.03 kg	3.03 kg
PROPELLANT TYPE	NQ/S53-12	NQ/S27-09	NQ/S27-09	NQ/S27-09
MUZZLE VELOCITY	1370 m/s	1370 m/s	670 m/s	670 m/s

*SH/Practice is L32A5

More recently the new APFSDS round designated the L23 has been introduced into service. In the future it is expected that the current 120 mm L11A5 tank gun will be replaced by a new 120 mm rifled high technology gun which will also be retrofitted to the Challenger MBT.

Mounted coaxially to the left of the main armament is a 7.62 mm L8A1 machine gun. The commander's cupola is provided with a 7.62 mm L37A1 machine gun which can be aimed and fired from within the tank. A 12.7 mm (0.50) L21A1 ranging machine gun is mounted over the main armament. Originally this was effective only out to 1800 metres but it is now effective out to 2500 metres. This has now been removed from all British Army Chieftain MBTs. Mounted either side of the turret is a bank of six electrically-operated smoke dischargers.

The gun control system is a Marconi Fighting Vehicle Gun Control Equipment (FV/GCE) No 7 Mk 4 which is a further development of the system used so successfully on the Centurion. This has the following modes of operation: stabilised power control, power control, emergency battery control and emergency hand control.

When originally introduced into service the Chieftain was provided with a 12.7 mm ranging machine gun (RMG) as the main means of aiming its 120 mm gun. For an APDS engagement the gunner fires short bursts from the RMG using four predetermined graticule marks. The burst which lands over the target indicates which main armament graticule mark should be used. Using this method the target can be engaged quite rapidly. For the lower velocity HESH ammunition up to 2000 metres the RMG is used for obtaining the close bracket required for this round which has a higher trajectory. The main armament is not fired until a hit is virtually a certainty.

In the early 1970s the Barr and Stroud Tank Laser Sight Unit was introduced; the first model was the No 1 Mk 1 (in production from 1973/74), which was followed by the No 1 Mk 2 (1974/76), No 3 Mk 1 (1976/78) and the No 4 Mk 1 (which entered production in 1978). The Tank Laser Sight Unit houses the laser transmitter module and optical system, the receiver system and the optical sight system. The line of sight in elevation is synchronised with the axis of the gun by means of a precision parallel linkage, and in azimuth by coincident turret mounting. Final boresighting is achieved by instrument-mounted controls. Gun laying is achieved through a ballistic graticule. Laser ranging may be initiated by the gunner or remotely by the tank commander; the range is displayed in the left eyepiece and remotely displayed at the commander's station. In a 'smoke' situation, target range uncertainty is effectively diminished by selection of first and last range logic. The laser has an operating range of 500 to 10 000 metres and is accurate to ±10 metres for 90 per cent of shots.

Chieftain MBT of British Army showing thermal sleeve for 120 mm L11A5 rifled tank gun (United Kingdom Land Forces)

Chieftain Mark 5 with all hatches closed showing external stowage (Royal Ordnance)

The British Army's Chieftain fleet (except Mk 1s) has now been retrofitted with the fully-integrated IFCS (Improved Fire-Control System) developed and manufactured by Marconi Command and Control Systems. The installation of this system has at last allowed the full potential of the 120 mm L11A5 gun to be exploited when firing at the halt or on the move. IFCS provides a significantly higher first-round hit probability on stationary tank targets of at least 3000 metres and on moving targets out to more than 2000 metres.

Originally developed for the Chieftain, the IFCS has now been adapted for use in other tanks with different armament and sights. The IFCS has already been installed in the Leopard 1 (with successful firings in 1979), and has been adopted for the Khalid and Challenger as the Computer Sighting System (CSS).

The IFCS uses the Marconi 12-12P digital computer, which is programmed for the specific combination of tank, gun and ammunition carried. It automatically gathers and updates information from various sensors, calculates the ballistic solution and correct laying offsets for each target engagement, and controls the automatic laying of the gun in line and elevation (with tracking of moving targets) in readiness to fire. Both gunner and commander have full fire controls, and the commander has override control and can manually insert data whenever desired.

The system comprises four sub-systems; the data handling sub-system (DHSS) with the 12-12P digital computer, commander's control and monitor unit, and the firing handles; the sighting sub-system with the Tank Laser Sight (TSL) and wiring ellipse electronics; the sensor sub-system of various sensors located about the tank: for example, wind direction and velocity, air temperature and pressure, trunnion tilt, angle of sight, charge temperature, barrel wear, target displacement and ammunition type, and processing electronics; and the gun control equipment (GCE) which has been uprated for IFCS as the FV/GCE No. 10 and No. 11.

During trials with the IFCS a Chieftain crew obtained nine first-round hits within 53 seconds at ranges of 1600 to 2900 metres in a 950 mil arc with three hits on each of the two turret targets (1 × 1.2 m) and one larger (1.6 × 2 m).

Marks of the basic Chieftain MBT
Mk 1 of which 40 were built and issued for training in 1965/66, 585 bhp engine

Mk 1/2 is Mk 1 brought up to Mk 2 standard and used for training

Mk 1/3 is Mk 1 with a new powerpack and used for training

Mk 1/4 is Mk 1/1 with a new powerpack and modified RMG, used for training

Mk 2 was the first model to enter service, first issued in 1967, with a 650 bhp engine

Mk 3 entered service in 1969, has improved auxiliary generator, 650 bhp engine, dry-air cleaner element, modified No 15 Mk 2 cupola with L37A1 7.62 mm machine gun, oil-filled top rollers, axle arms and track tensioner

Mk 3/G was a prototype only with turret air-breathing for engine aspiration

Mk 3/2 is Mk 3/G modified

Mk 3/S is production model of Mk 3/G with turret air-breathing and commander's firing switch

Mk 3/3 is Mk 3 with extended range RMG, fitted to accept the Barr and Stroud laser rangefinder, modified 720 bhp engine, new low-loss air cleaner system, turret aspiration and modified NBC pack

Mk 3/3P is Mk 3/3 export version for Iran

Mk 4, of which only two were built, had increased fuel capacity and other minor modifications

Mk 5 is a development of the Mk 3/3 with uprated 720 bhp engine and strengthened gearbox, gunner's telescope and commander's collimator fitted with graticule for use with extended range RMG ammunition, modified exhaust system, air cleaning filters for generator, battery heating and lagging, new type gun clamp to accept new thermal sleeve, modified charge bins, improved No 43 gunner's telescope mounting, improved stowage, 50 per cent reduction in RMG ammunition-carrying capacity, increase in APDS projectiles carried, No 37 Mk 4 commander's sight, stabilised infra-red detector, commander's machine gun elevation to 90 degrees and new NBC pack

Mark 5/2K is Mk 5 for Kuwait, produced by Royal Ordnance Leeds and Vickers at Elswick with final vehicles completed late in 1979

Mk 5/5P is a Mk 5 for Iranian Army

Mk 6 is Mk 2 with a new powerpack and modified RMG

Mk 7 is Mk 3 and Mk 3/S with an improved engine and modified RMG

Mk 8 is Mk 3/3 with above modifications

Chieftain Mk 5 MBT from rear with all turret hatches closed. NBC pack is mounted at turret rear (Royal Ordnance)

Chieftain ARV with Centurion MBT in background (Simon Dunstan)

Mk 9 is Mk 6 with IFCS
Mk 10 is Mk 7 with IFCS
Mk 11 is Mk 8 with IFCS
Mk 12 is Mk 5 with IFCS.

Variants

Re-engined Chieftain (Chieftain 800)
Shown for the first time at the 1980 British Army Equipment Exhibition was a Chieftain powered by a Rolls-Royce CV12 TCE 12-cylinder diesel developing 800 hp at 2300 rpm, coupled to a TN12 Merritt-Wilson gearbox with electro-hydraulic controls.

Chieftain with Hydrostrut Suspension
For trials purposes a Chieftain MBT has been fitted with the Hydrostrut suspension system developed by Royal Ordnance Leeds and Oceonics Vehicle Technology. The Hydrostrut features the hydrogas suspension units fitted to the Challenger MBT which were designed by Oceonics Vehicle Technology and built by Royal Ordnance Leeds. The Hydrostrut unit is mounted on a twin suspension bracket. No hull modifications are needed and many standard components, such as hubs and top rollers, are retained. Each road wheel is independently sprung and obviates the problem of the existing systems where travel is limited if two adjacent wheels rise together. To compensate for variations in ambient temperature, terrain profile or changes in vehicle weight, the gas pressure and therefore spring stiffness and ride height can be quickly adjusted in the field.

Chieftain/Challenger Armament (CHARM)
In the future the L11A5 gun will be replaced by the new L30 high-pressure rifled gun system in both Chieftain and Challenger, this system is called the L30 CHARM Chieftain/Challenger Armament.

Chieftain with Gas Turbine
Late in 1984 it was confirmed that a reconditioned Garrett Turbine Company GT601 gas turbine was to be supplied to the United Kingdom for installation in a Chieftain MBT for trials purposes. The engine will be coupled to the existing TN12 suspension.

Chieftain Armoured Recovery Vehicle (FV4204)
The Chieftain ARV was manufactured by Vickers at Elswick and was based on the chassis of the Mk 5 Chieftain MBT. The main double capstan winch with electro-hydraulic controls was provided with 122 metres of 28 mm diameter cable. The similar auxiliary winch was hydraulically operated and was provided with 260 metres of 11 mm diameter cable. Power for both winches is taken from a PTO on the main engine. Mounted at the front of the ARV was a hydraulically-operated dozer blade which, when lowered, allowed the vehicle to exert a pull of up to 90 000 kg. The Chieftains delivered to Iran had an Atlas AK 6000M crane which can lift a maximum load of 5803 kg. The Chieftain ARV has a crew of four and a loaded weight of 56 000 kg. Armament consists of a cupola-mounted 7.62 mm machine gun and smoke dischargers.

Armoured Repair and Recovery Vehicle
At present the British Army uses the FV434 armoured repair vehicle to change the powerpacks of the Chieftain MBT. The latter cannot however lift the complete powerpack of the new Challenger MBT and for this reason the Chieftain Armoured Repair and Recovery Vehicle (ARRV) has been introduced. This is essentially a Chieftain ARV fitted with a hydraulic crane that can lift a complete Challenger MBT powerpack. ARRVs will be conversions from existing ARVs.

Chieftain Armoured Vehicle-Launched Bridge (FV4205)
The Chieftain AVLB is basically a Chieftain MBT chassis without a turret and fitted with a hydraulic system for laying and recovering a bridge. The vehicle can carry and lay either a No 8 or a No 9 Tank Bridge. The No 8 Tank Bridge is carried folded and launched over the front of the vehicle. It has an overall length of 24.384 metres and can span a gap of up to 22.86 metres (hard banks) or 22.25 metres (soft banks). The No 9 Tank Bridge is carried horizontal and is swung vertically through 180 degrees and laid in position over the front of the vehicle. The No 9 Tank Bridge is 13.411 metres long and can span a gap of up to 12.192 metres (firm banks). The Chieftain AVLB (with No 8 Tank Bridge) weighs 53 300 kg and has a crew of three.

Chieftain Mk 6 AVLB
The Chieftain Mk 6 AVLB is an early Chieftain gun tank

Chieftain AVLB carrying No 8 Tank Bridge in folded position (Ministry of Defence)

Chieftain AVLB laying No 8 Tank Bridge in position (Ministry of Defence)

Chieftain AVLB crossing No 8 Tank Bridge it has just laid in position (Ministry of Defence)

converted to the AVLB role. It has a more powerful hydraulic pump and modified toe plate for mounting the Pearson Track Width Mine Plough (TWMP). The bridge boom also has a built-in intercom to assist in the picking up of laid bridges.

Chieftain Assault Vehicle Royal Engineers (FV4203)

This was a project only and did not enter service with the British Army. Most of the roles envisaged for it are carried out by the Combat Engineer Tractor.

Prototype of Chieftain SABRE with twin 30 mm self-propelled anti-aircraft gun system (Royal Ordnance)

Chieftain SABRE SPAAG

The Chieftain SABRE self-propelled anti-aircraft gun system is a joint development by Royal Ordnance Leeds, responsible for the Chieftain chassis, and Thomson-CSF of France responsible for the SABRE turret armed with twin 30 mm cannon. First prototype of the Chieftain SABRE was completed in late 1983. This is a private venture and has not so far entered production.

Chieftain 155 mm SPG

This is a Chieftain chassis fitted with the Vickers Shipbuilding and Engineering Ltd GBT 155 155 mm turret. It has not entered production.

SPECIFICATIONS

Model	Mk 3	Mk 5
CREW	4	4
COMBAT WEIGHT	54 100 kg	55 000 kg
UNLOADED WEIGHT	51 460 kg	53 500 kg
POWER-TO-WEIGHT RATIO	13.49 bhp/tonne	13.63 bhp/tonne
GROUND PRESSURE	0.84 kg/cm²	0.9 kg/cm²
LENGTH GUN		
forwards	10.79 m	10.795 m
rear	9.865 m	9.87 m
LENGTH HULL	7.52 m	7.518 m
WIDTH		
including searchlight	3.657 m	3.657 m
over skirts	3.504 m	3.504 m
over tracks	3.327 m	3.327 m
HEIGHT OVERALL	2.895 m	2.895 m
GROUND CLEARANCE	0.508 m	0.508 m
TRACK	2.718 m	2.718 m
TRACK WIDTH	610 mm	610 mm
LENGTH OF TRACK ON GROUND	4.8 m	4.8 m
MAX ROAD SPEED	48 km/h	48 km/h
FUEL CAPACITY	950 litres	950 litres
MAX RANGE		
road	400–500 km	400–500 km
cross-country	200–300 km	200–300 km
FORDING	1.066 m	1.066 m
GRADIENT	60%	60%
VERTICAL OBSTACLE	0.914 m	0.914 m
TRENCH	3.149 m	3.149 m
ENGINE	Leyland L60, 2-stroke, compression ignition, 6-cylinder (12 opposed pistons) multi-fuel	
ENGINE MODEL	No 4 Mk 6A	No 4 Mk 8A
OUTPUT	730 bhp at 2100 rpm	750 bhp at 2100 rpm
AUXILIARY ENGINE	Coventry Climax H30 No 4 3-cylinder, vertically-opposed compression ignition developing 23 bhp at 2000 rpm	

Model	Mk 3	Mk 5
TRANSMISSION	TN12 with 6 forward and 2 reverse gears plus emergency mechanical selection for 2nd gear forward and low reverse	
STEERING	Merritt regenerative incorporated in TN12	
CLUTCH	centrifugal	centrifugal
SUSPENSION	Horstmann	Horstmann
ELECTRICAL SYSTEM	28.5 V	28.5 V
BATTERIES	200 Ah (4 × 12 V) batteries in hull for engine starting and general electrical services. 100 Ah (2 × 12 V) in turret for radio load and emergency power supply to fighting equipment	
ARMAMENT		
(main)	1 × 120 mm	1 × 120 mm
(coaxial)	1 × 7.62 mm MG	1 × 7.62 mm MG
(anti-aircraft)	1 × 7.62 mm MG	1 × 7.62 mm MG
(RMG)*	1 × 12.7 mm MG	1 × 12.7 mm MG
SMOKE-LAYING		
EQUIPMENT	2 × 6 smoke dischargers mounted on each side of turret	
AMMUNITION		
(main)	53	64
(7.62 mm)	6000	6000
(12.7 mm)*	600	300
GUN CONTROL		
EQUIPMENT		
Turret power control	electric/manual	electric/manual
by commander	yes	yes
by gunner	yes	yes
Max rate power		
traverse	360° in 16 s	360° in 16 s
Gun elevation/		
depression	+20°/−10°	+20°/−10°
commander's override	yes	yes
Commander's fire-		
control override	yes	yes
Gun stabiliser		
vertical	yes	yes
horizontal	yes	yes
Range-setting device	yes	yes
Elevation quadrant	yes	yes
Traverse indicator	yes	yes

* When fitted with the IFCS the RMG and its ammunition is removed. IFCS is only in British Army Chieftains and not in Iranian or Kuwaiti vehicles.

Status: Production complete but can be resumed if further orders are received. In service with Iran, Iraq, Kuwait (165), Oman and the United Kingdom.

Manufacturers: Royal Ordnance Leeds. Vickers Defence Systems, Armstrong Works, Newcastle-upon-Tyne NE99 1CP.

Enquiries to Sales and Marketing Director, Royal Ordnance, Griffin House, The Strand, London WC2N 5BB, England.

Vickers Main Battle Tank Mark 7

Development

Vickers was one of the first companies in the world to have access to Chobham Armour, and immediately began to design and build a completely new tank, the Valiant, to use this armour to the full. Valiant is described in detail in its own entry.

Following a trial in the Middle East, interest was expressed in a tank which combined the firepower and turret system of Valiant with a more powerful engine. The most powerful tank engine available is the MTU 873 Ka 501 and Mark 7 was designed to use this engine. Full development began in 1984 and a prototype Vickers Mark 7 was demonstrated in Egypt in the summer of 1985.

Description

The Vickers Mark 7 is a conventional main battle tank carry-ing a crew of four and is divided into three compartments. The driver and 20 rounds of main armament ammunition occupy the front of the hull. The turret is mounted centrally and the engine and transmission are in the third compartment at the rear.

The driver sits in a reclining seat at the right hand side of the hull. His controls are very similar to those in an automatic transmission car, with steering by a wheel, and conventional foot-operated accelerator and brake pedals. On his left in the well protected hull front is a container with 20 rounds of main armament ammunition.

The welded steel turret has a layer of appliqué Chobham armour added on the front and sides and is mounted on a ballrace, the outer ring of which is fixed on the hull and incorporates a traversing rack.

The commander sits on the right, the gunner in front and below him, with the loader on his left. All three are positioned on a turntable which rotates with the turret, is supported on steadying rollers, is covered in non-slip aluminium tread-plate, and also carries stowage for ready use ammunition.

Vickers Mark 7 MBT undergoing trials in the United Kingdom with the turret traversed to right and showing roof-mounted SFIM commander's sight and Philips stabilised panoramic thermal sight

Vickers Mark 7 MBT with turret traversed to left and clearly showing thermal sleeve for 120 mm Royal Ordnance L11A5 rifled tank gun

Vickers Mark 7 MBT being put through its paces during initial mobility trials conducted in the United Kingdom in the summer of 1985. Turret is traversed to rear and 120 mm rifled tank gun is in travel lock

The complete weapon system is stabilised by the Marconi Command and Control Systems Centaur 1 fully integrated gun and fire-control system. The gun may be slaved to either the commander's gyrostabilised day sight or the gyrostabilised thermal sight or may be stabilised in space from a two axis gyro mounted under the breech.

The fully transistorised gun control equipment interfaces with the ballistic computer and gives rapid reaction and accurate aiming. It provides power drives actuated by the gunner's controller, with the commander having override facilities via his gyrostabilised sight controls. The fire-control computer is designed as an integral part of the Centaur 1 weapon control system. It operates in conjunction with the gunner's telescopic laser sight, the commander's gyrostabilised panoramic laser sight, the thermal imaging system and the gun control equipment.

The computer stores ballistic and other information. It receives target range from the gunner's or the commander's laser rangefinder. Target angular rate is automatically fed in as the gunner or commander track the target. The tilt of the gun trunnion axis is obtained from a tilt sensor mounted on the gun. The type of ammunition, barrel wear, charge temperature, etc are fed into the computer manually.

The system injects into the gunner's sight an aiming mark which is superimposed on the sight graticule, when the gunner acquires the target. He initiates the fire-control sequence by pressing the laser button as he starts to track the target. After about three seconds, when the gunner is satisfied with his tracking he releases his laser button.

As the corrections are computed the aiming mark moves ahead of the target and the computer, by injecting signals into the traverse and elevating systems, causes the gun to move and puts the aiming mark onto the target. The gunner makes any fine corrections and fires when ready.

The gunner is provided with a Vickers Instruments L31 telescopic laser sight as his main sight. This sight is mounted through the rotor coaxially with the main armament, thus eliminating the errors normally associated with mechanical linkages. The sight is monocular and has a magnification of ×10 and is fitted with an Nd Yag laser rangefinder and a cathode ray tube for injection of fire-control data.

In addition to his main sight the gunner is also provided with a Vickers Instruments GS10 periscopic sight. This sight is mounted in the turret roof and provides a wide-angle ×1 field of view and is used for surveillance and target acquisition.

The tank commander is provided with a ring of six fixed ×1 periscopes around his hatch to give all-round vision. The commander's main sight is a SFIM VS 580-10 panoramic sight which allows the commander to scan through a full 360 degrees without moving his head. Two degrees of magnification, ×3 and ×10, are provided and the gyrostabilised head enables the commander to hold the sight accurately on target from the moving vehicle. An Nd Yag laser rangefinder incorporated in the sight enables the commander to engage targets and fire on the move.

Indicators in the commander's sight's right eyepiece show the position of the vehicle axis, the sight axis and the gun axis. Fire-control information from the computer and laser is displayed in the left eyepiece.

When used in the surveillance mode the commander has the facility to align his main sight with any one of his six periscopes. This is achieved by pushing a button mounted under that periscope.

When firing on the move the commander commences an engagement by pressing his laser fire button; the laser does not fire but the computer is informed that a tracking sequence has commenced. He then tracks the target with his thumb controller. After a few seconds when he is satisfied that he has a steady track he releases the laser fire button and the laser fires and gives the target range to the fire-control computer. The computer calculates the super elevation from the range and lead angle from the target tracking rate. This information is fed into the gun control equipment and the turret is slaved in traverse and elevation to the correct aiming point. When this is achieved a ready to fire light is illuminated in his sight and he maintains his track. The commander can now press the firing switch; the gun will only fire when the gun and sight are in absolute alignment but the delay will be only milli-seconds.

In addition to these sighting systems, a gyrostabilised panoramic thermal sight (Philips UA 9090) is mounted on the turret roof. This provides a thermal picture on 625-line television monitor for both the commander and gunner. A graticule injected into the sight picture enables the sight to be used for engaging targets in the normal way. An auto-scanning device is provided to allow the crew members to rest. Changes in the thermal picture within a pre-set arc cause an alarm to sound.

Mounted on the main armament is a muzzle reference system designed to allow gun/sight alignment to be rapidly checked and, if necessary, adjusted from under armour. This system can be used with the gun at any angle of elevation.

The loader has a single-piece hatch cover that opens to the rear, in front of which is an AFV No 30 Mark 1 observation periscope.

Mark 7's main armament is the Royal Ordnance 120 mm L11A5 rifled tank gun, although a Rheinmetall 120 mm smooth-bore can be fitted if preferred. Both carry a muzzle reference system, fume extractor, and thermal sleeve. Either the commander or gunner can lay and fire the gun.

A 7.62 mm Hughes Helicopters Chain Gun mounted coax-ially to the left of the main armament is belt fed from an ammunition bin that is replenished by the loader. Because ammunition feed to this gun is electrical, a misfired round does not cause a stoppage.

The powerpack consists of the engine, gearbox and auxiliary equipment installed as a unit.

Power is provided by an MTU 873 Ka501 diesel, rated at 1500 bhp (1100 kW).

The engine is cooled by annular radiators mounted horizontally above the transmission. Two cooling fans mounted within the radiators are driven by hydraulic motors powered by an engine-driven pump. Cooling air is drawn by centrifugal fans through louvres in the top deck of the transmission compartment, blown through the annular radiators and expelled through louvres in the rear of the tank.

Power from the engine is transmitted by a torque converter to the gearbox and into the final drives.

The gearbox is the Renk HSWL 354/3. This unit contains the gearchange and steering mechanisms. Four forward and two reverse gears are provided. Gearchanging is automatic with an override for the driver. In the event of a system failure, one forward and one reverse gear can be manually selected.

Power from the gearbox is transmitted to the sprockets by two planetary final drive units.

The driver has a steering wheel which operates hydraulic valves on the steer unit in the gearbox casing. The hydro-static steering mechanism provides regenerative steering at all steering radii.

A dual main braking system is provided consisting of a hydro-dynamic retarder backed up by power operated disc brakes. The suspension is of the torsion bar type with seven dual rubber-tyred road wheels on each side, idler at the front, drive sprocket at the rear and four track return rollers. In addition the first, second, third, sixth and seventh wheel stations incorporate rotary shock absorbers. Upward movement of the suspension is limited by bump stops which provide a progressive deflection resistance up to the solid bump condition.

The Diehl rubber-bushed end-connector tracks can be fitted with rubber pads to reduce damage to road surfaces.

The Mark 7 has three features which reduce the likelihood of its detection by night sights and other heat sensing devices. These are its coat of infra-red reflective paint, the mixing of the hot exhaust gases with the cooling air before discharge and a new design of the thermal sleeve.

Standard equipment includes a fixed fire-extinguishing system in the engine compartment and NBC pack in the hull. The latter pressurises the interior of the vehicle to about 35 mm water gauge. A relief valve on the underside of the turret bustle vents excess air to the atmosphere. The pack can also be used for ventilation in which case the NBC filters are by-passed. Optional equipment includes air conditioning, an automatic fire detection and suppression system and a 12.7 mm anti-aircraft machine gun.

SPECIFICATIONS

CREW	4	ACCELERATION (0-100m)	11.8 seconds	AMMUNITION 120 mm	44 rounds 120 mm Rheinmetall or 38 rounds 120 mm Royal Ordnance
COMBAT WEIGHT	54 640 kg	FORDING	1.7 m		
UNLOADED WEIGHT	52 640 kg	GRADIENT	60%		
POWER-TO-WEIGHT		SIDE SLOPE	30%	7.62 mm	3000
RATIO	27.45 bhp/tonne	VERTICAL OBSTACLE	1.1 m	GUN CONTROL	
GROUND PRESSURE	0.84 kg/cm²	TRENCH	3 m	EQUIPMENT	
LENGTH		TURNING RADIUS	pivot	Turret power control	electric/manual
gun forwards	10.95 m	ENGINE	MTU MB 873 Ka 501 4-stroke,	by commander	yes
gun rear	9.77 m		12-cylinder turbo-charged	by gunner	yes
hull	7.72 m		diesel developing 1500 bhp	Gun elevation/	
WIDTH WITHOUT			at 2600 rpm	depression	+20°/−10°
APPLIQUE ARMOUR	3.42 m	TRANSMISSION	Renk HSWL 354/3	Commanders override	yes
HEIGHT			hydro-kinetic planetary gear	Commander's fire-	
top of commander's			shift with 4 forward and 2	control override	yes
sight	2.99 m		reverse gears	Gun stabiliser	
to turret roof	2.54 m	STERRING	hydrostatic	vertical	yes
FIRING HEIGHT	1.95 m	CLUTCH	torque converter	horizontal	yes
GROUND CLEARANCE	0.5 m	SUSPENSION	torsion bar	Elevation quadrant	yes
TRACK	2.785 m	ELECTRICAL SYSTEM	24 V	Traverse indicator	yes
TRACK WIDTH	635 mm	BATTERIES	8 × 12 V, 125 Ah		
LENGTH OF TRACK		ARMAMENT			
ON GROUND	4.945 m	main	1 × 120 mm		
MAX ROAD SPEED	72 km/h	coaxial	1 × 7.62 mm MG		
FUEL CAPACITY	1200 litres	anti-aircraft	1 × 7.62 mm MG		
ROAD RANGE	500 km	SMOKE LAYING	smoke dischargers either		
		EQUIPMENT	side of turret		

Status: Development complete, ready for production.

Manufacturer: Vickers Defence Systems, Armstrong Works, Scotswood Road, Newcastle-upon-Tyne NE99 1CP, England.

Vickers Valiant Main Battle Tank

Development

Following the announcement by the British Minister of Defence in June 1976 that Ministry of Defence scientists had developed a new form of tank armour that would be resistant to attack from all known anti-tank weapons, Vickers Defence Systems Division was provided with preliminary details of the armour, called Chobham, in May 1977.

By late in 1977 Vickers had completed outline schemes and specifications for a new 43-tonne tank incorporating the most sophisticated turret systems available.

By September 1978 the turret and hull had been completed and in June 1979 the chassis made its first running trials. During these extensive trials, which were completed by September 1979, the tank had been tested with two different models of the powerpack, one with a Rolls-Royce CV12 TCA Condor and the other with the General Motors 12V–71T engine.

The tank, by then named Valiant, was stripped down for inspection and re-assembled in December 1979 so that turret trials could be started early in 1980. Following these trials it was sent to the Royal Armoured Corps Armoured Trials and Development Unit at Bovington for a series of fightability trials. Following the successful conclusion of these trials the Valiant made its first public appearance at the 1980 British Army Equipment Exhibition at Aldershot in June.

By late 1982 the prototype of the Vickers Valiant MBT had completed over 4500 km of trials with very few changes to the basic hull apart from an additional periscope being added either side of the original wide-angle periscope for improved vision either side of the hull.

At the same time a successful series of trials at the Royal Armoured Corps gunnery range at Lulworth were carried out with the Valiant. These included firing APDS projectiles at simulated tank targets at ranges of 1015 and 1500 metres in daylight using the Philips UA 9090 thermal periscopic sight.

Early in 1983 Valiant was demonstrated in the Middle East armed with the Royal Ordnance 120 mm L11A5 rifled tank gun.

Vickers Valiant fitted with universal turret traversed to right, armed with Royal Ordnance 120 mm L11A5 rifled tank gun showing position of commander's sight in front of his cupola and thermal sight to left of loader's position

In the summer of 1985 the Vickers Valiant was one of the four tanks shortlisted by the Spanish Army.

Description

The all-welded aluminium hull of the Vickers Valiant is divided into three compartments: driver's at the front, fighting in the centre and engine at the rear. Chobham armour added to the front and sides of the aluminium hull provides protection from frontal attack over an arc of 60 degrees and lateral protection against hand-held infantry weapons.

The driver is seated at the front of the hull on the right side and has a single-piece hatch cover that lifts and swings to the right. To the front of it there is a single AFV No 44 Mark 2 modified periscope for driving in the closed down position which can be replaced by a Badger passive periscope for driving at night. An additional periscope is fitted either side

Vickers Valiant armed with Royal Ordnance 120 mm L11A5 rifled tank gun (not to 1/76th scale)

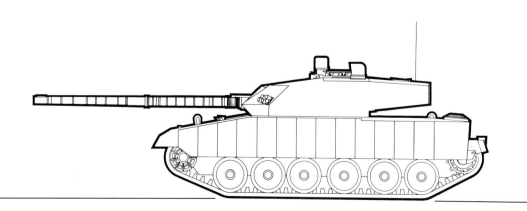

of the driver's main periscope for lateral ovservation. Should the driver hatch be covered by the turret at any time he can leave the vehicle via the fighting compartment. To the left of the driver are 30 rounds of 105 mm ammunition or 24 charges for the 120 mm L11A5 rifled tank gun.

The turret is identical to that used on the Vickers Mk 7 MBT and is fully described in the previous entry.

The powerpack consists of the engine and auxiliary equipment installed as a unit. Power is provided by a Rolls-Royce Condor CV12 TCA diesel, rated at 1000 bhp (746 kW), as an alternative, a General Motors 12V-71T two-stroke compression ignition diesel engine can be fitted.

The engine is cooled by twin radiators mounted horizontally on either side of the engine compartment, which are hinged to allow access to the engine compartment for maintenance.

Three cooling fans mounted over the gearbox compartment are driven by hydraulic motors powered by an engine-driven pump. Water is cooled by drawing air in through louvres, through the radiators and engine compartment and then discharging by mixed-flow fans through the outlet louvres over the gearbox compartment.

Power from the engine is transmitted by a resilient trailing link coupling through a centrifugal clutch into the gearbox and on to the final drives.

The TN12-1000 gearbox is an upgraded model of the one installed in the Chieftain and Vickers 37-ton MBT and combines the Wilson epicyclic gear change principle with the Merritt steering system to give six forward and two reverse gear ratios. Gear selection is normally automatic. A push switch on the left hand side of the driver's motorcycle type handlebar enables him to hold whichever gear he is in or to change down, thus allowing the driver to override the automatic gear change. In an emergency one forward and one reverse gear can be manually selected and an automatic sequential down change to neutral can be initiated by the driver or commander.

Power from the gearbox is transmitted to the sprockets on each side of the vehicle by a quill shaft coupling and final drive.

The driver steers by turning a handlebar. This actuates hydraulic motor cylinders which operate the hydraulic steer valve to control the pressure of the hydraulic fluid in the power steering system.

The main brakes are applied hydraulically, controlled by a hand lever on the left side of the driver's handlebar as on a motorcycle.

The suspension is of the torsion bar type with six dual rubber-tyred road wheels on each side, idler at the front, drive sprocket at the rear and three top rollers. The first, second and sixth road wheel stations mount a secondary torsion bar within the body of the axle arm and are brought into action by stops mounted on the hull plate. In addition the stations incorporate externally-mounted shock absorbers. Upward movement of the suspension is limited by bump stops which provide a progressive deflection resistance up to the solid bump condition. Hydro-pneumatic suspension with integral damping is also available for the Valiant MBT.

The tracks are made of cast manganese steel and when new each track has 98 links. Rubber pads can be fitted to reduce damage to road surfaces. The upper part of the track, idler

Vickers Defence Systems universal turret as installed on the Vickers Valiant showing main components of fire control systems

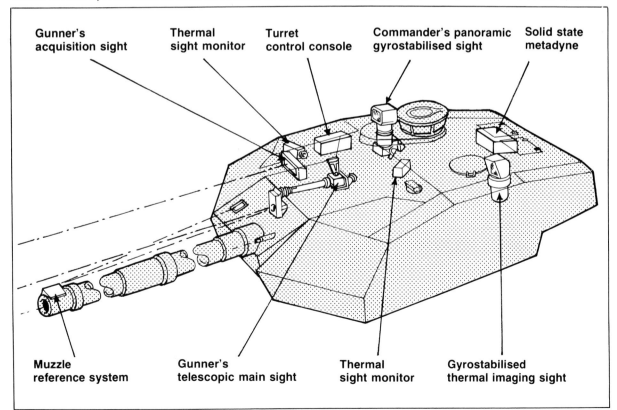

Gunner's acquisition sight

Thermal sight monitor

Turret control console

Commander's panoramic gyrostabilised sight

Solid state metadyne

Muzzle reference system

Gunner's telescopic main sight

Thermal sight monitor

Gyrostabilised thermal imaging sight

Vickers Valiant MBT fitted with universal turret armed with 120 mm L11A5 rifled tank gun manufactured by Royal Ordnance Nottingham. Note roof-mounted sights

wheels and top supporting rollers are enclosed and protected by fixed track guards and removable Chobham armour side plates.

The Valiant has two features that help to reduce its detection by night sights and other heat-sensing devices. These are its coat of infra-red reflective paint and the fact that the hot exhaust gases are mixed with the cooling air before being discharged.

Standard equipment includes a fixed fire-extinguishing system in the engine compartment and NBC pack in the turret rear. The latter pressurises the interior of the vehicle to about 70 mm water gauge. A relief valve on the underside of

the turret bustle vents excess air to the atmosphere. The pack can also be used for ventilation in which case the NBC filters are by-passed. Optional equipment includes heated clothing, fire-detection and suppression system and a 12.7 mm anti-aircraft machine gun.

Variants

Valiant 155 mm SPG
This would be the Valiant MBT chassis fitted with the 155 mm turret developed by Vickers Shipbuilding and

SPECIFICATIONS

		TRACK WIDTH	559 mm	BATTERIES	2 × 6TN in hull
		LENGTH OF TRACK ON		ARMAMENT	
CREW	4	GROUND	4.47 m	main	1 × 120 mm or 105 mm
COMBAT WEIGHT	46 000 kg	MAX ROAD SPEED	61.2 km/h	coaxial	1 × 7.62 mm MG
UNLOADED WEIGHT	43 400 kg	FUEL CAPACITY	1150 litres	anti-aircraft	1 × 7.62 mm MG
POWER-TO-WEIGHT		RANGE (at 32.2 km/h)	380 km	SMOKE-LAYING	
RATIO	21.74 bhp/tonne (with	FORDING	1.1 m	EQUIPMENT	smoke dischargers
	Rolls-Royce engine) or 19.89	GRADIENT	60%		either side of turret
	bhp/tonne (with General	SIDE SLOPE	30%		
	Motors engine)	VERTICAL OBSTACLE	0.914 m	AMMUNITION	
GROUND PRESSURE	0.89 kg/cm²	TRENCH	3 m	main	56 rounds 105 mm or 44
LENGTH		TURNING RADIUS	pivot		rounds 120 mm Rheinmetall
gun forwards, 105 mm	9.53 m	ENGINES	Rolls-Royce CV12 TCA		or 52 rounds 120 mm RO
gun forwards, 120 mm	10.62 m		2-stroke 12-cylinder	7.62 mm	3000 rounds
gun rear, 105 mm	8.59 m		diesel developing 1000	GUN CONTROL	
gun rear, 120 mm	9.68 m		bhp at 2300 rpm or	EQUIPMENT	
hull	7.36 m		General Motors	Turret power control	
WIDTH			12V-71T 2-stroke	by commander	electric/manual
without appliqué			compression ignition,	by gunner	yes
armour	3.03 m		12-cylinder diesel	Gun elevation/	yes
with appliqué armour	3.61 m		developing 915 bhp at	depression	+20°/−10°
HEIGHT			2500 rpm	commander's override	yes
to turret top	2.64 m	TRANSMISSION	TN12-1000 automatic with 6	Commander's fire-	
to top of commander's			forward and 2 reverse gears,	control override	yes
sight	3.1 m		with manual selection for	Gun stabiliser	
to top of thermal			emergency use	vertical	yes
sight hood	3 m	STEERING	Merritt regenerative	horizontal	yes
GROUND CLEARANCE	0.457 m	CLUTCH	centrifugal	Range setting	
TRACK	2.7 m	SUSPENSION	torsion bar	device	yes
		ELECTRICAL SYSTEM	24 V	Elevation quadrant	yes
				Traverse indicator	yes

Status: Development of 120 mm version was completed in 1982.

Manufacturer: Vickers Defence Systems, Armstrong Works, Newcastle-upon-Tyne NE99 1CP, England.

Vickers Valiant MBT fitted with universal turret armed with 120 mm L11A5 rifled tank gun which is equipped with Vickers Defence Systems Limited designed thermal sleeve. Note coaxial 7.62 mm Hughes Helicopters Chain Gun

Engineering Limited and is fully described in the entry for the Vickers Mk 3 MBT.

Vickers Valiant Armoured Recovery Vehicle

This would be fitted with a capstan winch with a nominal direct line pull of 30 tonnes capable of dealing with all normal recovery operations, but where necessary, the line pull can be increased to 75 tonnes by multi-reeving of the rope using recovery equipment provided with the vehicle. If required a hydraulically-operated crane can be fitted to facilitate removal and replacement of powerpacks in the field. For the recovery of light vehicles and to assist in main winch deployment an auxiliary winch with a 3 tonne pull is fitted.

Vickers Valiant Armoured Bridgelayer

This would be fitted with a Class 60 bridge which would be launched over the front of the vehicle and be 13.4 metres long.

Centurion Main Battle Tank

Development

In 1943 the Department of Tank Design was asked to start design work on a new heavy cruiser tank under the designation A41. This tank was required to have good armour protection, be armed with a 17-pounder gun and have a good cross-country performance: a high road speed was not considered essential at that time. The first mock-up of the A41 was completed in 1944 and six prototype tanks were completed in early 1945. These were sent to Germany but arrived too late to see any combat. The A41 later became known as the Centurion Mk 1 and the uparmoured A41A became the Centurion Mk 2, both armed with the 17-pounder gun.

The Centurion was first used in action by the British Army in Korea and has since seen combat in the Middle East (with Egypt, Israel, Iraq, Jordan and in the Lebanon), with the Indian Army during the Indo-Pakistan war, and in Viet-Nam with the Australian Army.

Throughout its life the Centurion has proved capable of being uparmoured and upgunned. It was originally armed with the 17-pounder which was replaced first by the 20-pounder and finally by the 105 mm L7 series gun which was subsequently adopted by many other countries and is now fitted to many tanks including the Leopard 1, Merkava, M48A5 (and other M48s), M60, Pz 61 and Pz 68, Type 74, S Tank, Vickers MBT, Vickers Valiant and the American M1. Other improvements carried out during its life included increased fuel capacity, contra-rotating commander's cupola

Centurion Mk 9 with 105 mm L7 gun and infra-red night vision equipment

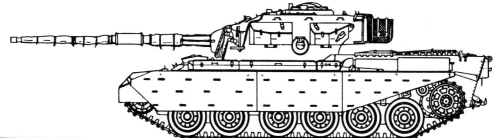

and improved stowage. All models of the tank used the same basic engine and transmission.

Production of the Centurion was undertaken by the Royal Ordnance Factories at Leeds and Woolwich, Vickers at Elswick and Leyland Motors at Leyland. The majority were built at Leeds and Elswick. Production of the Centurion was finally completed in 1962 by which time 4423 tanks had been built of which at least 2500 have been exported. In the British Army the Centurion was replaced from the late 1960s by the Chieftain.

CENTURION PRODUCTION

Years	Mark 1	Mark 2	Mark 3	Mark 5	Mark 7	Mark 8	Mark 9	Mark 10	Totals
1945/46		1							1
1946/47	48	57							105
1947/48	52	192	30						274
1948/49			139						139
1949/50			193						193
1950/51			229						229
1951/52			500						500
1952/53			573						573
1953/54			565		1				566
1954/55			359		154				513
1955/56			245	36	129	11			421
1956/57				176	168	51			395
1957/58				9	131	16			156
1958/59					78	16			94
1959/60					94	14	1	29	138
1960/61								110	110
1961/62								16	16
Totals	100	250	2833	221	755	108	1	155	**4423**

Description (Mk 13)

The all-welded hull of the Centurion is divided into three compartments: driver's at the front, fighting in the centre, and engine and transmission at the rear.

The driver is seated at the front of the hull on the right side and is provided with two hatch covers that open either side of his position, each with a periscope. To the left of the driver is ammunition.

The turret in the centre of the hull is of cast construction with the roof welded into position. There is an ammunition resupply hatch in the left side of the turret and stowage boxes on either side of the turret. Most vehicles have a wire stowage rack at the rear of the turret. The loader is seated on the left of the turret, commander on the right, and the gunner in front of and below the commander.

The commander's cupola can be traversed through 360 degrees by hand and is provided with split-hatches, periscopic sight with a ballistic pattern and seven periscopes for all-round observation. A searchlight mounted at the commander's station can be fitted with an infra-red filter. The gunner has a periscopic sight with ballistic pattern graticule, linked to a range drum for targets between 3000 and 8000 metres. The commander's and gunner's sights are linked by a heat-compensated bar.

The loader is provided with twin hatch covers that open front and rear and a single observation periscope.

The engine compartment at the rear is separated from the fighting compartment by a fireproof bulkhead. Air is drawn in through the engine deck louvres by two fans. Power is transmitted from the engine through the clutch to the transversely-mounted Merritt-Brown transmission. This is a combined change-speed and steering mechanism and incorporates a differential. Drive from the output epicyclic gears at each end of the gearbox is transmitted through an internally-toothed coupling ring and an externally-toothed driving shaft to the final drive.

The Horstmann suspension consists of three units on each side, each carrying two pairs of road wheels sprung by one set of concentric springs. The first and last road wheel units are fitted with shock absorbers. The drive sprocket is at the rear, idler at the front and there are six track return rollers, the four dual roller centre ones and the single front and rear ones which support the inside of the track only. The tops of the cast manganese steel tracks are covered by removable armour skirts which provide protection against HEAT projectiles.

As originally built the Centurion was not fitted with any infra-red night vision equipment but in the 1960s many Centurions of the British Army were fitted with infra-red driving lights, infra-red searchlight to the left of the main armament and infra-red sights for both the commander and gunner. The tank has no NBC system or amphibious capability although a deep fording kit was developed. A dozer blade

Centurion Mk 3 MBT with commander's hatch open (Ministry of Defence)

Type	APDS-T	APDS-T	APFSDS-T	DS/T	HESH	Smoke
DESIGNATION	L28A1	L52A1	L64	L45A1	L37	L39
WEIGHT OF COMPLETE ROUND	18.46 kg	19.14 kg	18 kg	14.91 kg	21.21 kg	26.35 kg
WEIGHT OF PROJECTILE	5.84 kg	6.48 kg	6.05 kg	3.91 kg	11.25 kg	19.58 kg
WEIGHT OF PROPELLANT	5.6 kg	5.6 kg	5.6 kg	3.9 kg	2.84 kg	0.4 kg
PROPELLANT TYPE	NQ/M11	NQ/M12	L	NQ/M07	NH 08	WM 04

can be mounted at the front of the hull for clearing obstacles and preparing fire positions. One of the shortcomings of the Centurion was its short operational range, although later production tanks had increased fuel capacity and the Mk 5 could tow a monowheel trailer full of fuel to increase its operational range. In addition to being used by the British Army the monowheel trailer was also used by Sweden and the Netherlands.

Main armament of the Centurion Mk 13 is the 105 mm L7A2 rifled tank gun which is provided with a fume extractor. It has an effective range of 1800 metres with APDS round or between 3000 and 4000 metres using HESH. A well-trained crew can fire eight rounds a minute.

The weapon is normally aimed using a 12.7 mm (0.50) ranging machine gun mounted coaxially with the main armament which has a maximum range of 1800 metres and fires in three round bursts using tracer ammunition. The gun is fully stabilised and the gunner can select any one of the following modes of operation: manual elevation and traverse, non-stabilised power traverse, stabilised powered elevation and traverse or emergency, single-speed power traverse.

The 105 mm gun fires the following types of ammunition, all of which are of the fixed type with the projectile securely attached to a brass cartridge case which contains the propellant and initiated by an electric primer (see Table above).

All of the above ammunition is manufactured by Royal Ordnance. The 105 mm gun can also fire ammunition manufactured by other countries including Canada, West Germany, Israel and the United States.

Mounted coaxially to the left of the main armament is a 7.62 mm (0.30) machine gun and there is a similar weapon on the commander's cupola for anti-aircraft use. Six electrically-operated smoke dischargers are mounted on either side of the turret.

The earlier 20-pounder (83.4 mm) gun fires the following types of ammunition: canister with a muzzle velocity of 914 metres a second, APDS-T with a muzzle velocity of 1432 metres a second and HE with a muzzle velocity of 601 metres a second and smoke with a muzzle velocity of 215 metres a second.

There have probably been more variants of the Centurion than any other post-Second World War vehicle in the MBT class. A full list of the gun tank models is given below followed by variants of the vehicle still in service; experimental vehicles have been excluded.

Centurion Gun Tank Models
Centurion Mk 1 armed with 17-pounder (76.2 mm) gun; none remains in service.
Centurion Mk 2 armed with 17-pounder (76.2 mm) gun; none remains in service.
Centurion Mk 3 armed with 20-pounder (83.4 mm) gun; none remains in service, most brought up to Mk 5 standard.
Centurion Mk 4 was to have been a close support model armed with 95 mm howitzer, but was not placed in production.

Centurion Mk 5 was designed by Vickers at Elswick and armed with a 20-pounder gun.
Centurion Mk 5/1 is Mk 5 uparmoured.
Centurion Mk 5/2 is Mk 5 with a 105 mm gun.
Centurion Mk 6 is a Mk 5 uparmoured, with additional fuel capacity at rear of hull and 105 mm gun.
Centurion Mk 6/1 is a Mk 6 with infra-red night vision equipment and stowage basket at rear of turret.
Centurion Mk 6/2 is Mk 6 with ranging machine gun for 105 mm gun.
Centurion Mk 7 was designed by Leyland and is designated the FV4007. Armed with a 20-pounder gun with fume extractor and carries 61 rounds of 20-pounder ammunition.
Centurion Mk 7/1 is a Mk 7 uparmoured and designated FV4012.
Centurion Mk 7/2 is a Mark 7 with a 105 mm gun.
Centurion Mk 8 was developed from the Mk 7 and has resiliently mounted gun mantlet with no canvas cover and the commander's cupola is contra-rotating. The commander can also raise his twin hatch covers in an umbrella fashion for improved visibility without exposing himself.

Centurion Mk 7 MBT with 20 pounder (83.4 mm) gun fitted with fume extractor (Ministry of Defence)

Centurion Mk 2 ARV

Centurion Mk 5 AVRE with dozer blade raised into travelling position (Ministry of Defence)

Centurion Mk 8/1 is Mk 8 uparmoured.
Centurion Mk 8/2 is Mk 8 with 105 mm gun.
Centurion Mk 9 is Mk 7 uparmoured and upgunned with 105 mm gun, designated the FV4015.
Centurion Mk 9/1 is Mk 9 with infra-red night vision equipment and stowage basket on rear of turret.
Centurion Mk 9/2 is Mk 9 with ranging machine gun.
Centurion Mk 10 is Mk 8 uparmoured, upgunned with 105 mm gun and has an ammunition capacity of 70 rounds, designated the FV4017.
Centurion Mk 10/1 is Mk 10 with infra-red night vision equipment and stowage basket on rear of turret.
Centurion Mk 10/2 is Mk 10 with ranging machine gun.
Centurion Mk 11 is Mk 6 with ranging machine gun, infra-red night vision equipment and stowage basket on turret rear.
Centurion Mk 12 is Mk 9 with infra-red night vision equipment, ranging machine gun and stowage basket on turret rear.
Centurion Mk 13 is Mk 10 with ranging machine gun and infra-red night vision equipment.

Centurion (Mk 5) Bridgelayer (FV4002)
As far as it is known none of these bridgelayers remains in service. In addition to being used by the British Army they were also used by Canada and Australia.

Centurion (Mk 5) Bridgelayer ARK (FV4016)
This was used only by the British Army and has been withdrawn from service.

Centurion (Mk 2) ARV (FV4006)
Until the introduction of the Chieftain ARV in 1975 the Centurion was the standard ARV of the British Army, and even today is still used in small numbers. The Mk 2 was preceded by the Mk 1 ARV but none remain in service. The ARV Mk 2 is essentially a Centurion MBT with its turret removed and replaced by an all-welded superstructure behind the driver's position. The commander's cupola can be traversed through 360 degrees and is fitted with a 7.62 mm (0.30) machine gun. Mounted at the rear of the hull are spades which are used to stabilise the vehicle when the winch is being used. The winch's 31 000 kg capacity can be increased with the aid of snatch blocks to a maximum of 90 000 kg. The vehicle has a loaded weight of 50 295 kg and a crew of four.

Centurion (Mk 5) AVRE (FV4003)
This is used only by the British Army and is basically a Mk 5 with its gun replaced by a 165 mm demolition gun and a hydraulic dozer blade mounted at the front of the hull. The AVRE can also tow a trailer carrying the Giant Viper mine-clearance equipment. The Centurion AVRE has a crew of five and weighs 51 810 kg loaded.

The Royal Engineers now also use the Centurion 105 mm gun tank to supplement the original Centurion 165 mm AVRE, the former is now referred to as the Centurion 105 mm AVRE and the latter the Centurion 165 mm AVRE.

Like the Centurion 165 mm AVRE the Centurion 105 mm AVRE can also be fitted with the Track Width Mine Plough and can tow a Royal Ordnance Giant Viper mine clearance system.

Centurion BARV (FV4018)
This is used only by the British Army and only 12 were built for use by amphibious forces. It is basically a Centurion tank with its turret removed and replaced by a superstructure that enables it to operate in water up to 2.895 metres deep. It has a crew of four, one of whom is a trained diver. Loaded weight is 40 643 kg.

Vickers Retro-fit for Centurion
Vickers, in conjunction with Marconi Command and Control Systems of Leicester and other component suppliers, has developed a series of retro-fit modifications designed to bring the Centurion into line with other modern MBTs. To replace the Meteor petrol engine and auxiliaries an integrated powerpack (V800) based on a General Motors 12V-71T diesel engine (or a Rolls-Royce CV12 TCE 750 hp engine) with a power output of 720 bhp has been developed. The installation of this powerpack results in both increased mobility and increased range of action. Maintenance is also facilitated since the powerpack which comprises radiators, fans and fan drives, alternators and heat exchanger can be removed and replaced in a few hours. Quick disconnect self-sealing couplings make it possible to change the powerpack without draining oils or coolant from the systems. The new powerpack can be used with the existing Z51R gearbox or alternatively a TN12 semi-automatic six-speed gearbox

Centurion Beach Armoured Recovery Vehicle (BARV) pushing a landing craft off the beach (MoD)

Vickers V-800 powerpack installed in Centurion MBT supplied by Vickers to Swiss Army

Centurion 105 mm AVRE fitted with Track Width Mine Plough and towing a Royal Ordnance Giant Viper mine clearance system (Terry J Gander)

Centurion chassis fitted with Marconi Command and Control Systems Marksman twin 35 mm anti-aircraft turret

can be installed. New final drive gears are also available which will further increase the maximum speed.

The Control Engineering Department of Marconi Command and Control Systems, Leicester, offers a new gun control and stabilisation system to replace the obsolete thermionic equipment, with greater reliability, better maintenance facilities and an improved performance. The cubicle is completely redesigned to use plug-in modules and solid-state components and new duplex controllers and a modern gyro unit are also supplied.

If the Centurion is not equipped with a 105 mm L7 series gun one can be fitted, in conjunction with upgunning a ranging machine gun, or alternatively a laser rangefinder can be provided. To bring the commander's station up to modern standards a new cupola is under development which comprises a dual magnification (×1 and ×15) sight together with all-round viewing periscopes. The cupola will be available with normal gear or contra-rotating drives. In addition several other improvements such as a revised ventilation system and passive night vision equipment are available.

The Vickers concept is that any combination of these modern facilities can be incorporated and retro-fit kits will be available so that customers can modernise Centurions in their own workshops. Sweden has had one of its Centurions brought up to the new standard and Switzerland has had two Centurions modernised by Vickers. But as of December 1985 no country had purchased this kit in quantity.

A Centurion has been used for a series of highly successful trials with the Marconi Command and Control Systems Simplified Fire-control System 600 which has now been adopted by India for its Vickers Mark 1 MBTs and by Nigeria for its new Vickers Mark 3 MBTs.

Many countries have modified their Centurions to meet their own specific requirements. Details of the modifications carried out by Austria, Denmark, Jordan, Netherlands, Sweden, Switzerland and South Africa are given in the second part of this book. Details of the Israeli Upgraded Centurion are given in this part of this book under Israel.

Centurion with Marksman anti-aircraft turret
A Centurion chassis has been used for initial firing trials of the private venture Marksman twin 35 mm anti-aircraft gun turret.

PERFORMANCE COMPARISON		V800 Powerpack		
	Meteor Engine Mk IVB	Z51R gearbox existing final drives	Z51R gearbox modified final drives	TN12 gearbox modified final drives
POWER	650 bhp at 2550 rpm	715 bhp at 2500 rpm	715 bhp at 2500 rpm	715 bhp at 2500 rpm
MAX TORQUE	1550 lb/ft at 1600 rpm	1740 lb/ft at 1600 rpm	1740 lb/ft at 1600 rpm	1740 lb/ft at 1600 rpm
MAX SPEED	34.6 km/h	33.47 km/h	30.1 km/h	40.1 km/h
FUEL CONSUMPTION				
road	0.184 km/litre	0.389 km/litre	0.389 km/litre	0.389 km/litre
cross-country	0.094 km/litre	0.166 km/litre	0.166 km/litre	0.166 km/litre

Model	Mk 5	Mk 13
CREW	4	4
COMBAT WEIGHT	50 728 kg	51 820 kg
POWER-TO-WEIGHT RATIO	12.81 hp/tonne	12.54 hp/tonne
GROUND PRESSURE	0.9 kg/cm²	0.95 kg/cm²
LENGTH GUN FORWARDS	9.829 m	9.854 m
LENGTH HULL	7.556 m	7.823 m
WIDTH	3.39 m	3.39 m
HEIGHT without AA MG	2.94 m	3.009 m
GROUND CLEARANCE	0.457 m	0.51 m
TRACK	2.641 m	2.641 m
TRACK WIDTH	610 mm	610 mm
LENGTH OF TRACK ON GROUND	4.572 m	4.572 m
MAX ROAD SPEED	34.6 km/h	34.6 km/h
FUEL CAPACITY	458 litres	1037 litres
MAX ROAD RANGE	102 km	190 km
FORDING	1.45 m	1.45 m
with preparation	2.74 m	2.74 m
GRADIENT	60%	60%
VERTICAL OBSTACLE	0.914 m	0.914 m
TRENCH	3.352 m	3.352 m
ENGINE	Rolls-Royce Mk IVB 12-cylinder liquid-cooled petrol developing 650 bhp at 2550 rpm	
AUXILIARY ENGINE	Morris USHNM 4-cylinder petrol, 20 bhp at 2500 rpm	
TRANSMISSION	Merritt-Brown Z51R manual with 5 forward and 2 reverse gears	
STEERING	mechanically operated, controlled differential	
CLUTCH	triple dry plate	triple dry plate
SUSPENSION	Horstmann	Horstmann
ELECTRICAL SYSTEM	24 V	24 V
BATTERIES	4 × 6 V, 115 Ah	4 × 6 V, 115 Ah
ARMAMENT		
main	1 × 83.4 mm	1 × 105 mm
coaxial	1 × 7.62 mm MG	1 × 7.62 mm MG
anti-aircraft	1 × 7.62 mm MG	1 × 7.62 mm MG
ranging MG	none	1 × 12.7 mm MG
SMOKE-LAYING EQUIPMENT	2 × 6 smoke dischargers either side of turret	
AMMUNITION		
main	65	64
7.62 mm	4250	4750
12.7 mm	none	600
GUN CONTROL EQUIPMENT	electric/manual	electric/manual
Max rate power traverse	360° in 26 s	360° in 26 s
Gun elevation/ depression	+20°/−10°	+20°/−10°
commander's override	yes	yes
Gun stabiliser		
vertical	yes	yes
horizontal	yes	yes
Range setting device	yes	yes
Elevation quadrant	yes	yes
Traverse indicator	yes	yes
ARMOUR		
Hull glacis	76 mm*	118 mm*
Hull nose	76 mm*	76 mm*
Hull sides front	51 mm*	51 mm*
Hull sides		
rear upper	38 mm*	38 mm*
rear lower	20 mm*	20 mm*
Hull floor	17 mm*	17 mm*
Turret front	152 mm*	152 mm*
* Estimated		

Status: Production complete. In service with Denmark, India (not in active service, for sale), Israel, Jordan, Netherlands, Kuwait (very few), Singapore (but based in Taiwan for training), South Africa (from India, Iraq, Jordan and United Kingdom), Somalia (from Kuwait), Sweden and Switzerland.

Manufacturers: Leyland Motors, Leyland, Royal Ordnance Factory, Leeds, Vickers Limited, Elswick and Royal Ordnance Factory, Woolwich.

Vickers Main Battle Tank

Development

The Chieftain MBT was designed to meet the requirements of the British Army in the late 1950s. Realising that several countries would not buy such a heavy and expensive tank, Vickers designed a new 37-tonne tank armed with the 105 mm gun from the Centurion and the engine, transmission, brakes, steering and fire-control system of the Chieftain. The use of these Chieftain components in a tank weighing only 37 tonnes improved their reliability and durability.

In January 1961 a team of defence experts headed by the them Indian Army Chief of Staff, Lt General L.P. Sen, visited both the United Kingdom and West Germany to examine tank designs which could be produced in India. The Vickers proposal was accepted and in August 1961 an agreement was signed between Vickers and the Indian Government under which the company would establish a factory in India for the production of the Vickers MBT.

The first two prototypes of the Vickers MBT were completed in 1963, one of which was retained in the United Kingdom and the other sent to India. Vickers established a production line at its Elswick works in 1964 and the first production tank was delivered to India in 1965. In the meantime the factory at Avadi, near Madras, was built and the first Vijayanta (as the Indians call the Vickers tank) rolled off the production line in January 1965. Initial production tanks were built of components supplied from the United Kingdom but gradually more and more parts of the tank (including the engine and main armament) were built in India. By the time production of the Vijayanta was completed in India it is believed that between 1200 and 1500 vehicles had been built. The Vijayanta still has the original ranging machine gun but after evaluating several systems late in 1980 India selected the British Marconi Command and Control Systems SFCS 600 fire-control system for installation in the tank. An initial batch of 70 systems supplied from the UK. In 1968 Kuwait placed an order for 70 Vickers Mark 1 MBTs which were delivered between 1970 and 1972.

In 1975 Vickers rebuilt the company demonstrator Mk 1 with the Leyland L60 engine being replaced by the General Motors 12V-71T turbo-charged diesel developing 720 bhp at 2500 rpm, but retaining the TN12 transmission. This increased the power-to-weight ratio to over 18 bhp/tonne, as

Vickers MBT Mk 3 with thermal sleeve for main armament

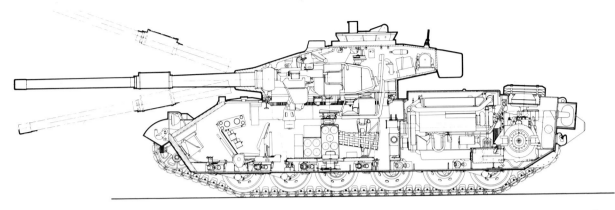

well as increasing the maximum road speed to over 50 km/h and increasing maximum operational road range.

In 1977 Kenya placed an order for 38 Vickers Mk 3 MBTs plus three ARVs, which were all completed by late 1980. In December 1978 Kenya placed a second order for 38 Vickers Mk 3 MBTs plus four ARVs which were delivered from 1981 to 1982.

In August 1981 the Nigerian Government placed an order worth some £60 million with Vickers Defence Systems Limited for 36 Vickers Mark 3 MBTs, five ARVs and six bridgelayers, with first deliveries being made in mid-1983. The MBTs are fitted with the General Motors 12V-71T diesel engine, Pilkington PE Condor commander's day/night sight and the Marconi Command and Control Systems SFC 600 fire-control system. Early in 1985 Nigeria placed a repeat order for Vickers MBTs with first deliveries taking place in 1985. The Vickers Mk 3 MBT has also been demonstrated in Thailand.

Description (Mk 1)

The all-welded rolled steel hull of the Vickers MBT is divided into three compartments: driver's at the front, fighting in the centre and the engine and transmission at the rear.

The driver is seated at the front of the hull on the right side and is provided with a single-piece hatch cover that opens to the right. Forward of this hatch cover is a single AFV No 44 Mk 2 wide-angle observaion periscope for when the hatch is closed, this can be replaced by a passive periscope for driving at night. To the left of the driver are stowed 25 rounds of ammunition.

The all-welded turret has an ammunition reloading hatch in the left side and a stowage basket at the rear. The loader is seated on the left of the turret and the commander and gunner on the right.

The commander is provided with a single-piece hatch cover that opens to the rear, a sight with a magnification of ×10 and six periscopes for all-round observation. The gunner is seated in front of and below the commander and is provided with a single sighting telescope with a ballistic graticule. The loader has a two-piece hatch cover that opens front and rear and is provided with an observation periscope in front of his position.

The engine, transmission, steering system and brakes are at the rear of the hull. The complete powerpack consisting of the L60 engine, transmission, radiators, fans, coolant and oil filter can be removed from the tank as a complete unit. Cooling air is drawn by way of the louvres, through the

radiators and engine compartment and is discharged by fans through outlet louvres over the gearbox compartment.

The TN12 gearbox combines the Wilson epicyclic gear change principle with Merritt steering system and provides six forward and two reverse speeds. Input to the transmission incorporates a centrifugal clutch and an input-driven pump provides oil pressure for gear engagement. Steering is controlled by hydraulically-applied disc brakes with a mechanical interlock to prevent simultaneous engagement.

In addition to the belt-driven 24-volt generator on the engine an auxiliary three-cylinder engine suitable for operation on the same fuels as the main engine drives a second generator when the main engine is not running.

Pilkington PE Condor commander's combined day/night sight from rear as fitted to Mk 3 Vickers MBT

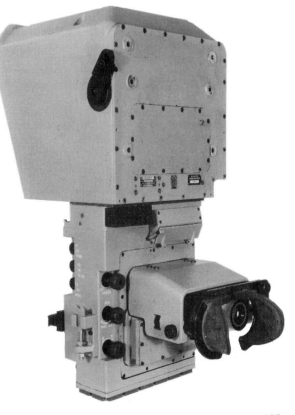

Vickers Mk 3 MBT without thermal sleeve for main armament and track guards not fitted during pre-delivery trials in UK

The torsion bar suspension system consists of six dual rubber-tyred road wheels with the idler at the front, drive sprocket at the rear and three track return rollers. Suspension units one, two and six incorporate secondary torsion bars which are brought into action by stops mounted on the hull. The first, second and sixth road wheel stations are provided with a hydraulic shock absorber. The tracks are of cast manganese with removable rubber pads.

Standard equipment for the Mk 1 includes fire warning and internal fire-fighting systems. Optional equipment included an NBC system, night vision equipment and a flotation screen carried collapsed around the top of the hull which would take between 15 and 30 minutes to erect. The tank would then be steered and propelled in the water by its tracks at a speed of 6.4 km/h. Some Indian vehicles have an infra-red/white searchlight mounted to the left of the main armament.

Main armament consists of a 105 mm L7A1 gun which is normally aimed using a 12.7 mm (0.50) ranging machine gun which is mounted coaxially with the main armament. This has a maximum range of 1800 metres and fires three-round bursts of tracer ammunition. The 105 mm gun fires the following types of ammunition, all of which are of the fixed type with the projectile securely attached to a brass cartridge case which contains the propellant and is initiated by an electric primer (see Table below).

During trials a Vickers MBT engaged ten targets at ranges of between 600 and 1000 metres in 55 seconds. Of 44 rounds of ammunition carried five rounds are under the gun, eight on the turntable floor, three on the left side of the turret and 25 to the left of the driver.

The tank is fitted with the Marconi Command and Control Systems EC517 gun control and stabilisation system which has three modes of operation: non-stabilised, stabilised and emergency. Mounted to the left of the main armament is a 7.62 mm (0.30) machine gun and a similar anti-aircraft weapon is mounted at the commander's station. Mounted

Vickers Mk 3 MBT from rear with 105 mm gun in travelling lock, track guards have yet to be fitted

either side of the turret are six electrically-operated smoke dischargers.

Variants

Vickers MBT Mk 2
This was a project only and was basically a Mk 1 with two integral missile launchers either side of the turret rear for the British Aerospace Swingfire ATGW missile.

Vickers MBT Mk 3
This is currently in production in the United Kingdom for Nigeria and has a redesigned turret with a cast front welded to armoured plate to give increased ballistic protection, new powerpack and a new fire-control system.

Description (Mk 3)
The all-welded rolled steel hull of the Vickers MBT is divided into three compartments: driver's at the front, fighting in the centre and the engine and transmission in the rear.

The driver's compartment is on the right, with a single-piece hatch cover opening to the right. Forward of the cover is a single AFV No 44 Mark 2 wide-angle periscope for closed-down driving. This can be replaced by a passive periscope for driving at night. To the left of the driver are stowed 25 rounds of 105 mm ammunition.

The turret has a cast front welded to armour plate to give improved ballistic protection. It has an ammunition reloading hatch in the left side and a stowage basket on the rear. The loader sits on the left of the turret and the commander and gunner on the right.

Type DESIGNATION	APDS-T L28A1	APDS-T L52A1	APFSDS-T L64	DS/T L45A1	HESH L37	Smoke L39
WEIGHT OF COMPLETE ROUND	18.46 kg	19.14 kg	18 kg	14.91 kg	21.21 kg	26.35 kg
WEIGHT OF PROJECTILE	5.84 kg	6.48 kg	6.05 kg	3.91 kg	11.25 kg	19.58 kg
WEIGHT OF PROPELLANT	5.6 kg	5.6 kg	5.6 kg	3.9 kg	2.84 kg	0.4 kg
PROPELLANT TYPE	NQ/M11	NQ/M12	L	NQ/M07	NH 08	WM 04

The commander's cupola has 360-degree hand traverse and has a rear-opening single-piece hatch cover. The commander has a Pilkington PE Condor combined day/night sight; this has day magnifications of ×1 and ×10 and a night magnification of ×4. Using the Condor, the commander can aim and fire the main armament at night or in poor light. The sight has an injected ballistic graticule from the collimator, a range readout from the laser rangefinder, and controls for operating the laser and for laying and firing the main armament. The commander also has six periscopes for observation.

The gunner has a Vickers Instruments L23 periscopic sight, with magnifications of ×1 and ×10, incorporating a Nd Yag laser rangefinder and a ballistic graticule. The gunner's sight is linked to the gun by a temperature-compensated link bar and to a collimator in the commander's cupola. The collimator projects an illuminated ballistic graticule image into the field of view of the commander's sight when the cupola and the turret are lined up.

The loader has a single-piece hatch cover that opens forward and an AFV No 30 Mark 1 observation periscope.

The main armament is the 105 mm L7A1 gun which was originally developed for Centurion and is now fitted to many other tanks. The L7A1 fires APFSDS, APDS, HEAT, HESH, HE, Smoke and Canister rounds.

The tank is fitted with the Marconi Command and Control Systems EC 620 gun control and stabilised system which has three modes of operation: non-stabilised, stabilised and emergency.

A computerised fire-control system is fitted to give the best chance of a first round hit. The Marconi Command and Control Systems SFC 600 is used for its simplicity which allows quick and accurate firing and requires the minimum of training.

The 12.7 mm ranging machine gun is retained. It is a very effective heavy machine gun for use against lightly-armoured and soft-skinned vehicles. It also provides a back-up in the event of failure of the laser rangefinder or fire-control computer.

The secondary armament is a coaxially-mounted 7.62 mm machine gun. A further 7.62 mm machine gun is provided on the commander's cupola, in front of and to the left of the hatch. This weapon can be elevated from −10 degrees to the vertical, and can be mechanically cocked, aimed and electrically fired from under armour. A spotlight is fitted to the cross shaft of the machine gun mounting. Elevation is achieved by the commander's sight elevation gear, thus the machine gun and the spotlight follow the commander's line of sight through all angles of elevation.

Fifty rounds of 105 mm ammunition are carried, 18 rounds in the turret below the ring, 25 stowed horizontally in the front of the hull and seven stowed vertically in the hull centre section.

Electrically-operated smoke dischargers are fitted on each side of the turret.

The engine, transmission, steering system and brakes are at the rear of the hull. The complete powerpack consisting of the engine, radiators, coolant and oil filter can be removed as a complete unit. All connections to the powerpack are by means of self-sealing couplings, plugs and sockets so that the powerpack can be readily removed from the vehicle for major overhauls. By the use of suitable extension leads the engine can be run up alongside the vehicle for short periods.

A choice of engines is offered. In the Kenyan and Nigerian vehicles a Detroit Diesel 12V-71T, two-stroke, turbo-charged diesel develops 720 bhp. Alternatively a Perkins/ Rolls-Royce CV12 TCA, four-stroke, turbo-charged diesel developing 800 bhp can be fitted. Both these engines have given several thousand km of reliable service in Mark 3 and other vehicles. Details of these engines are as follows:

Vickers Mk 3 MBT as built for Kenyan Army

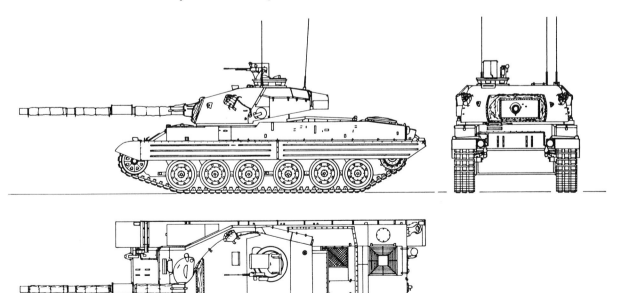

Type	VR800	V800
ENGINE MAKE	Rolls-Royce	General Motors
DESIGNATION	CV-12 800E	12V-71T
CONFIGURATION	12-cylinder, 60°V formation, 4-stroke diesel	12-cylinder, 60°V formation, 2-stroke diesel
PISTON DISPLACEMENT	26.1 litres	13.97 litres
HORSEPOWER	800 bhp at 2300 rpm	720 bhp at 2500 rpm
TORQUE	2800 Nm at 1700 rpm	2350 Nm at 1800 rpm
COMPRESSION RATIO	14:1	17:1
AIR CLEANER	2-stage cyclone/filter	2-stage cyclone/filter
ENGINE LUBRICATION	dry pump system	dry pump system
MAX ROAD SPEED	62 km/h	50 km/h

The TN12 V5 automatic gearbox combines the Wilson epicyclic gear change principle with the Merritt steering system and provides six forward and two reverse gears. The driver can initiate an emergency sequential downchange to first and also engage one forward and one reverse gear manually. Input to the transmission is by a centrifugal clutch; an input-shaft driven pump provides oil pressure for gear engagement. Steering is controlled by hydraulically-applied disc brakes with a mechanical interlock to prevent simultaneous engagement. The final drive gear ratio has been raised to take advantage of the extra power available.

Cooling air is drawn in through inlet louvres over the engine compartment, through the radiators and engine compartment and is discharged by fans through outlet louvres over the gearbox compartment.

Optional equipment includes added passive night vision equipment, deep wading and flotation equipment, full NBC filtration and pressurisation, heater, air-conditioning, contra-rotating gear for the commander's cupola, and an automatic fire detection and suppression system. A 12.7 mm machine gun can also be fitted on the commander's cupola in place of the standard 7.62 mm machine gun.

Vickers Armoured Bridgelayer

The Vickers Armoured Bridgelayer (VAB) is designed to transport, launch and recover a tank bridge which is 13.41 metres long and provide a clear span of military bridge classification of class 60/70. The bridge is launched over the front of the vehicle with the bridge launching equipment hydraulically operated with power supplied by a pump driven from a PTO from the main engine. As an alternative, the bridgelayer can incorporate a horizontally launched bridge.

Vickers AVLB based on Mk 3 chassis

Vickers Armoured Recovery Vehicle with stabilising blade in raised position and carrying a spare powerpack on hull top

Vickers Mark 3 MBT chassis with Vickers Shipbuilding and Engineering GBT 155 155 mm turret

Nigeria has placed orders for 12 bridgelayers of the standard type with the first of these being delivered in 1984.

Vickers Armoured Recovery Vehicle

The Vickers Armoured Recovery Vehicle is based on the Vickers MBT Mk 3 hull. Three were ordered by Kenya (two with a crane and one without a crane) and were delivered in 1980. In 1978 a further four were ordered (two with a crane and two without a crane) for delivery between 1981/82. Nigeria has placed orders for a total of 10 armoured recovery vehicles. The vehicle has three compartments: winch compartment at the front with the driver to the left of the winch, the other three crew members in the centre of the vehicle and the engine and transmission at the rear.

The main winch is of the capstan type with a nominal direct line pull of 25 000 kg working in conjunction with the earth anchor spade fitted to the front of the vehicle. Where necessary the line pull can be increased to a nominal 65 tons by multi-reeving of the rope using recovery equipment provided with the vehicle. The vehicle is provided with a full range of recovery equipment including pulleys, cables and tow bars and is also equipped with a crane capable of lifting 4000 kg to 3.62 metres which is primarily intended for removing/replacing the V800 power pack, or a TN12 transmission. The vehicle has a weight of 36 800 kg and is armed with a 7.62 mm machine gun and two six-barrelled smoke dischargers.

Vickers 155 mm SPG

Vickers Defence systems have proposed that the Vickers Mark 3 MBT chassis could be fitted with the private venture Vickers Shipbuilding and Engineering GBT 155 155 mm turret. This can also be mounted on other chassis including the M48, M60, Chieftain, Centurion and Leopard 1. The 155 mm weapon has an elevation of +70 degrees and a depression of −5 degrees, with turret traverse being a full 360 degrees. Both manual and automatic loading systems are available with a maximum possible range of 24 000 metres with the HE and 30 000 metres with a rocket assisted projectile. The four man crew in the turret consists of the commander, layer and two loaders.

Vickers anti-aircraft tank

This is a Vickers Mark 3 chassis fitted with the Marconi Command and Control Systems Marksman twin 35 mm turret which for firing trials has been installed on a Centurion MBT chassis.

SPECIFICATIONS

Model	Mk 1	Mk 3
CREW	4	4
COMBAT WEIGHT	38 600 kg	38 700 kg
UNLOADED WEIGHT	36 000 kg	36 100 kg
POWER-TO-WEIGHT RATIO	16.83 bhp/tonne	18.6 bhp/tonne
GROUND PRESSURE	0.87 kg/cm²	0.79 kg/cm²
LENGTH GUN FORWARDS	9.728 m	9.788 m
LENGTH HULL	7.92 m	7.561 m
WIDTH	3.168 m	3.168 m
HEIGHT		
overall without AA MG	2.64 m	3.099 m
to turret roof	2.438 m	2.476 m
GROUND CLEARANCE	0.406 m	0.432 m
TRACK	2.533 m	2.533 m
TRACK WIDTH	520 mm	520 mm
LENGTH OF TRACK ON GROUND	4.28 m	4.28 m
MAX SPEED		
road, forward	48 km/h	50 km/h
FUEL CAPACITY	1000 litres	1000 litres
MAX ROAD RANGE	480 km	600 km
FORDING	1.143 m	1.143 m
GRADIENT	60%	60%
SIDE SLOPE	30%	30%
VERTICAL OBSTACLE	0.914 m	0.914 m
TRENCH	2.438 m	3.1 m
ENGINE	Leyland L60 Mk 4B 6-cylinder water-cooled multi-fuel developing 650 bhp at 2670 rpm or Rolls-Royce CV12 TCA 12-cylinder turbo-charged diesel developing 800 bhp at 2300 rpm	General Motors 12V-71T turbo-charged diesel developing 720 bhp at 2500 rpm
TRANSMISSION	TN12 with centrifugal clutch and Merritt regenerative steering system, 6 forward and 2 reverse speeds	
SUSPENSION	torsion bar	torsion bar
ELECTRICAL SYSTEM	24 V	24 V
BATTERIES	4 × 6 V, 115 Ah	4 × 12 V, 200 Ah
ARMAMENT		
main	1 × 105 mm	1 × 105 mm
coaxial	1 × 7.62 mm MG	1 × 7.62 mm MG
anti-aircraft	1 × 7.62 mm MG	1 × 7.62 mm MG
RANGING MACHINE GUN	1 × 12.7 mm MG	1 × 12.7 mm MG
SMOKE-LAYING EQUIPMENT	6 smoke dischargers mounted either side of turret	

Model	Mk 1	Mk 3
AMMUNITION		
main	44	50
7.62 mm	3000	5000
12.7 mm	600	1000
GUN CONTROL EQUIPMENT		
Turret power control	electric or manual	electric or manual
by commander	yes	yes
by gunner	yes	yes
Max rate of power traverse	360° in 13 s	360° in 13 s
commander's override	yes	yes
Gun elevation/ depression	+20°/−7°	+20°/−10°
Commander's fire-control override	no	yes
Gun stabiliser		
vertical	yes	yes
horizontal	yes	yes
Range setting device	yes	yes
Elevation quadrant	yes	yes
Traverse indicator	yes	yes
ARMOUR		
Hull nose	80 mm	80 mm
Hull glacis	60 mm	60 mm
Hull sides front and intermediate	40 mm	40 mm
Hull sides rear	30 mm	30 mm
Hull top	25 mm	25 mm
Hull floor	17 mm	17 mm
Hull rear	20 mm	20 mm
Turret front	80 mm	n/a
Turret sides	40–60 mm	n/a
Turret rear	40 mm	40 mm
Turret top	25 mm	25 mm

Status: In service with India (Mk 1), Kenya (Mk 3), Kuwait (Mk 1) and Nigeria (Mk 3). Production continues in United Kingdom for Nigeria.

Manufacturer: Vickers Defence Systems, Armstrong Works, Scotswood Road, Newcastle-upon-Tyne NE99 1CP, England.

Tank Test Bed Program

Development/Description

On 22 June 1982 TACOM awarded a $12.9 million three year contract to the General Dynamics, Land Systems Division to design and build a Tank Test Bed (TTB). Unsuccessful bidders for this contract were AAI, FMC and Pacific Car and Foundry. It had been expected that two companies would be chosen to build prototypes but budgetary considerations meant that only one contractor could be selected.

The TTB will be based on the automotive components of the M1 MBT and armed with a modified 120 mm M256 Rheinmetall smooth-bore gun as fitted to the M1A1, first production models of which were completed by General Dynamics, Land Systems Division in August 1985.

The TTB will have a new automatic loader, advanced surveillance technology and a three man crew all of whom will be seated in the front of the hull for improved protection. In a separate compartment behind the crew will be an ammunition basket and an automatic loader, with the externally-mounted gun being positioned above the turret ring.

The removal of the turret will enable the TTB to have a much lower silhouette and also weigh about 15 per cent less than the current M1 and allow for increased armour protection to cope with anticipated future threat weapons.

The main and secondary armament will be aimed by surveillance sights/tv cameras provided at both the commander's and gunner's positions, with each equipped with a tv monitor.

General Dynamics, Land Systems Division, as prime contrator, awarded two sub-contracts to Rheinmetall of West Germany and FMC Northern Ordnance Division, for the construction of working models of an automatic loader for the TTB. At a later date Western Gear was also included.

All three models were evaluated by TACOM and Western Gear was subsequently awarded a contract to build a complete working system which was due to be integrated into the TTB in 1985.

Meanwhile TACOM and Litton Systems Inc with Pietzsch Corporation of West Germany as major subcontractor, have designed the Surrogate Research Vehicle (SRV). The SRV will simulate the TTB concept as well as other possible Close-Combat Vehicle (CCV) configurations.

TACOM modified the hull while Pietzsch built the turret and associate test equipment. The SRV was completed early in 1983 and delivered to Fort Knox for two months of initial trials. The TTB simulation exercise was completed in June 1983. The SRV is essentially a M1 hull with a low turret module with externally-mounted laser main gun simulator and modular crew stations and surveillance sights. The latter can be moved to various locations throughout the vehicle to find the best position.

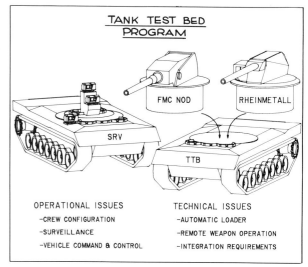

Model of the Tank Test Bed (TTB) armed with 120 mm M256 smooth-bore gun (US Army)

The first phase of the SRV was completed early in 1984 and was to validate the design of the TTB external gun concept and evaluate the operational feasibility to remote surveillance sighting concepts.

Phase II was to start in the summer of 1985 and evaluate an advanced closed-hatch surveillance system built by Emerson Electric Company. Phase III will include development of an automatic cuing system.

Status: Development.

Manufacturer: General Dynamics, Land Systems Division, PO Box 1743, Warren, Michigan 48090, USA.

Future Close-Combat Vehicle System

In May 1980 the United States Army Tank Automotive Command Concepts Laboratory held a pre-solicitation conference to discuss future close-combat vehicles to succeed the M1 MBT, M2 IFV and M3 CFV. Representatives from more than 90 companies were given briefings on future combat vehicle technology by representatives from TACOM and ARRADCOM. Briefings were also given on future operational concepts for the mid-1990s by representatives from the Infantry Center and the Armor Center.

Seven proposals were then received from industry and evaluated by a joint DARCOM/TRADOC team. Based on its evaluations and other considerations, four contractor teams were selected and in January 1981 Chrysler (now Land Systems Division of General Dynamics), FMC, Pacific Car and Foundry and Teledyne Continental were awarded contracts for the FCCVS. Each of the winning teams consists of at least one experienced vehicle designer or system integrator, system analyst in terms of operational concepts and threats, and a fire-control member.

Early in 1982 a draft of the study and concepts was presented to the review board at TACOM with the final report two months later. At the same time as the four teams carried out their studies, TACOM's Exploratory Development Division, with other supporting elements within the Command and ARRADCOM, carried out its concept studies.

In the spring of 1982 the contractor's concepts and in-house concepts were delivered and during the spring and summer they were evaluated and rated by a team of DARCOM and TRADOC experts. The FCCVS program initiated a second phase study from October 1982 to December 1983. The second phase explored technologies projected for the early 21st century.

It is expected that a series of testbeds may be built as a result of the analysis of the vehicle concepts generated by the FCCVS program. Design, fabrication and evaluation of these testbeds will form the technical basis for formulating the specifications for future close combat vehicles.

The end product will be a family of vehicle design concepts which will replace the M1/M2/M3 family of close combat vehicles.

FCCVS guidelines included the following desired capabilities:
(1) Family of vehicles probably subdivided into two or more weight classes which will reduce the associated logistical burden of supply, maintenance and training
(2) Countermeasures against smart and top attack
(3) Active and passive countermeasures against threat acquisition systems
(4) Offensive capability against hardened enemy positions
(5) Mobility for the infantry compatible with that of armour
(6) Kill the enemy as far forward as acquisition systems permit without exposing friendly systems to detection/killing
(7) Survivability and sustainability in NBC environment
(8) When sophisticated primary systems fail, continue to function at a creditable degraded level with unsophisticated back-up systems
(9) Refuel and rearm rapidly and without crew exposure
(10) Built in test, diagnostic and training equipment
(11) Self-defence against helicopter threat
(12) Crew and systems protection (compartmentalisation, fire suppressants, low vulnerability propellants and fuel)
(13) Decontamination capability
(14) Strategic and tactical transportability
(15) Self-contained mine detection, clearing/defeating capability
(16) Protection against mines
(17) Operate on the dirty battlefield (smoke, obscurants, night, rain, snow)
(18) Appliqué armour to respond to changing threats or meet transportability requirements
(19) Reduce soldiers' burdens/dangers through robotic devices
(20) Protection against directed energy weapons, both laser and RF
(21) Fight and survive in the urban environment
(22) Complexity hidden from the operator
(23) Command and control from each vehicle type
(24) Reduction of emissions that create attackable signatures
(25) Avoid being seen (stealth-type measures)
(26) Attack the flank, rear, top and bottom of enemy vehicles
(27) Defeat or neutralise targets with non-penetrating means as well as through brute force techniques
(28) Survivability through high levels of mobility and agility
(29) Use of close combat direct fire weapons as last resort
(30) Minimise the number of types of ammunition required
(31) Detect mines and NBC threats remotely
(32) PK:PH of friendly main weapon approach 1:0
(33) Acquire and engage multiple targets simultaneously
(34) Minimise vulnerability of critical components
(35) Self-contained land navigation systems
(36) Data processing equipment handles routine reporting (position, logistic status, readiness status, etc)
(37) Quick replacement of hardware parts (engines, transmission and filters etc)
(38) Improved engine performance, multi-fuel capability, high efficiency
(39) Video displays for Battlefield C^3
(40) Ergonomics designed for continuous buttoned-up operation on contaminated battlefield
(41) Passive identification of friend or foe
(42) Reconfiguration capability, for changing roles of missions, through the exchange of major components and gun systems
(43) Commonality of fire controls throughout the family
(44) Commonality of drive train components for both weight classes through duplication of components
(45) On board protected facilities and supplies for crew requirements sufficient for 72 hours.

M1 Abrams MBT

Development

Following the demise of the US-German MBT-70 in January 1970 the United States Army went on to develop a more austere version called the XM803. This was cancelled by the United States Congress in November 1971 on the grounds that it was unnecessarily complex, excessively sophisticated and too expensive. Congress did not dispute that the Army required a new tank, but they were concerned about its cost.

The XM1 Program was established in December 1971 and in February the following year the Army activated a task force with the user, trainer and developer participating to formulate the concept for the new battle tank. This report was published in August 1972 and the proposed characteristics were then reviewed to eliminate unnecessary features and reduce costs to the minimum. The final programme was contained in a Development Concept Paper, as amended, which was approved by the Deputy Secretary of Defense in January 1973.

In June 1973 contracts for the prototype development validation phase of the new tank, called the XM1, were awarded to the two prime contractors. Each contractor was required to develop a tank which met the material need requirements while remaining within an average 'design-to-unit hardware' cost of $507 790 in 1972 dollars for production tanks. Each contractor was required to deliver to the Army one prototype tank, one automotive test rig and one hull and turret for ballistic tests. The Defense Division of the Chrysler Corporation was awarded a contract worth $68.1 million, and the Detroit Diesel Allison Division of the General Motors Corporation was awarded one worth $87 million.

In February 1976 the Army accepted the prototype vehicles from both contractors and operational and engineering testing was conducted through to April 1976.

In July 1976 it was announced that the Army had decided to delay the decision as to the winner of the XM1 competition to late that year after the two competing contractors had submitted additional alternative proposals. The Secretary of the Army stated that 'This additional step represents an extension of the validation phase of the XM1 tank program and will call for the companies to submit revised proposals in which each will be asked to bid on the basis of both advanced engine technology and new key components as those which dominate field maintenance and logistics support in the field and which will lead to a higher degree of standardisation within NATO. This would permit the final selection to be made before the end of the calendar year.'

In accordance with the December 1974 MoU a comparative test and evaluation of the Leopard 2 American or Austere

M1 Abrams MBT from above with commander's, gunner's and driver's hatches in open position (US Army)

Version (AV), was conducted between September and December 1976, utilising the same criteria and constraints as used with the two American prototypes.

In November 1976 the Secretary of the Army announced that the Chrysler Corporation's prototype had been selected to enter Full Scale Engineering Development (FSED), even though the Leopard 2 (AV) was still being tested. The original bids, submitted in June were for $221 million from Chrysler and $208 million for General Motors but when the new bids were submitted Chrysler had dropped its bid to $196 million and the General Motors bid had increased to $232 million.

Major sub-contractors for the M1 MBT are:
Avco Lycoming Division, Stratford, Connecticut (engine); Cadillac Gage Company, Warren, Michigan (turret drive and stabilisation system); Computing Devices Company, Ottawa, Canada (ballistic computer); Detroit Diesel Allison Division, Indianapolis, Indiana (transmission and final drives); Hughes Aircraft Company, Culver City, California (laser rangefinder and thermal imaging system); Kollmorgen Corporation, Northampton, Massachusetts (gunner's auxiliary sight) and Singer Kearfott Division, Clifton, New Jersey (line-of-sight data link).

Four contractor-operated plants supply components to the Lima and Detroit facilities: Scranton Defense Plant, Scranton, Pennsylvania (suspension parts); Huntsville Electronics

M1 MBT

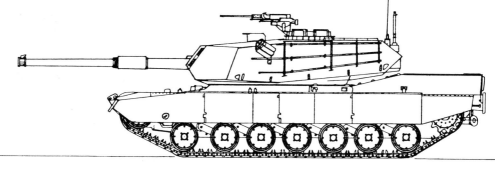

XM1 (now M1) MBT turret assembly at Lima Army Tank Plant, Ohio

Division, Huntsville, Alabama (electronic test equipment); Sterling Defense Plant, Sterling Heights, Michigan (sighting equipment and wire harnesses); and the Detroit Arsenal Tank Plant, Warren, Michigan (suspension components, gun recoil mechanisms and machine parts).

Chrysler was awarded a three-year contract worth $196.2 million for the FSED phase, during which 11 XM1 pilot vehicles with their associated spares were produced at the then Chrysler-run Detroit Arsenal Tank Plant. The first pilot was completed in February 1978 and the last in July 1978.

During the three-year FSED phase the 11 prototypes underwent intensive developmental and operational testing (DT/OT II) under a variety of operational conditions. The OT II (Operation Test II) was conducted by the United States Army Operational Test and Evaluation Agency (OTEA) at Fort Bliss, Texas, from May to December 1978, to provide data and associated analysis on the operational effectiveness and military utility of the XM1 MBT. During the test period six XM1 and five M60A1 (RISE) tanks were tested and compared in areas of survivability, hit performance, fightability, target acquisition, human factors and mobility. The tank was also tested in the areas of reliability,

Crew stations on the M1 MBT (US Army)

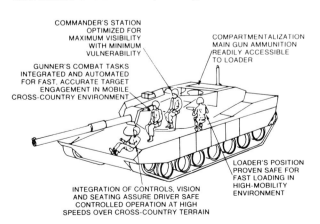

Avco-Lycoming AGT-1500 gas turbine as installed in M1

availability, maintainability, and logistics support. During trials with the 11 pre-production tanks there were problems with the gas turbine air filtration system, transmission, tracks and fuel supply system. As a result, three XM1s were modified and tested in the second half of 1979 and most of the problems were overcome. A new steel sprocket hub with mud discharge ports, hull-mounted scraper to remove mud and sand as the track turns and inside steel blocks and an outside retaining ring to prevent inside and outside throwing of the track. To help align the track and prevent damage to the suspension in the case of an inside throw, a new inside steel plate was mounted above the final drive. The suspension torsion bars were re-indexed at each road wheel and a more robust pressure valve applied to the track adjusting arm, which redistributed ground pressure and increased track tension and helped prevent the tendency towards thrown tracks. Turbine blade failures due to entry of dust and other matter through the seals in the engine air induction and filtration system were solved by fitting positive seals throughout the system.

By early 1982 Operational and Development Test III had been completed. During this testing 54 early production M1s fired 40 000 rounds of main gun ammunition and travelled over 330 000 km. The developmental and operational tests showed that the M1 met or exceeded the requirements established for major characteristics.

The dust ingestion problem had been solved but the M1 did not meet the operating range requirement, established in 1972, of 443 km travelling at a speed of 40 km/h on level secondary roads. This requirement was met during earlier testing, but the solution to the track-throwing problem, tightening track tension, resulted in lower fuel economy. At a speed of 48 km/h the engine and transmission operated more efficiently meaning fuel economy, and at 48 km/h the 443 km operational range can be exceeded.

In the areas of RAM-D, the M1 met or exceeded 12 of the 13 requirements. The only requirement not met was the track life and a new track is being developed and tested to meet this requirement.

In March 1982, Chrysler sold its tank building subsidiary (Chrysler Defense Incorporated) to General Dynamics for $348.5 million.

Production is being undertaken at the Lima Army Tank Plant in Lima, Ohio, with the first production tank completed in February 1980, and assembly at the General Dynamics-operated Detroit Arsenal Tank Plant in 1982. The original intention was to procure 3312 M1s at a cost of $4900 million, but in 1978 this figure was increased to 7058 by the end of fiscal year 1988 and in 1984 was increased to 7467. Production increased from 30 a month in 1981 to 60 a month in 1982 which was maintained until January 1984 when production increased to 70 vehicles a month and is expected to remain at this figure.

By the end of February 1985 a total of 2500 M1 tanks had been delivered with 19 battalion equivalents being fielded. Eleven battalion equivalents had been fielded in Europe, seven at Fort Hood and one with the National Guard at Fort Bragg. Worldwide fleet availability in early 1985 consistently exceeded the Department of the Army goal of 90 per cent.

Description

The hull and turret of the M1 is of advanced armour construction similar to the Chobham armour developed in the United Kingdom and also used on the Challenger and Leopard 2 MBTs. This gives protection against ATGWs and other battlefield weapons.

The driver is seated at the front of the vehicle in the centre and operates the vehicle from a semi-reclining position when driving with the hatch closed. Steering is accomplished by rotating a motorcycle type T-bar which actuates the steering lever on the transmission to produce the steering speed bias of the track. At both ends of the T-bar are twist grip controls which serve the throttle for the electronic fuel management system. The condition of fluid levels, filters, batteries, electrical connectors and circuit breakers are displayed on the driver's maintenance monitoring panel. The driver is provided with a single hatch opening to the right with three integral periscopes for observation when the hatch is closed. The centre periscope can be replaced by an image intensification periscope for night driving.

The commander and gunner are seated on the right of the turret and the loader on the left. The commander is provided with six periscopes which cover 360 degrees, as well as a sight with a magnification of ×3 for the 12.7 mm machine gun mounted over his position and an optical extension of the gunner's primary sight. The gunner has a primary sight (GPS) with dual day optics with a magnification of ×10 (narrow field of view), magnification of ×3 (wide field of view), close-in surveillance magnification of ×1 and an 18-degree field of view, thermal imaging night vision optics with a magnification of ×10 (narrow field of view), magnification of ×3 (wide field of view), sight stabilisation in elevation and a Hughes laser rangefinder. The gunner's auxiliary sight (a Kollmorgen model 939) has a magnification of ×8 and an 8-degree field of view. The loader is provided with a periscope

Hughes Aircraft Company technician displays the sight unit for M1 MBT. Hughes' Electro-Optical and Data Systems Group at El Segundo

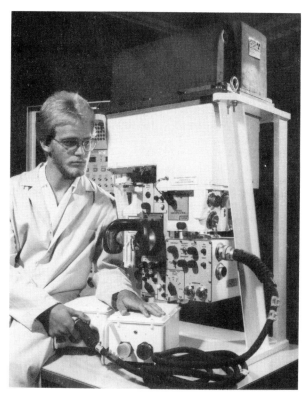

M1 Abrams MBT showing its cross-country mobility

with a magnification of ×1 which can be traversed through 360 degrees.

The fire-control system includes the laser rangefinder, full solution solid-state digital computer and stabilised day/thermal night sight. The stabilisation system permits accurate firing-on-the-move and the gunner merely places his graticule on the target, uses the laser rangefinder (Neodymium YAG) to determine the range, the computer then determines and applies the weapon sight offset angles necessary to obtain a target hit and the gunner opens fire. The main armament is equipped with a muzzle reference system to measure the bend of the gun. Information from a wind sensor mounted on the turret roof and a pendulum static cant sensor at the turret roof centre is fed automatically to the computer together with inputs from the laser rangefinder and the lead angle. The following data is manually set: battle sight range, ammunition type, barrel wear, muzzle reference compensation, barometric pressure and ammunition temperature.

The infra-red Thermal Imaging System (TIS) has been developed by the Hughes Aircraft Company and produces an image by sensing the small difference in heat radiated by the objects in view. The detected energy is converted into electrical signals which are displayed on a cathode ray tube, similar to a tv picture and the image displayed is projected into the eyepiece of the gunner's sight. In addition, the sight displays target range information and indicates the existence of more than one return, data which is received from the Hughes laser rangefinder. Ready-to-fire indication and confirmation that the systems are working properly are also provided.

The thermal imaging system generates a graticule pattern boresighted to the laser rangefinder, as well as computer symbology. This allows the gunner to operate the TIS just as he would the day sight. The infra-red sight is based on use of common modules, components standardised to specifications of the US Army Night Vision and Electro-Optics Laboratories.

The digital fire-control sub-system is produced in Canada by Computing Devices Company, a division of Control Data Canada Limited. The fire-control computer hardware consists of an electronics unit and a separate data entry and test panel. The electronic unit contains the computing element, the power regulators and interfaces with other elements of the fire-control system. The entry and test panel contains the keyboard, control switches and indicators, and a numeric display. The fire-control computer carries out a continuous monitoring of its internal function and memory, and provides a visual display of any malfunction. A manually initiated self-test facility gives fault diagnosis in either unit of the system to the replaceable sub-assembly level.

Power for the electro-hydraulic gun and turret drive system is provided by an engine-driven pump through a slip ring in the turret/hull interface, to a power valve in the manifold beneath the main armament.

The crew compartment is separated from the fuel tanks by armour bulkheads. Sliding armour doors and spall-protected boxes isolate the crew from on-board main armament ammunition explosion. An automatic HALON fire-extinguishing system in the tank reacts to the outbreak of a fire in three milliseconds and extinguishes fires in less than two-tenths of a second. Ready-use ammunition is stowed in the turret bustle and in the event of penetration by a HEAT projectile, the explosion would blow off the top panels with the crew being protected by the access doors, provided they were closed.

The M1 is powered by an Avco-Lycoming AGT-1500 gas turbine which, according to the manufacturer, can operate for up to 19 300 km before requiring an overhaul. The engine operates primarily on diesel or kerosene-based fuel, but can operate on petrol during emergency conditions. Approximately 70 per cent of the engine accessories and components can be removed without removing the powerpack from the tank. The complete powerpack can be removed and replaced in less than an hour compared with four hours for the current M60 series. The gas turbine delivers more horsepower to the sprocket than a comparable diesel engine because of the low cooling requirement. The exhaust for the gas turbine is at the rear of the hull with the air inlet on the hull top.

The engine is coupled to a Detroit Diesel X-1100-3B fully automatic transmission with four forward and two reverse speeds. The transmission also provides integral brakes, variable hydrostatic steering and pivot steering.

The improved torsion bar suspension has rotary shock absorbers at the first, second and seventh road wheel stations with 381 mm of road wheel travel compared with 162 mm in the current M60 series. The top of the suspension is covered by armoured skirts that hinge upwards to allow access to the suspension for maintenance. The drive sprocket is at the rear with the idler at the front and there are two return rollers. Standard equipment includes an AN/VDR-1 (RADIAC)

M1 Abrams MBT from rear with turret traversed left and showing extensive external stowage on turret bustle (US Army)

133

M1A1 MBT with 120 mm Rheinmetall-designed smooth-bore gun

Radiological Warning Device, chemical agent detector kit, a collective NBC protection unit and personnel heaters.

The turret has been designed to accept the standard 105 mm M68 series gun or the German Rheinmetall 120 mm smooth-bore gun which has the American designation M256.

The 105 mm M68E1 gun will fire the standard ammunition as used for the M60 as well as the more recent M735 APFSDS-T, with depleted uranium penetrator and corresponding training projectiles. Of 55 rounds of 105 mm ammunition carried 52 will be compartmentalised, 44 rounds stowed in the turret bustle, 22 on the left side and 22 on the right, three stowed horizontally in spallproof containers on the turret basket and the remaining eight stowed in the hull.

The USA has decided to adopt the 120 mm Rheinmetall smooth-bore gun for the M1. The final production decision was taken in December 1984 and the first two production tanks with the 120 mm smooth-bore gun were completed on schedule in August 1985 under designation of the M1A1. Under the royalty agreement signed with Rheinmetall the United States Army will pay the company $30 million for US defence purposes, three per cent of the cost of each gun is provided under grant aid of up to a maximum of $25 million and royalties of five per cent with a limit of $25 million on any guns sold for export under Foreign Military Sales. The 120 mm RDTE cost estimate (escalated $ in millions) was:

	Gun and ammunition	Integration	Total
FY78	6.1	6.2	12.3
FY79	21.2	12.4	33.6
FY80	22.9	18.1	41.0
FY81	29.6	31.8	61.4
FY82	26.3	60.3	86.6
FY83	26.6	27.5	54.1
FY84	9.3	45.4	54.7
FY85	0.5	12.6	13.1
Total	142.5	214.3	356.8

The first barrel of the M256 was completed at Watervliet Arsenal in the first half of 1980 and was then shipped to Aberdeen Proving Ground for tests and subsequent safety release. It was intended to use an American designed breech but during the development process West Germany reduced the number of parts in their breech and improved its reliabil-

ity. A decision was then taken to use the West German breech on the XM256. The first M1 of 14 prototypes with the 120 mm XM256 gun began trials in the first half of 1981 under the designation M1E1 which was subsequently standardised as the M1A1.

Gun/turret integration is being carried out by General Dynamics, Land Systems Division. The new gun mount is similar to that employed on the basic 105 mm M1 MBT. Software changes were made to the computer on completion of firing table data collection. The ammunition racks, blow-off panels and crew compartment sliding door have been redesigned.

Honeywell Defense Systems Division is the systems manager for 120 mm ammunition for the M1A1. The ammunition has a combustible cartridge case with a metal case base that is ejected during recoil. Types of 120 mm ammunition fired by the M1A1 are as follows:

M827 APFSDS-T, type classified in 1983, similar to West German round but uses a one-piece depleted uranium (DU) round instead of the two-piece tungsten configuration of the West German round.

M829 APFSDS-T, type classified in FY1985, standard combat round.

M830 HEAT-MP-T, similar to West German round, type classified in FY1985.

M831 HEAT-TP-T, training round for M830, type classified in 1984.

M1 MBT being unloaded backwards from Lockheed C-5A transport aircraft

General Dynamics, Land Systems Division M1 Abrams MBT firing its 105 mm M68 rifled tank gun

M865 TPFSDS-T, type classified in July 1984, for basic gunnery practice and can be used on most gunnery ranges in the USA and Europe.

XM866, interim training round, TPFSDS-T

Mounted coaxially to the right of the main armament is a 7.62 mm M240 machine gun, the Belgian FM MAG, and a similar weapon skate-mounted on the left side of the turret for the loader can be elevated from −30 to +65 degrees, total traverse being 265 degrees. A total of 11 400 rounds of 7.62 mm machine gun ammunition is carried. Mounted at the commander's station is a standard 12.7 mm (0.50) Browning M2 HB machine gun which can be elevated from −10 to +65 degrees and can be traversed through 360 degrees. This weapon has powered and manual controls for traverse and manual controls for elevation. A total of 1000 rounds of 12.7 mm machine gun ammunition is carried. Mounted on either side of the turret is a British-designed (L8A1) six-barrelled smoke discharger designated the M250.

Variants

Improved M1 MBT
First Improved M1 was completed in December 1984 and final deliveries are expected to be made in February 1986. The Improved M1 is essentially the M1 with improved armour protection.

M1A1 MBT
First two production M1A1s were completed in August 1985 and of the original anticipated buy of 7085 tanks, 3790 were expected to be M1s. In addition to improved armour protection of the Improved M1, the M1A1 has the 120 mm Rheinmetall smooth-bore gun and an integrated NBC system. This provides the crew with conditioned air for breathing and also supplies cooling or heating for the crew as required while they are wearing their protective suits and face masks.

M1A1 with Block II Improvements
First production models of this version are expected to be completed in mid-1988 and will feature all of the improvements of the M1A1 plus an improved commander's weapon

station, eye safe CO_2 laser rangefinder, fast refuel capability (increased from 50 to 200 gallons per minute) and driver's thermal viewer.

The commander's station will have a panoramic sight, automatic search and detection capability, improved target designation and handoff capability and an improved computer.

M1A1 with Block III improvements
This will enter production in 1989 and have all of the improvements of the previous models plus some others.

M1A1 for US Marine Corps
The US Marine Corps has decided in principle to purchase the M1A1 to replace its current 716 series M60A1 MBTs. The US Marine model will be similar to the M1A1 but have a deep fording kit that would include a cap for the gun barrel, engine exhaust tower on the hull rear and two inlet towers on the left side to the turret rear. This would enable it to ford to a depth of 2 metres with towers being removed by traversing the turret once ashore.

M1 Abrams Bulldozer Kit
In 1978 the Defense Division of the Chrysler Corporation (now the Land Systems Division of General Dynamics) studied the possibility of adapting the M9 bulldozer kit to fit the M1 MBT. The result of this study was that a recommendation was made that a new kit be designed with a revised mouldboard geometry to improve the driver's vision and the overall system performance and yet take advantage of the low profile of the M1. It was also recommended that improved hydraulic components be used allied to a rapid coupling and release mechanism.

Design of the new bulldozer kit was undertaken by the Belvoir Research and Development Center at Fort Belvoir and late in 1981 the Center awarded a production contract to build a prototype kit to Barnes and Reinecke Inc, and this prototype was tested at Fort Knox in mid-1984.

The M1 Abrams bulldozer kit fits onto the MBT's lifting eyes and towing lugs and is powered by the tank's 24-volt electrical system.

Tank Test Bed
The chassis of the M1 MBT is also being used as the basis for the Tank Test Bed (TTB) for which there is a separate entry earlier in this section.

M1 AVLB
In 1983 Bowen-McLaughlin-York (BMY) was awarded a contract for the development of the Heavy Assault Bridge (HAB) based on the chassis of the M1 MBT. BMY is teamed with Israel Military Industries and the prototype will be delivered to the US Army within 35 months and then undergo 12 months of extensive trials.

The three-part bridge will, when opened out, be able to span a gap of 30.48 metes compared to the 19.2 metres of the current AVLB based on the M48/M60 chassis, and will be able to take vehicles weighing up to 70 (US) tons.

M1 Mineclearing Vehicle
The mine roller kit developed by Chrysler (now General Dynamics Land Systems Division) for the M60 MBT has already been successfully tested fitted to the M1 MBT.

(Data in brackets relates to M1A1 where different)

CREW	4	GRADIENT	60%	AMMUNITION			
COMBAT WEIGHT	54 545 (57 154) kg	VERTICAL OBSTACLE	1.244 (1.066) m	main	55 (40)		
POWER-TO-WEIGHT		TRENCH	2.743 m	12.7 mm	1000		
RATIO	27 (26) hp/tonne	TURNING RADIUS	pivot to infinitely	7.62 mm	11 400		
LENGTH GUN			variable	smoke grenades	24		
forwards	9.766 (9.828) m	ENGINE	Avco Lycoming	GUN CONTROL			
rear	8.971 (9.033) m		AGT-1500 gas	EQUIPMENT			
LENGTH HULL	7.918 m		turbine developing	Turret power control	electro-hydraulic/		
WIDTH	3.653 (3.657) m		1500 hp at 3000 rpm		manual		
WIDTH REDUCED	3.479 m	TRANSMISSION	Detroit Diesel	by commander	yes		
HEIGHT			X-1100-3B automatic	by gunner	yes		
to turret roof	2.375 (2.438) m		with 4 forward	Max rate of			
overall	2.885 (2.886) m		and 2 reverse	power traverse	(tracking) 4.2°/s		
FIRING HEIGHT	1.89 m		gears		(slew rate with		
GROUND CLEARANCE		STEERING	hydrostatic		stabilisation) 42°/s		
hull centre	0.482 m	FINAL REDUCTION		Max rate of			
hull sides	0.432 m	RATIO	4.3:1 (4.67:1)	power elevation	(tracking) 1.4°/s		
TRACK WIDTH	635 mm	BRAKING SYSTEM	hydro-mechanical		(slew rate with		
LENGTH OF TRACK		SUSPENSION	advanced torsion bar		control handles)		
ON GROUND	4.65 m	ELECTRICAL SYSTEM	24 V		22.5°/s		
MAX SPEED		BATTERIES	6 × 12 V		(slew rate with		
road	72.421 (66.77) km/h	ARMAMENT			stabilisation		
cross-country average	48.3 km/h	main	1 × 105 mm		commands) 42°/s		
on 10% grade	32.2 (27.51) km/h		(1 × 120 mm)	Gun elevation/			
on 60% grade	8.3 (6.59) km/h	coaxial	1 × 7.62 mm MG	depression	+20°/−9°		
ACCELERATION		anti-aircraft			(+20°/−10°)		
0 – 32 km/h	7 (6.8) s	commander	1 × 12.7 mm MG	Gun stabiliser			
FUEL CAPACITY	1907.6 litres	anti-aircraft loader	1 × 7.62 mm MG	vertical	yes (sight)		
MAX ROAD RANGE	498 (465) km	SMOKE-LAYING		horizontal	yes (turret)		
FORDING	1.219 m	EQUIPMENT	6 smoke dischargers				
with preparation	2.375 m		either side of turret				
			and integral engine				
			smoke generators				

Status: First production tanks were completed in February 1980. In service with US Army.

Manufacturer: Production is undertaken at the Lima Army Tank Plant in Lima, Ohio, and from 1982 at the Detroit Arsenal Tank Plant. Prime contractor is General Dynamics, Land Systems Division, PO Box 1743, Warren, Michigan 48090, USA.

Teledyne Continental High Performance M60 MBT

Development

The High Performance M60 MBT has been developed as a private venture by the General Products Division of Teledyne Continental Motors. It is essentially an M60 series MBT fitted with a new powerpack, new suspension and, as an option, additional armour. These modifications can be carried out on existing M60 series (eg M60, M60A1 or M60A3) or incorporated in new production tanks. The Teledyne Continental High Performance M60 is also known as the Super M60.

The company leased an M60A1 from the US Army in 1978 for the development of this model but so far the Army has not evaluated the High Performance M60 MBT.

Description

The engine fitted is the AVCR-1790-1B 12-cylinder, air-cooled, fuel injected and turbo-charged diesel which is a modification of the standard AVDS-1790-2C diesel and develops 1200 hp at 2400 rpm compared with the 800 hp at 2400 rpm of the latter engine. Most of the components, apart from the pistons, are the same as in the AVDS-1790 of which over 32 000 have been built.

The variable compression ratio (VCR) pistons allow the engine to adjust compression ratios to vehicle load demands. Teledyne Continental also developed the 1500 hp AVCR-1360 which powered the American version of the MBT-70 as well as the General Motors entry in the XM1

MBT competition. More recently the engine has been fitted in the US Army High Mobility Agility Test Vehicle which also has hydro-pneumatic suspension.

The engine is coupled to a West German Renk RK-304 transmission which is fully automatic instead of the manual Allison CD-850 installed in the standard M60 series and incorporates a torque converter and lock-up clutch. Its steering system provides two steering radii per gear range (eight total) for greater manoeuvrability. As the range selection is automatic there is no need for the driver to downshift, the transmission when he encounters a tight turn as in the case of the standard M60. With the RK-304 pivot steer can be accomplished at two different speeds. The RK-304 also has a hydraulic retarder which provides braking when the vehicle is being driven downhill.

Relatively little modification is required for installing the new powerpack, but includes new mountings, replacing the existing air-inlet grilles by an improved design which allows greater air-flow for the new higher capacity air cleaner, replacing an access door over the engine by a grille and some modifications to the fuel tanks. The final drive ratio has been changed from 5.08 to 4.27:1.

PERFORMANCE COMPARISON

Model	Basic M60	High Performance M60
Maximum road speed	48.2 km/h	74 km/h
Acceleration, 0–32 km/h	15 s	9 s
Power-to-weight ratio	14.1 hp/t	23.1 hp/t

Frontal view of High Performance M60 MBT with appliqué steel armour package

To allow the vehicle to use its high speed over rough terrain the original torsion bar suspension has been replaced by an hydro-pneumatic suspension system that gives the tank the capability to negotiate marginal terrain without hull bulldozing.

The hydro-pneumatic suspension system was originally developed by the National Waterlift Company and has been installed on other vehicles including the HIMAG (Model 2867), General Motors XM1 (Model 2857) and Centurion (Model 2869). The Model 2880 is being proposed for the M1 MBT, the Model 2884 is being offered for vehicles in the 20 to 22-tonne range. The High Performance M60 has the Model 2866 which has already been tested in three M60 MBTs covering some 18 000 km and allows a vertical road wheel travel of 343 mm compared with the 163 mm of the basic M60.

Over Profile IV cross-country terrain the M60 with hydro-pneumatic suspension achieved a speed of 38.62 km/h compared to the basic M60 with torsion bar suspension which achieved a speed of 14.48 km/h.

In addition to allowing a higher cross-country speed and giving a better ride for the crew, the hydro-pneumatic suspension system also allows the tank to fire on the move with increased accuracy and tests have shown that the crew can load and fire the main armament while the tank is running over rough terrain at speeds of up to 32 km/h.

The hydro-pneumatic suspension units are externally mounted and provide for vehicle springing and damping. The unit is sealed and protected with a low-pressure relief valve to prevent over pressurisation of the hydraulic system. Disabled unit tests have confirmed that the tank can get home without difficulty.

The High Performance M60 can also be fitted with a new low profile commander's cupola and an appliqué steel armour package. The latter covers the complete turret including the mantlet, sides, rear and top, hull glacis and front deck on either side of the driver's hatch and new side skirts.

The new spaced appliqué armour provides additional protection against high velocity kinetic energy weapons, shaped charge warheads and artillery projectiles. The High Performance M60s armour package includes:

Appliqué armour
Turret (frontal arc protection from 125 mm weapons)
Turret (top and side protection from 30 mm weapons)
Hull (front and glacis protection for kinetic and HEAT weapons)

Side skirts
Track and hull (protection from HEAT warheads)
Special high-hardness steel plates and composite ceramic modules provide added protection to the turret, gun mantlet and hull. These plates, up to 22 mm thick, have a Brinell Hardness Number exceeding 500. Similar plates add to the protection of the turret top and engine compartment.

Side skirts increase the protection to the hull, tracks and the suspension system. Constructed with a layer of Sital type material sandwiched between two high-hardness steel plates, the side skirts resist penetration of shaped charge weapons. The skirts are modular for easy access to the hydro-pneumatic suspension units and track.

The vehicle can also be fitted with an automatic fire suppression protection system and automatic NBC protection. The latter has been designed for the High Performance M60 by Engineered Air Systems Incorporated and is a positive-pressure filtration system that removes toxic agents from air entering the tank. The system provides clean filtered air to the crew compartment and to the ventilated face pieces of the tank crew in an NBC environment. The system also provides ventilation air to the crew compartment when the vehicle is in a non-toxic environment.

The High Performance M60 is equipped with a full solution Laser Tank Fire-Control System (LTFCS). This fully integrated system has been designed to increase survivability and first round hit capabilities and to provide the gunner with a simplified firing sequence. The target is acquired, ammunition selected, laser rangefinder activated, firing button depressed and the gunner then observes the hit.

The LTFCS includes a Nd-YAG laser, second generation image intensifier or thermal imager, built in fault isolation, full solution system, full back up modes, simplified controls and M35 gunner's sight modified to include laser visual unit.

The weapon/turret stabilisation system provides the High Performance M60 with the ability to fire on the move while travelling over rough terrain or during evasive manoeuvring. During cross-country operations, the Super M60 has an 80 per cent hit probability at 1000 metres. The stabilisation system automatically keeps the weapon precisely oriented allowing the gunner to keep on target in spite of vehicle roll, pitch and yaw positions. The new system uses state-of-the-art electronic and hydraulic components to provide a high level of reliability.

Acceleration comparison of High Performance and standard H60 MBTs

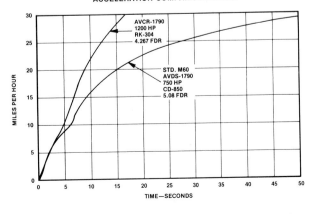

ACCELERATION COMPARISON CHART

Engine compartment of High Performance M60 MBT

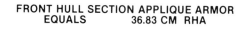

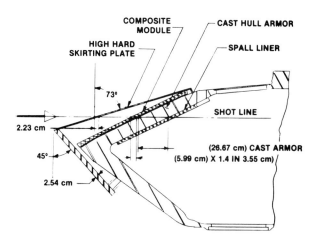

SPACED APPLIQUE ARMOR
EQUALS   40.64 CM RHA

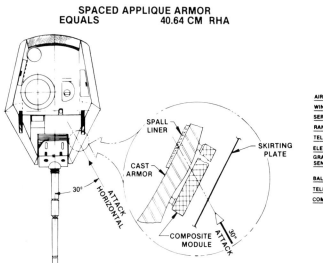

SUPER M60 LTFCS LAYOUT

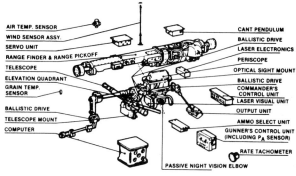

High Performance M60 MBT fitted with appliqué steel armour package and low profile commander's cupola

To complement the improvements in mobility and armour protection, Teledyne Continental has also designed a special diesel smoke generator system for the diesel engine. This is an add-on system with off-the-shelf components and is mounted at the rear of the engine compartment. It can be installed in under eight manhours and to do so it is not necessary to remove the engine or turret. Smoke can be produced any time the vehicle's engine is running by the simple flick of a toggle switch.

Variants

Teledyne Continental is now offering modernisation packages for a wide range of AFVs including the T-54/T-55, Centurion, AMX-30 and M47/M48. These packages can include advanced appliqué armour, fire-control system (such as the Belgian SABCA), turret and weapon stabilisation, hydro-pneumatic suspension (as on Super M60 and Jordanian Centurions), fire suppression system, passive night vision devices, NBC protection, new powerpack and higher capacity final drives.

SPECIFICATIONS
(where different from M60A1)

COMBAT WEIGHT	56 300 kg
POWER-TO-WEIGHT RATIO	21.3 hp/tonne
LENGTH HULL	7.086 m
WIDTH	4.191 m
HEIGHT	2.921 m
MAXIMUM SPEED	
road	74 km/h
cross-country	48 km/h
10% grade	32 km/h
60% grade	7.2 km/h
ACCELERATION	
0 to 32 km/h	9 s
ENGINE	Teledyne Continental AVCR-1790-1B 12-cylinder, air-cooled fuel injected turbocharged diesel developing 1200 hp at 2400 rpm
TRANSMISSION	Renk RK-304 hydromechanical, fully automatic, four forward and two reverse gears
TORQUE CONVERTER	two-stage with lockup
FINAL REDUCTION RATIO	4.27:1
SUSPENSION	hydro-pneumatic
SMOKE-LAYING EQUIPMENT	smoke generator in engine compartment

Status: Development complete. Ready for production.

Manufacturer: Teledyne Continental Motors, General Products Division, 76 Getty Street, Muskegon, Michigan 49442, USA.

M60 Series of Main Battle Tank

Development

Early in 1956 it was decided that the M48 tank should be further developed to produce an improved tank with increased operational range and mobility which would require a minimum of refuelling and servicing as well as incorporating an improved main armament.

In November 1956 a decision was taken to install an AVDS-1790-P compression ignition engine in an M48 tank, which was subsequently tested at Yuma Test Station during the summer of 1957. As a result of a meeting in February 1958, three M48 tanks (designated the M48A2E1) were rebuilt to incorporate the new powerpack contemplated for use in the new tank which had been designated the XM60. These prototypes were tested at Yuma, Fort Churchill, Fort Knox and in the Eglin Air Force Base climatic hangar.

During October and November 1958 several main armament candidates were tested at Aberdeen Proving Ground and based on the test results the British 105 mm L7A1 barrel with the American T254E2 breech was selected as the main armament for the XM60 and designated the M68 cannon.

In February 1957 the M60 (XM60) vehicle characteristics and production planning schedules were established and in March 1959 the M60 was classified as Standard A.

The initial bid package for the production of M60 tanks was released in April 1959 and in June 1959 a production contract was awarded to Chrysler Corporation (now taken over by General Dynamics, Land Systems Division), Delaware Defense Plant, for the production of 180 M60 MBTs. In August 1959 an engineering release bid package was released for the second production buy of M60s to be built at Delaware. Subsequent production buys, beginning with October 1960 production, were made from the Chrysler Corporation Detroit Tank Plant, where production of the latest model, the M60A3, continues today (but see under M60A3).

The M60 entered service with the United States Army in 1960 and from October 1962 the tank was succeeded in production by the M60A1 (development designation M60E1). The M60A1 has the same basic chassis as the M60 but a redesigned 'needle nose' turret with greater ballistic protection and other modifications. It carries 63 rounds of 105 mm ammunition rather than 60 as carried by the older M60. For most of the 1960s and early 1970s production of the M60A1 was maintained at a very low rate, the minimum necessary to sustain the production base.

As a result of the Middle East War of 1973 a major effort was undertaken to increase production of the M60A1 for two reasons: to replace M60A1 tanks supplied to Israel and to increase war reserve stocks which were then very low. It took some time to build up production of the M60A1 owing, in the main, to a shortage of hull and turret castings. By 1975 production had been boosted to 48 tanks per month, which increased to 72 a month in 1977 and 104 a month in December 1977. Peak production rate was achieved in October 1978 at 129 tanks a month. Production continued at a high rate until April 1979 when it started to drop and by the summer of 1980 it was running at 50 vehicles a month. The last M60A1 was completed in May 1980 and all production after this date was of the M60A3.

As of late 1985 the Detroit Tank Plant was producing M60A3s for the export market and M1A1 MBTs for the US Army.

Production of the M60A3 was expected to be completed in May 1985 after over 15 000 M60 series MBTs had been built but in May 1985 the US Department of Defense notified Congress of a letter of offer for 94 M60A3 MBTs for Egypt at a cost of $165 million.

M60A3s being produced early in 1985 were for Saudi Arabia. More recently Taiwan has been purchasing M60A3 hulls from General Dynamics, Land Systems Division.

The fiscal year 1980 request was for 116 M60A3s for the

Side view of M60A1 MBT (US Army)

United States Army and a further 444 for foreign military sales, which were built between April 1981 and July 1982. There was no United States Army funding for M60A3 production after fiscal year 1980 but in fiscal year 1981 167 M60A3s were built for foreign military sales between July and November 1982. Funding for modifications to the M60 will continue for some time. The majority of this funding is being used to procure kits for M60A1 to M60A3 conversions at both Anniston and Mainz Army Depots.

At the start of fiscal year 1985 the M60A3 TTS fleet size was 3191 and about 460 are now being converted every year.

Description (M60A1)

The hull of the M60A1 is made of cast sections and forged floor plates welded together. It is divided into three compartments: driver's at the front, fighting in the centre and the engine and transmission at the rear.

The driver is seated at the front of the vehicle and is provided with a single-piece hatch cover that opens to the right. Three M27 periscopes are mounted forward of his hatch and an M24 infra-red periscope can be installed in a mount in the centre of his hatch cover for driving at night. The M24 is now being replaced by the Baird-Atomic AN/VVS-2 night viewer which is of the passive rather than infra-red type. A hull escape hatch is provided near the driver's position.

The all-cast turret is in the centre of the vehicle with the loader on the left and the commander and gunner on the right. There is an external stowage basket at the rear of the turret. The loader is provided with a single hatch cover that opens to the rear with an integral M37 periscope that can be traversed through 360 degrees.

The commander has a cupola that can be traversed through 360 degrees by hand, a single-piece hatch cover that opens and swings to the rear, an M28C sight in the forward part and eight vision blocks for all-round observation. The M28C can be replaced by an M36 infra-red periscope or an M36E1 passive periscope for night vision. The gunner is seated in front of and below the commander and is provided with an M31 periscope with a magnification of ×8 and an M105D telescope with a magnification of ×8 and a 7.5-degree field of view. The M31 periscope can be replaced by

M60A1 with infra-red/white light searchlight mounted above 105 mm gun but without 12.7 mm machine gun fitted in commander's cupola

140

M60A1 MBT fitted with hydraulically-operated dozer blade (US Army)

M60A3 MBT (left) compared to M1 MBT (right). Both are armed with the same 105 mm M68 rifled tank gun (US Army)

an M32 infra-red periscope or an M35E1 passive periscope for night engagement of targets. The M17A1 or M17C rangefinder has a magnification of ×10, a 4-degree field of view and a range of between 500 and 4400 metres.

The engine compartment at the rear of the hull is separated from the fighting compartment by a fireproof bulkhead, and is equipped with a fire-extinguishing system.

The torsion bar suspension system consists of six dual rubber-tyred road wheels with the idler at the front, drive sprocket at the rear and three track return rollers. The first, second and sixth road wheel stations are provided with a hydraulic shock absorber.

The NBC system of the M60 is of the central air filtration type which pipes fresh air to each crew member via a tube. A full range of night vision equipment is fitted as standard including an infra-red searchlight over the main armament. The latter is either the AN/VSS-1 or the more recent AN/VSS-3A. The former is a 2.2-kilowatt Xenon unit that provides a narrow or wide beam of high-intensity visible or infra-red light. A 50 per cent increase in light intensity can be temporarily provided for 15 to 20 seconds by overriding the searchlight. It has a narrow beam width of 0.5 to 0.75 degree

and a wide beam width of 15 degrees. The AN/VSS-3A can be used in both the visible or infra-red modes with three types of beam, compact, spread or variable width.

The crew compartment is provided with a heater and a RADIAC NBC detector can be fitted if required. The tank can ford to a depth of 1.219 metres without preparation and with preparation to a depth of 2.438 metres. For deep fording a snorkel is attached to the commander's cupola enabling it to ford to a depth of 4.114 metres. The tank can also be fitted with an M9 bulldozer blade on the front of the hull for preparing fire positions and clearing obstacles.

Main armament of the M60, M60A1 and M60A3 tanks is a 105 mm M68 rifled tank gun with a bore evacuator. A well-trained crew can fire between six and eight rounds per minute. Of the 63 rounds of ammunition carried, 26 are carried in the forward part of the hull, to the left and right of the driver's position, 13 in the turret for ready use, 21 in the turret bustle and the remaining three under the gun.

The 105 mm gun can fire the following types of fixed ammunition:

APDS-T (M728) with the complete round weightin 18.95 kg and a muzzle velocity of 1426 metres a second.

APFSDS-T (M735/M735A1). The M731 has a tungsten alloy penetrator while the more recent M735A1 has a staballoy core within the standard penetrator (the latter was not adopted for service). Training version of the M735 is designated M797.

APFSDS-T (M774). Follow on to the M735, with monobloc staballoy penetrator.

APFSDS-T (M833) with monobloc staballoy penetrator, under development.

APDS-T (M392A2) with the complete round weighing 18.6 kg and a muzzle velocity of 1458 metres a second.

APERS-T (M494) with the complete round weighing 24.5 kg and a muzzle velocity of 821 metres a second.

HEAT-T (M456 series) with the complete round weighing 21.78 kg, muzzle velocity 1173 metres a second and a maximum range of 8200 metres.

TP-T (M467) with the complete round weighing 20.412 kg, muzzle velocity of 730 metres a second and a maximum range of 9510 metres.

TP-T (M490) with the complete round weighing 20.412 kg, muzzle velocity of 1170 metres a second and a maximum

Latest production version of the M60 series tanks is the M60A3 with many improvements including a tank thermal sight (TTS)

M60A1 MBT being fitted with turret at Detroit Tank Plant (US Army)

General Defence Corporation, Flinchbaugh Division, manufactured 105 mm M735 APFSDS-T projectile which has a tungsten alloy penetrator

range of 8207 metres (training round for M456).
TPDS-T (M724) with the complete round weighing 14.515 kg, muzzle velocity of 1507 metres a second and a maximum range of 2000 metres (training round for M392A2).
TPFSDS-T (M797) training round for M735, M774 and M833 rounds.
Smoke WP-T(M416) with the complete round weighing 20.68 kg, muzzle velocity of 731.5 metres a second and a maximum range of 9150 metres.

Mounted in the commander's cupola is an M85 12.7 mm (0.50) machine gun with an elevation of +60 degrees and a depression of −15 degrees. Mounted coaxially to the left of the main armament is a 7.62 mm M73 machine gun, currently being replaced by the M240 weapon which is the Belgian MAG-58.

A number of M60A1s are being updated with the RISE engine, main armament fully stabilised in both elevation and traverse, top-loading air cleaner fitted, new T142 tracks and improved night vision equipment. Additional details of this programme are given in the entry for the M60A3.

M60A1 with Mine-clearing Rollers

Following successful trials with prototype vehicles, a number of M60A1 tanks are now being fitted with roller mine-clearing equipment similar to that installed on Soviet T-54 and T-55 MBTs.

The mounting kit consists of a hydraulic release system which is operable from the driver's seat, lower glacis mounting bracket, and linkages which tie the system together.

In order to install the mounting kit the tank must be prepared by welding on the components of the M60 retrofit kit. The roller kit includes a left side pushbeam/carriage assembly, a right side pushbeam/carriage assembly and a dogbone/chain assembly attached to each pushbeam.

Each system uses two roller carriages of five wheels located in front of each track, the rollers clearing a path in front of each track and activates pressure-fuzed mines.

Total system weight is less than 10 tonnes and can be mounted in the field by a tank crew in less than 15 minutes and released from the inside of the tank in less than 30 seconds.

Note: An M48 mounting kit is also available, differing in using the lower glacis mounting structure to couple the rear of the pushbeams to the tank. The M48 roller kit is identical to the M60 roller kit. The system has also been successfully tested on the more recent M1 MBT.

ROBAT

Late in 1981 mine neutralisation equipment being developed by the US Army and Marine Corps was used in the US Army's first field test of a Robotic Counter-Obstacle Vehicle. For the demonstration, a modified M60A2 tank chassis with the turret removed was fitted with a mine-clearing roller, a Marine Corps M58A1 mine-clearing line charge and a Clear Lane Marking System (CLAMS). An M113 APC was outfitted with remote control systems for the test.

The two vehicles, operated by personnel 1.6 km from the site, were used in a simulated combat scenario. Observers had detected enemy minefield laying operations and the robot vehicles were dispatched to counter the threat. The

Frontal view of M60 MBT (US Army)

M60A1 fitted with front-mounted roller type mine clearing equipment

M60A1 from rear showing turret basket (US Army)

APC was used to attack the enemy position and draw suppressive fire while the counter obstacle vehicle cleared a path through the minefield. The Counter Obstacle Vehicle located the boundary of the enemy minefield by using the clearing roller to detonate one of the mines. It then backed up and breached the minefield by projecting the rocket propelled mine clearing charge. After clearing a path, the vehicle marked the safe lane as it moved through the minefield. When the cleared path was marked, the APC safely followed the counter obstacle vehicle across the minefield.

The first two prototypes of the Robotic Obstacle Breaching Assault Tank were completed early in 1985. These have mine clearance rollers mounted at the front of the hull and the same mine clearance kit mounted on top as fitted to the US Marine Corps LVTP7A1 amphibious assault vehicles.

M9 Bulldozer Kit

This has been developed as a depot retrofit package and is used to give already fielded M60 tanks bulldozing capabilities similar to those of the M728 Combat Engineer Vehicle.

M60A2

This model has now been phased out of service with the US Army. A total of 526 M60A2s were built and most have now been sent back to the Anniston Army Depot where they will be converted to other uses such as AVLB, M728 Combat Engineer Vehicles or Counter Obstacle Vehicles.

M60A3

The M60A3 (development designation M60A1E3) is a product-improved M60A1 and some of the improvements in

M60A3 MBT fitted with thermal sleeve for 105 mm M68 gun and covers over searchlight and British supplied smoke dischargers (Simon Dunstan)

the tank, for example the add-on-stabilisation system, RISE engine, and the smoke grenade launchers were first fitted to the M60A1 some years ago.

The first M60A3s completed at the Detroit Arsenal Tank Plant in February 1978 were the first of a low rate of initial production quantity of 296 M60A3s which were funded in fiscal year 1976 transitional quarter and fiscal year 1977. In 1978 the M60A1 monthly production rate was 116 tanks at Detroit. The first M60A3 tanks were delivered to Europe in mid-1979 and issued to the 1st Battalion of 32nd Armored. It was announced in mid-1979 that the two M60A1 tank battalions in South Korea would be re-equipped with M48A5 tanks as used by the National Guard, ensuring uniformity between South Korean and United States armoured units. The Army has 5400 M60A3 TTS tanks of which 1686 are new production M60A3s, 114 are M60A1 passive tanks field retrofitted to M60A3 TTS configuration, and 3600 conversions carried out by the Mainz Army Depot in West Germany and Anniston Army Depot in the USA. In January 1983 Saudi Arabia placed an order for 100 M60A3 MBTs.

The main improvements are in the fire-control system as a Hughes laser rangefinder with a maximum range of 5000 metres replaces the optical rangefinder, and a solid-state computer replaces the mechanical computer. Following successful trials with 20 prototype units Hughes was awarded its first production contract for the laser rangefinder in 1976. The contract was for 69 units at a total cost of $11 million. Range data is fed to the computer and, with other data such as cross-wind velocity, air temperature, gun trunnion tilt, air density, altitude, target tracking rate and ammunition ballistics, provides the correct azimuth and elevation firing commands to the tank gunner and commander. The improvements in the fire-control system, combined with the passive night sight, improve the night-fighting capabilities of the tank.

The fire-control system is composed of two major subsystems, the AN/VVG-2 laser rangefinder and the M21 ballistic computer. The laser/sight sub-system is composed of two main units: a commander's integrated laser/sight with control unit and a laser electronics unit. Range may be fed automatically to the computer or, if more than one return is received, the commander may select the range return based on his assessment of the situation. Since the gunner's sight is boresighted with the laser rangefinder, either the commander or the gunner can fire the laser and/or the gun.

The computer sub-system includes the ammunition selector sensors. The commander or gunner may select one of the four basic types of ammunition to be used. The computer stores solutions for six ammunition types with the four basic types to accommodate ammunition stored in different locations. The switch at the bottom of the ammunition select unit is used to set up conditions according to whether the tank is moving or stationary. The computer is a solid-state hybrid and processes all the input data and commands the sight lines for laying the gun.

The top half of the gunner's control unit panel contains three manual inputs: air temperature, pressure altitude (slowly varying inputs, not required to be very accurate), and manual range in case the laser fails. The rate unit, crosswind sensor and the cant unit are automatic. The rate unit is used against moving targets from a stationary tank. When the tank is moving it is switched out and replaced by input from the gun stabilisation system gyros, since inertial tracking rates are required. The crosswind sensor can be stowed horizontally and is spring mounted to prevent damage when the tank encounters low branches. Since it is the only unit not under armour, a circuit in the computer continuously monitors its output and can switch to manual input in the event of a failure. The cant unit senses gun trunnion roll.

A row of lights on the top of the gunner's control unit is for self-test. Either a green 'System OK' light is lit, or a light comes on indicating which unit is faulty. A red light indicates failure of the system and an orange light indicates that the system will continue to function, but less accurately. This self-test system removes the trouble-shooting burden from the tank crew, and replacing system units in the field is simple. The bottom half of the panel, which is normally covered, is used for boresighting, zeroing, manual crosswind input (if desired) and the switch to select the four basic ammunition types.

At the beginning of fiscal year 1980 AN/VGS-2 Tank Thermal Sights (TTS) were added, which not only improved the night fighting capability of the tank but also enabled the tank to see through smoke and ground cover. The AN/VSG thermal imaging equipment replaced the gunner's passive night vision periscope. Technical details have not been released but may reasonably be expected to be no less than those achieved by other land battlefield IR systems based on the TI range of infra-red modules, developed by Texas Instruments Equipments Group, including the AN/TAS-4, AN/TAS-5 and AN/TAS-6.

M60A1 MBT armed with 105 mm gun

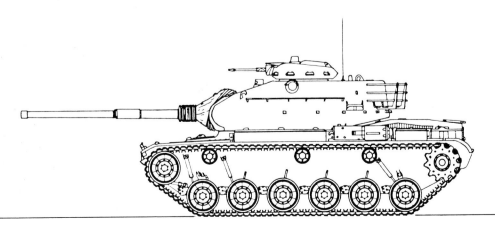

M728 Combat Engineer Vehicle in travelling configuration with A-frame lowered over rear and dozer blade raised (British Army Berlin)

The United States Army considers the M60A1 inferior to the Soviet T-64/T-72 and the M60A3 equal to it.

The full list of M60A3 improvements is as follows:
Main armament fully-stabilised in both elevation and traverse*
Top-loading air cleaner installed*
AN/VSS-1 searchlight replaced by AN/VSS-3A on passive tanks
T97 tracks replaced by T142 tracks with removable pads*
AVDS-1790-2C RISE (Reliability Improved Selected Equipment) engine fitted*
Thermal shroud for main armament
Laser rangefinder
650-amp oil-cooled alternator
Solid-state computer
Passive night vision devices, followed by thermal sights
Coaxial machine gun replaced by M240(MAG-58) weapon
British six-barrelled smoke dischargers fitted to either side of turret
Engine smoke generator
Automatic HALON fire-extinguishing system (not yet incorporated)
* also fitted to late production M60A1s.

Another improvement added to the M60A3 in the near future will be new final drives.

As the M60A3 fleet will remain in worldwide service for many years M1-type system improvements to enable the tank to remain effective on the battlefield will probably be developed.

The 105 mm Tank Gun Enhancement Programme has been funded and will have a longer barrel than the current M68 gun and fire a new range of ammunition with greater penetration characteristics.

All new production M60A3 tanks are now being fitted with the Teledyne developed engine exhaust smoke system and older tanks are being retrofitted. Fuel is sprayed into the exhaust manifold, creating smoke.

The existing manual fire-extinguishing system is being replaced by an automatic HALON system similar to the new M1 MBT's, which uses sensors to detect heat and light from a fire and automatically releases the HALON fire suppressant.

It is expected that in future a chemical alarm and a heading reference unit will be fitted to the M60A3; two types of heading reference have been evaluated, a magnetic indicator and a gyrocompass.

For trials purposes, three M60A1 tanks were fitted with a hydro-pneumatic suspension system developed by the National Water Lift Company. These tanks were successfully tested at both Aberdeen Proving Ground and Fort Knox and showed a significant improvement over the existing suspension system on the M60A1 and M60A3. But due to the high cost of retrofitting the Army fleet of M60s it was decided to retain the existing suspension system rather than adopt the hydro-pneumatic type. Teledyne Continental is now offering this as part of the High Performance M60 package described in the previous entry in this section.

In mid-1984 the Combat System Test Activity (CSTA) of the Test and Evaluation Command (TECOM) at Aberdeen Proving Ground, said that among the new systems being tested and considered to extend the service life of the M60 series for a further 20 years were a hydro-pneumatic suspension system, enhanced armour protection, changes in main gun, digital computer to replace present analogue computer, new transmission and a carbon dioxide laser rangefinder to replace the current ruby laser system.

TACOM and General Dynamics have also developed an improved air-filtration system for the M60 series called the Vehicle Exhaust Dust Ejector System (VEDES) which is being retrofitted to the fleet commencing in late 1984.

The automatic fire extinguishing system is expected to be retrofitted starting with the M60A3 in fiscal year 1987.

M60 AVLB

The M60 Armored Vehicle Launched Bridge is an M60 fitted with a hydraulic launching mechanism and an aluminium scissors bridge which is launched over the front of the vehicle and weighs 14 470 kg. The bridge takes two minutes to lay and when open has an overall length of 19.202 metres and can span a gap of up to 18.288 metres. The M60 AVLB weighs 55 746 kg with the bridge and 41 685 kg without it. By 1983 some 400 M60 AVLBs had been built. In 1985 Anniston Army Depot started a programme to convert M60A2s into M60A1 AVLBs.

M728 Combat Engineer Vehicle

The Combat Engineer Vehicle was developed under the designation T118E1 and was standardised in 1963 as the

Prototype of the ROBAT vehicle fitted with mine clearing rollers at front of hull and mine clearing charge on roof

M728. It entered production in 1965 and entered service with the US Army in 1968. By 1983 over 300 vehicles had been completed.

The M728 is armed with a short-barrelled 165 mm M135 demolition gun which fires the M123A1 HEP (or HESH) round. A 7.62 mm machine gun is mounted coaxially to the main armament and a 12.7 mm machine gun is mounted in the commander's cupola for ground and anti-aircraft use.

Mounted at the front of the hull is a hydraulically-operated dozer blade which is used for clearing obstacles and preparing fire positions. Pivoted towards the front of the turret is an A-frame which can be folded back over the rear of the turret when not required. The two-speed winch at the rear of the turret has a maximum capacity of 11 340 kg. An infra-red searchlight similar to that fitted to the M60A1 is mounted over the main armament of the M728. The M728 weighs 52 163 kg loaded and has a crew of four: commander, gunner, loader and driver.

SPECIFICATIONS

Model	M60	M60A1	M60A3
CREW	4	4	4
COMBAT WEIGHT	49 714 kg	52 617 kg	52 617 kg
UNLOADED WEIGHT	45 631 kg	48 684 kg	48 684 kg
POWER-TO-WEIGHT RATIO	15.08 bhp/tonne	14.24 bhp/tonne	14.24 bhp/tonne
GROUND PRESSURE	0.8 kg/cm²	0.87 kg/cm²	0.87 kg/cm²
LENGTH GUN FORWARDS	9.309 m	9.436 m	9.436 m
LENGTH HULL	6.946 m	6.946 m	6.946 m
WIDTH	3.631 m	3.631 m	3.631 m
HEIGHT	3.213 m	3.27 m	3.27 m
FIRING HEIGHT	2.095 m	2.095 m	2.093 m
GROUND CLEARANCE	0.463 m	0.463 m	0.45 m
TRACK	2.921 m	2.921 m	2.921 m
TRACK WIDTH	711 mm	711 mm	711 mm
LENGTH OF TRACK ON GROUND	4.235 m	4.235 m	4.235 m
MAX ROAD SPEED	48.28 km/h	48.28 km/h	48.28 km/h
FUEL CAPACITY	1457 litres	1420 litres	1420 litres
MAX ROAD RANGE	500 km	500 km	480 km
FORDING	1.219 m	1.219 m	1.22 m
with preparation	2.438 m	2.438 m	2.4 m
with snorkel	4.114 m	n/app	n/app
GRADIENT	60%	60%	60%
SIDE SLOPE	30%	30%	30%
VERTICAL OBSTACLE	0.914 m	0.914 m	0.914 m
TRENCH	2.59 m	2.59 m	2.59 m
TURNING RADIUS	pivot to infinity on all models		
ENGINE	Continental AVDS-1790-2A		AVDS-1790-2D
	12-cylinder air-cooled diesel developing 750 bhp at 2400 rpm		
TRANSMISSION	General Motors Corporation, cross-drive, single-stage with 2 forward and 1 reverse ranges		
SUSPENSION	torsion bar	torsion bar	torsion bar
ELECTRICAL SYSTEM	24 V	24 V	24 V
BATTERIES	6 × 12 V, 100 Ah	6 × 12 V, 100 Ah	6 × 12 V, 100 Ah
ARMAMENT			
main	1 × 105 mm	1 × 105 mm	1 × 105 mm
coaxial	1 × 7.62 mm MG	1 × 7.62 mm MG	1 × 7.62 mm MG
anti-aircraft	1 × 12.7 mm MG	1 × 12.7 mm MG	1 × 12.7 mm MG
AMMUNITION			
main	60	63	63
7.62 mm	5950	5950	5950
12.7 mm	900	900	900
GUN CONTROL EQUIPMENT			
Turret power control	electro-hydraulic/manual in all models		
by commander	yes	yes	yes
by gunner	yes	yes	yes
Max rate power traverse	360° in 15 s	360° in 15 s	360° in 15 s
Gun elevation/ depression	+20°/−9°	+20°/−10°	+20°/−10°
Commander's override	yes	yes	yes

Model	M60	M60A1	M60A3
Commander's fire-control override	yes	yes	yes
Gun stabiliser			
vertical	no	yes*	yes*
horizontal	no	yes*	yes*
Range setting device	yes	yes	yes
Elevation quadrant	yes	yes	yes
Traverse indicator	yes	yes	yes
ARMOUR	no details released, but armour protection is considered an improvement over M48 series, especially over frontal area and turret		

* As originally built, the M60A1 was not fitted with a gun stabilisation system but these are now being retrofitted to most models.

Status: In production. In service with Austria (120 M60A1s and 50 M60A3s), Egypt (in March 1980 Congress was informed of a proposed letter of offer to Egypt for 244 M60A3s at a total cost, including ammunition, training, spare parts and support equipment of $454.1 million. Later in 1980 a further 67 M60A3s were ordered in lieu of 130 M48A5s. In 1981 the US Department of Defense notified Congress of a letter of offer to Egypt for 128 M60A3 MBTs plus spares at a cost of $240 million. In April 1982 220 additional M60A3 tanks were ordered at a cost of $336 million. This brought total sales of M60A3 to Egypt to 659 tanks. In May 1985 the Department of Defense announced a letter of offer for a further 94 M60A3s at a cost of $165 million), Iran (M60A1), Israel (M60, M60A1 and M60A3, 200 of latter delivered from mid-1981), Italy (200 M60A1 were built under licence in Italy by OTO-Melara with 100 being supplied from USA), Jordan (in February 1980 Congress was informed of a letter of offer to Jordan for 14 M60A1/M60A3 tanks at a total cost of $20 million and later in the same year a further 100 were ordered to replace M48s which were then passed to Lebanon; in July 1981 the US Department of Defense notified Congress of a letter of offer to Jordan for 118 M60A3 tank conversion kits at an estimated cost of $60 million), Oman (6 delivered in 1980), South Korea (few), Saudi Arabia (158 delivered in late 1970s with a further 100 ordered in 1983 and delivered in 1984–85), Singapore (M728 CEV and M60 AVLB only), Spain (AVLBs), Sudan (in October 1981 the US Department of Defense notified Congress of a letter of offer to Sudan for 20 M60A3 MBTs plus spares at a total cost of $36 million, which was accepted), Tunisia (in July 1981 the US Department of Defense notified Congress of a letter of offer to Tunisia for 54 M60A3 MBTs at a cost of $92 million, which was accepted), United States (Army and Marines) and Yemen Arab Republic (North) (64 M60A1s).

Manufacturer: Detroit Tank Plant which is now operated by General Dynamics, Land Systems Division, PO Box 1743, Warren, Michigan 48090, USA.

M48 Series of Main Battle Tanks

Development

When the Korean War broke out in 1950 there was no medium tank in production in the USA, although the T42 medium tank was under development. To meet the urgent need for a modern tank, the turret of the T42 was mounted on the chassis of the M46, which was a development of the M26 Pershing heavy tank of the Second World War, and this was

M48A2 tank with turret being removed by an M578 armoured recovery vehicle (US Army)

accepted for limited service as the M46A1. Production vehicles were designated the M47 and even though it was only an interim design production amounted to 8576 tanks.

In October 1950 Detroit Tank Arsenal began design work on a new tank armed with a 90 mm gun and in December the same year the Chrysler Corporation was awarded a letter of intent to design the new tank under the designation T48. Design work began in late December and six prototypes were built, the first being completed in December 1951. Before the prototypes had been completed, in March 1951 the Fisher Body Division of the General Motors Corporation and the Ford Motor Company at Livonia were both given a production contract for the tank. Chrysler's first production M48 rolled out of the Delaware Tank Plant and was christened by Mrs George S Patton Junior on 1 July, 1952.

The first production M48s were completed in 1952 and it soon became apparent that it had been a mistake to place the production orders before the tank had been thoroughly tested. The Army justified the decision on the grounds that they had no idea how long the Korean War was going to last and there was a distinct possibility that the Third World War could have broken out in the early 1950s. Most of the early M48s had to be subsequently rebuilt before they could be issued to the units and until the introduction of the diesel-engined M48A3 the operating range of the tank was very small.

Total production of the M48 series amounted to 11 703 units, of which about 6000 were built by the Chrysler Corporation at the Delaware Defense Plant which continued

production until 1959. Alco Products of Schenectady also built a number of M48A2 tanks.

Many components of the M48 are also used in the M88 ARV as well as the M53 SPG, and further development of the tank resulted in the M60 series which is currently being manufactured by the General Dynamics, Land Systems Division, Detroit. Initial production of the M60 MBT was in fact undertaken at the Delaware plant but in 1959 a decision was taken that all future production would be undertaken at the Detroit Plant.

Description (M48A3)

The cast hull of the M48 is boat-shaped with additional sections welded into position. A hull escape hatch is provided in the floor of the tank. The turret is a one-piece casting.

The driver is seated at the front of the hull in the centre and is provided with a single-piece hatch cover that opens to the right, forward of which are three M27 periscopes. For driving at night an M24 infra-red periscope is placed in the turntable located in the driver's hatch.

The other three crew members are in the turret with the commander and gunner on the right and the loader on the left. The commander is provided with an M1 cupola that he can traverse by hand through 360 degrees. This cupola is also fitted to the M48A1, M48A1C and the M67 flamethrower tanks, and is equipped with five vision blocks and an M28C sight for controlling the 12.7 mm (0.50) machine gun. The M28C has a magnification of ×1.5 and a 48-degree field of view. The coincidence rangefinder is operated by the tank

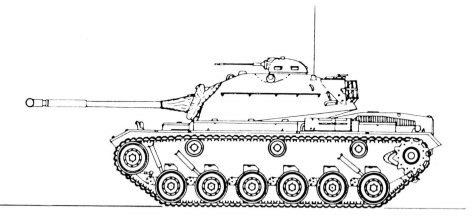

commander and has a maximum range of 4400 metres and a magnification of ×10. The gunner is seated forward and below the commander and has a roof-mounted periscope sight with a ×8 magnification and a telescope with a similar magnification that is linked to the main armament. The ballistic computer is an electro-mechanical device which has been designed to compute super-elevation angles for the main armament. It receives information in the form of shaft rotation from the rangefinder. The data is then applied to the ammunition data and ballistic corrections which have been rendered manually into the computer by the gunner. The end product is the super-elevation angle which is transmitted through the ballistic drive to the periscope. The ballistic drive also transmits the same super-elevation angle to the rangefinder which is operated by the tank commander. The loader is provided with a single-piece hatch cover that opens to the rear. Mounted to the rear of the turret is a dome-shaped ventilator and a stowage basket is provided at the rear of the turret.

The engine is mounted to the immediate rear of the bulk-head that separates the engine and fighting compartments and the transmission is at the rear of the vehicle. The engine compartment is equipped with fire extinguishers but there is no fire warning system. Power is transmitted to the final drives through the cross-drive transmission, which is a combined transmission, differential, steering and braking unit.

The torsion bar suspension consists of six dual rubber-tyred road wheels with the idler at the front, drive sprocket at the rear and five return rollers. Some earlier versions of the M48 tank were fitted with a tensioning idler between the drive sprocket and the sixth road wheel station. Hydraulic shock absorbers are provided for the first, second and sixth road wheel stations.

Infra-red driving lights are fitted as standard and most models have an infra-red/white light searchlight mounted over the main armament, which has a maximum range of 2000 metres. Standard equipment includes an NBC system, heaters, external infantry phone and provision for installing a dozer blade on the front of the hull. The M48, M48C and M48A1 are fitted with the M8 blade weighing 3980 kg and the M48A2, M48A3 and M48A5 with the M8A1 blade which weighs 3810 kg.

The tank can ford to a depth of 1.219 metres without preparation and to 4.438 metres with a deep-fording kit. Before deep fording all the openings are sealed and an exhaust extension is fitted vertically to the right rear engine grille, and the bilge pump switched on.

Main armament of the M48A3 is an M41 (T139) 90 mm gun, which consists of the barrel, evacuator chamber, blast deflector, and breech mechanism assembly. The breech-block is of the vertical sliding type with an inertia percussion firing mechanism. The barrel has a life of 700 equivalent full charge rounds. The following types of fixed rounds can be fired, but it should be noted that not all are currently in use:

APERS-T (M580) with the complete round weighing 18.71 kg, muzzle velocity of 914 metres a second, effective range 3000 metres.

APC-T (M82) with the complete round weighing 19.39 kg, muzzle velocity of 793 metres a second, maximum range of 19 570 metres.

AP-T (M77) with the complete round weighing 19.06 kg, muzzle velocity of 822 metres a second, maximum range of 11 269 metres.

AP-T (M318) with the complete round weighing 19.94 kg, muzzle velocity of 853 metres a second and a maximum range of 21 400 metres.

Canister (M336) with the complete round weighing 18.86 kg, muzzle velocity of 874 metres a second, effective range 183 metres.

Canister (M377) with the complete round weighing 17.82 kg, muzzle velocity of 899 metres a second, maximum range 365 metres.

HE-T (M71) with the complete round weighing 18.68 kg, muzzle velocity of 823 metres a second, maximum range of 17 800 metres.

HEAT-T (M431) with the complete round weighing 14.96 kg, muzzle velocity of 1219 metres a second, maximum range 8138 metres.

HVAP-T (M332A1) with the complete round weighing 18.37 kg, muzzle velocity of 1165 metres a second, maximum range 15 700 metres.

TP-T (M353) with the complete round weighing 19.91 kg, muzzle velocity of 914 metres a second, maximum range 21 031 metres.

Smoke WP (M313) with the complete round weighing 19.29 kg, muzzle velocity of 822.9 metres a second, maximum range 17 717 metres.

Nineteen rounds of 90 mm ammunition are stowed to the left of the driver with a further 11 rounds to his right, eight horizontally on the turret floor, 16 stowed vertically around the turret ring and the remaining eight for ready use in the turret.

Mounted coaxially to the left of the main armament is a 7.62 mm M73 machine gun (earlier models have the 7.62 mm (0.30) M1919A4E1 weapon) and mounted in the commander's cupola is a 12.7 mm (0.50) Browning M2 HB machine gun which can be elevated from −10 to +60 degrees, and can be aimed and fired from within the cupola.

Variants

M48

This was the first production model of the series and has the following distinguishing features: small driver's hatch, five track return rollers, no tensioning idler, no dust shields on the fenders, 'T' or cylindrical type blast deflector on the barrel and the commander's cupola has the 12.7 mm machine gun on an open mount rather than in a fully enclosed cupola as later production tanks in this series.

M48C

This is identical to the M48 but has a hull of mild steel and is therefore unsuitable for combat. This model is used for training only and has the letter C embossed on the right front of the hull meaning that the tank is non-ballistic.

M48A1

This model has larger driver's hatch, fully enclosed commander's cupola, fender dust shields, rear track idler wheel, five track return rollers and a 'T' type blast deflector. In 1964 Bowen-McLaughlin-York was awarded a contract to remanufacture 313 M48A1 tanks at its York, Pennsylvania, plant.

M48A2

Development of this model began in 1954 under the designation T48E2. The first production order was awarded to Alco

Products Incorporated of Schenectady, New York in 1955, followed two years later by an order to the Chrysler Delaware Defense Plant (Lenape Ordnance Modification Center) at Newark, Delaware. Major differences between this and earlier models can be summarised as a fuel injection system for the engine, larger fuel tanks, improved engine deck to minimise infra-red detection, constant-pressure turret control system, improved fire-control system, modified commander's cupola, stowage basket mounted at turret rear, and the main armament fitted with a 'T' type blast deflector. The suspension was also modified and jettisonable long-range fuel tanks could be fitted at the rear.

M48A2C

This is almost identical to the M48A2 apart from slight differences in the optical and fire-control equipment. Most models do not have the track tensioner wheel.

M48A3

This had the development designation of the M48A1E2 and is basically a rebuild of the earlier M48A1 and M48A2 tanks. Major differences are the replacement of the petrol engine by the same diesel engine as installed in the M60A1 MBT, improved fire-control system and commander's cupola modified by mounting a circular ring with vision blocks between the roof of the turret and the base of the commander's cupola. Most M48A3s have only three track return rollers and no rear idler. In addition they have 'T' type blast deflectors and fender dust shields.

M48A3 MBT (US Army)

M48A2 MBT from top with turret traversed to rear (US Army)

M48A2 MBT with turret traversed to front (US Army)

In 1967 Bowen-McLaughlin-York was awarded a contract to remanufacture and modify 578 M48A1 tanks to M48A3 configuration. Under this programme the company rebuilt the vehicles and performed extensive modifications in accordance with 74 US Government designed kits. The principal change to this vehicle was the replacement of the petrol engine with the Continental AVDS-1790-2A diesel engine. Both remanufacture and modification were carried out in York, Pennsylvania.

The Red River Army Depot converted 400 M48A1s to M48A3 standard while the Anniston Army Depot converted 800 M48A1s to M48A3 standard.

M48A4
It was intended that turrets removed from M60s after they had been fitted with the new turret mounting the Shillelagh missile system would be fitted to older M48 chassis to be designated the M48A4. But this project was cancelled after six prototypes had been completed.

M48A5
From October 1975 the Anniston Army Depot started to modernise older M48A1 and M48A3 tanks to a new standard called the M48A5. By the end of fiscal year 1977 764 had been converted, by the end of fiscal year 1978 1454, and a total of

1864 at the end of fiscal year 1980. The Anniston Army Depot converted 2064 M48A1/M48A3s to M48A5 configuration with final deliveries taking place in December 1979. As of early 1985 the US Army had 1601 M48A5s in service. The first unit to receive the M48A5 was the South Carolina Army National Guard which took its first delivery in December 1975. Unit cost of the M48A1 modification was $240 000 and of the more recent M48A3 was $130 000. It took about three months to convert an M48A3 and four months to convert an M48A1. Major modifications required to convert an M48A1 to the M48A5 standard are top-loading air cleaner, top deck grille, engine and transmission shroud, gun travel lock, exhaust grilles, powerpack (new engine fitted), final drives, tow pintle, engine and transmission mounts, hull turret seal, torsion bar knockout, bulkhead, drain valves, fuel tank and lines, track support rollers and shield, turret basket, modified turret ammunition stowage, T142 track, double bump spring and forward arm, driver's controls, driver's escape hatch, modified hull ammunition stowage, fire extinguisher, hull armour, heater, stowage boxes, driver's periscope, gun shield and cover, turret and gun control, 105 mm M68 gun (as in M60 series), composite headlamp, 2.2 kW searchlight, nylon ballistics shield, M114 mount and M105 telescope and graticule kit, M13B1 quadrant elevation, M10A6 ballistics drive, M32 and M118 periscope mount, M13B1C computer cam kit, M17B1C rangefinder and M28C periscope, M104A1 periscope mount, turret electrical kit, cupola adapter ring and retaining ring, turret manual drive and traverse gear box, turret stowage, searchlight stowage and cargo rack screen. Major modifications to convert the M48A3 to the M48A5 are the turret electrical kit, turret stowage, top-loading air cleaner, gun travel lock, solid state regulator, turret basket, T142 track, ammunition stowage, 105 mm gun, gun shield and cover, M87 gun mount, graticule kit and computer cam kit. The fully enclosed commander's cupola was replaced by an Israeli-designed cupola which is manufactured by Associated Steel Foundries in Israel. First American-produced cupolas were delivered in mid-1976. A 7.62 mm M60D machine gun is mounted externally at the commander's station and there are two mounting positions provided at the loader's hatch for his 7.62 mm M60D machine gun, to provide suppressive fire against enemy troop and ATGW positions.

M67/M67A1/M67A2 Flamethrower Tanks
None of these remain in service with the US Army or Marine Corps.

M48 Armoured Vehicle Launched Bridge
This is basically an M48 with its turret removed and fitted with a scissors bridge that is launched hydraulically over the front of the vehicle in three minutes. The bridge weighs 14 470 kg and has an overall length when opened out of 19.202 metres, can span a gap of up to 18.288 metres and has a maximum capacity of 60 000 kg. The M48 AVLB has a crew of two men and weighs 55 746 kg with the bridge and 41 685 kg without it.

Local modifications
A number of countries have, or are, carrying out modernisation programmes on their M48s to extend their operational life into the 1980s and 1990s. These countries include West Germany, Greece, Iran, Israel, South Korea, Spain and Turkey.

M48 AVLB in travelling configuration (Michael Ledford)

M48 AVLB laying its scissors bridge in position (US Army)

Brief details of these programmes are given under the respective country entries in the second part of this book.

New Powerpacks

NAPCO and Teledyne of the United States and GLS and Wegmann of West Germany have all developed new power-packs for the M48 tank. Teledyne Continental's kit, which has already been adopted by a number of countries, uses the AVDS-1790-2C engine. Wegmann have provided 170 of their kits to Turkey. This kit also includes the installation of the 105 mm gun as fitted in the 650 M48A2GA2s supplied to the Federal German Army. For trials purposes FFG of West Germany have installed a GT601 gas turbine in a M48 tank of the West German Army. This was tested alongside an M48 with an MTU MB 837 Ea-500 V-8 diesel engine developing 550 kW and coupled to a CD-850-5/6 transmission.

M48 Division Air Defense Gun System

The Sgt York twin 40 mm Division Air Defense Gun (DIVAD) based on a modified M48A5 tank chassis was cancelled in August 1985 after more than 50 systems had been delivered.

Trials Versions

Over the years there have been numerous trials versions of the M48 including various models fitted with AT systems, mine-clearing equipment and one was also used to test the Avco AGT-1500 gas turbine subsequently installed in the M1 MBT now in production by General Dynamics.

M48A5 with 105 mm gun and two 7.62 mm M60D machine guns mounted externally on turret roof, one for commander and one for loader (US Army)

SPECIFICATIONS

Model	M48	M48A1	M48A2	M48A3	M48A5
CREW	4	4	4	4	4
COMBAT WEIGHT	44 906 kg	47 173 kg	47 173 kg	47 173 kg	48 987 kg
UNLOADED WEIGHT	42 240 kg	43 999 kg	43 999 kg	44 452 kg	46 287 kg
POWER-TO-WEIGHT RATIO	18.03 hp/tonne	17.17 hp/tonne	17.39 hp/tonne	15.89 hp/tonne	15.89 hp/tonne
GROUND PRESSURE	0.78 kg/cm²	0.83 kg/cm²	0.83 kg/cm²	0.83 kg/cm²	0.88 kg/cm²
LENGTH GUN FORWARDS	8.444 m	8.729 m	8.686 m	8.686 m	9.306 m
LENGTH HULL	6.705 m	6.87 m	6.87 m	6.882 m	6.419 m
WIDTH	3.631 m	3.631 m	3.631 m	3.631 m	3.631 m
HEIGHT OVERALL	3.241 m*	3.13 m	3.089 m	3.124 m	3.086 m
GROUND CLEARANCE	0.393 m	0.387 m	0.385 m	0.406 m	0.419 m
TRACK	2.921 m	2.921 m	2.921 m	2.921 m	2.921 m
TRACK WIDTH	711 mm	711 mm	711 mm	711 mm	711 mm
LENGTH OF TRACK ON GROUND	4 m	4 m	4 m	4 m	4 m
MAX ROAD SPEED FORWARDS	41.8 km/h	41.8 km/h	48.2 km/h	48.2 km/h	48.2 km/h
FUEL CAPACITY	757 litres	757 litres	1268 litres	1420 litres	1420 litres
MAX ROAD RANGE					
without external tanks which could be fitted to M48A1 and M48A2	113 km	113 km	258 km	463 km	499 km
FORDING	1.219 m	1.219 m	1.219 m	1.219 m	1.219 m
with preparation	2.438 m	2.438 m	2.438 m	2.438 m	2.438 m
GRADIENT	60%	60%	60%	60%	60%
VERTICAL OBSTACLE	0.915 m	0.915 m	0.915 m	0.915 m	0.915 m
TRENCH	2.59 m	2.59 m	2.59 m	2.59 m	2.59 m
ENGINE					
all Continental 12-cylinder air-cooled	AV-1790-5B/7/7B/7C	AV-1790-7C	AV-1790-8	AVDS-1790-2A	AVDS-1790-2D†
Type	petrol	petrol	petrol	diesel	diesel
Output	810/2800 hp/rpm	810/2800 hp/rpm	825/2800 hp/rpm	750/2400 hp/rpm	750/2400 hp/rpm
Auxiliary engine	General Motors Corporation Model A-41			none	none
TRANSMISSION (model)	CD-850-4/4A/4B	CD-850-4B	CD-850-5	CD-850-6	CD-850-6A
TYPE	planetary gear shift with hydraulic torque converter with 2 forward and 1 reverse (low, high and reverse)				
STEERING	cross-drive differential in all models				
ELECTRICAL SYSTEM	24 V	24 V	24 V	24 V	24 V
BATTERIES	4 × 12 V	4 × 12 V	4 × 12 V	6 × 12 V	6 × 12 V
ARMAMENT					
main	1 × 90 mm	1 × 90 mm	1 × 90 mm	1 × 90 mm	1 × 105 mm
coaxial‡	1 × 7.62 mm MG	1 × 7.62 mm MG	1 × 7.62 mm MG	1 × 7.62 mm MG	1 × 7.62 mm MG
anti-aircraft§	1 × 12.7 mm MG	1 × 12.7 mm MG	1 × 12.7 mm MG	1 × 12.7 mm MG	2 × 7.62 mm MG
SMOKE-LAYING EQUIPMENT	none	none	none	none	M239 smoke grenade launchers and engine smoke laying system
AMMUNITION					
main	60	60	64	62	54
7.62 mm	5900	5900	5590	6000	10 000
12.7 mm	180	500	1365	630	none
GUN CONTROL EQUIPMENT					
Turret power control	electro-hydraulic with manual for emergency use				
by commander	yes	yes	yes	yes	yes
by gunner	yes	yes	yes	yes	yes
Max rate of power traverse	360° in 15 seconds for all models				
Gun elevation/depression	+19°/−9°	+19°/−9°	+19°/−9°	+19°/−9°	+19°/−9°
commander's override	yes	yes	yes	yes	yes
Commander's fire-control override	yes	yes	yes	yes	yes
Gun stabiliser					
vertical	no	no	no	no	no
horizontal	no	no	no	no	no
Rangefinder	M13	M13	M13A1	M17B1C	M17A1 or M17B1C
Gunner's telescope	M97C	M97C	M97C	M105	M105D
Elevation quadrant	M13A1	M13A1	M13A1	M13A3	M13B1
Traverse indicator	yes	yes	yes	yes	yes
ARMOUR					
Hull front	101/120 mm	101/120 mm	101/120 mm	101/120 mm	101/120 mm
Hull sides front	76 mm	76 mm	76 mm	76 mm	76 mm
Hull sides rear	51 mm	51 mm	51 mm	51 mm	51 mm
Hull top	57 mm	57 mm	57 mm	57 mm	57 mm
Hull floor	12.7/63 mm	12.7/63 mm	12.7/63 mm	12.7/63 mm	12.7/63 mm
Hull rear	44 mm	44 mm	44 mm	44 mm	44 mm
Turret front	110 mm	110 mm	110 mm	110 mm	110 mm
Turret sides	76 mm	76 mm	76 mm	76 mm	76 mm
Turret rear	50 mm	50 mm	50 mm	50 mm	50 mm
Turret top	25 mm	25 mm	25 mm	25 mm	25 mm

Status: Production complete. In service with West Germany (including 105 mm armed versions), Greece (including 105 mm versions), Iran (including M48A5), Israel (105 mm versions), Jordan, South Korea (including M48A5), Lebanon, Morocco (including 105 mm versions), Norway, Pakistan, Portugal (M48A5 from West Germany), Somalia, Spain (including M48E and M48A5), Taiwan, Thailand (55 M48A5s), Tunisia, Turkey, USA and Viet-Nam.

Manufacturers: Chrysler Corporation, Delaware, Ford Motor Company, Michigan, Fisher Body Division of General Motors Corporation, Michigan and Alco Products of Schenectady. Although no longer in production, the Systems Technical Support (engineering) work for the M48A5 is still being done by General Dynamics Land Systems Division.

(Please see notes at top of next page)

† M48A3 conversion uses AVDS-1790-2A engine while M48A1 conversion uses
AVDS-1790-2D engine.
‡ As originally built coaxial machine gun was 7.62 mm (0.30) M1919A4E1 but those
still in service with US Army now have 7.62 mm M73 machine gun
§ Browning 12.7 mm (0.50) M2 HB machine gun, except M48A5.

M47 Medium Tank

Development

The heaviest tank in the US Army at the end of the Second
World War was the M26 Pershing. A total of 2428 Pershing
tanks was built by the Detroit Tank Plant (run by the
Chrysler Corporation) and the Grand Blanc Tank Arsenal
(run by the Fisher Body Division of General Motors Corporation). In May 1946 the designation of the Heavy Tank
M26 was changed to Medium Tank M26. Further development of the M26 resulted in the M46 (M26E2), which had a
new engine and cross-drive transmission and a new gun.

In 1949 a decision was taken to design three new tanks, the
T41 light, which became the M41 Bulldog, T42 medium and
the T43 heavy, which became the M103. When the Korean
War broke out the following year the T42 was not ready for
production so the turret of the T42 tank (with gun T119) was
mounted on the chassis of the M46 tank. This combination
was known as the M46E1 and accepted for limited service as
the M46A1. The front hull armour of the M46 was improved
in the M46A1 by eliminating the ventilator housing between
the driver's and bow machine gunner's position and increasing the front slope angle of the armour.

Production of the M47 was undertaken by the Detroit
Tank Plant (which built 3440 by November 1953) and the
American Locomotive Company (which built over 5000).
Total production amounted to 8676 units. The M47 did not
see combat in Korea and was soon replaced in the regular
Army by the M48, development of which started late in 1950
by Chrysler. The majority of M47s were subsequently sup-
plied to other countries under the Mutual Aid Program.

Description

The hull of the M47 is made of armoured plate and cast
armour sections welded together and reinforced, and has
three compartments, driver and bow machine gunner at the
front, fighting in the centre and the engine and transmission
at the rear.

The driver is seated at the front of the vehicle on the left
side with the bow machine gunner to his right. Both men are
provided with a single-piece hatch cover that opens to the
outside of the vehicle with an integral M13 periscope. Both
the driver and bow-gunner are provided with a hull escape
hatch.

The cast turret is mounted in the centre of the hull with the
commander and gunner on the right and the loader on the
left. The commander is provided with a single-piece hatch
cover that opens to the rear and five vision blocks are
arranged around the sides and behind his position. Mounted
to his front is an M20 periscope and a similar periscope is
provided forward, and slightly below the commander's position for the gunner. The M20 periscope has two built-in
optical systems, a ×1 system for wide-angle observation and
a ×6 for sighting distant objects and ranging on targets. The
M12 stereoscopic ballistic computing rangefinder is mounted
in the forward part of the turret and is used by the gunner
who, through the use of various adjustment knobs, indexes
the proper ammunition, sets the ballistic correction, ranges

and tracks the target, and boresights the gun for firing. The
loader is provided with a single-piece hatch cover that opens
to the right front and an M13 periscope mounted forward of
his hatch. The turret has an overhanging bustle with the
dome-shaped turret ventilator mounted in the roof at the
rear. A light steel stowage box is provided at the rear of the
turret.

The engine compartment is at the rear of the vehicle and
separated from the fighting compartment by a bulkhead. The
engine transmits power via the cross-drive transmission to
the final drives. The torsion bar suspension consists of six
dual rubber-tyred road wheels with the idler at the front and
the drive sprocket at the rear. There are three track return
rollers and an adjustable tensioning wheel between the sixth
road wheel and the drive sprocket. Hydraulic shock absorbers are provided for the first, second, fifth and sixth road
wheel stations. The steel tracks have rubber blocks and when
new each track has 86 links.

The main armament of the M47 consists of a 90 mm gun
M36 (T119E1) in a mount M78. The main components of the
gun are the blast deflector (depending on the type of tank this

Top view of M47 without M2 12.7 mm (0.50) HB machine gun
fitted for anti-aircraft defence (US Army)

M47 medium tank with 7.62 mm (0.30-inch) bow machine gun not installed (US Army)

can be of the 'T', cylindrical or as fitted to the M46 tank), evacuator chamber and the barrel mechanism. The mount consists of the shield group and the recoil mechanism assembly. The recoil mechanism is of the concentric hydrospring type and the breech-block is of the vertical sliding type. Once a round is loaded into the breech, a closing mechanism closes the breech which is re-opened automatically during counter-recoil of the gun. The empty cartridge case is ejected into the spent bag under the gun. The barrel has a life of 700 rounds and can fire the following types of ammunition (not all of these rounds are currently in use and the ranges quoted are with the weapon at maximum elevation, effective anti-tank range is 2000 metres):

APC-T (M82) with the round weighing 19.39 kg, muzzle velocity of 792 to 853 metres per second and a maximum range of 19 568 metres

APERS-T (XM580E1) with the round weighing 18.71 kg, muzzle velocity of 914.4 metres per second and a maximum range of 4400 metres

AP-T (M77) with the round weighing 19.06 kg, muzzle velocity of 822 metres per second and a maximum range of 11 269 metres

AP-T (M318) with the round weighing 19.94 kg, muzzle velocity of 853.4 metres per second and a maximum range of 19 568 metres

Blank (M394) with the round weighing 3.733 kg

Canister (M336) with the round weighing 18.86 kg, muzzle velocity of 874 metres per second and a effective range of 183 metres

Canister (M377) with the round weighing 17.82 kg, muzzle velocity of 899 metres per second and a effective range of 365 metres

Dummy (M12) with the round weighing between 19.06 and 19.95 kg

HE (M71) with the round weighing between 18.68 and 19.01 kg, muzzle velocity of 823 metres per second and a maximum range of 17 716 metres

HEP-T

M47 medium tank without anti-aircraft machine gun

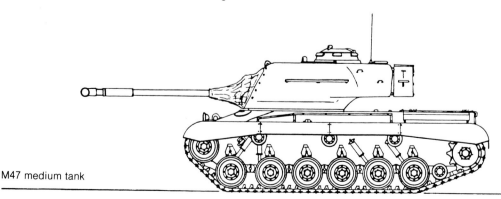

M47 medium tank

HE-T (M71A1) with the round weighing between 17.59 and 17.93 kg, muzzle velocity of 731 metres per second and a maximum range of 15 550 metres
HEAT (M348A1) (fin-stabilised) with the round weighing 15.78 kg, muzzle velocity of 853 metres per second and a maximum range of 11 896 metres
HEAT (M431) with the round weighing 14.96 kg, muzzle velocity of 1219 metres per second and a maximum range of 8138 metres
HVAP-T (M304) with the round weighing 16.84 kg, muzzle velocity of 1021 metres per second and a maximum range of 13 835 metres
HVAP-T (M332A1) with round weighing 18.37 kg, muzzle velocity of 1165 metres per second and a maximum range of 15 362 metres
HVTP-T (M333A1) with the round weighing 14.28 kg, muzzle velocity of 1165 metres per second and a maximum range of 14 356 metres
HVTP-T (M317) with round weighing 17 kg, muzzle velocity of 1021 metres per second and a maximum range of 13 835 metres
TP-T (M353) with round weighing 19.91 kg, muzzle velocity of 914.4 metres per second and a maximum range of 21 031 metres
The M71 TP round has no tracer
Smoke WP (M313) with round weighing 19.29 kg, muzzle velocity of 822.9 metres per second and a maximum range of 17 716 metres.

Of 71 rounds of 90 mm ammunition carried 11 are in the turret bustle for ready use. A 7.62 mm (0.30) M1919A4E1 machine gun is mounted coaxially to the left of the main armament and a similar weapon is mounted in the bow of the tank on the right side. Some countries have taken out the bow machine gun enabling the number of 90 mm rounds to be increased from 71 to 105. A 12.7 mm (0.50) Browning M2 HB machine gun is mounted on the roof of the tank for anti-aircraft use.

The M47 is not fitted with an NBC system and as built was not provided with any infra-red night vision equipment, although some countries have since fitted it. The tank can be fitted with the M6 dozer blade. Thirty-one pre-production dozer blades were built followed by 468 production models.

Variants
Many companies have carried out various modifications to the M47 to extend its life including Austria (new powerpack), France (105 mm gun), Israel (RKM conversion with new powerpack and 105 mm gun), Italy (105 mm gun and new powerpack) and the United Kingdom (installation of Swingfire ATGWs), but none of these entered service. Details of the Iranian M47M (also used by Pakistan) are given under Iran in Part 2. Details of Spanish M47E are given in this Part.

NAPCO M47s
In 1984 NAPCO of the USA purchased 101 M47 medium tanks in a US Army property disposal sale. These tanks are ex-Italian Army and one has now been sent to NAPCO's facilities in Hopkins, Minnesota while the remaining 100 are still in Italy.

SPECIFICATIONS (data in square brackets relates to M47M where different from M47)

CREW	5 [4]	TRENCH	2.59 m	GUN CONTROL	
COMBAT WEIGHT	46 170 [46 814] kg	TURNING RADIUS	skid turns	EQUIPMENT	
UNLOADED WEIGHT	42 130 kg	ENGINE	Continental AV-1790-5B	Turret power control	hydraulic/manual
POWER-TO-WEIGHT			[AVDS-1790-2A, 750 bhp at	Max rate power traverse	360° in 10 s
RATIO	17.54 [16.11] hp/tonne		2400 rpm], 7 or 7B, V-12,	Max rate power elevation	4°/s
GROUND PRESSURE	0.935 kg/cm²		4-cycle, air-cooled petrol	Gun stabiliser	
LENGTH GUN			developing 810 bhp at	vertical	none
forwards	8.508 [8.553] m		2800 rpm	horizontal	none
rear	7.09 m	AUXILIARY ENGINE	Wisconsin TFT 2-cylinder	Elevation quadrant	T21
LENGTH HULL	6.307 [6.267] m		petrol	Traverse indicator	T24
WIDTH	3.51 [3.39] m	TRANSMISSION	Allison model CD-850-4	ARMOUR	
WIDTH OVER TRACKS	3.377 m		[CD-850-6A], 4A or 4B cross	Hull front	101 mm at 60°
HEIGHT			drive with 2 forward and 1	Hull front lower	76/89 mm at 53°
to turret top	2.954 m		reverse ranges	Hull sides front	76 mm
overall including		SUSPENSION	torsion bar	Hull sides rear	50.8 mm
A/A MG	3.352 [3.397] m	ELECTRICAL SYSTEM	24 V	Hull top	22 mm
commander's cupola	3.016 m	BATTERIES	4 × 12 V	Hull floor front	25.4 mm
GROUND CLEARANCE	0.469 m	ARMAMENT		Hull floor rear	12.7 mm
TRACK	2.794 m	main	1 × 90 mm	Turret mantlet	115 mm
TRACK WIDTH	584 mm	coaxial	1 × 7.62 mm (0.30) MG	Turret front	101 mm at 40°
LENGTH OF TRACK		bow	1 × 7.62 mm (0.30) MG	Turret sides	63.5 mm at 30°
ON GROUND	3.911 m		[none]	Turret rear	76.2 mm at 30°
MAX ROAD SPEED	48 [56.3] km/h	anti-aircraft	1 × 12.7 mm (0.50) MG	Turret top	12.7 mm
early model	58 km/h	SMOKE-LAYING			
FUEL CAPACITY	875 [1476] litres	EQUIPMENT	none		
MAX RANGE	130 [600] km	AMMUNITION			
FORDING	1.219 m	main	71 [79]		
GRADIENT	60%	7.62 mm	4125		
VERTICAL OBSTACLE	0.914 m	12.7 mm	440		

Status: Production complete. In service with Greece, Iran, Italy, Pakistan, Somalia, South Korea, Spain, Sudan (17 were delivered from Saudi Arabia in 1981), Taiwan, Turkey and Yugoslavia.

Manufacturers: Detroit Tank Plant and American Locomotive Company.

PART 2

PRESENT AND POSSIBLE FUTURE MBT OPERATORS

Afghanistan

The order of battle of the Afghanistan Army includes 11 infantry divisions and three armoured divisions which, like the rest of the Army, are under strength due to the internal problems within the country. The armoured divisions, which to all intents and purposes are brigades, are the 4th and 15th based in the capital Kabul and the 7th based at Kandahar. All three are organised along Soviet lines.

Total tank strength includes 50 T-34/85s, about 400 T-54/T-55s and around 100 more modern T-62/T-72.

The Soviet Union invaded Afghanistan on 27 December 1979 and total Soviet military strength is estimated to be around 120 000 officers and men, including supporting units. There is one Soviet Army HQ, two motorised rifle and one airborne divisions, one air assault and two motorised rifle brigades.

Albania

Between 1949 and 1961 Albania was a Soviet satellite but in 1961 the country broke with the Soviet Union and in 1968 withdrew from the Warsaw Pact. Since 1961 Albania has been aligned with China and any future procurement of MBTs will probably come from this source.

Albania has one tank brigade which is believed to consist of three tank battalions and one motor rifle battalion. If the tank battalion follows Chinese lines it would have 33 MBTs, although from information in the West it would seem that there is only sufficient tanks to form two operational battalions.

The country took delivery of some 110 T-34/85 tanks but under half this number are now operational. Fifteen Chinese supplied Type 59 and a similar number of Soviet T-54 MBTs are also in service with the Albanian Army.

Algeria

When Algeria became independent from France in 1962 it took over some French AFVs including AMX-13 light tanks, M8 Greyhound and Panhard AML light armoured cars. In the early 1960s some 200 T-34/85 tanks were supplied by the Soviet Union, but all of these are now either in reserve or are used for training.

From 1964 the Soviet Union provided a large number of tanks and in 1985 front line strength consisted of 300 to 400 T-54/T-55s, 300 T-62 and 100 of the more modern T-72 with first of latter delivered in 1980.

Today the Algerian Army is known to have two armoured brigades, five mechanised brigades and eight motorised infantry brigades. Each of the former is believed to have three battalions of MBTs so giving Algeria a total of nine tank battalions. These are believed to be organised along Soviet lines with each having 31 MBTs with three companies of ten tanks and one at battalion HQ.

From the above it can be seen that Algeria has taken delivery of far more tanks than required to equip its known tank battalions. The remainder of the tanks are either in reserve, held for shipment to other countries in the Middle East or each of the eight motorised infantry and five mechanised brigades has an integral or attached tank battalion. If the

latter is correct and they are organised along Soviet lines it would account for a further 341 MBTs.

Angola

When Portugal withdrew from Angola in 1975 it left behind a small number of light armoured vehicles including Panhard AML (4×4) armoured cars and Panhard M3 (4×4) armoured personnel carriers.

In 1985 it was reported that Angola had 263 T-54/T-55 MBTs and 153 of the older T-34/85s. Between 90 and 100 of more modern T-62/T-72 MBTs are believed to be in service.

A number of Soviet-supplied tanks were destroyed by South African Eland armoured cars (French Panhard AML-90 manufactured under licence in South Africa by Sandock-Austral) when they operated deep in Angola in 1976 in support of UNITA/FNLA units. In 1981 South Africa captured and destroyed a number of T-34/85 tanks during operations against SWAPO bases in Southern Angola.

Angola has two motorised brigades each of which comprises two infantry and one tank battalion. Each of the latter comprises three companies each of ten tanks plus a single tank at battalion HQ, thus giving each battalion a front line strength of 31 tanks. There are also 17 infantry brigades, ten tank battalions plus anti-aircraft and artillery battalions.

Angola has some 20 000 Cuban and 500 East German and Soviet advisors and it is believed that many of the tanks are manned by Cubans as there are insufficient Angolans trained to operate them.

Angolan T-34/85 tanks captured by South African forces. Note long-range fuel tanks at hull rear

Argentina

Argentina has no MBTs but about 125 Sherman tanks are in service. These were modernised in the 1970s and fitted with French Poyaud 580 V8 S25 diesel engines developing 570 hp.

To meet the requirements of the Argentinian Army the West German company of Thyssen Henschel designed and built the TAM medium tank and the VCTP armoured personnel carrier. Production of these is now underway in Argentina and it is believed that about 150 TAMs have now been built. Export sales have been made to Panama and Peru. Details of TAM are given in Part 1.

The order of battle of the Argentinian Army includes two armoured cavalry brigades each of which has two armoured cavalry regiments, one tank regiment and one artillery battalion.

Australia

Australia has only one tank battalion, the 1st Armoured Regiment, Royal Australian Armoured Corps, based at Puckapunyal.

This regiment has a HQ with two MBTs, three Sabre tank squadrons and a technical squadron.

Each tank squadron has a HQ with two MBTs and one MBT with a dozer blade and three tank troops each with three MBTs. The HQ squadron has a quartermaster troop, transport troop, reconnaissance troop and a special troop with two AVLBs. The technical squadron has a special equipment troop and three tank squadron technical sections each of which includes an ARV. Total strength of the regiment is 47 MBTs, three ARVs and two AVLBs.

For many years the regiment used the British Centurion MBT with 135 gun tanks, seven ARVs and four bridgelayers being procured, including some from New Zealand.

Between 1972 and 1973 Australia evaluated the M60A1 and the Leopard 1 MBTs and subsequently placed an order with West Germany for the supply of 90 Leopard 1A3 MBTs, six ARVs and five AVLBs; these were delivered to Australia between 1976 and 1978.

The Leopard 1A3s of the Australian Army were delivered with a number of changes including a Belgian SABCA fire control system, tropical kit, improved turret and trunnion bearings, modifications to the fire control system to enable APFSDS rounds to be fired, improved combustion cleaners and external stowage boxes on hull sides. A small quantity of dozer blades were also ordered.

As can be seen from the figures, sufficient tanks and specialised vehicles are available to form another regiment should this be required. More recently three of the Leopard MBTs have had their turrets removed and are in service in the driver training role, with the turrets being used for instructional training.

In Australian Army service the Leopard variants are designated as follows: Leopard AS 1 MBT, Leopard AS 1 armoured recovery vehicle medium, Leopard AS 1 AVLB Leopard AS 1 medium tank dozer.

Leopard 1 driver training tank of Australian Army (Paul Handel)

Leopard AS 1 medium tank dozer of Australian Army with dozer blade raised (Paul Handel)

Austria

When Austria became independent following the withdrawal of American, British, French and Soviet occupation troops, the Austrian Army was formed. Initial tank equipment included 27 Soviet T-34/85s and 56 Charioteer tank destroyers which were supplied by the United Kingdom in 1956. None of these remain in service today.

These were followed by an initial batch of 150 M47 tanks which were supplied by the United States and issued to the 10th, 33rd and 34th Tank Battalions. Later additional M47s were supplied and some sources have given a total of 320 which appears to be far too high. For trials purposes one M47 was fitted with the powerpack of the M60A1 but this was not adopted. As far as it is known, no M47 tanks remain in service with the Austrian Army.

Between 1962 and 1963 120 M60A1s were delivered by the United States and more recently 50 M60A3s were acquired at a total cost of $47.2 million.

In 1980 the United States Congress was advised of a letter of offer to Austria valued at $117 million for 120 M60A3 turrets, 80 M60A1 turrets and 120 modification kits, but this letter of offer was not taken up. The basic idea was that the existing M60A1s would have been brought up to M60A3 standard and the old turrets used in the static defence roles.

Today the Standing Alert Force Austrian Army includes three mechanised infantry brigades, 3rd, 4th and 9th, each of which has a staff battalion (including signals, engineer, anti-aircraft, supply/transport, reconnaissance and medical companies), tank battalion, mechanised infantry battalion, anti-tank battalion with SK 105s and an artillery battalion.

The tank battalion has a staff company and three tank companies with two tanks at company HQ and three platoons of five tanks each, giving the battalion a total of 51 M60A1/M60A3 tanks.

An interesting feature of the Austrian Army is that it uses old tank turrets embedded in concrete for the static defence role; these include Centurion turrets with 105 mm L7 guns, Charioteer with 20 pounder (83.4 mm), M47 with 90 mm guns and T-34/85 with 85 mm guns.

In April 1984 it was confirmed that Austria was purchasing 120 Centurion tanks from the Netherlands and their

turrets will be used in static defence role. A further 180 turrets may be purchased from the Netherlands for similar purposes.

Bahrain

At present Bahrain has no MBTs but in November 1985 the US Department of Defense announced a letter of offer to the country for the supply of 54 M60A3 MBTs at a cost of $90 million, including ammunition and training.

Bangladesh

The Bangladesh Army has two armoured regiments, one of which is believed to be equipped with 30 T-54/T-55 tanks supplied by Egypt in 1974 and the other with 20 Chinese Type 59 tanks and six ex-Pakistani Army M24 Chaffee light tanks.

Belgium

The Belgian Army order of battle includes one armoured and three mechanised brigades fully manned and one mechanised brigade and one motorised brigade in reserve. These are organised into two divisions, 1st Division (1st Mechanised and 7th Mechanised Brigades and 10th Reserve Mechanised Brigade) and the 16th Division (4th Mechanised, 17th Armoured and 12th Reserve Motorised Brigade). The 16th Division, less the reserve motorised brigade is forward deployed in West Germany.

The armoured brigade consists of a HQ company, two armoured battalions, two armoured infantry battalions, anti-tank battalion, artillery battalion, engineer, medical, supply/transportation and maintenance companies.

Each armoured battalion has a HQ and HQ support company with one MBT and two ARVs plus a reconnaissance platoon with CVR(T), and three armoured companies. Each of the latter has an MBT at company HQ and four platoons of three tanks. This gives the battalion a total strength of 40 MBTs plus one ARV.

The mechanised infantry brigade is similar to the armoured brigade but has only one tank battalion and different equipment in some of the support battalions (eg anti-tank and artillery).

Belgium was the first country to order the Leopard 1 MBT after West Germany and placed its first order in 1967. The first deliveries took place in 1968.

The Belgian vehicles had their 7.62 mm Rheinmetall MG 3 machine guns replaced by 7.62 mm FN MAG weapons plus minor stowage changes. From 1975 the tanks were fitted with stowage boxes similar to those of the Dutch Leopards, thermal sleeve for the main armament and Cadillac Gage weapon stabilisation system. The initial third were also fitted with the Belgian SABCA fire control system which has also been adopted by Australia and Canada.

The SABCA FCS consists of a laser rangefinder, seven sensors, an analogue computer and an optical sight. The computer determines the angles between the line of sight and the gun axis from information it receives about the range of the target and other variables. The output of the computer is transformed through a two-degrees-of-freedom gimballed mirror system, with torque dc motor drives and a compen-

M60A3 MBT of Austrian Army fitted with infra-red/white light searchlight over main armament and thermal sleeve for latter; 12.7 mm cupola-mounted MG is not fitted (Austrian Army)

Leopard 1s of Belgian Army without thermal sleeve for main armament (C R Zwart)

sated resolver feedback network, into a displacement of cross-hairs in the gunner's sight. When the cross hairs are brought back on to the target, the gun is laid with the correct target elevation (or super-elevation) and azimuth. The sensors measure ambient temperature, air pressure, temperature in the ammunition stowage area, gun wear, cross wind, trunnion cant or tilt and rate of turret traverse. Early in 1980 the Belgian Government placed an order for the second and third batch of SABCA FCS for Belgian Army Leopard 1s. Following trials with a prototype Leopard 1 fitted with the West German Blohm and Voss add-on armour, as already installed on West German and Dutch Leopard 1 MBTs, the Belgian Army is expected to refit all of its tanks at the Rocourt Arsenal in Belgium.

The Belgian Army has a total of 334 Leopard 1 MBTs, 36 Leopard ARVs, six AEVs, 12 driver training tanks and 55 Gepard twin 35 mm self-propelled anti-aircraft guns.

Brazil

At present Brazil has no MBTs in service. ENGESA and Bernardini of Brazil have developed MBTs to the prototype stage to meet requirements of both home and export markets. Details of these are given in Part 1.

Bulgaria

The Bulgarian Army is unique among the Warsaw Pact in that it has no tank divisions, having five tank brigades and eight motorised rifle divisions, which are organised along

Soviet lines. It is not thought that these units are up to full strength. There are no Soviet units stationed in Bulgaria.

Each motorised rifle division has three motorised rifle regiments, one tank regiment and one artillery regiment. Each motorised rifle regiment has one battalion of 40 tanks while the tank regiment has 95 tanks. The latter has two tanks at HQ and three tank battalions each with 31 tanks, one at HQ and three tank companies each with ten tanks.

Total tank strength includes some 300 T-34/85s which are used mainly for training, 1500 T-54/T-55s and a few more modern T-62s and T-72s.

Burma

This country has no MBTs as such although about 25 obsolete British-built Comet tanks remain in service.

Canada

The Canadian Armed Forces has one brigade group deployed in Europe and two brigade groups plus a special force in Canada.

The 4th Brigade Group in Europe is stationed in West Germany and has one armoured regiment (Royal Canadian Dragoons), two mechanised infantry battalions, one artillery regiment and one engineer regiment plus supporting units.

The armoured regiment has a regimental HQ with two Leopard 1A3 MBTs, two M577s and two M113s, one reconnaissance squadron with HQ and three troops of Lynx

Canadian Leopard C1 fitted with front-mounted dozer blade and PZB 200 passive searchlight above and coaxial with main armament (Canadian Armed Forces)

logistic supplies, training, ammunition and other equipment.

The first Leopard 1A3s, called the C1 by the Canadians, were handed over in June 1978. Under the terms of the contract Krauss-Maffei took Canada's entire fleet of European Centurion tanks. Some of the turrets of these vehicles, complete with 105 mm guns, were subsequently sold to Austria where they are used in the static defence role.

In January 1984 it was announced that Oceonics Vehicle Technology was undertaking a study on behalf of the Canadian Armed Forces for using the company's hydro-pneumatic suspension system as a possible replacement for the torsion bar suspension system currently fitted to the Canadian Leopard 1 MBTs. This study forms part of the Canadian MBT improvement programme.

As can be seen from the above figures less than half the Leopards are in service, the remainder are used in Canada at Gagetown for training or held in reserve in Europe. The two other brigades in Canada are equipped with the Armoured Vehicle General Purpose range of 6 × 6 vehicles which were manufactured under licence from MOWAG of Switzerland.

command and reconnaissance vehicles, three armoured squadrons and one armoured defence group with TOW ATGW. Each armoured squadron has a HQ element with one Leopard 1A3 and one M577 command post and four troops each of four Leopard 1A3s. This gives the battalion a total of 53 Leopard 1A3 tanks.

For many years Canada used the Centurion MBT and in the 1970s selected the Leopard 1A3 fitted with the Belgian SABCA fire control system. Total value of the Canadian order, for 114 MBTs, six bridgelayers and eight ARVs, was $187 million, of which $115 million was for the vehicles, $2.7 million for the loan of 35 Leopards until the Canadian Leopards were ready and the remaining $69.3 million for

Central African Republic

In 1982 Libya supplied the Central African Republic with a quantity of military equipment including four T-55 tanks.

Chile

Chile has two armoured regiments which by Western standards are battalions and these are equipped with some 70 M4 Sherman tanks (these being supplied by the United States in the 1950s, although some reports have stated that an addi-

Leopard armoured vehicle launched bridge of the Canadian Armed Forces in travelling configuration (Canadian Armed Forces)

tional 60/70 vehicles have been received from other sources) and 21 AMX-30 MBTs. Chile did order 50 AMX-30 MBTs from France but in March 1982 France announced that it had suspended delivery of the remaining 29 vehicles.

Chile is known to have taken delivery of a quantity of M51 105 mm Sherman tanks from Israel; these are believed to be the 60/70 vehicles mentioned above.

China (People's Republic)

The Chinese Army is the largest in the world and its front line strength includes some 13 armoured divisions with 119 (some sources have recently suggested 130) infantry divisions and possibly some independent tank regiments.

Each armoured division has an HQ element with one MBT, signals battalion, engineer battalion, anti-aircraft battalion, reconnaissance company, guard company, chemical warfare company, artillery regiment, mechanised infantry regiment and three tank regiments. Each tank regiment has 100 tanks, one at regimental HQ and three tank battalions each with 33 tanks. This gives the armoured division a total strength of 301 tanks.

Each infantry division has one tank/assault gun regiment with 32 medium tanks and ten assault guns (eg Soviet supplied SU-100s).

Most sources give China a total tank strength of between 11 000 and 12 000 vehicles which would seem to be more than enough to equip the known tank units leaving plenty in reserve. If the above organisation is correct, 3913 tanks are in the 13 armoured units and 3808 in the infantry divisions.

It is estimated that some 9000 Type 59 MBTs are in service plus around 1000 T-34/85s and at least 2000 more recent Type 69s. Small numbers of T-54s were supplied by the Soviet Union in the 1950s. It is probable that the T-34/85 tanks are now used for training while some Soviet IS-2 heavy tanks may also be in reserve or used for training.

Congo

The order of battle of the Congo Army includes one armoured battalion whose equipment includes 35 Soviet supplied T-54/T-55 tanks and 15 Chinese Type 59 tanks.

Cuba

The Cuban Army order of battle includes one armoured division, three mechanised divisions and 13 infantry divisions (of which eight are reserve and only manned on mobilisation).

Each mechanised division consists of one tank regiment, three mechanised infantry regiments, one artillery regiment, one air defence regiment, one reconnaissance battalion, one engineer battalion, one signals battalion, one NBC defence company, one maintenance battalion, one support company and one transportation battalion.

An armoured division is similar to the mechanised division except that it has three tank regiments and one mechanised infantry regiment and a medical company rather than a battalion.

Each tank regiment has one armoured reconnaissance, engineer, maintenance, supply, transportation and signals companies plus chemical defence platoon, medical platoon, two air defence batteries and three tank battalions.

T-55 MBT of Czechoslovakian Army fitted with long-range fuel tanks at hull rear

Each tank battalion has one tank at battalion HQ and two tank companies each with ten tanks. Each company has one tank at company HQ and three platoons each with three tanks. Each battalion may have one company of SU-100 assault guns in place of a company of tanks and it is possible that each tank battalion has an additional tank company which is not normally manned.

Regular infantry divisions usually have one tank regiment of three tank battalions.

Total tank strength includes about 300 T-34/85s, 350 T-54/T-55s, 150 T-62s (delivered in 1975) and 40 T-72s (first observed with the armoured division stationed near Havana in 1980–81). It is not thought that any of the IS-3 heavy tanks remain in front line service but may be used in static defence role.

Czechoslovakia

The Czechoslovakian order of battle includes five motorised rifle (2nd, 3rd, 15th, 19th and 20th) and five tank (1st, 4th, 9th, 13th and 14th) divisions, with two of the latter being at Category II status, eg manned at 50 per cent of establishment but having full complement of equipment. Czechoslovakian units are organised along Soviet lines.

In addition there are three Soviet motorised rifle (16th, 55th and 66th) and two tank (10th and 31st) divisions stationed in Czechoslovakia, these being known as the Soviet Central Group of Forces in Czechoslovakia, with HQ at Tabor.

In the post-war period Czechoslovakia produced the T-34/85 tank and the SU-100 tank destroyer on the same chassis, mainly for the export market, especially the Middle East. From the mid-1960s the country produced the T-55 for both home and export markets and between 1976 and 1980

production of tanks was, according to American reports, running at about 800 a year in Czechoslovakia and Poland. Czechoslovakia is known to have produced some T-62 MBTs.

In 1979/80 the Martin Machine Tool Enterprise in Martin started tooling up to produce the Soviet-designed T-72 MBT. The transmission is produced by CKD-Praga which managed T-34/85 production in Czechoslovakia.

According to the 1983 edition of *Soviet Military Power* published by the US Government, only 100 T-72s were produced in Czechoslovakia and Poland during 1982. It also stated that production of the older T-55 was still being undertaken outside of the USSR (for example in Czechoslovakia and Poland) at the rate of 500 per year, presumably for the export market.

The 1985 edition of *Soviet Military Power* stated that production of MBTs in the Warsaw Pact, excluding the USSR was a total of 550 in 1983 and 450 in 1984.

Current Czechoslovakian tank strength is believed to include just over 3000 T-54/T-55 and about 600 T-62/T-72 tanks.

Cyprus

The Greek-Cypriot National Guard has one armoured battalion whose equipment includes about ten T-34/85 tanks.

Denmark

The Danish Army order of battle includes five mechanised brigades, four active and one reserve, each of which has one tank battalion, two mechanised battalions, one motorised battalion, one artillery battalion, reconnaissance company and the normal support elements.

Danish Centurion with 105 mm L7 series gun and 12.7 mm Browning M2 HB anti-aircraft MG (Ministry of Defence)

Each tank battalion has two tank companies of 11 MBTs plus an armoured infantry company with M113s and M125 mortar carriers, a motorised infantry company and a HQ company. The mechanised battalions have two armoured infantry companies, a tank company of 11 MBTs, motorised infantry company and a HQ company.

The active brigades use the Leopard 1 and the Centurion armed with the 105 mm L7 gun while the reserve brigade uses the Centurion with the old 20 pounder (83.4 mm) gun.

Denmark ordered 120 Leopard 1s in June 1974 which were delivered between March 1976 and November 1978. Unlike other users of the Leopard 1, Denmark did not order any specialised versions of the Leopard such as the ARV or bridgelayer. Danish Leopard 1s have the drivers periscopes fitted with washers and wiper blades.

The Danish Army took delivery of 200 Centurion Mk 3 MBTs and a small quantity of Centurion Mk 2 ARVs, in the mid-1950s which were funded by the United States under the Mutual Defense Assistance Program (MDAP). These were later brought up to Mk 5 and Mk 5/2 (105 mm L7 standard). By 1985 about 90 Centurions remained in service. One local modification is the installation of a 12.7 mm Browning M2 HB anti-aircraft machine gun on the commander's cupola and some also have a Leopard 1 type infra-red/white light searchlight mounted over the main armament. In 1983 it was announced that the Danish Army was to upgrade its Centurions by replacing existing gunners sight by a Ericsson sight with integrated laser rangefinder. This sight has magnifications of ×1 and ×10 and a range of from 200 to 9990 metres, and is accurate to 10 metres. This has also been ordered by Sweden for its Centurions.

Egypt

The Egyptian Army order of battle includes three armoured divisions (each with two armoured and one mechanised brigade), six mechanised infantry divisions (each with two mechanised and one armoured brigade), three infantry divisions (each with two infantry and one mechanised brigade), two Republican Guard brigades, one independent armoured brigade, two independent mechanised infantry brigades and five independent infantry brigades.

Each armoured brigade consists of three tank battalions, one anti-aircraft company, one motorised rifle company and one reconnaissance company. A mechanised brigade consists of three mechanised infantry battalions, one mortar company, one anti-tank company with ATGWs, one anti-aircraft company and one reconnaissance company. Each infantry division and has one tank battalion.

At present it is believed that each tank battalion is organised along Soviet lines with 31 tanks, one tank at battalion HQ and three companies of ten tanks, one at company HQ and three platoons each of three tanks. With the influx of so much American equipment it is probable that the whole structure of the Egyptian armoured corps will change and each battalion be modelled along American lines with 54/58 tanks.

In 1983 the Egyptian Ministry of Defence announced that an agreement had been reached with Romania for the production of the M-77 (or TR-77) MBT in Egypt as well as the manufacture of spare parts for these and Soviet supplied T-54/T-55 Egyptian Army tanks. The M-77 is essentially a modernised Soviet T-54/T-55 and available details of this tank are given under Romania.

Total Egyptian front-line tank strength is believed to consist of 900 T-54/T-55s (some of which have recently been supplied to Iraq), 700 T-62s and 659 M60A3s. In May 1985 the Pentagon announced a letter of offer to Egypt for an additional 94 M60A3 tanks at a cost $165 million. In early 1984 the American Kollsman Instrument Company was awarded a two-year contract valued at $5 million for the installation of a maintenance facility in Egypt to support the repair of the M60A3 Integrated Tank Fire Control System.

Egypt has also sent a T-55 to the United Kingdom to have a 105 mm L7A3 rifled gun installed. Details of this conversion are given in the entry for the Soviet T-54/T-55 in Part 1.

In the 1970s several hundred Egyptian T-54/T-55/T-62 MBTs were fitted with West German AEG/Telefunken white/infra-red searchlights to the right of the main armament and some were also fitted with the Iskara laser rangefinder. Some Egyptian T-62s have also been fitted with two launchers either side of the turret rear for ground-to-ground smoke rockets.

Late in 1984 the Egyptian Defence and War Production Minister stated that $216 million had been allocated for the design and development of a new Egyptian MBT. It is believed that the Egyptian requirement is for an MBT weighing about 46 tonnes, equipped with a 120 mm smooth-bore gun and powered by a 1200 hp diesel engine.

T-55 of Egyptian Army on parade in Cairo (Egyptian Army Official)

T-54 of Egyptian Army captured by Israel with 12.7 mm DShKM anti-aircraft gun removed (Israeli Ministry of Defence)

Late in 1984 General Dynamics Land Systems Division was awarded a $150 million contract to build a new tank plant outside Cairo. The facility will be called Factory 200 and will initially overhaul US supplied M60A3 and M88A1 armoured vehicles. It is expected to become operational in 1987 and any new Egyptian tanks will be built there.

In 1984 the General Products Division of Teledyne Continental Motors was awarded a contract by the Egyptian Army to modernise a T-54 tank. This work is being carried out in the USA and will include the installation of the AVDS-1790-2C diesel engine developing 750 hp coupled to the CD-850 series fully-automatic transmission.

The existing torsion bar suspension will be replaced by Teledyne Model 2880 in-arm hydro-pneumatic suspension units for greater cross-country mobility. The Soviet 100 mm gun will be replaced by the 105 mm M68 in a new mount and other equipment to be installed includes a muzzle reference system, image intensification periscope for tank commander, modernised gunner's station with digital fire-control system and laser rangefinder integrated into gunner's sight, NBC system and a Halon fire-suppression system.

Ethiopia

The order of battle of this country includes three motorised infantry and 12 infantry divisions. There are 20 tank battalions with each infantry division having one tank battalion and each mechanised infantry division having two tank battalions. It is believed that the tank battalions are organised along Soviet lines with each having one MBT at battalion HQ and three companies each with ten tanks.

Ethiopia is believed to have 800 T-54/T-55 MBTs. There may be about 50 T-34/85 tanks used for training. As far as it is known no M47 tanks remain in service.

Egyptian Army T-55 MBT fitted with Royal Ordnance Nottingham 105 mm L7 series rifled tank gun

Finland

This country has only one armoured brigade which is stationed at Parola and has one tank battalion and supporting units. There is no armoured corps as such as the armour belongs to the infantry. Some reports have indicated that an additional tank battalion can be raised on mobilisation. Tank strength consists of between 75 and 100 T-54/T-55 MBTs which were supplied by the Soviet Union. In 1984 Finland ordered a quantity of T-72 MBTs from the Soviet Union.

In the 1950s the United Kingdom supplied some Comet medium tanks and Charioteer tank destroyers but these have now been phased out of service.

T-54 of Finnish Army with 12.7 mm DShKM anti-aircraft MG in position on turret roof (Finnish Army)

AMX-30 MBTs of French Army on parade in Paris (GIAT)

France

The French Army is at present undergoing a major reorganisation and when complete will consist of six armoured divisions, one air mobile division, one light armoured division and seven infantry divisions.

Of these the so-called Battle Corps will consist of six armoured divisions, two infantry divisions (with VABs) and two infantry divisions.

The Fast Intervention Force (FAR) will consist of the 4th air mobile division (Nancy), 6th light armoured division (Nimes) and three infantry divisions, the 11th Parachute Division (Toulouse), 9th Marine Infantry Division (St Malo) and 27th Alpine Division (Grenoble). The FAR does not have any MBTs in its tables of organisation and equipment.

On full mobilisation an additional eight infantry divisions will be formed.

Of the 15 peacetime divisions, three armoured divisions will be based in West Germany, with an additional armoured regiment and infantry regiment in West Berlin.

Each armoured division consists of a HQ, two mechanised infantry regiments, one VAB (4 × 4) regiment, two tank regiments, reconnaissance company, artillery regiment, anti-tank company, engineer regiment and command and support regiment (which includes signals, maintenance, transport and medical units). Total AMX-30 MBT strength of the armoured divisions is 148 in all.

Each tank regiment has an HQ element with two AMX-30s and four tank companies and one mechanised infantry company. Each tank company has an HQ element with one AMX-30 and four tank platoons each with three AMX-30s. This gives each tank regiment a total of 54 AMX-30 MBTs.

Each mechanised infantry regiment has two tank companies each of which consists of an HQ element with one AMX-30, three tank platoons each with three AMX-30s and a mechanised infantry platoon.

As of 1985 the French Army had a total of 1173 AMX-30 series MBTs plus 134 ARVs and other variants. A total of 271 AMX-30 B2 MBTs are being delivered to French Army with a further 693 existing AMX-30s being converted to upgraded configuration. The AMX-30 series will be supplemented from the early 1900s by the EPC now under development by the AMX/GIAT.

Germany, Democratic Republic (East)

The National People's Army (NVA – Nationale Volksarmee) is considered to be the most reliable among the Warsaw Pact forces and has in recent years been issued with the latest Soviet equipment.

The country is divided into two military regions. Northern group of forces with HQ at Neubrandenburg controls the 1st Motorised Rifle Division at Potsdam, 8th Motorised Rifle Division at Schwerin and the 9th Armoured Division at Eggesin. Southern group of forces has the HQ at Leipzig and controls the 4th Motorised Rifle Division at Erfurt, 11th Motorised Rifle Division at Halle and the 7th Armoured Division at Dresden.

The tank divisions have three tank and one motorised rifle regiments while the motorised rifle divisions have one tank and three motorised rifle regiments. All of these are organised along Soviet lines and at Category 1 status (eg fully equipped and manned).

The total tank strength is believed to be around 1500 T-54/T-55s, with a small number of T-62s and about 1500 T-34/85s which are used for training or held in reserve. The T-72 is now being introduced in significant numbers having made its first public appearance during a parade held in East Berlin in October 1979 to celebrate the 30th anniversary of the foundation of the German Democratic Republic.

East Germany also houses the largest contingent of Soviet forces in the Warsaw Pact. In 1979 the Group of Soviet Forces Germany (GSFG) had some 11 tank and nine motorised rifle divisions, plus supporting units, all of which were at Category I. Since then some units have been withdrawn eastward with much publicity, although the remaining units have in turn been strengthened to more than compensate for the forces withdrawn. The list on the right relates to the position before the reductions.

BLG-60 bridgelayer of East German Army

Polish built T-55(M) of East German Army fitted with 12.7 mm DShKM anti-aircraft MG (traversed to rear) and hull-mounted dozer blade. Note stowage box on left side of turret and protective covers over externally-mounted infra-red searchlights

T-72 MBT of East German Army showing dozer blade under nose of vehicle

Group of Soviet Forces, Germany

Headquarters	Zossen-Wünsdorf
34th Gun Artillery Division	Potsdam
1st Guards Tank Army	Dresden
6th Guards Tank Division	Lutherstadt-Wittenberg
7th Guards Tank Division	Dessau Rosslau
9th Tank Division	Riesa
11th Guards Tank Division	Dresden-Klotzsche
27th Guards Motorised Rifle Division	Halle
2nd Guards Tank Army	Fürstenberg
16th Guards Tank Division	Neustrelitz
21st Motorised Rifle Division	Perleberg
25th Tank Division	Vogelsang-Berlin
94th Guards Motorised Rifle Division	Schwerin
3rd Shock Army	Magdeburg
10th Guards Tank Division	Krampnitz
12th Guards Tank Division	Neuruppin
47th Guards Tank Division	Hillersleben
207th Guards Motorised Rifle Division	Stendal
8th Guards Army	Weimar-Nohra
79th Guards Tank Division	Jena
20th Guards Motorised Rifle Division	Grimma
39th Guards Motorised Rifle Division	Ohrdruf
57th Guards Motorised Rifle Division	Naumberg-Saale
20th Guards Army	Eberswalde
6th Guards Motorised Rifle Division	Bernau
14th Guards Motorised Rifle Division	Jüterbog
35th Motorised Rifle Division	Döberitz

As of 1985 the GSFG consisted of ten tank, nine motorised rifle and one artillery divisions plus one air assault brigade, three SSM brigades, five artillery brigades and five attack helicopter regiments.

Germany, Federal Republic

Following its recent reorganisation the West German Army now has a total of 36 regular brigades; 17 armoured (each with two tank, one mechanised infantry, one mixed combat and one artillery battalion, one anti-tank company, one reconnaissance platoon plus engineer, maintenance, medical and support companies), 15 armoured infantry (similar to armoured brigades but with one tank and two mechanised battalions instead), three airborne and one mountain brigade. These are organised into 12 divisions (six armoured, four mechanised infantry, one mountain and one airborne), which make up three Corps.

The armoured division contains two armoured brigades, one armoured infantry brigade, armoured reconnaissance and anti-aircraft battalions, artillery regiment, engineer, signal, maintenance, transport/supply and medical battalions, aviation, MP and NBC companies. The armoured infantry division is similar but has one armoured and two armoured infantry brigades. Excluding artillery and support units, an armoured brigade has two tank regiments/battalions each with 41 MBTs, one mechanised infantry battalion with 35 infantry fighting vehicles and one mixed combat battalion with 28 MBTs and 11 infantry fighting vehicles.

A mechanised infantry brigade has one tank regiment/battalion with 41 MBTs, two mechanised infantry battalions with 34 infantry fighting vehicles each and one mixed combat battalion with 24 infantry fighting vehicles and 13 MBTs.

Each West German tank battalion consists of two tanks at HQ and three tank companies; each of the latter has an HQ element with one tank and three platoons (or troop) each with four tanks, so giving the battalion a total strength of 41 MBTs. The mixed battalion of both armoured and infantry brigades is formed in wartime.

In addition the strength of the Territorial Army includes 12 home defence brigades each with two tank, two infantry and one artillery battalion. Of these 12 home defence brigades, one is at 85 per cent of wartime strength, three at 65 per cent of wartime strength and two at 52 per cent of wartime strength. The remaining six are not manned but the equipment is already in position.

It is also planned that all of the armoured brigades will be equipped with the Leopard 2 (with the exception of two which will have the Leopard 1A4), while the armoured infantry brigades have the Leopard 1s and the home defence brigades the M48s.

By 1985 total armoured strength of the West German Army consisted of some 1400 Leopard 2s (with a total of 1800 to be delivered by 1986), 945 M48A2 (see below) and 2437 Leopard 1 MBTs (details of the individual marks are given in the entry for the Leopard 1 in the first part of this book). Variants used by the West German Army include 544 armoured recovery vehicles, 36 armoured engineer vehicles, 105 Biber bridgelayers, 420 Gepard twin 35 mm self-propelled anti-aircraft guns and 60 unarmed training tanks. West Germany also uses a number of M48 series AVLBs.

Leopard 2 MBT of West German Army in latest camouflage scheme

West German M48A2GA2 with 105 mm L7A3 gun and other modifications

Leopard 1A3 of Greek Army

Of the 945 M48A2s Wegmann of Kassel has rebuilt 650 to a new configuration known as the M48A2GA2 with the first of these being delivered in 1978. This has the 90 mm gun replaced by a 105 mm L7A3 rifled gun as installed in the Leopard 1, thermal sleeve for main armament, new travelling lock, new commander's cupola, modified ammunition stowage, passive night vision equipment for the driver (BM8005 image intensification periscope) and gunner (PZB 200 passive TV aiming and observation unit), and modifications to the fire control system. Four West German type smoke dischargers are mounted either side of the turret and an infrared/white light searchlight is mounted above the main armament, similar to that of the Leopard 1. Basic data of the M48A2GA2 is: loaded weight 47 800 kg, length gun forwards 9.35 m, length gun rear 8.1 m, height 2.9 m. Ammunition stowage is 46 rounds of 105 mm and 4750 rounds of 7.62 mm; of the latter 2250 rounds are in the turret and 2500 in the hull.

For the future the West German Army has a requirement for about 1300 Leopard 3 MBTs (in service from 1999), 1700 120 mm armed tank destroyers (in service from 1994) and 796 anti-tank/anti-helicopter vehicles (in service from 1990s).

Greece

The Greek Army includes one armoured division, one mechanised division, 11 infantry divisions, one parachute/commando division, five armoured brigades, two mechanised brigades, four armoured reconnaissance battalions plus aviation, artillery and air defence units.

The armoured division consists of a HQ company, three armoured regiments, reconnaissance battalion, artillery regiment, engineer, signals, medical and supply battalions plus an aviation company.

The armoured regiments have two tank and one mechanised infantry battalions. The tank battalion has an HQ element with one to three MBTs and three tank companies each with two tanks at HQ and three platoons each with five tanks. This gives the tank battalion a strength of between 52 and 54 tanks. The reconnaissance battalion has three reconnaissance companies with three platoons each consisting of an HQ element, one squad with two M48 tanks, two reconnaissance squads with jeeps, one mechanised infantry squad and one mortar squad with 81 mm mortars.

The infantry division has a HQ company, infantry regi-

AMX-30 MBTs of Greek Army

ment of three battalions, one tank battalion (same as in armoured division but also has a reconnaissance company similar to that in the armoured division), artillery regiment and supply battalion.

Total tank strength of the Greek Army includes about 400 M47s (most of which were supplied by the United States with the remainder by West Germany), 900 M48s (of which 204 are being brought up to M48A5 standard and 600 to M48A3 standard) and 285 AMX-30s (one batch of 170 and another of 115).

After inviting tenders for building a new tank production facility in Greece, the following were received by the end of April 1977: France with the AMX-30 and the AMX-13, West Germany with the Leopard 1 and the Thyssen-Henschel TAM, Italy with a modified version of the West German designed Leopard 1 and the United Kingdom with the Vickers Mark 3 and the Royal Ordnance Leeds with the Chieftain.

But in the end no facility was built in Greece and in April 1981 the Greek Government placed an order for 110 Leopard 1s valued at DM300 million with West Germany. The order comprised 106 Leopard 1A3 MBTs and four ARVs, plus an option on a further 113 vehicles. Deliveries commenced in February 1983 and were completed in April 1984 with Krauss-Maffei building 73 MBTs and Krupp MaK building 33 MBTs and four ARVs. Greek Leopard 1s have the EMES 12A3 fire control system and the PZB 200 LLLTV system.

Guinea

Guinea has one armoured battalion which is believed to be organised along Soviet lines and be equipped with some 45 T-34/85 and eight T-54/T-55 tanks.

Guinea-Bissau

Guinea-Bissau has one tank battalion which is equipped with about 30 T-54/T-55 and 15 T-34/85 tanks and this is believed to be organised along Soviet lines. One source does however

Hungarian T-72 MBT

T-54 MBT of Indian Army with US 12.7 mm Browning M2 HB anti-aircraft MG (Indian Army Official)

state that Guinea-Bissau has just one armoured squadron with about 10 T-34/85 tanks and 20 PT-76 light tanks.

Hungary

The Hungarian Peoples Army (MN – Magyar Nephadsereg) includes one tank division (the 5th) and five motorised rifle divisions (4th, 9th, 12th, 17th and 27th), all of which are organised along Soviet lines. Two Hungarian divisions took part in the Soviet invasion of Czechoslovakia in 1968. It is believed that the single tank division and two of the motorised rifle divisions are at Category 2 status (full scale of equipment but only 70 per cent of manpower) while other three motorised rifle divisions are at Category 3 status.

Total tank strength is believed to include some 1400 T-54/T-55s and at least 200 T-72s which entered service in 1979. Some T-34/85s are held in reserve and used for training.

The Soviet Southern Group of Forces is stationed in Hungary with its HQ at Budapest and consists of two tank divisions (2nd and 5th) and two motorised rifle divisions (35th and 102nd).

India

The Indian Army order of battle includes two armoured divisions (the 1st and 6th), one mechanised division, 19 infantry divisions, 10 mountain divisions (without any tanks), ten independent infantry brigades, seven independent armoured brigades, one mountain brigade, one parachute brigade, three independent engineer brigades and eight independent artillery brigades.

It is believed that each armoured division has two armoured brigades (with a total of six armoured regiments), one infantry brigade (with three battalions), artillery and support elements.

Each armoured brigade has three tank regiments plus an HQ element. Each tank regiment has a HQ company and three tank companies. Each of the latter has an HQ element with three tanks and four platoons of three tanks, giving the regiment a total of 45 tanks.

Infantry divisions have one tank regiment which is organised along similar lines to that in the armoured brigades.

Total Indian tank strength consists of about 1500 Vijayantas, 1000 T-54/T-55s (provided from the late 1960s) and about 300 T-72s. All of the Centurions have now been phased out of service.

Indian T-54/T-55 tanks have had their Soviet 12.7 mm DShKM anti-aircraft machine guns replaced by 12.7 mm Browning M2 HB weapons as fitted to other Indian MBTs, and it is probable that the coaxial weapons are also now Browning machine guns. India placed sheet metal tubes over the 100 mm barrels to resemble the bore evacuator of the L7 gun to serve as a means of distinguishing Indian T-54/T-55 tanks from Pakistani Type 59 MBTs.

There is a separate entry in the first part of this book on the Vijayanta MBT and current and future Indian tank developments.

Iran

In November 1985 the war between Iran and Iraq was still continuing and it is therefore impossible to give an accurate order of battle of the Iranian Army.

Western sources give the Iranian Army a total strength of seven infantry divisions, one special forces division (23rd), three mechanised divisions, an unknown number of independent armoured and infantry brigades and an Independent Coastal Force. In addition there is the Revolutionary Guard Corps which has a total of at least ten divisions organised in brigades.

During the fighting in the early part of 1985 in the Huwaiza marshes battle, the Iraqi Army identified the following Iranian divisions, in addition to the 23rd Special Forces Division: the 5th, 7th, 14th, 25th, 31st and 41st Khomeini Guard's divisions, as well as the 3rd, 8th, 19th and 27th brigades from the following Khomeini Guard's divisions, 21st, 28th, 92nd and 77th regular divisions.

Prior to the Iraq/Iran war the Iranian Army had four armoured and four infantry divisions plus independent brigades. Each armoured division had two armoured

brigades each of which had two tank battalions, one mechanised infantry battalion, one artillery battalion and a company of engineers. Armoured divisions had Chieftains and M60A1s while infantry divisions had M47Ms.

Prior to the conflict the Iranian army had 707 Mk 3/3P and Mk 5/5P Chieftains, 187 improved Chieftains, 40 Chieftain ARVs, 460 M60A1s, 400 M47s and 240 M48 series tanks.

Many of these have been lost although the Iranian Army has obtained new tanks from other sources as well as capturing a significant number of Iraqi vehicles.

By late 1985 Iranian strength is believed to include 250 M60A1, 300 Chieftains, 200 M47M and M48A5s and perhaps 250 Type 59/T-54/T-55/T-62/T-72 tanks captured from Iraq. Unconfirmed reports state that Iran has ordered 100 TAMs from Argentina as well as 200 tanks from China who is already supplying Iraq with Type 69s.

Between 1970 and 1972 Bowen-McLaughlin York established a vehicle overhaul and repair facility in Iran. This first brought the Iranian M47 tanks up to M47M standard and later Iranian M48A2 series up to M48A5 series. The plant also undertook work for Pakistan including upgrading their M47s to M47M standard and M48A2s to M48A5 standard. As far as it is known this plant is still operational although all of the BMY staff have long since gone. It no longer undertakes work for Pakistan and it has been reported that at the time of the revolution some Pakistani tanks were still in the facility and that these were never returned.

The M47M has the following components which are also interchangeable with the M48A3 and M60A1 MBTs: engine, transmission, gun elevating and traversing components, personnel heater, engine top deck and hull rear doors, air cleaners, machine gun ammunition racks, tail and warning lights, gauge instrument panel, driver's master control panel, tachometer with hour meter, speedometer with odometer, turret accessories control box, fire extinguisher control, drain valve and shock absorbers.

The bow machine gun has been removed and the gunner's position used to carry 22 rounds of 90 mm ammunition. The M47M carries 79 rounds of 90 mm ammunition compared to 71 rounds of the basic M47. The M47M can be fitted with the

M47M as used by Iran

T80E6 steel track or the T84E1 rubber track. The auxiliary compensating idler wheels, support arms and torsion bars which are between the No 6 road wheel and the drive sprocket have been removed. New M60 series shock absorbers have been fitted permitting greater vehicle speed and mobility.

The larger capacity fuel tanks, coupled with the improved fuel economy of the diesel engine, have increased the operational range of the M47M to 600 km, a dramatic improvement over that of the original M47. Specifications of the M47M are given in the entry for the M47 medium tank in the first part of this book.

Iraq

The Iraqi Army order of battle is believed to include six armoured divisions (each with one or two armoured and one mechanised brigades), five infantry divisions, five mechanised or motorised infantry divisions, two special forces divisions (each with three brigades), four mountain divisions, the Presidential guard (two armoured, one commando and one infantry brigade), perhaps 10 reserve brigades and a large number of volunteer brigades.

It is believed that the armoured division equate to a Soviet tank division except that it has two tank regiments not three and no integral SSM or MRL. The mechanised division is similar to the Soviet motorised rifle division but is thought to have only two motorised rifle regiments (not three as in the Soviet) and also no SSM or MRL.

In view of the fighting between Iraq and Iran, the present ORBAT of the Iraqi Army and the exact number of vehicles that it operates must be treated with caution. Front line armoured strength is believed to include 1200 T-54/T-55, 1000 T-62, 600 T-72, 400 to 500 Type 59, 200 plus Type 69 (with 100 mm gun) and between 50 and 200 Romanian M-77 MBTs. Significant numbers of M60A1, M47M, M48s, Chieftains and Soviet T-series tanks have been captured. Apart from the T-series vehicles it is not thought that any of these captured vehicles have entered service with the Iraqi Army.

Iraq has also received the first of 85 155 mm GCT self-

Centurion MBT (left) and M60A1 (right) MBTs of Israeli Army, both of which are armed with the proven M68 gun which is essentially the British 105 mm L7 series (Kensuke Ebata)

propelled guns from France on the AMX-30 tank chassis and 18 Roland 2 systems on the AMX-30 chassis. A small quantity of AMX-30 ARVs are also in service.

A number of reports have stated that some of the captured Chieftains have been passed on to Jordan who already operates a more advanced version called the Khalid.

Israel

The Israeli Army is believed to comprise some 33 armoured brigades (each of which has three tank and one mechanised infantry battalion in M113s), 11 armoured divisions, five mechanised infantry brigades, five parachute brigades, 15 artillery brigades and about 12 border/territorial infantry brigades. In peacetime it is probable that only five armoured, four infantry and two airborne brigades are kept at full strength. The armoured divisions are formed from the brigades depending on the mission but could consist of three armoured brigades, one artillery brigade, reconnaissance

T-55 MBT of Iraqi Army

M60A1 MBT of Israeli Army fitted with Israeli RKM mine clearing rollers

battalion (with MBTs and APCs), engineer battalion and other supporting units.

Each armoured brigade has an HQ element, three tank battalions, one mechanised infantry battalion (with M113 series APCs), reconnaissance company and a 120 mm mortar battalion. Each tank battalion has an HQ element with three MBTs and four tank companies each consisting of an HQ element with two tanks and three platoons each with three tanks. This would give the tank battalion a total of 47 tanks.

Total Israeli tank strength is believed to consist of about 1100 Centurions (all of which have been re-built to the Upgraded Centurion configuration which is fully described in the first part of this book), 650 M48s (all of which are to M48A5 configuration with 105 mm gun, diesel engine and a low profile commander's cupola), 1200 M60A1/M60A3s, plus small numbers of M728 Combat Engineer Vehicles and M60 AVLBSs), and 400 Merkava MBTs, with the latter seeing combat for the first time during the invasion of the Lebanon in the summer of 1982.

About 250 T-54/T-55 and 150 T-62 MBTs are held in reserve.

A few Sherman tanks are also in service, these being used mainly by the territorial/infantry brigades, although some of these vehicles have also been passed on to the Christian faction in Southern Lebanon. There is a separate entry on the Sherman and many of the specialised versions developed by Israel in the first part of this book.

Israeli M48, M60, Centurion and Merkava tanks can be fitted with dozer blades and mine clearing rollers developed

by Urdan. Details of these are given in the entry for the Israeli Upgraded Centurion in the first part of this book.

M60A1 MBT of Israeli Army fitted with Blazer add-on reactive armour, new commander's cupola, 7.62 mm machine guns at commander's and loader's stations and 12.7 mm machine gun over 105 mm gun which has a thermal sleeve

M60A1 MBT of Israeli Army fitted with Blazer add-on reactive armour, 7.62 mm and machine gun mounts and banks of ten smoke dischargers mounted either side of 105 mm M68 gun

Israeli T-54 and T-55

The Israeli Army captured large numbers of T-54 and T-55 tanks during both the 1967 and 1973 conflicts, many of which have been modified for their own use. These modifications which have not been carried out on every Israeli T-54 or T-55 include replacing the 100 mm gun by a 105 mm rifled gun, the coaxial machine gun by a 7.62 mm (0.30) Browning machine gun and the 12.7 mm DShKM anti-aircraft machine gun by a 12.7 mm (0.50) Browning M2 HB machine gun, new fire-control and electrical system, air-conditioning system, new radio mounts on turret rear, American infantry telephone on hull rear, Browning 0.30 machine gun at loader's station, exhaust outlet angled upwards, additional track stowage, fire-extinguishing system installed and new night vision equipment. These tanks are designated the TI-67.

Israeli T-54/T-55 Model S

This was announced in 1984 and in addition to all of the previous modifications such as replacement of the 100 mm gun by the 105 mm rifled gun, it has many other improvements including the American General Motors 8V-71T engine developing 609 hp, new semi-automatic hydro-mechanical transmission equipped with a torque converter, new air cleaners as fitted to the Israeli M60 and Merkava tanks, Blazer reactive armour added to the hull and turret, Cadillac Gage weapon stabilisation system, installation of EI-Op computerised Matador fire-control system, new low-profile commander's cupola, infra-red detectors, passive night vision equipment for commander, gunner and driver, fire detection and suppression system, new turret basket and extensive external stowage, modernised driver's station including replacement of sticks by a steering wheel and

improved suspension. These as well as modernised T-62s are now being offered for export.

Italy

The Italian Army has 24 brigades of which 18 are in the northern part of the country and the remaining six in the south. There are five armoured, seven mechanised, two independent mechanised, four independent motorised, five Alpine and one airborne brigade. There is also a heavy support brigade with Lance SSMs, HAWK SAMs and heavy artillery.

Italy is divided into six military regions, I with HQ at Turin, V with HQ at Pauda, VII with HQ at Florence, VIII with HQ at Rome, X with HQ at Naples and XI with HQ at Palermo.

There are three Corps, 3rd, 4th and 5th. The 5th Corps has its HQ at Vittorio Veneto and has the Ariete armoured division with HQ Pordenone, Mantova (HQ at Udine) and Folgore (HQ at Treviso) mechanised divisions plus associated supporting units.

The 4th Corps defends the Alps and has five Alpine brigades.

The 3rd Corps has its HQ in Milan and consists of the Centauro (HQ in Novara) mechanised division and the Cremona (HQ in Turin) motorised brigade.

There are also independent mechanised brigades, which are not assigned to NATO, Granatieri di Sardegna (in Rome), Pinerolo (in Bari), as well as three independent motorised brigades, Friul in Florence, Acqui in L'Aquila and Aosta in Messina. In addition there is the Folgore airborne brigade at Pisa and the Serenissima marine regiment which has one tank and three infantry battalions.

The Ariete armoured division, which is equipped with the M60A1, has two armoured and one mechanised brigade plus a reconnaissance battalion (with one company of tanks and two of infantry), artillery regiment, engineer battalion, aviation squadron, signals battalion and a supply battalion. The mechanised divisions have one armoured and two mechanised brigades and the same supporting units as the armoured divisions.

Italian-built Leopard 1 MBT with thermal sleeve for 105 mm gun, infra-red/white light searchlight fitted with track skirts removed

The armoured brigade has two tank battalions and one mechanised infantry battalion while the mechanised brigade has two mechanised infantry battalions and one tank battalion.

All tank battalions have one tank at battalion HQ and three tank companies. Each of the latter has one tank at company HQ and three platoons each with five tanks, giving the battalion a total of 49 tanks.

Each of the independent mechanised and motorised brigades has one battalion of M47 tanks.

Total Italian tank strength consists of some 500 M47s (800 were supplied by the United States but 100 have since been supplied to Spain for conversion into specialised vehicles), 300 M60A1s and 920 Leopard 1s (plus 69 ARVs and 12 AEVs with another 160 specialised versions built in Italy by OTO-Melara).

In 1956 Italy, France and West Germany drew up a requirement for a European MBT which would be well armed, lighter and more mobile than other tanks then in service.

In the end France placed the AMX-30 in production, West Germany placed the Leopard 1 in production while Italy obtained a licence to manufacture the M60A1 from the United States. A total of 200 were built in Italy by OTO-Melara for the Italian Army with a further 100 being supplied direct from the United States.

In the summer of 1964 Italy evaluated the Leopard 1 in Sardinia and after many delays in 1970 placed an order for 800 Leopard 1 MBTs, the first 200 of which were to be supplied from West Germany by Krauss-Maffei and the remaining 600 to be built under licence in Italy by a consortium headed by OTO-Melara. In addition 69 ARVs and 12 AEVs were ordered from Krupp MaK of West Germany which built all of the specialised versions of the Leopard 1.

The first Italian-built Leopard 1 was completed in 1974 and the last of the original order for 600 in 1978. Since then a further order was placed for 120 which were delivered in 1982.

OTO-Melara has recently built 160 specialised versions based on the hull of the Leopard 1 MBT including 64 bridgelayers, 68 ARVs and 28 AEVs. Co-producers to OTO-Melara are FIAT which supplies the engine, suspension and track, Lancia which supplies the transmission and major sub-contractors include Fucine Breda which provides the forged steel gun barrel and the cast turret.

For trials purposes Italy has ordered four sets of the West German Blohm and Voss add-on armour system as installed on Dutch and West German Leopard 1 MBTs.

Production of the new OTO-Melara/FIAT MBT for the Italian Army is expected to commence in 1987 with first deliveries due in 1988. First order is for 200 vehicles which will replace part of the remaining M47 fleet. A new 8 × 8 tank destroyer with a 105 mm gun is also being built.

Japan

The Japanese Ground Self-Defence Force order of battle includes one armoured division (7th), 12 infantry divisions (1st, 2nd, 3rd, 4th, 5th, 6th, 8th, 9th, 10th, 11th, 12th and 13th), two composite brigades, one airborne brigade, one artillery brigade, five engineer brigades and a single signals brigade.

The 1st, 2nd, 3rd, 4th, 6th, 11th and 13th infantry divisions each have four infantry regiments, one artillery regiment, one tank battalion, one anti-tank company, one reconnaissance company, engineer battalion, plus transport, aviation, medical and other supporting units. The other five infantry divisions (5th, 8th, 9th, 10th and 12th) are similar but have only three infantry regiments.

The 7th armoured division has three infantry regiments mounted in armoured personnel carriers, one tank battalion, one self-propelled artillery regiment plus supporting units.

The tank battalion has a HQ company with four tanks and four tank companies. Each of the latter has a HQ with two tanks and three platoons of four tanks giving the battalion a total strength of 60 tanks.

Total armoured strength of the Japanese Ground Self-Defence Forces consists of 500 (out of 559 built) Type 61 and 600 Type 74 MBTs, with the latter expected to increase to a total of 850 by 1988.

Jordan

The Jordanian Army has recently been reorganised and re-equipped and now consists of two armoured divisions, two mechanised infantry divisions, two air defence brigades, 16 artillery battalions, a special forces brigade and a number of independent brigades and units.

Each armoured division consists of three armoured brigades each of which has two tank battalions, one mechanised infantry battalion with M113s, a battalion of 155 mm M109A1 self-propelled howitzers and supporting units. At division level there is a battalion of 10 203 mm M110 self-propelled howitzers and an anti-aircraft battalion.

Each mechanised infantry division consists of two infantry brigades each of which has two mechanised infantry battalions, one tank battalion and same supporting units as the armoured division.

The Khalid and Tariq tanks are used by the armoured divisions while the M60A1 are used by the mechanised infantry divisions.

In late 1985 Jordan had 278 Khalid tanks (plus some Chieftain armoured recovery vehicles), 293 Tariqs and 200

Upgraded Centurion of Jordanian Army with new power-pack, Cadillac Gage weapon stabilisation system, new suspension and night vision equipment

M60A1/M60A3 MBTs. About 150 to 170 M47/M48A5 tanks are held in reserve, with some of the latter already being handed over to Lebanon several years ago.

Each Jordanian tank battalion has 44 tanks, two at battalion HQ and three tank companies, each of the latter has two MBTs at company HQ and four platoons each of three tanks.

All Centurions have now been upgraded and fitted with the Belgian SABCA fire control system (described in this section under Belgium), Teledyne Continental AVDS-1790-2C engine, CD-850-6A transmission, Cadillac Gage weapon stabilisation system. Teledyne Continental hydropneumatic suspension and passive night vision equipment.

Kampuchea

The order of battle of Kampuchea includes one armoured regiment whose equipment includes 10 T-54/T-55 tanks and 10 PT-76 light amphibious tanks.

Last Kenyan Vickers Mk 3 MBT and ARV await delivery at Vickers Defence Systems new Armstrong facility in November 1982

Kenya

When Kenya became independent its Army consisted mainly of infantry battalions with logistic support. In 1977 a Somali force crossed the border in Northern Kenya and in the same year Kenya placed an order with Vickers Defence Systems of the United Kingdom for 38 Vickers Mk 3 MBTs plus 3 ARVs which were all completed by 1980 and formed the

country's first tank battalion. In December 1980 the country ordered a further 38 Vickers Mk 3 MBTs, plus four ARVs which were delivered from 1981. The last two vehicles, an Mk 3 MBT and an ARV were completed at Vickers Defence Systems new Armstrong works in November 1982. These two tank battalions form an armoured brigade. It is believed that Kenya has a requirement for a third battalion of Vickers Mk 3 MBTs but there is insufficient funding at present to allow these to be purchased.

Vickers Mk 3 MBT of Kenyan Army

Korea, Democratic People's Republic (North)

The North Korean Army is one of the largest in Asia and its order of battle includes 24 infantry divisions, two armoured divisions (stationed near the South Korean border), five motorised and mechanised infantry divisions, seven independent armoured brigades, nine independent infantry brigades, 22 special operation brigades, plus air defence and artillery divisions and over 20 reserve infantry divisions and ten tank training battalions of which nine are believed to be equipped with the T-34/85.

The armoured division has three armoured regiments, an armoured infantry regiment, reconnaissance battalion, artillery regiment, anti-aircraft battery and support units. Each armoured regiment has three armoured battalions each of which has 31 MBTs plus a reconnaissance company, armoured infantry company, anti-aircraft battery and an engineer company. The armoured infantry regiment has three armoured infantry battalions, reconnaissance platoon, anti-aircraft battery, multiple rocket launcher battery, 76 mm gun battery, mortar battery and an engineeer company. Total MBT strength of the armoured division is 283.

The independent armoured brigades have three tank battalions, an armoured infantry battalion, reconnaissance battalion, anti-aircraft battery and an engineer company. Each tank battalion has 31 MBTs.

Each infantry division has one battalion of tanks with one at the battalion HQ, plus an ARV, and three companies each with 10 tanks. The motorised infantry divisions also have a single tank battalion.

It is reported that total North Korean tank strength now consists of about 175 Chinese Type 59 MBTs, 300 T-34/85s (used mainly for training), 2000 T-54/T-55s and about 400 T-62s, with the latter now being made under licence in North Korea. Late in 1985 South Korean sources stated that North Korea had organised and deployed another armoured corps to the rear of the DMZ consisting of three armoured divisions.

It is believed that North Korea now deploys four Corps along the border with South Korea, 1st, 2nd, 3rd and 5th Corps. To the rear of these infantry corps are deployed the Special Corps and the 3rd, 7th and 8th armoured corps. Based on this more recent information North Korea must have anything up to at least 12 armoured divisions.

M48s of South Korean Army (via Kensuke Ebata)

Korea, Republic of (South)

The South Korean Army has a front-line strength of two mechanised infantry divisions, 19 infantry divisions, seven special warfare brigades plus air defence (gun and missile), surface-to-surface missile and army air defence brigades.

Reserves include at least 23 infantry divisions. These are all organised into three Army HQs (1st, 2nd and 3rd) and five Corps. In addition there is the Combined Field Army (ROK/USA) which includes the American 2nd Infantry Division stationed around Camp Casey-Uijongbu which has two battalions of M60A3 tanks.

Each mechanised infantry division has three brigades each of which consists of three battalions of mechanised infantry, three battalions of motorised infantry, three tank battalions, one reconnaissance battalion, one field artillery brigade of four battalions, one engineer battalion, one signals battalion, one aviation detachment, one chemical support detachment, one TOW ATGW company and one combat service command.

Each infantry division has three infantry regiments, one reconnaissance battalion, one tank battalion, one engineer battalion, one divisional artillery group, one signals battalion, one aviation group, one chemical support detach-

M48A5 of South Korean Army with side skirts

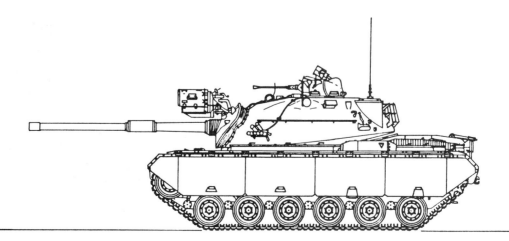

M48A5s of South Korean Army fitted with 105 mm M68 guns and side skirts (via Kensuke Ebata)

ment, one TOW ATGW company (not in all divisions yet) and one combat service support command.

Each tank battalion has a HQ and three tank companies with each of the latter having two tanks at HQ and four-five tank platoons, giving the battalion a total of 66 tanks.

The United States supplied South Korea with between 500 and 600 M47 medium tanks but it is believed that only between 300 and 400 of these are now operational. About 1100 of the later 90 mm M48 were supplied of which 800 to 900 are operational with about 600 of these having been brought up to M48A5 standard. In addition to being fitted with 105 mm gun, the South Korean M48A5s also have the diesel engine, infra-red driving lights, infra-red searchlight over main armament, smoke dischargers either side of turret and side skirts that are hinged at top to allow access to suspension and tracks for maintenance. These were originally converted with the aid of kits supplied by the United States but kits were subsequently produced in South Korea with major sub-contractors being:–

JE-IL Precision Co Ltd: Hull and turret electrical kit
Kangwon Industrial Co Ltd: Top engine deck grille, elbows of air cleaner, commander's cupola, hull welding and machining, engine and transmission mounts
Korea Heavy Industries and Construction Co Ltd: Track shoes
Ssangyong Heavy Industries Ltd: Continental AVDS-1790-2D diesel engine
Tong Myung Heavy Industries Co Ltd: Turret and gun control equipment
Miki Chemical Co Ltd: Road wheel assembly

Some of the M47s have been converted to the recovery role with the 90 mm gun removed and winch installed in the turret. Mounted at the front of the hull is an A-frame with the winch cable being taken out through the front of the turret. This vehicle is primarily used for changing vehicle components in the field as there are insufficient ARVs in service.

Under contract to the South Korean Government, General Dynamics, Land Systems Division, has designed and built the XK-1 MBT which is now being built in South Korea. Details of this are given in Part 1.

M47 armoured recovery vehicle of South Korean Army (via T Bell)

Kuwait

When Kuwait gained its independence from the United Kingdom in June 1961 it came under almost immediate pressure from Iraq which resulted in British troops being quickly dispatched to the country. Included in the latter were Centurion Mk 8/1s of C Squadron, 3rd Carabiniers, who arrived by sea from Aden. Their 25 Centurions were left behind when the crisis was over so that they would be ready for immediate use should the situation deteriorate again. At a later date these were handed over to Kuwait and a further 25 Centurions were supplied. Most of these have now been disposed of to Somali and only ten are now thought to remain in service.

In 1968 Kuwait placed an order for 70 Vickers Mk 1 MBTs which were delivered between 1970 and 1972. During the last Middle East conflict these were driven from Kuwait to Syria under their own power and back again when the conflict was over. Although there have been many problems with the Chieftain powered by the Leyland L60 engine there appears to have been little trouble when this engine has been installed in the lighter Vickers Mk 1 MBT.

In the late 1970s Kuwait ordered 165 Chieftains from the United Kingdom, most of which were built by Vickers at Elswick with final deliveries taking place in 1979. These are based on the Mk 5 and designated the Mk 5/2K but are not fitted with the Marconi Radar Systems light projector on the left side of the turret. It is probable that these will be fitted with passive night vision equipment in the future and a more advanced fire control system as they do not have the Marconi Command and Control Systems Improved Fire Control System which has now been retrofitted to most Chieftains of the British Army.

The Kuwait Army has two armoured and one mechanised infantry brigades and a surface-to-surface missile battalion.

Vickers Mk 1 MBTs of Kuwaiti Army

Laos

Armoured vehicles used by this country include about 30 Soviet supplied T-34/85 and T-54/T-55 MBTs.

Lebanon

Owing to the current political situation in this country no exact details of tank strength are available. In 1982 the United States supplied the Lebanon with 34 M48A5s with additional vehicles being supplied by Jordan. It is believed that the Army has about 50 M48A5s with a similar number in reserve. Other factions in the country also have tanks including the Lebanese Forces Militia (perhaps M48s), South Lebanon Army (Shermans from Israel and T-54), Druze (T-54/T-55 and T-34/85) plus others.

Libya

The strength of the Libyan Army includes some 20 tank battalions which are organised along Soviet lines with each having one MBT at battalion HQ and three tank companies each with ten tanks. This gives a front line active strength of 620 tanks There are also 30 mechanised infantry battalions, two anti-aircraft battalions, ten field artillery battalions plus the National Guard Brigade. HQs exist for one tank and one mechanised infantry division.

For some years Libya has been purchasing tanks and other military equipment on a large scale, far more than it can operate and maintain and for this reason much of it remains in storage and unused.

Total tank strength is now believed to be around 3000 vehicles including 250 T-72s, 2000 T-54/T-55s (mostly the latter) and 750 T-62s. A few T-34/85s may be used for training.

Chieftain Mk 5/2K awaiting delivery from Royal Ordnance Leeds. Note the absence of light projector on left side of turret (R O Leeds)

Mali

Mali was a French colony until indpendence in 1966 and since then most aid and equipment has been supplied by the Soviet Union including a single tank battalion that has a small number of T-54/T-55 tanks plus the remains of 30 to 40 T-34/85 tanks supplied many years ago. This battalion is probably organised along Soviet lines with 31 tanks.

Malaysia

The Federation of Malaysia was formed in 1963 and comprises Malaya, Sarawak and Sabah (previously British North Borneo). Singapore was a member of the Federation until 1965 when it seceded.

At the present time Malaysia has no tank units but has a requirement for at least one tank battalion. The known contenders for this contract include the Thyssen-Henschel TH-301, Vickers Mk 3, AMX-32, Cadillac Gage Stingray and OF-40 plus others that are still on the drawing board.

Mongolia

The Mongolian Army has four infantry divisions each of which has a number of tank battalions organised along Soviet lines with 31 tanks per battalion. It is believed that total tank strength includes about 650 T-54/T-55 and T-62 tanks.

Morocco

The Moroccan Army has been engaged in fighting the Polisario guerillas in the Sahara for some years and has been expanded and re-equipped with Austrian, French, South African and American equipment.

Morocco is believed to have at least five tank battalions. Two of these are thought to be organised along Soviet lines with 31 T-54/T-55 tanks per battalion, these being the remains of some 100 to 120 vehicles supplied by Czechoslovakia and the USSR in the 1960s.

The other three tank battalions are thought to be organised along American lines with each battalion having 54 M48 tanks. About 180 M48 series tanks have been supplied by the United States and most of these have been brought up to M48A5 standard with new engine and 105 mm gun.

In 1981 the US Department of Defense announced a letter of offer to Morocco for 108 M60A3 MBTs at a cost of $182 million including spares and training, but this was never taken up.

Mozambique

In the 1970s Mozambique received significant amounts of military equipment from the Soviet Union and other members of the Warsaw Pact and the country acted as a base for guerillas operating against the then Rhodesia (now Zimbabwe).

It has been reported that about 150 T-34/85, 200 T-54/T-55 and a small number of T-62 MBTs have been supplied and that some of these, specifically the T-34/85s were for use by the guerilla forces.

The Mozambique Army order of battle is believed to include one tank brigade, two independent mechanised battalions, seven infantry brigades plus artillery units.

Each infantry brigade consists of one tank battalion (believed to be organised along Soviet lines), three infantry battalions, two artillery battalions, one air defence battalion plus other supporting units including logistics.

Netherlands

The regular Netherlands Army has two armoured and four mechanised brigades with one armoured brigade (41st) and support units being forward deployed in West Germany. Upon mobilisation a further armoured brigade, two mechanised and one independent infantry brigade would be added. In April 1984 it was announced that the Netherlands was to sell 120 Centurion tanks to Austria for £3800 each with the possibility of an additional 180 vehicles. On arrival in Austria these have had their turrets removed and used in static defence positions.

Each armoured brigade has a HQ and HQ company, two armoured battalions, an armoured infantry battalion, reconniassance company, artillery battalion, anti-tank company, engineer company, anti-aircraft battery, signals company and supply battery.

The armoured battalion has a HQ company with two Leopard 1 MBTs and three Leopard ARVs and a reconnaissance platoon with three command and reconnaissance vehicles, and three armoured companies. Each of the latter has a HQ with two Leopard 1 MBTs and three platoons each with five Leopard 1 MBTs. This gives the tank battalion a total strength of 53 Leopard 1 MBTs and three Leopard ARVs.

The mechanised infantry brigade is similar to the armoured brigade except it has one tank battalion and two infantry battalions. One of the latter was equipped with the AMX VCI tracked APC and the other with the DAF YP-408 (8 × 6) APC, but these are both now being converted to the FMC tracked AIFV.

Today the Dutch Army tank fleet consists of 300 Centurion and 468 Leopard 1 vehicles, plus specialised versions and over 350 Leopard 2s.

Centurion Mk 5/2 of Dutch Army without track skirts fitted (Royal Netherlands Army)

Leopard 2 MBT of Royal Netherlands Army (Michael C Klaver)

In the early 1950s the Netherlands procured 591 Centurion gun tanks plus 44 Mk 2 ARVs. A further batch of 70 Mk 7 gun tanks followed but these were sold with American approval in the early 1960s as the UNF design was not compatible with the original batch. 343 Centurions were brought up to Mk 5/2 standard with 105 mm L7 series guns, 216 retained the old 20 pounder (83.4 mm) gun, 16 were fitted with an old Sherman dozer blade and 16 were fitted with an M48 type AVLB. A further 122 Mk 5s were sold to Israel, again with US approval, when the Leopard 1 was introduced into service. These ten brigades form 1(NL) Corps which was established in November 1952 and is the Dutch contribution to NATO ground forces in the central region. Of the ten brigades, nine of these are formed into three divisions, these being the 1st Division (13th armoured, 11th, and 12th mechanised brigades) with HQ in Schaarsbergen, 4th Division (41st armoured, 42nd and 43rd mechanised brigades) with HQ in Harderwijk and 5th Division (51st armoured, 52nd and 53rd mechanised brigades) with HQ in Stroe. The 1st and 4th Divisions are fully operational with the 5th being formed on mobilisation.

After evaluating the Chieftain, Leopard 1 and MBT-70 between 1967 and 1968, the Netherlands placed an initial order for 400 Leopard 1s in 1968. This was followed by further orders for the Leopard MBT and specialised variants and in the end 468 Leopard 1 MBTs, 52 ARVs, 14 bridgelayers, 12 driver training vehicles and 65 twin 35 mm self-propelled anti-aircraft gun systems were acquired. The MBTs were delivered from 1969 to 1971 and many components were made by the DAF company in Holland.

The Dutch vehicles have different radios, Dutch type smoke dischargers, three stowage panniers and different exhaust covers. The 7.62 mm MG was replaced by a 12.7 mm Browning M2 HB MG at the commander's station. At a later date the tanks were fitted with an American Honeywell gun stabilisation system, modified optical sights to enable British L52 APDS ammunition to be fired, and a passive periscope for the driver.

All 468 Leopard 1s of the Dutch Army are now being modified by 574 Tankwerkplaats at Leusden and fitted with applique armour provided by Blohm and Voss of West Germany. This is similar to that fitted to the Leopard 1A1A1 of the West German Army. When modified they are designated the Leopard 1-V with the latter standing for Verbeterd, or improved. New track skirts are also being fitted. When the Leopard 1s are being up-armoured, the EMES 12A3 (Dutch configuration) gunner's fire control system is being installed. The EMES 12A3 is supplied by Honeywell, Zeiss with Old Delft as the major Dutch sub-contractor.

Following a competition between the United Kingdom (L64), Israel (M111) and the United States (M735) for a new APFSDS round for the 105 mm L7 guns, the British L64 was selected as the replacement for the L52 APDS round currently used by the Dutch Army.

In March 1979 the Netherlands placed an order for 445 Leopard 2s to replace the 369 Centurion MBTs and 130 AMX-13 light tanks. First vehicles were delivered in 1982 with final deliveries due in 1986. The Dutch vehicles have Belgian 7.62 mm FN MAG machine guns. Dutch smoke dischargers, night vision equipment and radios. The Dutch Army's 41st Amoured Brigade, based in West Germany, is the first unit to be re-equipped with the Leopard 2. When the Leopard 2 was introduced the armoured squadrons now have four platoons each of four tanks in place of the current three platoons with five tanks.

Centurion AVLB of Dutch Army

Nigeria

The order of battle of the Nigerian Army includes one armoured division which is said to consist of four armoured and one mechanised brigade plus a reconnaissance battalion, engineer battalion and an artillery brigade, two mechanised divisions, one composite division and a Guards brigade with one armoured reconnaissance battalion and three infantry battalions. Many of the armoured units have light armoured vehicles. Tanks in service include remains of 100 T-54/T-55 and some 40 Vickers Mk 3s with more still to be delivered.

In August 1981 Nigeria placed an order with Vickers Defence Systems of the United Kingdom for the supply of 36 MBTs, six ARVs and five AVLBs worth some £60 million. The MBTs are powered by the General Motors 12V-71T diesel engine, and fitted with Pilkington PE Condor commander's day/night sight and the Marconi Command and Control Systems SFC 600 fire-control system. They also have the Vickers L22 sight which incorporates the Simrad LV352 laser rangefinder. Early in 1985 Nigeria placed a repeat order for a similar number of Vickers Mk 3 MBTs, ARVs and bridgelayers with first deliveries made in 1985.

Nicaragua

Owing to the present situation in Nicaragua the exact order of battle of the Nicaraguan Army is uncertain but is believed to include at least five armoured battalions whose equipment includes about 120 T-54/T-55 plus a few Shermans supplied by the United States many years ago.

Norway

The Royal Norwegian Army operates a total of 38 M48s and 78 Leopard 1 MBTs which are organised into one tank company for the brigade group based on the north of the country and one company for the all arms group based in southern Norway. In addition there are seven independent armoured squadrons in various parts of the country, five

Norwegian M48 showing 12.7 mm (0.50-inch) anti-aircraft machine gun on commander's cupola (Royal Norwegian Army)

Norwegian Leopard 1 fitted with West German Hoffmann-Werke AFV gunfire simulator over 105 mm gun and stowage box on glacis plate (Ministry of Defence)

being equipped with the Leopard 1 and two with the M48.

From November 1966 Norway tested the Leopard 1 at the Trandum Armour School and the Snoeheim Cold Weather Command and on 22 November 1968 placed an order for 78 Leopard 1s which were delivered between 1969 and 1971. In addition six ARVs were ordered from Krupp-MaK of Kiel. The Leopard 1s are similar to the first production batch of Leopard 1s for the West German Army as Norway requested no special modifications to the vehicles. In recent years M48s have been brought up to M48A5 standard with 105 mm gun and diesel engine in place of original petrol engine.

Oman

In 1980 a decision was taken to incorporate MBTs into the Sultan of Oman's Land Forces (SOLF) which at that time operated Alvis Saladin (6 × 6) armoured cars.

In August six American M60A1s were delivered and formed as the Oman Tank Force/6th Tank Squadron.

In August 1981 12 Chieftain Mk 7/2C MBTs were supplied by the British Army on a loan basis and formed into E Squadron, as by that time the Saladins (now replaced by the Alvis Scorpion) had been formed into A, B and C squadrons. The Chieftains made their first public appearance during the National Day Parade held in October 1981.

More recently Oman has taken delivery of 27 new Chieftains from Royal Ordnance Leeds known as the Qayis Al Ardh. These, like the Alvis Scorpions, have the Vickers Instruments L20 sight which incorporates a Ferranti Type 520 Mk 2 laser rangefinder. The Omani order of battle now includes one armoured regiment with two tank squadrons and an artillery battery with M109A2.

Pakistan

The Pakistani Army order of battle includes two armoured divisions (1st and 6th), 16 infantry divisions, four independent armoured brigades and eight independent infantry brigades.

Pakistani Army Type 59 MBT with standard 100 mm gun (via G Jacobs)

The armoured divisions are believed to have six tank regiments, the armoured brigades three and each infantry division one. Each tank regiment has three MBTs at HQ and three tank companies each with three tanks at HQ and four platoons of three tanks giving each regiment an authorised strength of 48 tanks. It has however been reported that tanks are in such short supply that each regiment now has only 38 tanks.

Pakistan has fought two major campaigns with India in 1965 and 1971 and lost significant numbers of tanks in both. In the 1950s most of its vehicles were supplied by the United States including large numbers of M47 and M48 tanks. From 1965 however all vehicles came from China including large numbers of Type 59 tanks. Prior to the Iranian revolution the BMY company of the United States constructed a plant in Iran for the rebuilding of Iranian M47s to the M47M standard (qv this section under Iran). Pakistan had its remaining M47s brought up to M47M standard in the early 1970s after which the M48s were brought up to M48A5 standard, although it has been said that some vehicles were still in Iran at the time of the revolution.

Following the Soviet invasion of Afghanistan, Pakistan has again started to receive American military assistance and late in 1982 the Pentagon informed Congress that it intended to sell 100 M48A5s to Pakistan at a cost of $80 million.

With Chinese assistance Pakistan has established the Heavy Rebuild Factory at Taxila. This facility covers some 48 acres and is capable of rebuilding tanks and powerpacks as well as manufacturing individual optical and electrical components.

It is believed that the total front line strength of the Pakistani Army consists of 800 to 1000 Chinese supplied Type 59s, 40 to 50 T-54/T-55s, 150 M47Ms and about 350 M48A5s.

Vickers Instruments L20 sight which incorporates a Ferranti Type 520 Mk 2 laser rangefinder

M48 tank of Pakistani Army knocked out by Indian forces in the Western sector in 1971 (Indian Army Official)

Of these the first 145 M48s were rebuilt to M48A5 configuration between 1977 and 1979 with a further 100 being supplied from the United States in 1982 at a cost of $71 million and another 100 in 1984.

Panama

Early in 1984 it was reported that Panama had placed an order with Argentina for the supply of 60 TAM 105 mm tanks and a small quantity of VCTP armoured personnel carrier versions to form a single armoured battalion.

Peru

The Peruvian Army order of battle includes three armoured divisions, although by Western standards they are in fact brigades.

Total armoured strength is believed to include between 250 and 300 T-54/T-55s which were supplied by the Soviet Union in the early 1970s and the remainder of some 60 M4 Sherman tanks supplied by the United States in the 1950s. The Soviet Union is known to have offered Peru the more recent T-62 MBT but the problems with the original T-54/T-55 vehicles and the country's lack of foreign exchange have so far prevented this and other modernisation programmes. In mid-1983 Peru placed an order for 80 TAMs with deliveries expected to take place in 1985.

Poland

The Polish Army order of battle includes five tank (5th, 10th, 11th, 16th and 20th) and eight motorised rifle (1st, 2nd, 3rd, 4th, 8th, 9th, 12th and 15th) divisions, all of which are organised along Soviet lines. The Soviet Southern Group of Forces is stationed in Poland and consists of two tank (2nd and 5th) divisions.

Total tank strength includes some 3500 T-54/T-55 and 100 T-72 MBTs; the latter will rapidly increase as production

Soviet supplied T-55 MBT in service with Peru (US Department of Defense)

builds up in Poland. A few T-34/85s are probably used for training to conserve track life on the more modern vehicles.

Poland produced the T-34/85 from 1951 to 1956 and the T-54 and T-54M from 1956 to 1965 at Labedy. This was followed in production by the T-55 which has been built for both the Polish Army and for export, mainly to other members of the Warsaw Pact. Many of the Polish vehicles were fitted with a large stowage box mounted on the left side of the turret (see photograph in this section under East Germany). Production of the T-55 has now been completed in Poland and the tank facility at Katowice started tooling up to produce the T-72 MBT in 1979 with first production tanks being completed the following year. According to United States Department of Defense figures between 1976 and 1980 combined tank production of Czechoslovakia and Poland amounted to 800 vehicles a year.

Portugal

The First Independent Mixed Brigade, which is NATO earmarked, includes one tank battalion equipped with 66 M48A5 tanks armed with 105 mm guns.

Qatar

This country has one tank battalion, the equipment of which includes 24 AMX-30S MBTs and one AMX-30D armoured recovery vehicle supplied by France in the mid-1970s. The MBTs are probably the AMX-30S version which is also used by Saudi Arabia and has been modified specifically for operations in the desert.

Romania

The order of battle of the Romanian Army includes two tank and eight motorised rifle divisions which are organised along Soviet lines.

Romania is a member of the Warsaw Pact but its forces took no part in the invasion of Czechoslovakia in 1968 and in recent years has tended to lean more to the West and China. The army is mainly defensive and it is not thought that it would fight outside of its own borders in the future. There have been no Soviet troops stationed in Romania since 1958 and its forces have not taken part in the annual Warsaw Pact exercises in recent years.

Tank strength includes some 200 T-34/85s which are used mainly for training, 1300 T-54/T-55s, a few T-62s, about 30/40 T-72s purchased in 1979–80 and several hundred M-1977 (or M-77) MBTs.

The M-1977 was seen for the first time during a parade held in Bucharest in 1977 and is believed to be a rebuilt T-55. It has six road wheels instead of five as on the T-54/T-55, side skirts similar to those fitted to the British Chieftain and Centurion, new 12.7 mm anti-aircraft machine gun with some ammunition boxes mounted externally on the sides of the turret similar to those of the T-64 and T-72 MBTs, and improved cooling for the engine, which is not thought to have been replaced. The M-1977 (also referred to as the TR-77 or M-77) has also been supplied to Iraq and Egypt

Romanian M-1977 (modified T-55) MBTs showing side skirts and six road wheels during a parade held in Bucharest

Saudi Arabia

The strength of the Saudi Arabian Army includes three armoured brigades (with a fourth now being formed), one infantry brigade, three mechanised brigades, one airborne brigade, one Royal Guard regiment, plus field and air defence battalions.

Total tank strength includes some 290 AMX-30Ss (plus ARVs, bridgelayers, 155 mm GCT self-propelled howitzers, Shahine SAM systems and AMX-30S DCA twin 30 mm self-propelled anti-aircraft guns, also on an AMX-30S type chassis) and 150 M60A1s (plus some M728 combat engineer vehicles). In 1983 Saudi Arabia placed an order with the United States for 100 M60A3 MBTs with tank thermal sights and these have now been delivered.

Saudi Arabia was to purchase 86 M60A3 chassis mounted with a Swiss Oerlikon-Bührle twin 35 mm turret as fitted to the Gepard self-propelled anti-aircraft gun system but this was subsequently dropped.

Saudi Arabia was also supplied with about 75 M47 tanks in the 1950s and recently some of these have been given to Sudan and Somalia. It is not thought that any M47s remain operational with the Saudi Army.

Saudi Arabia has a requirement for a new MBT and in 1985 tested two British Royal Ordnance Challenger MBTs, one ENGESA EE-T1 Osorio MBT and one GIAT AMX-40 MBT.

Singapore

Singapore is known to have eight M728 Combat Engineer Vehicles and 12 M60 AVLBs, and 60 Centurion MBTs have been purchased and are kept in Taiwan for training as there is insufficient space on Singapore to conduct realistic training with MBTs. In addition the Army has some 300 French-built AMX-13 light tanks with 75 mm guns.

Somali Democratic Republic

In the 1960s and early 1970s the Somali Army was trained and equipped with weapons provided by the Soviet Union. Following the heavy fighting between Somalia and Ethiopia in 1977, in which Somalia lost a good deal of equipment, supplies were stopped by the Soviet Union.

Today the order of battle of the Somali Army includes three tank/mechanised brigades and about 20 infantry bat-

talions. Armoured strength is said to consist of about 40 T-34/85s (out of some 200 plus supplied) and about 50 T-54/T-55 (out of 100 T-54/T-55 and supplied). It is a matter as to how many of these are operational as no spares have been supplied by the Soviet Union for some six years.

Saudi Arabia is providing some funding for the re-equipment of the Somali Army but so far most of this appears to have been for FIAT trucks, FIAT/OTO-Melara 6616 armoured cars and FIAT 6614 armoured personnel carriers.

Saudi Arabia has transferred a number of M47 tanks to Somali (with first batch consisting of 17 vehicles with total now believed to be as many as 100), Kuwait is believed to have supplied 35 Centurions.

South Africa

In the early 1950s the United Kingdom supplied South Africa with some 200 Centurion Mk 3 MBTs which were to be used by a South African armoured division as part of a British Commonwealth contingency force for employment in the Middle East. These were subsequently upgraded to Mk 5 standard but following the Suez campaign 100 were sold to Switzerland.

In the 1970s the remaining Centurions, plus vehicles obtained as scrap from Iraq (very small number), India (various figures have been quoted with 90 being the most common) and Jordan (41 Mk 7), were rebuilt at 61 Base Workshop in Verwoerdurg and fitted with a new powerback and standard 105 mm tank gun. These are called the Olifant (Elephant) and total South African tank strength is now put at 300 Centurions.

During the fighting in Angola no South African tanks were deployed as the Eland armoured cars with their 90 mm guns were more than adequate to deal with the T-34/85 and few T-54 tanks used by Angola.

Upon mobilisation South Africa would field one armoured and one infantry division which would have a total of four motorised brigades, one armoured brigade (with two tank battalions) and one mechanised brigade (with one tank battalion). A small number of Centurion tanks have been deployed with the 61st Mechanised Battalion Group of the South African Army in South West Africa.

Olifant MBT of South African Army with turret traversed to rear and showing 105 mm gun (South African Army)

Specifications of Olifant MBT

COMBAT WEIGHT	56 000 kg
POWER-TO-WEIGHT RATIO	13.39 hp/tonne
LENGTH	8.61 m
WIDTH	3.39 m
HEIGHT	2.94 m
MAXIMUM ROAD SPEED	45 km/h
FUEL CAPACITY	1240 litres
MAXIMUM RANGE	250 km
GRADIENT	60 per cent
TRENCH	3.45 m
ENGINE	diesel developing 750 hp
ARMAMENT	
main	1 × 105 mm
coaxial	1 × 7.62 mm MG
anti-aircraft	1 × 7.62 mm MG
AMMUNITION	
main	72

Spanish AMX-30 fitted with British Weston Simfire tank gunnery and tactical training system

Spain

The Spanish Army order of battle includes the Immediate Intervention Force, the Territorial Defence Force (to disband), the General Reserve Force, a few independent units and the Overseas Forces. The first of these includes one armoured, one motorised and one mechanised division, armoured cavalry, parachute, airportable and artillery brigades plus a number of specialised regiments such as multiple rocket launchers and light anti-aircraft. All MBTs are concentrated in the Immediate Intervention Force.

The armoured division consists of two armoured brigades (of which one is in cadre form) and one mechanised brigade. The mechanised division consists of two mechanised (of which one is in cadre form) and two motorised brigades, and the motorised division consists of two motorised brigades plus another in cadre form. Each division also has one artillery regiment, a light anti-aircraft gun regiment, a light

cavalry squadron (the equipment of which includes the M41 light tanks) plus supporting units.

Each armoured brigade consists of two battalions of M48s, one mechanised infantry battalion with M113s and an artillery battalion with three batteries each with six M109A1 155 mm self-propelled howitzers.

The mechanised brigade has one tank battalion (with M47 or AMX-30E), three mechanised infantry battalions, and an artillery battalion.

The motorised division has a single tank battalion (with M47 or AMX-30E), three motorised battalions and an artillery battalion with 105 mm M101 series towed howitzers.

Each tank battalion has three tanks at HQ and three tank companies each with a total of 17 tanks giving a strength of 54 tanks, eg the same as an American tank battalion.

The Spanish Army use of tanks is unusual in that some

Talbot rebuilt M47E1 with powerpack and turret traversed to rear with 90 mm gun in travel lock

belong to the infantry (seven battalions with AMX-30E, M47E and M48E) and some to the cavalry.

The Spanish cavalry consists of four light armoured cavalry regiments, one equipped with AMX-30E MBTs and M113A1 armoured personnel carriers and three with M47E MBTs and M113A1 armoured personnel carriers. There are also 11 ight cavalry groups of which nine are equipped with M41 light tanks and AML 60/90 4 × 4 armoured cars and two with just AML 60/90s, of which one is with the Legion.

There are also seven armoured cavalry regiments, three with M47E MBTs and M113A1 armoured personnel carriers, two with M47E MBTs and BMR-600 (6 × 6) armoured personnel carriers and two with M48E MBTs and M113A1 armoured personnel carriers. Of these the two with M48E/M113A1 are based at Ceuta and Melilla, the three with M47E/M113A1 are with the cavalry brigade and the remaining two with M47E/BMR-600 are with the mountain division.

The armoured cavalry brigade has a total of 170 MBTs and consists of a HQ and HQ squadron, one light armoured cavalry regiment, three armoured cavalry regiments, one artillery regiment with 36 self-propelled howitzers and an engineer battalion.

In 1985 the Spanish Ministry of Defence stated that the total front-line tank strength of the Spanish Army consisted of 127 M41 light tanks, 375 M47, 164 M48 and 299 AMX-30 MBTs.

AMX-30E

Following delivery of the first 19 vehicles from France, Spain built the AMX-30 under licence from 1974 under the designation AMX-30E. Initially these tanks were built from components supplied by France but gradually the Spanish content increased until about 85 per cent of the tank was built in Spain. Ten AMX-30D ARVs were also supplied direct from France.

It is estimated that five tanks were completed in Spain in 1974, 21 in 1975, 52 in 1976, 66 in 1977 and at least 80 in 1978. Production of the AMX-30 was completed in Spain in 1983.

The Spanish tanks are almost identical to the French models but have a 7.92 mm MG 42 machine gun in place of the 7.62 mm weapons and other minor differences. Production of the AMX-30 was undertaken by the Alcalá de Guadaira factory of Empressa Nacional Santa Barbara (ENSB), with Empressa Nacional de Optica (ENOSA) providing the optical equipment and Experiences Industriales SA(EISA) the electrical and hydraulic equipment.

In 1980 Spain purchased the entire licence from GIAT of France in order to continue development of the tank itself.

Spanish M48 tanks

A total of 18 M48s of the Spanish Marines have been retrofitted by Chrysler with an AVDS-1790 series diesel engine but retain their 90 mm guns. Fifty-four Spanish Army M48A1s have been brought up to M48A5 standard with 105 mm guns, with a similar number converted more recently. Spain has also purchased a number of M48A2 tanks from West Germany and these are being brought up to M48A5 standard.

Spanish M47 tanks

Some 560 M47s were supplied to Spain by the United States and 330 of these have now been selected for rebuilding. The first 110 are designated the M47E, the second 110 the M47E1

and the third batch the M47E2. It is believed that these have a new diesel engine and at least one batch has been fitted with the West German Rheinmetall 105 mm 105-30 gun which fires standard 105 mm tank ammunition. In 1981 an additional 100 ex-West German and Italian M47s were purchased as scrap and may be rebuilt with new engines and converted into engineer and recovery vehicles. The former are very similar in appearance to the AMX-30D and Leopard 1 ARVs with a dozer/stabilising blade at the front of the hull and a crane pivoted at the front of the hull on the right side.

Note:

The Spanish Foreign Legion also operates the AMX-30E and the Spanish Marines operate 18 M48E tanks with 90 mm guns.

Sudan

Sudan has two armoured brigades each of which is believed to have two tank and one mechanised infantry battalion. Armoured equipment includes 17 M47s (supplied by Saudi Arabia in 1980), 20 T-34/85s (out of 70 supplied in 1958–59 and probably now relegated to training), 60 T-54s and 60 T-55s. In October 1981 the US Department of Defense advised Congress of a letter of offer to Sudan for 20 M60A3 MBTs plus spares at a cost of $36 million, and these have now been delivered. China is believed to have supplied 20 Type 59 MBTs to Sudan.

For much of the 1960s Sudan obtained all of its military equipment from the Soviet Union but in recent years has purchased equipment from China, France and the United States. Saudi Arabia is also providing military equipment as well as funding some of the American purchases. The main external threat to Sudan is Libya, which has already backed a number of unsuccessful coups that have taken place in the Sudan.

Centurion MBT of Swedish Army fitted with 105 mm gun and machine gun mounted externally at commander's cupola (Swedish Army)

Sweden

The Swedish Army, when mobilised, would field four armoured brigades, one mechanised brigade, five Norrland brigades, 19 infantry brigades plus 60 independent armoured, infantry, air defence and artillery battalions.

Each armoured brigade has a HQ and HQ company, three armoured battalions, reconnaissance company two anti-tank companies, artillery battalion, engineer battalion and supply battalion.

Each armoured battalion has a HQ and HQ company, two tank companies, two armoured infantry companies, one howitzer battery and one supply battery. Each tank company has an HQ element with one tank, four tank platoons each of three tanks and one mechanised infantry platoon. This gives the battalion a total of 26 tanks, or 78 per brigade.

The infantry and Norrland brigades do not have any MBTs but have an assault gun company with 12 Ikv-91 tank destroyers.

Swedish armoured strength consists of 300 S-tanks and a similar number of British-supplied Centurions.

Sweden originally ordered 88 Centurion Mk 3 tanks in the early 1950s which were subsequently given the Swedish Army designation of Stridsvagn 81 (Strv 81 for short). These were followed by a large number of Mk 5s in the mid-1950s. In 1958 Mk 10s were ordered with 105 mm L7 guns which were delivered from 1960 and designated the Stridsvagn 101. From 1962 the earlier Centurions were refitted with the 105 mm gun and then designated the Strv 102. Sweden is now the only known user of the mono-trailer which carries additional fuel. Sweden also used the Centurion Mk 2 ARV under the designation of the Bargninstanvagn 81 (Bgtv 81). The Swedish Centurions also have different radios, Browning machine guns made in Sweden (designated the Ksp m/39), special track link ice peg, crew heater and facility to warm engine.

After evaluating Centurions fitted with new powerpacks by Vickers Defence Systems of the UK and Teledyne Continental of the US, the latter was selected in 1982, late in 1981 the Swedish FMV awarded a contract worth some SKr 150 million to Bofors for the upgrading of the Swedish Centurion Strv 101 and Strv 102 MBTs.

This programme is being carried out in two stages covering firepower and mobility. The first retrofitted vehicle was delivered to the Swedish Army early in 1983.

Bofors Aerotronics is providing a new fire control system based on its export version computer. A new gun control equipment, including solid-state amplifiers, a gyro-unit and a new gunner's and commander's control handles will also be in the package.

The gunner's sight is replaced by a new Ericsson sight incorporating a laser rangefinder. Additional details of this sight are given in this section under the Danish Centurions.

A modified cupola retaining the existing commander's sight but including an armoured hood to provide protection when observing head out is also being installed.

Bofors Ordnance will provide the Lyran twin launcher for the 71 mm illuminating system with a range of 1300 metres.

Late in 1982 the Swedish Army placed an order worth Skr 180 million with Detroit Diesel Allison (CD-850-6A automatic transmission) and Teledyne Continental (AVDS-1790-2C diesel engine) to be used in the Strv 101 and Strv 102 MBTs.

Chassis conversion will be carried out by Hägglund and Söner while integration of the chassis and turret will take place in Southern Sweden at a government facility.

Early in 1985 the Swedish armed forces successfully completed trials of a Centurion MBT with the British hydro-strut suspension system which has been developed jointly by Oceonics Vehicle Technology and Royal Ordnance Leeds. This has also been tested on a British Army Chieftain MBT and the private venture Royal Ordnance Chieftain 900 MBT. The hydro-strut suspension system can be installed on an existing Centurion in just one day with no modifications being required to the hull.

Switzerland

The Swiss Army order of battle includes three Field Army Corps (FAK – Feldarmeekorps) and one Mountain Army Corps (Geb AK – Gebirgsarmeekorps). 1st Field Army Corps contains the 1st Mechanised and 2nd and 3rd Field Divisions, 2nd Field Army Corps the 4th Mechanised and 5th and 8th Field Divisions and 4th Field Army Corps the 11th Mechanised and 6th and 7th Field Divisions. The 3rd Mountain Army Corps has no armoured units and contains the 9th, 10th and 12th Mountain Divisions. The 1st, 2nd and 4th FAK defend the northern part of Switzerland while the 3rd Geb AK defends the south. Most of the Swiss Army is made up of reservists.

Leopard 2 MBT of Swiss Army showing Bofors Lyran launcher on left side of turret (Swiss Army)

Swiss Centurion Pz 57/60 fitted with 105 mm gun and new smoke dischargers (Swiss Army)

Swiss Centurion Mk 2 ARV (Entpannungspanzer 56) (Swiss Army)

Each mechanised (or armoured) division has a HQ, two armoured regiments, one motorised infantry regiment, one howitzer regiment, one artillery regiment, one anti-aircraft battalion, one engineer battalion and one signals battalion.

The armoured regiment has a HQ which also contains the four Brückenlegepanzer 68 armoured bridgelayers (based on the Pz 68 MBT chassis), two armoured battalions, regimental mortar company and an anti-tank company. Each armoured battalion has a HQ and support company, two tank companies, two armoured infantry companies and a mortar company. Each tank company has an HQ element with one tank and three platoons each with four tanks making a total of 13 tanks per company or 26 tanks per battalion.

The field (or infantry) division has the following: three infantry regiments, two armoured battalions, one anti-tank company, artillery regiment, anti-aircraft battalion, engineer battalion and a signals battalion. One of the armoured battalions is identical to that of the mechanised divisions with a total of 26 tanks. The other battalion is however different as it has an HQ company, three armoured companies and one armoured infantry company. Each armoured company has

an HQ element of one tank and three platoons each of four tanks, thus giving the battalion 39 tanks compared to the 26 of the normal battalion. Each of the three infantry regiments is normally given one of these armoured companies for close support.

The armoured battalions of the field divisions normally have the Centurions while the mechanised divisions have the Swiss built tanks. In addition each Field Army Corps has a central reserve of two tank battalions.

Total armoured strength of the Swiss army consists of:–
300 Centurions
150 Pz 68 Mark 1s
50 Pz 68 Mark 2s
110 Pz 68 Mark 3s
60 Pz 68 Mark 4s

The first batch of the 100 Centurions were purchased from the United Kingdom as Mk 5s and delivered in 1956–57. These were followed by a further 100 Mk 7s and in 1961, 100 Centurion Mk 5 (Mk 3s upgraded) were purchased from South Africa making a total of 300 MBTs. The Mk 5s were designated the Pz 55 and the Mk 7 the Pz 57; all were subsequently fitted with the 105 mm L7 series gun and redesignated the Pz 55/60 and Pz 57/60. In addition they have Swiss driving lights, Swiss radios, MG 51 machine guns and 8.05 cm 1951 smoke dischargers. Switzerland also purchased 30 Centurion Mk 2 ARVs which are designated the Entpannungspanzer 56.

Switzerland has had two of its Centurions upgraded by Vickers (as described in the Centurion MBT entry) Saurer of Switzerland has also offered a retrofit package to the Swiss Army as have Teledyne Continental of the United States and Israel with its Upgraded Centurion (qv). In 1983 the proposal to upgrade the Centurion tank was stopped.

The Swiss Army has a requirement for a new MBT for the late 1980s. After studying various proposals and designs submitted with the Swiss defence industry a decision was taken in 1979 to order an MBT from abroad that had already been developed.

After evaluating the United States M1 (105 mm gun) and West German Leopard 2 (120 mm gun), the latter was accepted for service with the Swiss Army. The first 35 will be delivered from West Germany in 1987 and remaining 345 will be built in Switzerland with final deliveries taking place in 1993.

Syria

The Syrian Army order of battle includes five armoured divisions (each with three armoured and one mechanised brigades), three mechanised divisions (each with two armoured and two mechanised brigades), one special forces division, two independent mechanised brigades, plus artillery, air defence and surface-to-surface brigades. There are also reserves of nine infantry and mechanised brigades.

An armoured brigade has an HQ element with two MBT, three tank battalions, one mechanised infantry battalion, one reconnaissance company and one anti-aircraft company.

Each tank battalion has an HQ element with one tank and three tank companies. Each of the latter consists of a HQ element with one tank and three platoons each of three tanks. This gives a total of 31 tanks per battalion (same as the Soviet Union). Some reports have said that the battalion has four tank companies, which would give the battalion 41 tanks.

The mechanised brigade has an HQ element, two mechanised infantry battalions, one tank battalion (but with five tank companies), anti-tank company with BRDM-2 (4 × 4)/*Sagger*, mortar battery and anti-aircraft battery.

Each division would also have an engineer battalion, artillery brigade, anti-aircraft battalion and other supporting arms.

Total strength of the Syrian tank force is believed to include about 1800 T-54/T-55s, 1300 T-62s, 1100 T-72s and a few T-34/85s, the latter being used for training.

Syria is believed to be actively considering installing a new fire control system in her T-54/T-55/T-62 fleet as well as a passive night vision system for the commander, gunner and driver.

Taiwan

The order of battle of the Taiwanese Army includes 12 heavy infantry divisions, six light infantry divisions, six mechanised and two airborne brigades, four tank groups plus artillery, air defence and army aviation units. A further nine infantry divisions exist in cadre form.

The army has some 300 M48A2s and possibly 100 plus M47s, but there is considerable doubt about the latter. Light tanks are more suitable for use in Taiwan and for this reason some 1100 M24 Chaffee and M41 Walker Bulldog tanks are in service.

In mid-1984 it was announced that the Pentagon had awarded General Dynamics Land Systems Division a contract for the supply of 75 M60A3 assembly-ready hulls to Taiwan at a cost of $12.2 million and in January 1985 a further 140 were ordered at a cost of $21.1 million. These will be fitted with engines, transmissions and turrets in Taiwan.

In 1981 Teledyne Continental were awarded a contract by Taiwan to provide kits for a small number of M48A2s to be fitted with a new powerpack consisting of a Teledyne Continental AVDS-1790-2D diesel coupled to a CD-850-6A transmission. No improvements so far have been made to the tank's fire control system and the tank still retains its old 90 mm gun.

Tanzania

Tanzania has one tank battalion which is equipped with 30 Type 59 tanks supplied by China plus Scorpion CVR(T), Type 60 and Type 62 light tanks. It is reported that some 300 T-54/T-55 tanks were delivered to Tanzania for use by ZAPU forces against the then White regime in Rhodesia. These were never supplied and are believed to remain in Tanzania. As the country faces no external threat at the present time it would appear unlikely that these tanks have been taken into service with the Tanzanian Army.

Thailand

It was not until the Vietnamese invasion of Cambodia (now Kampuchea) that Thailand took steps to form its first MBT battalion as up until that time its heaviest AFVs were the American supplied M41 Walker Bulldog light tanks. The order of battle of the Thai Army today includes one armoured division which has one tank, one cavalry and one mechanised regiments, one cavalry division, seven infantry divisions (each of which has one tank battalion), two special forces divisions, one Royal Guard plus artillery, air defence and engineer units.

A total of 95 M48A5 MBTs are in service; 55 of these were delivered in 1979 to 1981, with the remaining 40 from 1984. Thailand has large numbers of M41, M24 and Scorpion light tanks which are more suited to much of the Thai terrain than MBTs.

Thailand has a requirement for over 100 new MBTs and has evaluated the Vickers Mk 3, OF-40, Leopard 1 and SK 105 so far, but as of November 1985 no orders had been placed.

Togo

This country has seven T-34/85 and two T-54/T-55 tanks in service.

Tunisia

For many years the only MBTs operated by Tunisia were 13 M48s supplied by the United States under MAP in 1972–74. In July 1981 the Pentagon advised Congress of a letter of offer for the supply to Tunisia of 54 M60A3 MBTs at a total cost of $92 million, including training and support and these have now been delivered.

The order of battle of the Tunisian Army includes one Sahara brigade, one para-commando brigade, two combined arms brigades, plus engineer, reconnaissance, field artillery and anti-aircraft regiments/battalions.

Each of the two combined arms brigades has two mechanised infantry battalions and one armoured battalion. It is believed that one of the latter has the M60A3 and the other M48A5, AMX-13 and M41s. It is probable that the M60A3 battalion is organised along United States lines with a HQ and HQ company which would include three M60A3s in headquarters tank section, three tank companies each with 17 M60A3s and one combat support company. Each tank company has two M60A3s at company HQ, with one of these being equipped with a dozer blade, and three tank platoons each with five M60A3s.

Turkey

The Turkish Army's order of battle includes one armoured division, two mechanised infantry divisions, 14 infantry divisions, five to six armoured brigades, four mechanised brigades and 11 infantry brigades, one commando brigade, one parachute brigade. Corps units (there are ten Corps HQs) include ten tank battalions, 20 anti-aircraft battalions and 30 field artillery battalions. There are also surface-to-surface missile battalions.

The armoured division has two armoured brigades, one armoured infantry brigade, reconnaissance battalion, artillery regiment, engineer battalion, signals battalion and medical, maintenance and supply companies. The armoured brigade has two tank battalions, one mechanised infantry

M48 tank of Turkish Army modernised by Wegmann of West Germany and fitted with a new diesel engine and 105 mm gun with thermal sleeve

battalion plus maintenance, engineer, medical, reconnaissance, transportation and supply companies.

The tank battalion has an HQ element with two MBTs and three tank companies, each with a MBT at company HQ and three platoons of five tanks. The reconnaissance battalion has three reconnaissance companies each with two tanks at company HQ and three platoons each with five tanks.

The mechanised infantry division is similar to the armoured division but has one armoured and two armoured infantry brigades (eg reverse of armoured division), plus similar supporting units.

Each of the infantry divisions has one tank battalion which has a similar organisation to that of the above. In the reconnaissance platoon of each infantry battalion are seven tanks, normally M47s.

Total tank strength of the Turkish Army now consists of some 700 M47s (out of 1340 supplied) and about 2700 M48s (out of some 2800 supplied by West Germany and the United States). It is reported that Turkey has a few Sherman tanks in reserve.

Wegmann of West Germany equipped five Turkish M48s with a diesel engine and 105 mm gun as fitted to the 650 M48A2GA2s it supplied to the West German Army. It was then awarded a contract by the West German government to provide 170 kits, plus personnel support, to enable Turkey to carry out the work itself. West Germany has for some time provided assistance to the Turkish Army, including the transfer of equipment such as M48A2 tanks that were being phased out of service with the German Army. The 1983–84 plan included some DM 32.7 million for the Turkish tank maintenance plants at Arifiye and Kayseri as well as the provision of spare parts for the M48 and Leopard 1.

Under an agreement signed in Bonn in November 1980, Turkey received from 1982 77 Leopard 1A3 MBTs (54 to be built by Krauss-Maffei and 23 by Krupp-MaK) and four ARVs (to be built by Krupp-MaK). These MBTs are fitted with the EMES 12A3 fire control system and PZB 200 LLLTV system.

In recent years Turkey has commenced a major modernisation programme to upgrade its fleet of M48A2 tanks to the M48A5 standard with diesel engine, 105 mm gun and passive night vision equipment.

In 1981 orders were placed for 348 kits to convert M48A1s to M48A5 standard followed by another 52 in 1982, 518 in August 1982 and 600 at a cost of $129 million in 1984. Late in 1985 the Pentagon announced a letter of offer to Turkey for 590 conversion kits to convert M48A1 tanks to M48A5 configuration at a cost of $79 million.

Uganda

As far as it is known Uganda has no tank units, although a few T-34/85s, T-54s and some Israeli supplied Shermans may remain from those acquired many years ago.

Union of Soviet Socialist Republics

The Soviet order of battle includes 51 tank divisionns, 141 motorised rifle divisions, seven airborne divisions, eight air assault brigades, 16 artillery divisions, plus artillery brigades, and independent tank, artillery, surface-to-surface missile, anti-tank, air defence, signals, electronic warfare and other supporting regiments and brigades. Special forces include Spetsnaz with 16 brigades. These have three degrees of combat readiness which are Category I which are at 75 to 100 per cent of authorised manpower with all required equipment. Category II which are at 50 to 75 per cent of authorised manpower with all required equipment. Category III have only about 25 per cent of authorised strength and their equipment includes older vehicles.

Soviet divisions are believed to be deployed as follows:

East Germany	10 tank divisions
	9 motorised rifle divisions
	1 artillery division
	1 air assault brigade
Poland	2 tank divisions
Hungary	2 tank divisions
	2 motorised rifle divisions
Czechoslovakia	2 tank divisions
	3 motorised rifle divisions

Baltic military district (HQ Kaliningrad)
    3 tank divisions
    6 motorised rifle divisions
    2 airborne divisions
    2 artillery divisions

Belorussian military district (HQ Minsk)
    10 tank divisions
    4 motorised rifle divisions
    1 artillery division

Carpathian military district (HQ Lvov)
    4 tank divisions
    7 motorised rifle divisions
    2 artillery divisions

Kiev military district (HQ Kiev)
    6 tank divisions
    4 motorised rifle divisions
    1 artillery division

Leningrad military district (HQ Leningrad)
>9 motorised rifle divisions
>1 airborne division
>1 artillery division
>1 air assault brigade

Moscow military district (HQ Moscow)
>2 tank divisions
>6 motorised rifle divisions
>1 airborne division

Odessa military district (HQ Odessa)
>8 motorised rifle divisions
>1 airborne division
>1 artillery division

Ural military district (HQ Sverdlovsk)
>1 tank division
>4 motorised rifle divisions

Volga military district (HQ Kuybyshev)
>4 motorised rifle divisions

North Caucasus military district (HQ Rostov)
>1 tank division
>7 motorised rifle divisions
>1 artillery division

Trans-Caucasus military district (HQ Tbilisi)
>12 motorised rifle divisions
>1 artillery division

Turkestan military district (HQ Tashkent)
>6 motorised rifle divisions

Central Asian military district (HQ Alma Ata)
>1 tank division
>6 motorised rifle divisions
>1 artillery division

Siberian military district (HQ Novosibirsk)
>6 motorised rifle divisions
>1 artillery division

Transbaykal military district (HQ Chita)
>2 tank divisions
>8 motorised rifle divisions
>1 artillery division

Far Eastern military district (HQ Khabar Ovsk)
>2 tank divisions
>22 motorised rifle divisions
>1 artillery division

Mongolia military district (HQ Ulan Bator)
>2 tank divisions
>3 motorised rifle divisions

Units deployed to Afghanistan include two motorised rifle divisions, one airborne division, one air assault and two motorised rifle brigades plus smaller and support units.

There are three types of Soviet division, tank, motorised rifle and airborne, but only the first two of these have tanks. In recent years the organisation of these divisions has been

Soviet Army T-55 MBTs with laser rangefinders mounted over their 100 mm guns advance under cover of smoke during training

changed and the examples given below are for the new divisions, the older ones have less tanks.

The motorised rifle division has a division HQ and HQ company, two motorised rifle regiments with BTR-60/BTR-70 series APCs, one motorised rifle regiment with BMPs, tank, artillery and SAM-6 regiments, plus FROG, multiple rocket launcher, anti-tank, reconnaissance, engineer, signal, motor transport, chemical defence and medical battalions, artillery command battery, mobile field bakery and a helicopter squadron.

The BTR-60/BTR-70 equipped motorised rifle regiment has a regimental HQ, three motorised rifle battalions, tank battalion, 122 mm howitzer battalion, anti-aircraft battery, anti-tank missile battery, engineer company, signal company, chemical defence company, motor transport company, maintenance company, medical company and a service and supply platoon. The only tanks are in the tank battalion which has a total of 40 MBTs with one MBT at battalion HQ and three companies each with one tank at HQ and three platoons each of four tanks. The BMP equipped motorised rifle regiment has a similar tank battalion with a total of 40 MBTs.

The tank regiment has a regimental HQ which includes one MBT, three tank battalions, one self-propelled howitzer battalion, anti-aircraft missile/artillery battery plus reconnaissance, engineer, signal, chemical defence, motor transport, maintenance and medical companies and a service and supply platoon.

Each tank battalion has a battalion HQ, HQ and service platoon and three tank companies. There is one MBT at battalion HQ and one MBT at company HQ with each company having three platoons each of three tanks. This gives the battalion a total of 31 MBTs and the tank regiment a total of 96 MBTs. In addition there are six MBTs in the reconnaissance battalion.

The tank division has three tank regiments, one motorised rifle regiment with BMP, one artillery regiment and one anti-aircraft regiment. All of the supporting units are the same as the motorised rifle division except that it does not have an anti-tank battalion.

The tank division has a total of 328 tanks, 282 in three tank regiments, 40 in the tank battalion of the motorised rifle regiment and six in the reconnaissance battalion. Each tank regiment has one MBT at regimental HQ and three tank battalions. Each of the latter has a total of 31 MBTs with one at battalion HQ and three tank companies each of which

Production of Ground Forces Material

USSR/NSWP

Equipment type	1980		1981		1982		1983		1984	
	USSR	NSWP	USSR	NSWP	USSR	NSWP	USSR	NSWP	USSR	NSWP
Tanks	3100	700	2000	500	2500	600	2700	550	3200	450
Other AFVs	6500	1300	5200	1300	4500	1400	4500	1300	3800	1200
Towed field artillery	1400	175	1600	150	1800	250	1700	300	1600	250
Self-propelled field artillery	900	50	950	50	850	150	750	200	1000	300
Multiple rocket launchers	700	150	700	150	700	100	700	100	600	100
Self-propelled anti-aircraft guns	300	100	300	50	200	50	100	0	50	0
Towed anti-aircraft guns	0	150	0	250	0	200	0	225	0	225

Source: *Soviet Military Power 1985* (US Department of Defense)

have ten tanks, eg one at company HQ and three platoons each of three tanks.

It is estimated that the Soviet Union has over 50 000 MBTs including the T-54/T-55/T-62/T-64/T-72 and the new T-74. In addition numbers of T-34/85, T-44, IS-3 and T-10/T-10M tanks are used for training, militia or held in reserve. The Soviet Navy Infantry (Marines) has five regiments/brigades each of which is about 3000 men strong. Each includes a single tank battalion organised along army lines with 31 T-54/T-55 tanks.

United Arab Emirates

The United Arab Emirates (UAE) was formed in 1976 by the merging of the former Trucial States of Abu Dhabi, Ajman, Dubai, Fujairah, Ras al Khimah, Sharjah and Umm al Qaiwain. The order of battle includes an armoured brigade.

Some years ago Abu Dhabi took delivery of 64 AMX-30 MBTs and four AMX-30D armoured recovery vehicles from France which are now believed to be organised into two tank battalions.

In 1981 Dubai took delivery of the first of 18 Italian OTO-Melara OF-40 Mk 1 MBTs and more recently has taken delivery of an additional 18 OF-40 Mk 2 MBTs and three armoured recovery vehicles on the same chassis. The original Mk 1 OF-40s have now been brought up to Mk 2 standard which includes a stabilisation system for the main armament, modified fire control system and a LLLTV with camera mounted coaxial with the 105 mm gun on right side of mantlet, all OF-40's form a single tank battalion.

United Kingdom

The Cavalry elements of the British Army comprise the Household Cavalry (two regiments), the Royal Armoured Corps (17 regiments) and two Yeomanry regiments. The latter are equipped with the CVR(W) Fox (4 × 4) and based in the United Kingdom; in time of war these would probably be deployed to West Germany.

Until recently there were two types of armoured regiment, Type A (BAOR) with a total of 74 Chieftain MBTs and four Chieftain ARVs and Type B (UK) with a total of 42 Chieftain MBT and three Chieftain ARVs.

OF-40 Mk 1 MBT of United Arab Emirates (Dubai)

Today there is basically one type of armoured regiment, the Type 57. This consists of a regimental HQ with one MBT, three Sultan command vehicles, one Spartan APC and three Ferrets, a reconnaissance troop with eight CVR(T) Scorpions, and guided weapons troop with two Ferret scout cars and nine FV438s armed with Swingfire ATGWs, HQ squadron, light aid detachment with one FV434, one Chieftain ARV, one Ferret and one Samson and four armoured squadrons.

Each armoured squadron has a squadron HQ with two MBTs and one Ferret, LAD section with one Chieftain ARV, one FV434 and one FV432, one admin troop and four tank troops each with three MBTs.

Total equipment in the armoured regiment is 57 MBTs, five Chieftain ARV, three Sultans, eight Scorpions, one Spartan, one Samson, five FV432 ambulances, four FV432s, five FV434s, nine FV438s, ten Ferrets and 58 trucks and Land-Rovers.

Of the 19 regular regiments, 14 are equipped as armoured (eg tank) regiments and five as armoured reconnaissance regiments with Scorpion CVR(T). Of these 13 regiments (11 armoured and two reconnaissance) are based in West Germany with six remaining in the United Kingdom.

Of the six regiments based in the United Kingdom, two are in training role at Bovington and Catterick. There is also one armoured regiment in Southern England which only has three armoured squadrons as the fourth squadron is in West Berlin. The other three regiments are reconnaissance and provide detachments to NATO flanks, Cyprus, Falklands and Belize.

In the future it is planned to form a 12th armoured regiment in BAOR with Chieftains which will be manned by one of the regiments normally used in United Kingdom for training purposes.

By 1987 it is expected that six of the 12 armoured regiments in BAOR will have the Challenger with remaining regiments equipped with the Chieftain. Some sources believe that further Challengers will be ordered for a further three regiments to be equipped with Challenger.

British Army Chieftain MBT with turret traversed to rear while training in Canada. Every year a number of battalions from the British Army of the Rhine are sent to Canada for extensive training (United Kingdom Land Forces)

United States of America

The active United States Army has four armoured divisions, six mechanised divisions, one airborne division, one air assault division, two light infantry divisions (of which one is operational and one forming), two infantry divisions (which will be reorganised into light divisions), one high technology infantry division (forming), one independent armoured brigade, four independent infantry brigades, three armoured cavalry regiments, plus special forces, artillery, air defence and independent air cavalry brigades.

The armoured division normally has five mechanised infantry, six tank, four artillery (three of 155 mm M109A2 and one with 203 mm M110A2), air defence, NBC, engineer and signals battalions plus divisional HQ, military police company, support company, armoured cavalry squadron and aviation company. Each of the tank battalions has MBTs at battalion HQ, a combat support company the equipment of which includes two AVLBs (M48 or M60) and four tank companies each of which has 14 tanks, so giving the battalion a total of 58 MBTs. The armoured cavalry squadron equipment includes 43 MBTs and is used for reconnaissance, all the M551 Sheridan light tanks/assault vehicles having been phased out of service.

Under the old battalion arrangement each battalion had a total of 54 M60 series MBTs. Each of the Division 86 battalions has a total of 58 M60 or M1 tanks. There are two tanks at battalion HQ and four tank companies; each of the latter has two tanks at company HQ and three platoons each with four tanks. The scout platoon is identical to that in the divisional cavalry squadron and has six M3 Cavalry Fighting Vehicles. There is also a mortar platoon with six 4.2 inch (107 mm) mortars and other supporting units.

The mechanised infantry division is similar to the armoured division but has six mechanised and four tank battalions.

The infantry division has the same type of units as the armoured and mechanised divisions but the four artillery battalions consists of three towed 105 mm (now mostly 155 mm) and one towed 203 mm, eight infantry, one tank and one mechanised battalion.

The Regular United States Army is deployed as follows:

105 mm armed M1 Abrams MBTs line up at Fort Bragg, North Carolina, prior to target practice. This photograph clearly shows blow-out panels in roof of turret to rear of commander's and loader's cupolas

United States Army Europe

7th US Army		Heidelberg
Berlin Brigade	3 infantry battalions 2 companies of MBTs 1 battery of 155 mm SPH engineers and special forces	Clay Allee
32nd Army Air Defence Command		Darmstadt
10th Air Defence Artillery Brigade	2 HAWK and 2 Patriot battalions	
69th Air Defence Artillery Brigade	4 HAWK battalions	
94th Air Defence Artillery Brigade	2 Hercules (to disband) 2 HAWK battalions	
108th Air Defence Artillery Brigade	3 battalions of Vulcan/Chaparral (of which one is for 1st Armored Division)	
56th Artillery Brigade	4 Pershing battalions 1 infantry battalion	
V Corps		Frankfurt-am-Main
3rd Armored Division	5 mechanised infantry battalions 6 tank battalions 4 artillery battalions 1 air defence battalion 1 engineer battalion 1 cavalry squadron 1 aviation battalion	Frankfurt-am-Main
8th Infantry Division (mechanised)	6 mechanised infantry battalions (to be reduced) 5 tank battalions 4 artillery battalions 1 air defence battalion 1 engineer battalion 1 cavalry squadron 1 aviation battalion	Bad Kreuznach
V Corps Artillery	3 Lance SSM battalions 1 155 mm M109A2 battalion 4 M110A2 battalions	Babenhausen
11th Armored Cavalry Regiment	2 squadrons plus support	
130th Engineer Brigade	5 engineer battalions	
VII Corps		Stuttgart/Möringen
1st Armored Division	5 mechanised infantry battalions 6 tank battalions 4 artillery battalions 1 air defence battalion 1 engineer battalion 1 cavalry squadron 1 aviation battalion	Ansbach
3rd Infantry Division (mechanised)	6 mechanised infantry battalions 5 tank battalions 4 artillery battalions 1 air defence battalion 1 engineer battalion 1 cavalry squadron 1 aviation battalion	Würzburg
1st Infantry Division 3rd Brigade) (remainder of division is in USA)	2 mechanised infantry battalions 1 tank battalion 1 artillery battalion 1 cavalry troop 1 engineer company	
VII Corps Artillery	3 Lance SSM battalions	Augsburg

	7 M110A2 battalions	
	2 M109A2 battalions	
2nd Armored Cavalry Regiment	3 squadrons plus support	
7th Engineer Brigade	6 engineer battalions	

8th US Army, South Korea

		Yong San
2nd Infantry Division	2 tank battalions	Camp Casey
	5 infantry battalions	
	1 air defence battalion	
	4 artillery battalions	
	2 engineer battalions	
	1 cavalry squadron	
	various aviation units	

United States of America

CONUS (Continental United States)

I US Corps   Fort Lewis, Washington

9th Infantry (High Technology
  Motorised Division)
1st Brigade with three battalions of infantry
2nd Brigade with two battalions of infantry plus one of tanks
3rd Brigade with three battalions of infantry
4 battalions of artillery (3 with 155 mm M198 and one with MLRS and 105 mm towed)
9th Cavalry Brigade (Air Attack)
plus aviation, Ranger, HAWK battalion and a Chaparral battalion

7th Infantry Division	9 infantry battalions	Ford Ord, California
(became Light Division late 1985)	3 battalions of 105 mm towed artillery	
	plus aviation, air defence,	
	signals and engineer battalions	

172nd Light Infantry Brigade	3 infantry battalions	Fort Richardson
(Arctic)	1 field artillery battalion plus	
	engineer aviation units	

Between 1986 and 1987 6th Infantry Division (Light) will form with two brigades and replace 172nd Light Infantry Brigade

III Corps   Fort Hood, Texas
6th Cavalry Brigade (Air Combat)

1st Cavalry Division   Fort Hood, Texas
1st Brigade with two tank and one mechanised infantry battalions
2nd Brigade with two tank and one mechanised infantry battalions
Divisional troops include one air defence, one engineer, one aviation battalion, one armoured cavalry squadron and three artillery battalions (one with 203 mm M110A2/MLRS and the other two with 155 mm M109A2 self-propelled howitzers

2nd Armored Division   Fort Hood
1st Brigade with two tank and one mechanised infantry battalions
2nd Brigade with two tank and one mechanised infantry battalions
Divisional troops include one air defence, one engineer and one aviation battalion, one armoured cavalry squadron and three artillery battalions (one with 203 mm M110A2/MLRS) and the other two with 155 mm M109A2 self-propelled howitzers

1st Infantry Division (Mechanised)   Fort Riley, Kansas
1st Brigade with two tank and two mechanised infantry battalions
2nd Brigade with two tank and two mechanised infantry battalions
Divisional troops include one aviation and one engineer battalion, three battalions of artillery (one with 203 mm M110A2/MLRS) and other two with 155 mm M109A2 self-propelled howitzers, one armoured cavalry squadron (remainder of division is already in West Germany)

4th Infantry Division (Mechanised)   Fort Carson, Colorado
1st Brigade with two tank and two mechanised infantry battalions
2nd Brigade with one tank and two mechanised infantry battalions
3rd Brigade with one mechanised infantry and two tank battalions
Divisional troops include one aviation battalion, one armoured cavalry squadron, one air defence battalion, one engineer battalion and four battalions of artillery (one with 203 mm M110A2/MLRS) and other three with 155 mm M109A2 self-propelled howitzers

5th Infantry Division (Mechanised)   Fort Polk, Louisiana
1st Brigade with two tank and one mechanised infantry battalions
2nd Brigade with one tank and two mechanised infantry battalions
Divisional troops include one aviation battalion, one air defence battalion, one engineer battalion, one armoured cavalry squadron and three battalions of artillery (two with 155 mm M109A2 self-propelled howitzers and one with 203 mm M110A2/MLRS)

III Corps Artillery   Fort Sill, Oklahoma

9th Field Artillery Missile Brigade
2 battalions of Lance SSM and one battalion of Pershing SSM

75th Field Artillery Brigade
3 battalions of 155 mm M109A2 and one battalion of 203 mm M110A2

212th Field Artillery Brigade
2 battalions of 155 mm M109A2 and two battalions of 230 mm M110A2

214th Field Artillery Brigade
one battalion of 105 mm towed howitzers

Artillery School, Fort Sill
7 training battalions

2nd Armored Cavalry Regiment   Fort Bliss
3 armoured cavalry regiments

11th Air Defence Artillery Brigade   Fort Bliss
3 battalions of HAWK SAMs plus one battalion of Chaparral/Vulcan

1st Air Defence Artillery Training Brigade
3 battalions plus a Patriot battalion

XVII Airborne Corps   Fort Bragg, North Carolina

18th Field Artillery Brigade   3 battalions of 155 mm M198 towed howitzers
                                          1 air defence battalion with HAWK SAMs
                                          2 engineer battalions

82nd Airborne Division
1st Brigade with three airborne battalions and one anti-tank company
2nd Brigade with three airborne battalions and one anti-tank company
3rd Brigade with three airborne battalions and one anti-tank company
Divisional troops include three battalions of towed 105 mm M102 howitzers, one aviation, one air cavalry, one M551 Sheridan, one Vulcan 20 mm air defence and one engineer battalion

1st Special Operations Command Airborne

4th Psychological Warfare Operations Group

101st Airborne Division (Air Assault)   Fort Campbell, Kentucky
1st Brigade with three battalions
2nd Brigade with three battalions
3rd Brigade with three battalions
Divisional units include three battalions of 105 mm towed howitzers, four aviation battalions, one aviation company, one engineer battalion, one air defence battalion with towed Vulcans and one air cavalry battalion

24th Infantry Division (Mechanised)   Fort Stewart, Georgia
1st Brigade with two mechanised infantry and one tank battalion
2nd Brigade with two mechanised infantry and one tank battalion
Divisional assets include three battalions of artillery (one 203 mm M110A2s and two M109A2s), one aviation battalion, one air defence battalion with Vulcan/Chaparral and one armoured cavalry squadron

10th Light Infantry Division
Being formed by 1988, based at Fort Drum, New York

194th Armored Brigade (separate)   Fort Knox, Kentucky
With one mechanised infantry, two tank, and one field artillery battalions, one troop of cavalry and one engineer company

US Armor Centre and School   Fort Knox, Kentucky
11 tank battalions/cavalry squadrons (training)

197th Infantry Brigade (Separate) (Mechanised)   Fort Benning, Georgia
With two mechanised infantry, one tank and one field artillery battalions plus one cavalry troop and one engineer company

US Infantry School   Fort Benning
14 battalions including mechanised and airborne (training)

25th Infantry Division   Schofield Barracks, Hawaii
Will be converted to 15th Light Infantry Division. At present has some six infantry, three field artillery and one air defence battalions

Note: many of the above divisions and brigades have attached units and some have roundout units to bring them up to full strength. There are other training units including infantry and engineer

National Guard
26th Infantry Division   Boston, Massachusetts
28th Infantry Division   Harrisbury, Pennsylvania
29th Infantry Division (Light)   Fort Belvoir, Virginia (being formed)
35th Infantry Division (Mechanised)   Fort Leavenworth, Kansas
38th Infantry Division   Indianapolis, Indiana
40th Infantry Division (Mechanised)   Long Beach, California
42nd Infantry Division   New York City, New York
47th Infantry Division   St Paul, Minnesota
49th Armored Division   Austin, Texas
50th Armored Division   Somerset, New Jersey
8 separate infantry brigades
1 infantry group (scout)
6 infantry brigades (mechanised) separate
3 armoured brigades (separate)
4 armoured cavalry regiments
22 field artillery brigades (inc XI Corps artillery)
11th Air Defence Artillery Brigade (5 battalions)
In addition the National Guard has numerous other special forces, infantry battalions, engineer groups and battalions, field artillery battalions, aviation units, and many non-combat units.

Army Reserve
This includes 12 training divisions and three training brigades plus many independent brigades, battalions and companies.

  The United States Marine Corps has a total of 716 M60A1 MBTs which will be replaced from the late 1980s by 560 M1A1s.

US Army tracked battalions (Armour and Infantry) FY 80 to FY 86

Type	FY 80		FY 81		FY 82		FY 83		FY 84		FY 85		FY 86	
	A	R	A	R	A	R	A	R	A	R	A	R	A	R
M1 MBT	0	0	1	0	7	0	11	1	14	1	24	4	30	4
M60 MBT	53	20	52	26	46	33	42	34	40	34	30	31	24	31
M48 MBT	2	25	2	19	2	12	2	10	0	10	0	10	0	10
M2 IFV	0	0	0	0	0	0	0	0	5	0	9	1	11	1
M113 APC	58	45	58	45	58	45	59	45	39	45	37	42	35	43

A = active army
R = reserve army

As of late 1985 the US Army had just over 3000 M1s, 1600 M48A5s and about 8800 M60/M60A1/M60A3 MBTs.

Venezuela

The Army has one armoured brigade which includes two MBT and one light tank battalion. The former operates 81 AMX-30 MBTs and four AMX-30D ARVs which were built at the ARE in France and delivered in 1979–80.

The Venezuelan Marines are believed to operate a small number of M48A1 tanks which were supplied by the United States.

Viet-Nam

The Vietnamese Army order of battle includes one armoured division and 65 infantry divisions. It is believed that the armoured division is organised along Soviet lines and that each infantry division has one tank battalion of 31 tanks attached, one at battalion HQ and three companies each with ten tanks.

Total Vietnamese tank strength is reported to be around 2000 vehicles of all types including as many as 400 M48s (few if any operational) and 1600 T-34/85, T-54/T-55, T-62 and Type 59 tanks. Some T-54/T-55s have been fitted with additional armour.

Yemen Arab Republic (North)

The order of battle of the Yemen Arab Republic (North) includes one armoured brigade, five infantry brigades, one mechanised brigade, two special forces/parachute/commando brigades, one marine brigade, one central guard force, three artillery brigades and air defence units.

From available information total tank strength consists of about 500 T-54/T-55s (some supplied by Poland but most by Soviet Union), 100 T-34/85s (presumably used for training and 64 M60A3s (supplied by the United States in 1979–80 and paid for by Saudi Arabia).

Yemen: People's Democratic Republic (South)

Full details of the Army are not available but it is believed to include one armoured brigade, one mechanised brigade and ten infantry brigades. The latter have three battalions of infantry although it is reported that some are now being converted into mechanised brigades. It is probable that the armoured brigade has two or three battalions of tanks and one of mechanised infantry, with each tank battalion having 31 tanks as in a Soviet battalion.

Total tank strength is said to consist of between 400 and 500 T-54/T-55, T-62 and T-34/85s, with the latter being used for training. From these figures it appears that the country has far more tanks than it requires to equip the known units and therefore additional units could well have been formed.

Yugoslavia

The Yugoslav People's Army (YPA) is believed to consist of 12 infantry divisions (nine active and three reserve), nine independent infantry brigades, eight independent tank brigades, three mountain brigades plus air defence, artillery and anti-tank units. The tank brigades consist of three tank battalions, one or two motorised/mechanised infantry battalions, an artillery battery and supporting units. It is believed that the tank brigades are actually grouped in twos to form armoured divisions and some are based around Sisak (Croatia), Kragujevac (Serbia) and Skopje (Macedonia).

Each of the infantry divisions has one tank battalion. All Yugoslav tank battalions are believed to be organised along Soviet lines and each has 31 tanks, one at battalion HQ and three companies each with ten tanks.

Yugoslavia has six military regions, I (Belgrade), III (Skopje), IV (Split), V (Zagreb), VII (Sarajewo) and IX (Ljubljana) and each of these has one tank battalion as a central reserve for that military region.

Total Yugoslav tank strength is reported to consist of some 900 T-54/T-55, 150 T-74 and 300 T-34/85 tanks which would appear to be insufficient to fill all of the tank battalions. It could be that some of the tank units are not fully manned and use the remainder of the 630 Sherman (including Firefly) and 300 M47 tanks supplied by the United States in the 1950s. From the 1960s tanks were supplied by the Soviet Union.

Yugoslavia is known to have supplied replacement vehicles to some countries in the Middle East at the request of the Soviet Union and these may have been subsequently replaced by newer vehicles.

Shortly after the end of the Second World War Yugoslavia redesigned the Soviet T-34/85 medium tank to incorporate

an improved frontal hull design and a new turret. These were
not however produced in any quantity.

For some years there has been an agreement between the
Swedish company of L M Ericsson and the Yugoslav company of Iskara concerning the development and production
of lasers for a number of applications, including their use in
MBTs such as the T-54/T-55. It is reported that Yugoslavia
has supplied some laser rangefinders to Egypt for installation
in their T-54/T-55 MBTs.

In 1984 it was confirmed that production of the Soviet
T-72/T-74 was underway in Yugoslavia with first production
vehicles completed late the same year.

Prior to production commencing in Yugoslavia, the Soviet
Union provided Yugoslavia with a batch of at least 50
vehicles for training.

The version being produced in Yugoslavia is the late production model designated T-74 by the Soviet Union. This has
two banks of smoke dischargers mounted on the forward part
of the turret, five on the right and seven on the left. This
model is called the M-84 by the Yugoslav Army.

Yugoslavia took the decision to produce the Soviet
T-72/T-74 in 1977 and by 1979 all of the technical data
package had been received. First prototypes of the vehicle
were completed in Yugoslavia in 1982/83 and these incorporated a number of changes to meet specific Yugoslav Army
requirements and the installation of Yugoslav equipment.

Zambia

For many years Zambia's only armoured unit was A squadron of the Zambia Armoured Car Regiment which was
equipped with Soviet supplied BRDM-1 (4 × 4) and
BRDM-2 (4 × 4) amphibious reconnaissance vehicles and
British supplied Ferret (4 × 4) scout cars.

In the late 1970s some 70 T-54/T-55 MBTs were acquired
for use by ZAPU guerilla units operating against Rhodesia
(now Zimbabwe). As far as it is known these were never sent
to Rhodesia/Zimbabwe and it is possible that they have now
been taken into the Zambian Army. Some recent reports
have stated that Zambia now has one armoured regiment
which could consist of one armoured car and two tank battalions. Total front-line strength is now believed to consist of
30 T-54/T-55 tanks and a few Chinese Type 59s.

Zimbabwe

Prior to the formation of Zimbabwe (Rhodesia) about six
T-34/85 tanks were captured during a cross-border raid into
Mozambique and 15 T-54/T-55 tanks were obtained from
South Africa which acquired them from a merchant ship.
Other T-54/T-55 tanks were waiting in Mozambique, Tan-
zania (some estimates have quoted a figure of 300) and
Zambia (50 to 90) for use by guerilla units. But as far as it is
known these never went to Zimbabwe and were subsequently
incorporated into the respective armies or are still retained in
store.

The order of battle of Zimbabwe includes a single
armoured regiment whose equipment includes three T-34/85
tanks, 20 Chinese Type 59 tanks and eight to ten Soviet T-54
tanks.

Abbreviations

AA Anti-aircraft
AEV Armoured Engineer Vehicle
AFV Armoured Fighting Vehicle
AMX Atelier de Construction d'Issy-les-Moulineaux
AOS Add On Stabilisation
AP Armour Piercing
AP-T Armour Piercing – Tracer
APC Armoured Personnel Carrier
APC Armour Piercing Capped
APC-T Armour Piercing Capped – Tracer
APDS Armour Piercing Discarding Sabot
APDS-T Armour Piercing Discarding Sabot – Tracer
APERS-T Anti-Personnel – Tracer
APFSDS Armour Piercing Fin Stabilised Discarding Sabot
APFSDS-T Armour Piercing Fin Stabilised Discarding Sabot – Tracer
APFSDS-T(P) Armour Piercing Fin Stabilised Discarding Sabot – Tracer (Practice)
ARRADCOM Armament Research and Development Command
ARE Atelier de Construction Roanne
ARRV Armoured Repair and Recovery Vehicle
ARV Armoured Recovery Vehicle
ATGW Anti-tank Guided Weapon
ATR Automotive Test Rig
AV Armoured Vehicle
AVLB Armoured Vehicle Launched Bridge
AVRE Assault Vehicle Royal Engineers

BAOR British Army of the Rhine
BARV Beach Armoured Recovery Vehicle
bhp brake horse power
BITE Built In Test Equipment
BMY Bowen-McLaughlin-York

CCV Close Combat Vehicle
CHARM Challenger Chieftain Armament
CHARRV Challenger Armoured Repair and Recovery Vehicle
CHIP Challenger Improvement Programme
CLAMS Clear Lane Marking System
CET Combat Engineer Tractor
CEV Combat Engineer Vehicle
CFV Cavalry Fighting Vehicle

COTAC Conduite de Tir Automatique pour Char
COV Counter Obstacle Vehicle
CSS Computer Sighting System
CVR(T) Combat Vehicle Reconnaissance (Tracked)
CVR(W) Combat Vehicle Reconnaissance (Wheeled)

DARCOM US Army Materiel Development and Readiness Command
DASCU Digital Automotive System Control Unit
DCA Defense Contre Avions (anti-aircraft)
DFCS Digital Fire Control System
DHSS Data Handling Sub-System
DS Discarding Sabot
DS-T Discarding Sabot – Tracer
DTAT Direction Technique des Armements Terrestres
DT/OT Development Test/Operational Test
DU Depleted Uranium

EBG Engin Blindé Genié
ECCM Electronic Counter Counter Measures
EFCR Equivalent Full Charge Rounds
EPC Engin Principal de Combat (future MBT)
ESRS Electro Slag Refined Steel
EWK Eisenwerke Kaiserslautern Göppner

FCCVS Future Close-Combat Vehicle System
FCS Fire Control System
FCTR Fire Control Test Rig
FFR Fitted For Radio
FMS Foreign Military Sales
FN Fabrique Nationale
FSED Full Scale Engineering Development
FTS Future Tank Study
FV Fighting Vehicle
FV/GCE Fighting Vehicle Gun Control Equipment
FVRDE Fighting Vehicle Research and Development Establishment
FY Fiscal Year

GCE Gun Control Equipment
GCA Gearbox Controller Automatic

GCT Grande Cadence de Tir
GIAT Groupement Industriel des Armements Terrestres
GPS Gunner's Primary Sight
GST General Staff Target

HAB Heavy Assault Bridge
HB Heavy Barrel
HE High Explosive
HE-T High Explosive – Tracer
HEAT High Explosive Anti-Tank
HEAT-FS High Explosive Anti-Tank – Fin Stabilised
HEAT-MP-T High Explosive Anti-Tank-Multi-Purpose – Tracer
HEAT-MP-T(P) High Explosive Anti-Tank-Multi-Purpose – Tracer – Practice
HE-FRAG High Explosive Fragmentation
HE-FRAG(FS) High Explosive Fragmentation – Fin Stabilised
HEI High Explosive Incendiary
HEI-T High Explosive Incendiary – Tracer
HEP High Explosive Plastic
HESH High Explosive Squash Head
HESH-T High Explosive Squash Head – Tracer
hp horsepower
HQ Headquarters
HVAP-T High Velocity Armour Piercing – Tracer
HVTP-T High Velocity Target Practice – Tracer
HVSS Horizontal Volute Spring Suspension

IAI Israel Aircraft Industries
IEPG Independent European Programme Group
IFCS Improved Fire Control System
IFV Infantry Fighting Vehicle
IMI Israel Military Industries
IR Infra-Red

LAD Light Aid Detachment
LLLTV Low Light Level Television
LST Landing Ship Tank
LTFCS Laser Tank Fire Control System
LVTP Landing Vehicle Tracked Personnel

MBT Main Battle Tank

MCCS Marconi Command and Control Systems
MECU Main Engine Control Unit
MG Machine Gun
MoU Memorandum of Understanding
MRL Multiple Rocket Launcher
MRS Muzzle Reference System
MTU Motoren-und-Turbinen-Union
MVEE Military Vehicles and Engineering Establishment

NATO North Atlantic Treaty Organisation
NBC Nuclear, Biological, Chemical
NSWP Non-Soviet Warsaw Pact

OT Operational Test
OTEA Operational Test and Evaluation Agency
OVT Oceonics Vehicle Technology

PRI Projector Reticle Image
PTO Power Take Off

RAC Royal Armoured Corps
RAM(D) Reliability, Availability, Maintainability and Durability
RAP Rocket Assisted Projectile
RARDE Royal Armament Research and Development Establishment
RDTE Research, Development, Test and Evaluation
REME Royal Electrical and Mechanical Engineers
RISE Reliability Improved Selected Equipment
RMG Ranging Machine Gun
RO Royal Ordnance

ROBAT Robotic Counter-Obstacle Vehicle
ROC Republic of China
ROC Required Operational Characteristics
ROF Royal Ordnance Factories/rate of fire
ROKIT Republic of Korea Indigenous Tank
rpm rounds per minute/revolutions per minute
RSAF Royal Small Arms Factory

SABCA Société Anonyme Belge de Constructions Aéronautics
SAMM Société d'Applications des Machines Motrices
SFIM Société de Fabrication d'Instrument de Mesure
SAM Surface-to-Air Missile
SAPHEI Semi-Armour Piercing High Explosive Incendiary
SAPHEI-T Semi-Armour Piercing High Explosive Incendiary – Tracer
SFCS Simplified Fire Control System
SPAAG Self-propelled Anti-Aircraft Gun
SPG Self-propelled Gun
SPH Self-propelled Howitzer
SRV Surrogate Research Vehicle
SSM Surface-to-Surface Missile

TAM Tanque Argentino Mediano
TCM Teledyne Continental Motors
TI Thermal Imaging
TICM Thermal Imaging Common Modules
TIRE Thermal Infra-Red Elbow

TIS Thermal Imaging System
TLS Tank Laser Sight
TOGS Thermal Observation and Gunnery System
TOW Tube-Launched, Optically-Tracked, Wire-Guided
TP Target Practice
TP-T Target Practice – Tracer
TPFSDS-T Target Practice Fin-Stabilised Discarding – Sabot – Tracer
TRADOC Training and Doctrine Command
TTB Tank Test Bed
TTS Tank Thermal Sight
TWMP Track Width Mine Plough

USSR Union of Soviet Socialist Republics
UK United Kingdom
USA United States of America

VAB Vickers Armoured Bridgelayer
VARV Vickers Armoured Recovery Vehicle
VCR Variable Compression Ratio
VCG Véhicle de Combat du Genie
VCI Véhicle de Combat d'Infanterie Véhiculo Combate Infanteria
VEDES Vehicle Exhaust Dust Ejection System
VIRSS Visual and Infra-Red Smoke Screening System
VVS Vertical Volute Suspension

WP White Phosphorous
WP-T White Phosphorous – Tracer

YPA Yugoslav Peoples Army

Index

MBT types and main variants in alphabetical order of countries

Note: Type designations in bold print indicate principal models; page numbers in bold print relate to detailed descriptions.

Other armoured fighting vehicles and their variants in alphabetical order of countries